A **LEVEL**

EUROPEAN HISTORY

David Weigall
Head of History, Anglia Polytechnic University
and Michael Murphy

EDUCATIONAL

Letts Educational
Aldine Place
London W12 8AW
Tel: 020 8740 2266
Fax: 020 8743 8451
e-mail: mail@lettsed.co.uk

First published 1982
Reprinted 1983 (twice), 1985, 1986
Revised 1984, 1986, 1991
Reissued 1993
Reprinted 1994, 1996
Revised 1997
Reprinted 1998, 2000

Text © David Weigall, 1982, 1984, 1986, 1991, 1997

Typeset by Jordan Publishing Design

Design Watermark Communications Ltd (cover), Jonathan Barnard (text)

Illustrations Illustra Design

Design and illustrations © Letts Educational Ltd

British Library Cataloguing in Publication Data
A CIP record for this book is available from the British Library

ISBN 1 85758 602 6

Printed and bound in Great Britain by
The Bath Press, Bath

Letts Educational Ltd. a division of Granada
Learning Ltd. Part of the Granada Media Group.

visit www.letts-education.com for free education and revision advice

PREFACE

This book is designed to meet the needs of students covering the popular late modern period of European history for A-level, AS and Scottish Higher examinations. It is intended to be used as an aid throughout the course, as a book for constant reference and as something which will be particularly helpful for revision.

This book is a companion guide to *A-level British History*, which covers the modern period in Britain. In preparing this book we have received indispensable help and advice from A-level History examiners and specialist historians in schools, colleges and universities. This means that we have been able to benefit from the practical experience of teachers and examiners and the insights of professional historians.

Our particular thanks are due to Mr Harry Browne and to Dr Boyd Hilton for their invaluable contributions and advice throughout, to Mr Ritchie Greig for his advice and help over the Scottish syllabuses, and, for their special contributions to particular topics, to the following: Professor Norman McCord, Dr Stephen Beller, Mr Christopher Catherwood, Mr Alan Griffiths, Dr Eunan O'Halpin, Dr Martin Moriarty, Dr John Pollard, Dr David Stevenson and Dr Don Watts.

We are grateful, too, to the staffs of all the examination boards for their prompt helpfulness and advice.

We are, further, very indebted to all the staff of Letts Educational Ltd who have helped with this publication, and to their advisers, for their encouragement, expertise and forbearance. Rachel Grant deserves special mention for all her work with the new edition in two companion volumes.

Use of past questions

We are grateful to the examination boards for allowing us to use past A-level and Scottish Higher questions in this publication and to their subject officers for details and History syllabuses.

David Weigall
Michael J Murphy

CONTENTS

SECTION 1: STARTING POINTS

SECTION 2: A-LEVEL EUROPEAN HISTORY 1815–1993

SECTION 3: TEST RUN

STARTING POINTS

In this section:

How to use this book

The structure of this book

Syllabus checklists and paper analysis

Examination boards and addresses

Studying and revising History

The difference between GCSE and A/AS Level

Study strategies and techniques

Revision techniques

The examination

Examination techniques and question styles

HOW TO USE THIS BOOK

THE STRUCTURE OF THIS BOOK

The 15 chapters in this book do not pretend to be an introduction to all aspects of European History for the period since 1815. They concentrate, however, on topics which are essential to a proper understanding of the nineteenth and twentieth centuries and which, year after year, are recognised as such in the questions set by the examiners.

The period from the end of the Napoleonic Wars is an extremely popular and widely studied one. It is also a very complex one, for which there is a greater abundance of historical material than for any previous period. The chapters are intended to guide you to greater comprehension of the period and help you acquire and practice historical skills.

The years after 1815 were years of unprecedented and dramatic transformations, rapidity of social and economic development and of major political change. In many respects this period forms a natural unit of historical development for study. When one considers such topics as the growth of Nationalism, parliamentary democracy and Communism, it can also be seen to offer the basic background of knowledge for an understanding of present-day developments, institutions and ideas.

The chapter objectives provide a comprehensive synopsis for the chapter. It indicates what you should be looking out for in your reading and the considerations which your examiners, at the end of your course, will require you to bear in mind. It encourages you to approach your reading analytically, as explained in the following section. It also challenges you to relate various aspects to one another.

Before you embark on your reading for a given topic, you should read through the relevant list of study objectives very carefully to assess the full scope of the topic. When you have completed your reading and note-taking, check through the objectives and ask yourself if you have mastered enough knowledge and acquired enough understanding of what you have read to be able to give an account of each of them. When you have mastered all these points you should be confident that you will be prepared to answer questions on that topic at A-level, from whatever angle they may come.

The main text should be read as a supplement to your textbook and other reading. It is important to remember that the text is *not* an alternative to other reading but is a guide to what is of significance to your needs for A-level History. It is condensed and written with an emphasis on analysis of the topics, covering such considerations as the causes, effects and wider historical significance of events and developments. It includes definitions of key concepts and, organised under clear headings, will help you with the process of historical selection, comprehension, comparison and interpretation. Remember, though, that they are an aid for you to master A-level history and do not do all the work for you!

The chronologies include a list of events, enactments, etc. arranged by topic. Those in capitals are of special significance. These can help you make sure, with the help of your textbooks and other sources of information, that you make notes on these key facts.

As you work through your reading, it may be helpful to clarify the order of events by referring to the chronologies. The chronologies are also excellent memory aids during your pre-examination revision.

QUESTION PRACTICE

Each chapter contains a question section with worked answers divided under the following headings:

Tutorial note: an analysis of what the question is really getting at. This examines the wording of the question and any confusions that arise from it, points out any implications you should be aware of and also gives you general advice on how to answer the question.

You need to know about: a summary of those areas of the topic which you should have mastered in order to be able to answer the question proficiently.

Suggested essay plan: an essay plan showing you how to construct a comprehensive and relevant answer to the question. This shows you how to use evidence to present a historical argument – on the use of what you have read and learned to present a well-reasoned response to the question *as set*.

These are *not* full model answers. Examiners will be looking for knowledgeable, convincing, well-planned answers, but in history essay-writing at this level there is no such thing as an *exclusively 'right' answer*, in contrast to, say, the solution of mathematical problems. The suggested essay plans are presented, therefore, as exercises for you to consider, discuss and work through – and emphatically *not* as the only right answer. They should be studied when you have done your reading and note-taking and thought out the topic. Again, they are not intended as substitutes for your own efforts.

Remember that the construction, presentation and ordering of historical material are most important. Practice in constructing and appropriately supporting a historical argument is essential. Very often A-level History candidates fail to do justice to what they know because of weak presentation and incompleteness in their essays.

The illustrative questions are followed by question banks, consisting of document questions and further essay questions. Use the question banks at the end of each chapter to draw up your own essay plans. There is no more effective way of building up your confidence in your ability to use what you know to answer specific questions and to produce essays that are wholly relevant.

The document questions can be used either with your textbooks to hand as an exercise to find out more about the topic, or, after you have finished your reading for the topic, to test your grasp of it. Note how marks are weighted for these questions. They give you some indication of the amount of space you should be prepared to allocate to each. While the straightforward factual questions on the document, for which two marks are awarded, probably only require a few lines, you may well need to spend half a page or more on the demanding analytical question which offers eight marks.

The reading list at the end of each chapter refers you to a number of the most commonly used textbooks for nineteenth and twentieth-century European History outlines, as well as to titles recommended for *further* reading on the topic concerned. Wide reading is essential for a good, rounded grasp of history. In-depth study of History leads you beyond your textbooks to other sources. One of its major purposes is to encourage the spirit of enquiry.

Maps and diagrams are included where necessary and you should study them carefully when you are reading the text.

SYLLABUS CHECKLISTS AND PAPER ANALYSIS

The following details indicate relevant units for study for papers offered by the examining boards. For full information on the nature of the syllabus, papers on offer, objectives of courses and weighting of marks you should consult your teachers or lecturers, or the examining board concerned. What follows is based on the most recent information available to the authors. But syllabus and paper contents are liable to change and examination regulations or rubrics to be altered.

This list is therefore indicative rather than comprehensive or necessarily completely up-to-date in all particulars. Booklets containing all details are available from the individual boards.

Note, also, that this book will be useful for a number of courses other than A-level, for example access and return-to-study courses for the older student.

A-level Examinations

Associated Examining Board

Syllabus 0630	Paper 02 Period Study	British and European History c.1760–1980	Chapters 1–15
Syllabus 0630	Paper 04 Period Study	Aspects of World History	Chapters 14, 15 since 1945
Alternative Syllabus 0673	Paper 02 Period Study	British and European History c.1760–1980	Chapters 1–15
Alternative Syllabus 0673	Paper 04 Period Study	Aspects of World History	Chapters 14, 15 since 1945
Syllabus 0630	Paper 08 Depth Study	The Russian Revolution 1914–1933	Chapters 7, 10
Syllabus 0630	Paper 09 Depth Study	National-Socialist Germany 1933–1945	Chapters 12, 13

Edexcel, London Examinations (formerly ULEAC)

Syllabus A 9266	Paper 13	European History 1763–1975	Chapters 1–15
Syllabus B 9267	Paper 5	The Origins of the First World War 1878–1914	Chapter 8
Syllabus B 9267	Paper 6	Russia in Revolution 1894–1924	Chapters 7, 10
Syllabus B 9267	Paper 8	The Dictatorships in Europe 1919–39	Chapters 9–15
Syllabus D 9269	Paper 1	International Problems since 1931	Chapters 11–15
Syllabus D 9269	Paper 2	The World since 1945	Chapters 14, 15

Northern Examinations and Assessment Board

Syllabus A	Paper 1 Alternative D	Revolution, Conservatism and Nationalism in Europe 1789–1871	Chapters 1–7
Syllabus A	Paper 1 Alternative E	Rivalry and Conflict in Europe 1870–1939	Chapters 5–13
Syllabus A	Paper 1 Alternative F	The Reconstruction of Europe in the Twentieth Century 1914–1985	Chapters 8–15

Oxford and Cambridge Examinations and Assessment Council

Syllabus 9020	Paper 13	European History 1789–1964	Chapters 1–15
Syllabus 9020	Paper 14	European History 1450–1964	Chapters 1–15
Syllabus 9020	Paper 15	World Affairs since 1945	Chapters 14, 15
Syllabus 9020	Paper 21	The Origins of the Second World War 1929–39	Chapters 9, 12, 13
Syllabus 9930	Option C Unit 4	European and World History 1740–1980	Chapters 1–15
Syllabus 9930	Option D Unit 4	European and World History 1740–1980	Chapters 1–15
Syllabus 9625	Paper 6	European History 1661–c.1965	Chapters 1–15
Syllabus 9625	Paper 16	Russia in Revolution 1905–1921	Chapters 7, 10
Syllabus 9625	Paper 17	The Rise of Hitler and the Establishment of the Third Reich	Chapters 12, 13

Welsh Joint Education Committee			
Syllabus A	Paper A2 (3)	European Nationalism, 1848–1871	Chapters 1–6
Syllabus A	Paper A2 (4)	European Fascism, 1918–1945	Chapters 9, 11, 12, 13
Syllabus B	Paper A3 (C)	European History 1815–1914	Chapters 1–8
Syllabus B	Paper A3 (D)	European History 1900–1975	Chapters 7–15

Scottish Qualifications Authority (formerly SEB)		
Scottish Certificate of Education Higher Grade		
Option C: Later Modern History Section (b)	The Growth of Nationalism	Chapters 1–6 and 8–13
Option C: Later Modern History Special Topic 11	Appeasement and the Road to War	Chapters 13
Option C: Later Modern History Special Topic 12	The Origins and Development of the Cold War 1945–1985	Chapter 14

Certificate of Sixth-Year Studies		
Option (h)	Germany: Versailles to the Nuremberg Trials	Chapters 12, 13
Option (i)	Soviet Russia 1917–1956	Chapters 10, 14

Northern Ireland Council for the Curriculum Examinations and Assessment			
	Paper 1	European History c.1815–c.1914	Chapters 1–8
	Paper 1	European History c.1914–c.1964	Chapters 9–15
	Paper 2	German Unification c.1862–c.1871	Chapter 6

AS-level Examinations

Associated Examining Board		
Syllabus 0991	British and/or European History c.1760–1980	Chapters 1–15
Syllabus 0992	Aspects of World History since 1945	Chapters 14, 15

Edexcel, London Examinations (formerly ULEAC)		
Syllabus 8265	British and European History	Chapters 1–15

Oxford and Cambridge Examinations and Assessment Council			
Syllabus 8470/8392	Paper 20	European History	Chapters 1–15

EXAMINATION BOARDS AND ADDRESSES

AEB The Associated Examining Board
Stag Hill House, Guildford, Surrey GU2 5XJ

EDEXCEL Edexcel, London Examinations
Stewart House, 32 Russell Square, London WC1B 5DN

NEAB Northern Examinations and Assessment Board
Devas Street, Manchester M15 6EX

NICCEA Northern Ireland Council for the Curriculum Examinations and Assessment
29 Clarendon Road, Belfast BT1 3BG

OCEAC Oxford and Cambridge Examinations and Assessment Council
Syndicate Buildings, 1 Hills Road, Cambridge CB1 2EU
Ewert House, Ewert Place, Summertown, Oxford OX2 7BZ

SQA Scottish Qualifications Authority
Ironmills Road, Dalkeith, Midlothian EH22 1LE

WJEC Welsh Joint Education Committee
245 Western Avenue, Cardiff CF5 2YX

STUDYING AND REVISING HISTORY

THE DIFFERENCE BETWEEN GCSE AND A/ AS LEVEL

Before you start your A-level History course it is essential that you are clear about the sort of skills that are required. What qualities will the examiners will be looking for? What is being tested? How do the demands of A-level differ from those of any history you may have done before?

Anything you write, either in course essay work or for your exams, should display a sound factual grasp, a clear sense of the order of events and of their relationship to one another: you should be able to *describe* and to *narrate* accurately. But it is a great mistake to imagine that these skills alone will satisfy A-level History requirements. While a sound factual and chronological grasp is essential, it is only the beginning.

Historical analysis

As examiners' reports show, the most frequent failing among History candidates is an unwillingness, or inability, to *apply* what they know and to *analyse* it in the context and within the bounds of a specific question. It is not so much a lack of knowledge but an apparent absence of thought about that knowledge, and of practice in using it, which lose marks. These skills can only be mastered with practice and experience, not least in sorting out what is relevant in your reading. Answers to A-level History questions come from the process of selection and analysis.

The style and demands of these questions involve you in discussing, comparing, judging and justifying. A grasp of the narrative of historical events and the ability to prescribe are presupposed in the good A-level candidate. At GCSE the basic skills of memorising, understanding historical sequence and presenting it in an orderly fashion may be adequate accomplishments for examination success. This is not to say that the good GCSE candidate may not attempt more than this, either in course work or in exams. The A-level student, however, *must* attempt more and must always resist the temptation to drift into a *simply narrative* response to a question where *analysis* is required.

This is not to disparage narrative, nor to say that narrative and analysis cannot be very satisfactorily combined. They can; and in history – which is the study of individuals, institutions and developments in time – narrative sequence is an essential component. However, A-level History is not simply a matter of offering historical details but of using what you know in interpretation and explanation – not just of knowing but of giving the clearest indications that you understand the implications both of what you know and of the further questions to which that knowledge may give rise.

As the ULEAC examiners have stated, they are 'not looking for the mere regurgitation of received truths... . The highest marks are reserved for answers which clearly provide a cogent and coherent response to the question as set out on the examination paper, and which are supported by substantial illustrative material intelligently selected'. They warn that 'other work may display accurate and relevant knowledge but fails to use this knowledge as an effective contribution to an answer to the question set. Such work will be considered for Grade E equivalent but seldom more. On the other hand, any answer which shows real endeavour to focus relevantly on the question set, and achieves some success in this, will always be treated sympathetically'. NEAB is even more specific, saying that 45% of the marks awarded for an A-level History answer will be given for knowledge and 55% for the ability to assess evidence and to select and organise material. A-level History papers, it insists, demand more than narrative answers and a wholly narrative answer would only secure a maximum of 10 out of 25.

Historical assessment

A-level History requires the assessment of problems in their context. The demands of an A-level essay, in terms both of depth and of sophistication, mark a considerable advance on what you were prepared for in GCSE History. At GCSE you were expected to describe how the unification of Germany came about; at A-level you must be prepared, for example, to estimate the various contributory causes and to weigh their significance – to consider the extent to which it was the result of long-term economic developments, and the part played in it by French diplomatic calculations.

In addition to analysis and a capacity for well-supported and soundly constructed historical argument, you should be able to show an appropriate sense of historical period and a clear understanding of the framework of ideas and attitudes of the age about which you are writing. The good historian is able to intuit and to convey (1) a feeling of the way that people's minds reacted in a particular period, and (2) an understanding of their situation. He is able, in short, to display historical imagination.

The less able student all too often shows himself confined in his judgment by contemporary perspectives. This shows particularly in those essays where students deliver harsh (and often unsubstantiated) verdicts on past figures, institutions or developments. To criticise the past out of hand for not living by what you consider to be the values of the present demonstrates a failure of historical imagination. An intelligent appraisal of Metternich's policies after 1815 is not really helped by denouncing him, from the vantage of hindsight, for not grasping what would happen in Europe 50 years after the Congress of Vienna.

STUDY STRATEGIES AND TECHNIQUES

A-level History, particularly with all the '-isms' of the late modern period, requires you to be able to understand and handle concepts. Questions often demand a mastery of technical historical vocabulary, and the instructions of examiners to 'discuss', 'consider' and 'examine' make essential a high level of discrimination in the meaning of words and in their use in historical writing. An extremely common failing among history students is the misuse of staple words in the history textbook vocabulary – words such as *absolutist*, *totalitarian*, *radical*, *reactionary* and *protectionist*. An imprecise grasp of such concepts leads to confused and inadequate answers in course or examination work. You have only to consider the following A-level questions to appreciate that any proper answers to them are inconceivable without a clear definition in one's mind of what the concepts mean and imply in their context:

> To what extent were liberal ideas in Europe in the first half of the nineteenth century an expression of Romanticism rather than of the Enlightenment?

> 'A demi-semi-constitutional monarchy.' To what extent does this phrase appropriately summarise the achievement of the Dumas in the reign of Nicholas II?

It is not just misunderstanding and misuse of concepts which lead to poor and waffly answers and essays. Another frequent weakness is the attempt to explain historical events by the sweeping use of broad concepts, such as *Nationalism* and *technological change*, without using specific examples or sufficient discrimination between different sorts of nationalism or kinds of technological change. It is essential for you to master sufficient detail to be able to illustrate and clarify such general concepts.

Note that a good number of concepts are what have been called 'essentially contested'. For instance, the description 'democratic' has been frequently appropriated by authoritarian or totalitarian regimes (e.g. as in 'democratic centralism'), as well as Western-style pluralistic societies. Again, what an Athenian meant by 'democracy' two and a half thousand years ago is very different from contemporary representative democracy. It is very easy to misuse concepts, applying them anachronistically to a period in which they were not known, or undiscriminatingly, without pointing out that they denoted something quite distinct in the period you are writing about.

Historical debate and interpretation

The topics which you cover in your History course, and on which you will be questioned in the examination, may have produced considerable controversy and a wide variety of interpretations among historians. There are few entirely simple problems in modern history and you should be aware of the major debates, at least in outline. At A-level, one of the purposes of studying history is to introduce you to historical interpretation and to particular approaches to the study. The skill of constructing and sustaining a historical argument depends, in the first instance, on analysis and the sifting of available evidence. You will rapidly gain confidence in coming to terms with history through practice in evaluating the arguments for and against particular interpretations. You will also discover that it is ill-advised to opt unhesitatingly for one interpretation against all others unless you can sustain this view with a compelling display of evidence supporting it. At all events, one should avoid giving the impression of one-sidedness.

The wider context of 'factors'

Though the analytical approach to history will lead you to identify separate factors as in the causes of a war or revolution you should be prepared to discover the wider context, i.e. the interrelatedness and linkage between them, as well as identifying their individuality. Though they help to clarify and define, such categories as *economic*, *political*, *social*, *constitutional* and *ideological* overlap and, in explaining any event or development, are often found to be interrelated.

A rote learning approach to your studies tends, quite simply, to make for pedestrian and unimaginative answers when you come to write a course essay or take your examination. The uninspired reeling-off of factors will suggest that you have not thought either sufficiently deeply or thoroughly about what you have been studying.

The importance of relevance

The most frequent loser of marks at A-level is the sort of answer which is either plainly irrelevant to the question, or only of marginal relevance. Many students who may well have written comprehensive essays on a topic during their course are disconcerted to find that the questions in the examination cover aspects for which they were not prepared or are posed from an unexpected angle. All examiners are well aware that some candidates may have prepared a number of major topics and virtually memorised answers on them – quite frequently with stock quotations. In such papers a question on Cavour becomes *the* answer on Cavour. This fundamental failing goes back to the question of historical analysis.

You should remember that, in preparing course work and examinations, your historical material should always be shaped to provide a relevant answer, supported by apposite allusion and factual illustration. The narrative and descriptive parts of your essays should be at the service of your analysis of the question. In good historical writing, the writer is seen to be in control of the evidence in presenting a historical argument. It is obvious to the examiner which answers sort out the relevant considerations, make analytical use of reading, and display the skills of identifying the significant points and of relating them.

Note-taking and essay-writing skills

Every History student should have clear, comprehensive and well-ordered notes. These are essential both for course work and in preparing for examinations. In addition, practice in note-taking is of more general value, encouraging clear-headedness and mental discipline.

The key skills here are: selectivity, precision and neat presentation. Before you take notes from a chapter, pamphlet or article, read it through first to establish a general idea of its information and argument. Then carefully re-read and draft notes from this second reading. Finally, check through and see if you have missed anything of significance. If you have, amend your work accordingly. Keep your notes brief, to the point and, as far as possible, prepare them in your own words. Make sure you note down your source. Ensure above all that they are legible and comprehensible. For instance, if you use abbreviations, make sure you will be able to understand them when you come to write your essay or revise for the exam. Anything you note down should be instantly comprehensible afterwards.

Break your notes into clearly differentiated sections. The judicious use of underlining also helps. Underline the key points, but ensure you have significant factual illustration to support these points. For example, if you are noting down reasons for the revolutions of 1848, you will include economic and social causes, as well as listing the political discontents of that year. Good notes convey some idea of the variety of motivations and their interrelationship; and they give you plenty of hard facts to back up analysis. You will find effective notes absolutely invaluable when you come to revise. Re-reading your old essays before your exams is no alternative to having a file of lucid and pithy notes to hand! Finally, when you are note taking, remember to leave space in the margin or at the bottom of the page or section so that you can add any useful additional material from further reading. This is particularly helpful when you are refreshing your memory of a topic during revision.

A good essay needs reasoned judgement and a comprehensive range of evidence. Good note-taking is the first step. Before you put pen to paper for your essay make sure you have a clear idea of your answer to the question as set. Draft an essay plan when you have asked yourself what points you are going to make, how you are going to relate them in a coherent and relevant argument and what facts/ evidence you have to support your argument. Before you do this you should make sure that you have explored all the implications of the question before you and that you are ready to do them justice. When you write the essay out, express yourself as clearly and accurately as you can. It is essential for you to read it through when you have finished, checking for inaccuracies and vagueness of expression. You will find it useful also to list those books, articles or other sources of information you have used at the end of the essay, noting author, title, edition, place and date of publication, publisher and (where relevant) the pages consulted.

The questioning approach

The good student develops, from his reading and thought about the subject, a questioning habit of mind. He goes on from a question to ask further questions. He requires the clarification of any ambiguous term. To give an example: when faced with question on the causes or results of any particular event or development he will take care to distinguish between the immediate and the longer-term causes or results. If he is asked explain the outbreak of the First World War, he has an awareness of the far-reaching considerations – of all those things which produced the international climate in which the Powers were quite likely to go to war – as well as the immediate occasion, being the course of events following the assassination of Archduke Francis Ferdinand in 1914. The good answer illuminates the relations between the longer-term and the immediate causes.

Documents

You will be required to answer questions on source material/documents. This requires sharp critical assessment. As Marc Bloch the French historian noted, source material like this is a witness, 'and like most witnesses it rarely speaks until one begins to question it'. Faced with a document, one should ask the following questions: a) What kind of statement is it? b) What do we know about its author and the circumstances in which it was produced? c) Is it a primary or secondary source? d) Did it have an intended audience or readership? For instance, was it intended as a public statement, or purely as private comment, as in a diary which the author regarded as entirely personal and never intended to be published? e) Was it an immediate reaction to an historical event, or a later reflection, as with memoirs?

You must be able to evaluate the extract(s) and to interpret them. This is a two-way process. On the one hand, your knowledge about a particular historical event or development will help you to understand the source material before you. On the other, this material should add to and illuminate what you already know about it. You should ask yourself, then: how does this contribute to my understanding? How does my knowledge of the historical context enable me to interpret what is before me? You may have one or a variety of documents. The questions may simply test your factual grasp. They may probe your understanding of concepts. They may ask you to evaluate their reliability or perspective; or you may be asked to compare and contrast various accounts and/or assess to what extent they provide a full understanding and explanation. In your examination, the marks awarded for each of the questions on documents or statistical material will be specified after the question. The higher the marks, the more testing the question. The quality of your overall answer to a document question will be indicated by the way in which you are able to combine knowledge extracted from the documents themselves with wider appreciation of the historical context and other sources.

Projects

Several of the Examining Boards offer history candidates the opportunity of writing an individual assignment or personal study. This is a special test of your capacity for independent investigation and enquiry and many students find that this is one of the most fulfilling parts of their course and a real opportunity to display particular enthusiasm and investigative and evaluative skills on a topic which particularly interests them.

Ensure that you read carefully any instructions and advice from the Board on the kind of topic envisaged, the required length, scope, procedures for approval and rules for presentation. It is essential that you choose an appropriate topic, that you have a clear idea of the time you will have to allocate to it and that you have adequate and accessible sources for your research. You must discuss it thoroughly with your teacher or lecturer who will normally have to submit the topic for approval to the Examining Board.

Preparation of a good project requires considerable self-discipline, precision and close attention to detail and presentation. You will need to establish the answer to a variety of questions. Some are procedural, relating to approval of the idea, deadline for submission, whether or not you will have an interview on your project and are expected to bring your notes with you, whether you are to provide a log of your research. Others relate to the research and writing-up of your project, its parameters and the expectations of your examiners. What do they emphasize in their instructions?

One Board, for instance, specifies that you should place the problem investigated in its historical background and relate it to its context, meaning here both background and historical continuum. Another Board advises that you are likely to gain most from studies which ask a definitive question or attempt to solve a problem and that if you choose a local topic you should be prepared to relate it to the wider historical frame. Some topics may present themselves because you are aware of an interesting cache of documents or source material. Others offer themselves first in the form of a question which you would like to try and resolve.

Be absolutely clear about presentation. For instance, how will you be expected to present your footnotes and bibliography? Tidy professionalism is most important. However original your contribution, if it is submitted in an unclear and disorganized form it may well confuse and will certainly detract. A good project should be something standing in its own right, a product of considerable thought and academic self-criticism and of a willingness to re-write, the result of what Dr Samuel Johnson called 'slow diligence'. If you decide to take history either as a Single or Joint-Honour subject at university or college you will very likely have to prepare a dissertation in the course of your studies, usually in your last year. Previous practice in researching a topic thoroughly and presenting your conclusions in a cogent form will serve you in good stead.

Conclusion

A sound piece of work for A-level History shows an intelligent understanding of the past, a clear analysis based on a sound grasp of fact and a capacity for lucid expression. The criteria by which you are judged in the examinations are: relevance, accuracy and quantity of factual knowledge; effectiveness or presentation and the ability to communicate knowledge in a clear and orderly fashion with maximum relevance. You should show that you can present and justify a historical argument, that you are capable of exercising historical judgment and are aware of period and context. These skills can only be acquired over a period of time, with wide reading and much practice.

Two journals, *History Review* and *Modern History Review* are strongly to be recommended for the A-level History student. Not only do they include authoritative articles on historical topics; they also provide useful advice on historical skills and methods. Recent useful books include Mary Abbott (ed.) *History Skills* (London, Routledge, 1996); Derek Rowntree's *Learn How To Study* (3rd edition, London, Macdonald, 1988); R Brown and C Daniels *Learning History: A Guide to Advanced Study* (London, Macmillan, 1986); M Stanford *The Nature of Historical Knowledge* (Oxford, Blackwell, 1986); J A Clarke, V Crinnion and S M Harrison *The Modern History Manual* (Lancaster, The Framework Press, 1987) and A Marwick *The Nature of History* (3rd edition, London, Macmillan Education, 1989). Note, too, that examining boards publish and make available reports on how candidates collectively handle the questions they set. These are very instructive, both as to what the examiners expect and how candidates fall short.

REVISION TECHNIQUES

Effective revision for A-level History is not simply passive absorption, but a very active process. It is an opportunity for you to reassess what you have written in your notes and essay assignments, not just an exercise in re-reading.

You should remember, as explained in the previous section, that you are being examined not simply on your memory, but on your capacities for thought, analysis and judgment. After revising each topic, you should be able to feel confident that you will be capable of answering questions on it from whatever perspective they may come.

In order to encourage this confidence and flexibility of approach, you should practise drafting skeleton essay plans for past questions. List the main points you want to make in the order in which you will present them (remember that a clear structure is most important in essay-writing), and jot down key information to use in supporting them.

In drafting either full or outline answers in your revision, remember that your material should provide a fully specific and relevant answer. Any narrative and descriptive parts of your essays should be used to serve your analysis of the question. At the same time, though, you should never allow the weight of factual information to obscure the argument of your answer, neither should you assume that the examiner will be aware you know the facts if you have not stated them, or that he will find your assertions and generalisations self-evidently correct.

Further, you should allow yourself practice in fully answering questions under mock examination conditions, timing yourself for this exercise. Section 3 of this book contains a full mock European History examination for this purpose.

A planned programme

Revision should be clearly and systematically planned. If you are taking the summer A-level examinations, you should have covered the great majority of the syllabus topics by the end of the spring term (if you are taking the winter examinations, by the beginning of the autumn term). Draw up a schedule for your revision, starting, in the case of the summer examinations, at the beginning of April.

Try to give at least an hour to your History revision each day. Use your mock examination to highlight those topics which need more attention in your revision.

A clearly thought-out programme of revision is one which you can complete without panic and which you can combine with additional reading for the subject. Leave a period of, say, a week to a fortnight at the end for comprehensive re-revision, during which you can refine key points from your notes and clarify any final difficulties. A thorough schedule along these lines will give you the confidence which is such an important element in achieving success.

THE EXAMINATION

EXAM TECHNIQUES AND QUESTION STYLES

Some of the following points may appear very obvious to you. They are, nevertheless, frequently disregarded by candidates and neglect of them is again and again noted in examiners' reports as leading to poor or indifferent answers and to failure in the examination.

You should try and ensure that you observe the following rules:

❶ Read the rubric for each paper and section of paper very carefully and answer the full number of questions required of you. Pay particular attention to subdivisions, i.e. where you are asked to answer questions from more than one section.

❷ Be sure that you have an absolutely clear idea of what any question you choose to answer means and answer it *as set*. Pay particular attention to the precise requirements of the examiners, i.e. are you being asked to 'explain', 'comment upon', 'illustrate', etc.? If the wording of a question is genuinely ambiguous or confusing, be prepared to point this out in your answer.

❸ Choose the questions you are confident you can answer rather than those, however interesting, which you *think* you might be able to answer. Your answers should be pointed and precise. If you use quotes, make sure that they are pertinent to your argument. Do not quote in a random way simply to impress, because you will not. Avoid the vague, weak and general introduction to a question which does not go straight to the point.

❹ Attempt as far as possible to apportion your time equally between the questions, unless there are indications in the rubric or marks (as in some document questions) to the contrary. An overlong first answer only forces you to scramble to finish the last question. Far too many candidates every year submit scripts which show they have not properly familiarized themselves with exam conditions. Give yourself plenty of practice in writing against the clock.

❺ Answer all parts of the question. For instance, in the following question:
    Show why and how a 'cold war' developed after 1945. What were its consequences?

You should note *why*, *how* and *consequences*. The examiner will be looking for answers which deal with all three.

❻ This is equally true of questions which require you to 'compare' or 'contrast'. Candidates often fall down badly by simply concentrating on one side of the question and making only a passing reference to the other(s), e.g:
    Compare Bismarck's foreign policy with that of his successors under Kaiser William II.

Any treatment of this question which concentrates almost exclusively on Bismarck's foreign policy – however detailed and thorough – will not be even a partial answer: it will not really be an answer at all, since the purpose of the question is to elicit a comparison.

❼ Remember to use what you know to provide an answer which is strictly relevant to the question. It is useful to draft an essay outline and to check its relevance to the question, as set, before you answer it.

❽ Avoid essay conclusions which are simply repetitions of what you have already written.

❾ Provide a clear structure and sequence in your answer. The art of presenting a historical argument is extremely important.

❿ Always write clearly, avoiding vagueness either of expression or in factual allusions, e.g: Austria lost several battles – which battles, when and why?

⑪ In answering document questions, read the extract(s), not just the questions, very carefully. If asked to explain them, do so in your own words. Make sure the examiner sees that you understand what the document means and its relevance. Look out particularly for differences of emphasis or tone if there is more than one extract on a topic.

On no account leave your compulsory document question till last. The extracts will require careful reading and reflection. Examiners frequently comment how easily marks are lost in rushed answers to the document questions.

⑫ Give yourself time at the end to re-read what you have written, to correct any errors, or to make any necessary additions.

A-LEVEL EUROPEAN HISTORY 1815–1993

In this section:

Each chapter features:

- *Units in this chapter:* a list of the main topic heads to follow.

- *Chapter objectives:* a synopsis of the topics which will be covered in the chapter.

- *Commentary and chronology:* a concise text, analysing key concepts and incidents, followed by a list of significant events arranged in chronological order.

- *Worked questions and answers:* typical examination questions, with tutorial notes, an indication of the knowledge required and a suggested answer plan.

- *Question bank:* further examination questions for you to attempt.

INTRODUCTION

Europe during the nineteenth century underwent a process of political, economic and social change quite unprecedented in its rapidity. It was the first period in human history in which the pace of transformation was so rapid that society was vastly altered within one lifespan – a period in which human beings living at the same time were capable of acting as though they belonged to completely different eras.

This is not to say that these changes were unheralded. There had been remarkable discoveries in the 'scientific revolution' of the seventeenth century. During the period of the Enlightenment, thinkers had argued that there could be major progress and radical improvement for the human condition, and their ideas and criticisms had helped to sap confidence in the *Ancien régime*. But still, in the eighteenth century – in spite of notable advances – much of everyday life on the Continent was closer in its routines to the Middle Ages than to the twentieth century.

The essential agents of transformation and modernisation were the growth of industrialisation and the influence of the French Revolution. Britain was the first industrial nation. In the third quarter of the nineteenth century she was followed, among the major Powers, by France and Germany and – by the early twentieth century – by Russia. The respective scale and success of industrial development and the growth of population in the various countries affected the balance of power in Europe and were major elements in the imperialist expansion of the Powers.

At the end of the eighteenth century, France was Europe's leading country, its greatest military Power and the focus of its cultural life. By 1871, the year in which the new German Empire was proclaimed after France's defeat at the hands of Prussia, France had already lost that pre-eminence she had enjoyed in European affairs since the seventeenth century. During the first half of the twentieth century it was to be German aggrandisement, based on a rapidly increasing population, great economic advance and military efficiency which threatened the European balance and led to two wars.

The underlying developments during the nineteenth and twentieth centuries, which form the background to this book, were not only very rapid by comparison with previous centuries; they were also complex and closely interrelated. There was a very great increase in population in Europe of the order of about 40% during the first half of the nineteenth century. This – combined with industrialisation, urbanisation, the increase of communications and the much greater mobility of labour, the spread of education and the growing influence of public opinion – compelled change in the old social structures and led to the demand for social reforms. These were accompanied by a growing challenge to the political order and hierarchy and a demand for more representative government.

Though the economic structure of European life was still predominantly agricultural during much of the nineteenth century, the very great increase in population provided industry with both a labour force and a growing market. Industrial advance was stimulated by the revolution in transportation with, in particular, the notable growth of railway construction in the 1840s and 1850s (something which also, among other things, helped to transform military planning and strategy). Land, which had formerly been the basis of social organisation in all European states, became, therefore, relatively less important as industrialisation progressed and finance capital came to play an ever-increasing role. At the same time, as the sum total of human wealth dramatically increased and the social consequences of industrialisation became fully apparent, social reformers and radical politicians called more and more for the redistribution of wealth. Materialistic achievement was accompanied by growing criticism of the inequalities of wealth by the evolution of socialistic ideas and by demands for the organisation of state welfare.

In 1815 there were six great Powers in Europe – the multi-national empires, the Austrian, Russian and Turkish (all were to collapse during the First World War); the constitutional monarchies, Britain and France; and the dynastic state of Prussia. There was also the rest of Germany and the Italian peninsula, both divided into separate states. The unification of these territories were to be central events in the mid-nineteenth century.

The ideas of the French Revolution and the experience of Napoleonic rule left an indelible impression on European society. While the ideas of the French revolutionaries threatened the old social order with its hereditary hierarchy of status, they also posed a challenge to the European order of states.

The Revolution had proclaimed that the state belonged to the people and that the people correspondingly owed loyalty to the state. They were identified in the concept of the nation-state. As the century progressed, the national idea became the dominant force in international relations in Europe. More and more peoples came to be influenced by the idea that each nation has it own character and that each has the right to run its own affairs.

The nationalist idea presented a particular threat to those established monarchies where the unifying principle was loyalty to the dynasty, as with the Habsburg Empire. In the first half of the nineteenth century, Nationalism tended to go hand in hand with Liberalism in the revolts against the conservative order which followed the Vienna Settlement: major upheavals occurred in 1820, 1830 and, above all, in 1848.

The impact of industrialisation and the great population increase combined, then, with new political and social ideas and with cultural advance to transform Europe in the nineteenth century. Together with these developments went the general movement towards the consolidation of state power and extension of state controls over society, with the growth of professional bureaucracies. This was a process whose full implications were only to become apparent in the 20th century.

At the same time as the 19th century was witnessing the ascendancy of state power, it also saw the apogee of European influence across the globe and a burst of new imperial acquisition during its later years. The decades after 1900, however, witnessed a progressive eclipse of the European role in the world. Through the rise of other major Powers, the revolt of colonial dependencies against imperial rule, and the depredations of two world wars, the Western European nations, individually, could no longer aspire to their nineteenth-century status on the international scene.

CHAPTER 1

THE CONGRESS OF VIENNA AND CONCERT OF POWERS

Units in this chapter

Chapter objectives

❶ The events from the Treaty of Chaumont to the Treaty of Vienna; the nations represented at Vienna and the statesmen representing them; the divisions and alliances among these nations; the influence of Metternich, Castlereagh, Talleyrand and Gentz, especially.

❷ The terms of the Vienna Settlement as it affected France, the Netherlands, Germany, Italy, Poland and Norway; the movement of peoples and national boundaries; the respect for legitimacy; distrust of liberal and nationalist movements; fear of renewed French aggression (especially after the 'Hundred Days') and concern to preserve a balance of power between the states.

❸ The allegations that the Congress of Vienna, under Metternich's influence, tried to 'put the clock back'; alternative view that Napoleon had tried to put it forward too quickly; other alternative view that Metternich's real fault lay rather in trying to *keep* the clock back *after* 1815.

❹ The success of the Congress of Vienna in helping to ensure European peace for 40 years: no Power was utterly humiliated, so there were no extreme desires to upset the settlement; the general attitude of war-weariness after Napoleon.

❺ The formation of the Holy Alliance; Tsar Alexander's political ideas and ambitions; Metternich adopted the Alliance as a means to check Russia's south-eastern expansion; Castlereagh's attitude to the Alliance.

❻ The formation of the Quadruple Alliance as the basis for the Concert of Europe; Castlereagh's role in this.

❼ The career and political philosophy of Metternich; the interaction between his domestic and foreign policies; his desire to turn the Concert of Europe into a device to 'police' the world and to suppress revolutionary movements.

8 The Congress of Aix-la-Chapelle and the admission of France to the Concert of Europe.

9 The impact of revolutionary movements in Europe 1819–20 (the assassinations of Kotzebue and de Berry, Spanish and Neapolitan revolts, the rising of the Semenovsky regiment) and the Congresses of Troppau and Laibach.

10 The Congress of Verona sanctions French and Austrian intervention in Spain and Italy respectively, but keeps Russia out of Greece.

11 Canning's political philosophy, attitudes to Greece, Spain and the South American colonies; reactions to the Monroe Doctrine; declaration that the Concert of Powers is dead ('Each nation for itself…').

12 Concert of Europe threatened also by the conflict of interest of Russia and Austria; in 1812 Russia had reached the Danube, thus facing Austria across the Dobrudja, which Austria needed for commercial reasons. As Gentz pointed out, the end of Turkey would spell the end of Austria, so Russia's southern ambitions dismayed Metternich.

13 The revolutions of 1830; the Treaty of Münchengrätz resurrecting the Holy Alliance of Austria, Russia and Prussia – formally signifying the end of the post-Napoleonic Concert of Europe.

After the defeat of Napoleon the primary task of the Allies was to secure a lasting peace. The Vienna Settlement of 1815 inaugurated a period of political and social conservatism in Europe – a period in which the maintenance of international stability was closely linked with resistance to revolution within states. Diplomacy in this period – personified in the career of Metternich – worked to preserve the status quo.

The territorial settlement was not fundamentally shaken until the 1860s, when Germany and Italy were united, and there was no European-wide war until 1914. The Holy Alliance and the Quadruple Alliance were other significant agreements. The latter, among other things, provided for regular meetings between the Powers. At the first of these – at Aix-la-Chapelle in 1818 – France was readmitted to the Concert of Powers.

Great Britain progressively distanced herself from the continental states, however, over the question of the right of intervention in the internal affairs of other countries. This rift became fully apparent at the subsequent congresses of Troppau, Laibach and Verona.

The continuing underlying rivalries between the major Powers were clearly displayed over the Greek revolt. The post-Napoleonic Concert of Powers did not in practice outlive Tsar Alexander I, who died in December, 1825 – though there were later attempts to revive it in times of international crisis.

1.1 THE CONGRESS OF VIENNA

The statesmen who met at Vienna in 1814–15 to create the post-Napoleonic Europe were determined to ensure that no power would be able to dominate the Continent as Napoleon had done. They wanted to secure a lasting peace.

At the same time they were concerned with the maintenance of order within states and the prevention of revolution.

In the minds of all the statesmen of this period the threat of war and the fear of domestic political upheavals went together. In the shadow of the French Revolution and its Napoleonic aftermath, this is one of the reasons why peace was preserved for so long after 1815. There was no major conflict between the powers until the Crimean War of 1854–56.

Never before had so many rulers and principal ministers met to work out a comprehensive peace settlement. The key figures were the Austrian Foreign Minister

Metternich, the British Foreign Secretary, Castlereagh, Tsar Alexander I and the French representative, Talleyrand. It was Metternich who became most identified with the postwar order, regarded by some as the saviour of Europe from war and revolution and by others as the repressive upholder of the rights of monarchs and dynasties against the rights of peoples. This was not least because he survived as a statesman until the revolutions of 1848 and because the multinational Habsburg Empire which he served had most to lose through the revolutionary changes which he resisted.

Territorial changes

In 1815 there was no possibility of simply reconstructing the European map of 1789. A number of changes were irreversible. In Germany, for instance, 300 states had been reduced to only 39. The major territorial changes of the Congress were made with a view to preventing any future French expansion. The treaty of Chaumont of March 1814 had already indicated that Britain, Russia, Austria and Prussia were prepared to form a permanent league to contain France.

In order to achieve this the Kingdom of the United Netherlands was established in the north; the Kingdom of Savoy was enlarged to the south and the control of northern Italy was given to the Habsburgs in the form of the newly created Kingdom of Lombardy-Venetia. Swiss neutrality was guaranteed by the powers.

One of the most significant results of the settlement in the longer term was the strengthening of Prussia. Apart from her other acquisitions, she was given the Rhineland. This placed her in a position where she would have to take the lead in any future war against France. Her territories were now so distributed that by consolidating them she would bring about the economic unification of the greater part of Germany.

In the period after 1815, however, Austria remained the most powerful German state. She not only regained territory she had lost to Bavaria but received the Presidency of the German Confederation or Bund.

It is important to note that Metternich and Castlereagh, while anxious to defend Europe against any revival of French power, were also keen to safeguard Central Europe against any expansion of Russian power.

The major achievement on the Continent after Vienna was that both France and Russia appeared sufficiently contained to allow a balance of power to emerge.

The problems of Poland and Saxony

From the start there were serious rivalries between the victorious powers. By the winter of 1814 disagreement over Poland and Saxony had become so acute that it seemed quite possible that relations between Russia and Prussia on the one hand and Austria and Britain on the other would break down completely.

The large Polish state which Alexander wanted would have meant a considerable expansion of Russian power westwards. If Prussia had been allowed, as she wanted, to take Saxony, her position would have been greatly strengthened at the expense of Austria. Talleyrand intervened on this issue and in January 1815 Britain, France and Austria signed a secret agreement to resist the demands of Russia and Prussia by force of arms if necessary. In the event a compromise was arrived at over both territories and a Kingdom of Poland (Congress Poland) was set up under Alexander I with a constitutional regime.

1.2 THE HOLY ALLIANCE

There was widespread pessimism about whether peace could be preserved. In addition to the territorial and other agreements arrived at in Vienna, a number of other proposals were put forward. The most important of these were the Holy Alliance of

Alexander I and the Quadruple Alliance suggested by Castlereagh.

The Holy Alliance was conservative in a double sense:

❶ it set itself against changes of the European frontiers as laid down in 1815; and

❷ it was opposed to political changes *within* states.

In this Alliance the Russian, Austrian and Prussian leaders promised to treat one another in accordance with 'the sublime truths which the Holy Religion of our Saviour teaches' and to watch over their respective peoples 'as fathers of families'. All the European rulers were invited to subscribe to it and all did except the Sultan, the Pope and the Prince Regent. The last explained that such a personal agreement between monarchs was incompatible with constitutional government.

Absolute and constitutional government

Though it was privately dismissed by Metternich as a 'loud-sounding nothing', the Holy Alliance underlined a growing division between the absolute and constitutional monarchies. That is, Russia, Austria and Prussia on the one hand and Britain and France on the other. Liberals and constitutionalists who believed in representative government argued that it was an agreement between rulers, not peoples. In their view its alleged defence of 'decent Christian order' would be used as an excuse for repression within states.

1.3 THE QUADRUPLE ALLIANCE

By this the victorious powers pledged themselves to prevent any attempt by France to overthrow the peace settlement. Castlereagh regarded this as *the* essential arrangement on which all others must rest. It made provision for the periodic meetings of the powers. Other statesmen joined him in hoping that the settlement would signal the creation of a permanent system of consultation – a Concert of Europe.

The Concert of Europe

What was attempted here in the immediate postwar period was a system of collective security among governments: as opposed to free competition among states in pursuit of their individual interests, they would have to hold some common interest to be more important than individual state ambition. Underlying this was the spectre of revolution. Conflict between states would lead to revolution within states. The wider object of the peace-makers was, in the words of Gentz, Metternich's secretary, to contain the 'restlessness of the masses and disorders of our times.'

1.4 FOUR CONGRESSES

Four congresses were convened under Article VI of the Quadruple Alliance, but there were differences right from the start. The leaders of the conservative, absolutist monarchies argued that peace between states and social and political order within states could not be separated. They insisted on the right of intervention in the affairs of states. Britain – and this was clearly spelled out in Castlereagh's State Paper of May 1820 – held that there should be no general right of interference in the affairs of states.

The Congress of Aix-la-Chapelle

This marked the end of the postwar treatment of France as a defeated enemy. Though the Quadruple Alliance was renewed as a precaution against France, another alliance, the Quintuple, brought her in.

The Congress agreed, in return for final settlement of the indemnity, that the army of occupation should leave France. At the same time, a marked divergence opened up between Britain and Russia: the Tsar called for an international army to uphold the 'sacred principles of order'. Castlereagh replied that the British government would resist all efforts 'to provide the transparent parent soul of the Holy Alliance with a body'.

The Congresses of Troppau and Laibach

These underlined the growing difference of view between Britain and the continental Powers. Both concerned the issue of intervention. Austria was authorised to suppress the Naples uprising. The powers of the Holy Alliance affirmed their determination to intervene wherever a legitimate regime was in danger of being overthrown. Britain opposed the principle of intervention.

The Congress of Verona

In October 1822, following the revolt of the Spanish insurgents against King Ferdinand VII, the five Great Powers came together for what proved to be the last of the era's congresses which involved them all.

George Canning had taken the place of Castlereagh. In opposing the French intervention against the Spanish rebels, he completed the movement away from the Concert of Powers which Castlereagh had begun. Great Britain's constitutional and political system and her dominant interest in developing empire and commerce set her apart not only from Russia but from the other allies as well. Her independence was confirmed by her cooperation with the North American Republic to prevent continental intervention in the New World, on the principles expressed in the Monroe Doctrine.

Subsequent congresses and the Concert of Powers

The idea of a Concert of Powers survived the immediate post-Napoleonic period. There were subsequent congresses, such as those at Paris (1856) and Berlin (1878). A clear distinction should be drawn, though, between the subsequent international conferences of heads of states and the congress system.

The key question about the post-Napoleonic period was whether a *genuinely international system of peacekeeping* could be made to work. The attempt failed primarily because of the disagreement over intervention. The three major areas of disagreement were:
❶ The response of the Powers to revolts in Spain and Italy.
❷ The Greek War of Independence against Turkey. (If the Russians intervened to aid the Greek rebels the whole balance of power in Europe might be destroyed). (See Chapter 3, The Eastern Question to 1856.)
❸ The extent to which European powers should impose their will on colonial territories. President Monroe stated that the American continents were not to be considered for future colonisation by any European Power and he opposed intervention in already established settlements.

1.5 METTERNICH'S 'SYSTEM'

The revolutions of 1830 further widened the rift between the Powers and the division of Europe into liberal constitutionalist and conservative blocs. This put an end to

Metternich's hope of building a conservative Concert of Powers. His views had been formed by the cosmopolitan attitudes of the eighteenth century and the horror of revolution. His personal influence was particularly apparent in the German Confederation. He came to be seen as the arch-upholder of an oppressive order by the liberals and nationalists in the years before 1848. These emphasised the freedom of nations, the legal and political rights of individuals and constitutionalism. A balanced assessment of this period requires that such criticisms should be studied in the light of the very real achievement of the Vienna Settlement.

1.6 CHRONOLOGY

1814	March	THE TREATY OF CHAUMONT; arranged by LORD CASTLEREAGH, British Foreign Secretary, to prevent any break-up of the Fourth Coalition of Great Britain, Russia, Austria and Prussia against the Emperor Napoleon. Guarding against a separate peace with the French ruler, the alliance was to continue for 20 years. Allied entry into Paris.
	April	Napoleon abdicated unconditionally; the Allied Powers granted him the island of Elba as a sovereign principality.
	May	THE FIRST TREATY OF PARIS: France to retain her frontiers of 1792.
1815	June	THE CONGRESS OF VIENNA: the major decisions of peacemaking. The Congress was interrupted by the return of Napoleon from Elba and the 'Hundred Days', brought to an end by the battle of Waterloo (June 18th) and Napoleon's second abdication June 22nd. THE ACT OF THE CONGRESS OF VIENNA (June 8th).
	September	THE HOLY ALLIANCE: drawn up by TSAR ALEXANDER I. The Russian, Austrian and Prussian monarchs promised to treat one another in accordance with the 'sublime truths which the Holy Religion of Our Saviour teaches' and to watch over their respective peoples 'as fathers of families'. Subscribed to by all European rulers except the Prince Regent, the Pope and the Sultan of Turkey.
	November	THE SECOND PEACE OF PARIS: France restricted to the boundaries of 1790 and made to pay an indemnity for the war.
		THE QUADRUPLE ALLIANCE: between Great Britain, Russia, Austria and Prussia. Each of the signatories promised to supply 60,000 men should France attempt to violate the Treaty of Paris. This was concluded for 20 years for the preservation of the territorial settlement. The principle of government by international conference was agreed: the Powers to meet periodically to discuss common interests and problems.
1818		THE CONGRESS OF AIX-LA-CHAPELLE: arranged the withdrawal of allied troops from France and finally settled the French indemnity payments. France was admitted to the newly constituted QUINTUPLE ALLIANCE.
1819	July	THE CARLSBAD DECREES: following the murder of August von Kotzebue, previously a tsarist agent, by a patriotic student. These decrees were proposed by Metternich and sanctioned by the Germanic Confederation. They bound sovereigns to repress Liberalism. Control of universities; censorship and the establishment of an inquisition into secret societies.
1820–21		THE CONGRESSES OF TROPPAU AND LAIBACH: called on the insistence of Tsar Alexander, alarmed at the outbreak of revolts in Naples, Portugal, Piedmont and Spain. Metternich persuaded the three Eastern Powers, Prussia, Russia and Austria to accept the TROPPAU PROTOCOL. This was directed against revolts and uprisings which might disturb the European Peace. It stated that any state which had succumbed to revolution had ceased to be a member of the Holy Alliance and that the powers could intervene to restore order. Castlereagh refused to accept the policy of interference in the affairs of other states. This dissent was clearly expressed in the BRITISH STATE PAPER OF MAY 5th 1820.
1821	February	OUTBREAK OF THE GREEK REVOLT (see Chapter 3, The Eastern Question to 1856).
1822	October	THE CONGRESS OF VERONA: convened to deal with the situations in Spain and Greece. Lord Castlereagh's successor, GEORGE CANNING, denounced the 'European Areopagus'. Though unable to prevent French military intervention in Spain, he refused to cooperate with the other powers. Collapse of the Congress System.
1823	December	THE MONROE DOCTRINE: the background to this to be found in the threat of the Powers of the Holy Alliance to restore the Spanish American colonies to Spain and the aggressive attitude of Russia on the north-west coast of America. It stated that 'the American continents by the free and independent condition which they have assumed and maintained are henceforth not to be considered as subjects of future colonisation by any European powers.'

1825	August	Portugal recognised the independence of Brazil.
	December	Death of Tsar Alexander I.
1827	July	THE TREATY OF LONDON: between England, Russia and France to secure the independence of Greece.
1830	February	THE LONDON CONFERENCE: Greece declared independent under the joint protectorate of England, Russia and France.
1830–31		REVOLUTIONS: Parisian revolt of July 1830 against the policies of the Bourbon Charles X and his minister Polignac. Orleanist King Louis-Philippe succeeded to power. Rulers forced to abdicate and constitutions introduced in the German states of Brunswick, Hesse-Cassel and Saxony. Revolt in Brussels (August to September 1830) assisting the INDEPENDENCE OF BELGIUM. In Italy, risings in Modena, Parma and the Papal States. The Russian garrison driven out of Warsaw in November 1830. Revolutions suppressed during 1831. November 1831 Britain and France agree to the separation of Belgium and Holland.
1832	November	British and French capture Antwerp to force Holland to recognise the independence of Belgium.

Illustrative questions and answers

1 The Quadruple Alliance of 1815 agreed to 'reunions devoted to the great common interests' of its members. How far did the events of the next 10 years show that these members had very few 'great common interests'?

Tutorial note

This is a question on the workings of the Concert of Europe circa 1816–26; you must develop a narrative of events and analyse the differences of interest and ideas among the Great Powers.

You need to know about

Diplomacy 1816–26. Details of the various congresses. Attitudes to the Greek revolt and to international intervention in the internal concerns of small states.

Suggested answer plan

1 Assess the situation in 1815; the common fear of Napoleon and of possible French movement for revenge; financial and psychological war-weariness; this leading to a belief in institutionalised diplomacy.

2 The formation of the Quadruple Alliance; seen by Castlereagh as a counter to Alexander I's mystical Holy Alliance of Austria, Russia and Prussia, and as a means of containing Russian expansionism.

3 Metternich and Castlereagh were the most active members of the Alliance, but differed fundamentally over its purpose; Castlereagh saw it as an instrument to guarantee the territorial arrangements made in 1815; Metternich believed it constituted a licence to intervene in the domestic affairs of nations, and to suppress revolutionary movements.

4 Aix-la-Chapelle; concord maintained; agreement to admit France into the European concert.

5 1819–20 revolutionary movements: the Burschenschaft, the murders of Kotzebue and de Berry; Neapolitan revolution; military revolution in Spain and grant of a liberal constitution. All this turned Alexander I from liberalism to blackest reaction ('Today I deplore all that I said and did in 1815–18'); Alexander became Metternich's pawn; the Carlsbad Decrees.

6 British protests against the new direction of the Quadruple Alliance; Castlereagh's 1820 State Paper; the Congress of Troppau; alliance splits over Protocol; Congress of Laibach; Austria suppresses Italian revolutions; Canning – his policies were similar to Castlereagh's but more genuinely isolationist.

7   The Greek revolt: Britain and Austria combined to thwart Alexander; the Congress of Verona; sanctions interventions by France in Spain and by Austria in Italy, and the Congress of Verona allowed Canning to encourage Latin American colonies – but kept Russia out of Turkey.

8   Canning refused to attend 1824 Congress on South America – which marked the virtual end of Congress rule. In 1825 Prussia, Austria, France and Russia met but the meeting broke up in anger. In Canning's words: 'The age of the Areopagitica is gone by; each nation for itself, and God for us all'.

9   Conclusion: the proposition contained in the question is true; there were few *permanent* common interests. The Alliance operated so long as Britain, Austria, Prussia and Russia were afraid, first of Napoleon, then of a French war of revenge. By 1818 that fear had subsided. A common fear of Russia enabled Britain, Austria and France to combine at times after that and a common fear of revolution led to Austro-Russian cooperation from time to time. By 1826 the Alliance was virtually dead.

2   'I ruled Europe sometimes, but I never governed Austria.' How accurate is this assessment of Metternich's influence?

Tutorial note

The point is to compare Metternich's considerable success in manipulating international diplomacy, at least until the middle 'twenties, with his failure to secure necessary political and constitutional change within the Habsburg Empire; you need to explain what his ideals for the Empire were, and what he wanted to do.

You need to know about

Metternich's personality and policies. Austria's domestic power structure and politics. The Congress of Vienna, Concert of Europe and general European diplomacy 1815–48.

Suggested answer plan

1   Metternich was given to cryptic and melodramatic utterances (like 'I came into the world either too soon or too late'), so one has to be sceptical; nevertheless there is considerable truth in the proposition under discussion.

2   Metternich's career and political philosophy: a paternalist philosophy – he believed absolute power was essential for protecting the *people* against middle-class industrialists and constitutionalists; he realised that his views went against 'the spirit of the age'; supported police-state – though not a too severe one – and imposed censorship and repression.

3   The power structure in Austria and Metternich's position: he was believed to be all-powerful, and identified with the regime, so that his fall in 1848 was itself sufficient to satisfy many revolutionaries; but in fact he was much less powerful domestically than Finance Minister Kolovrat; power was centred in Coreisenregiment (Archduke Lewis, Kolovrat, Metternich), with Metternich the least powerful.

4   His lack of influence was shown by the suppression of his schemes for reform. For example, he wanted devolution of government to solve the nationalist problems; a Reichsrat, Council of State, and provincial diets; and privileges for German merchants in Budapest; all such schemes were thwarted by his rivals.

5   He tried to prevent the rise of capitalism, especially in agriculture; he clung to serfdom, but could not prevent the development of the money economy.

6   Metternich's boast about his European role also had some truth; as Austria's Foreign Minister he undoubtedly took the lead at Vienna; he succeeded for a while in turning the Concert of Europe into a policing institution against subversives (e.g. the Carlsbad Decrees) and also into a means for checking Russian expansion.

7   But all this was due to his able diplomacy, not to Austrian power; the balancing act was bound to fail – e.g. he encouraged France to intervene in Spain in order to persuade Alexander that Spain posed a serious revolutionary threat to world order, and succeeded in persuading Alexander not to add to the danger by assisting Greece; *but* France's invasion of Spain induced Canning to quit the Concert of Europe, which effectively undermined Metternich's influence.

8   So while Metternich exercised great influence, he never *ruled*. Moreover, his foreign policy reacted unfavourably on his domestic political ambitions. Austria's widespread European commitments meant that she could not be isolated. So western ideas of Nationalism and Liberalism infiltrated and doomed the regime.

3   How much attention did the Congress of Vienna pay to the principle of nationality?

Tutorial note

Having discussed what you understand by the principle of nationality, you should look in turn at the various problems with which the Congress had to deal, deciding how far they were respectful of Nationalism in each case. Distinguish between the attitudes of the different countries and statesmen. (See: Liberalism, Nationalism and the revolutions of 1848.)

You need to know about

Nationalist movements in the early nineteenth century. The ideas of Nationalism. The negotiations at Vienna and the Vienna settlement.

Suggested answer plan

1   Define what is meant by nationality in the early nineteenth century: Germany and linguistic-cultural nationalism; ideas of the power of the state, still mainly confined to the universities in 1815, but already given practical reality by the Prussian War of Liberation against Napoleon.

2   Similar liberation movement in Spain, where Nationalism was more liberal than in Germany; Napoleonic rule also awakened Nationalism in Italy; stirrings of nationality elsewhere.

3   The circumstances of 1814–15 treaty-making before and after the 'Hundred Days'; the countries represented at Vienna and statesmen representing them; secret diplomacy and behind-the-scenes alliances; the responsibility for the decisions contained in the Treaty.

4   Incorporation of Belgium in Holland: fear that France might soon overrun an independent Belgium; not really against Nationalism because few Belgians were *then* very concerned; it was to be Dutch misgovernment of Belgium (no religious toleration, religious equality, etc.) which caused the national revolution in 1830.

5   The German Confederation was at least a step towards unification compared with the Holy Roman Empire; no prospects of unification in 1815, whatever the Congress had done, because Germany was still very divided.

6   Italy: only Piedmont and the Papal States were *not* handed over to foreign rule; this was a clear frustration of nationalist sentiment, which Napoleon's influence there had stimulated.

7   The transfer of Norway from Denmark to Sweden was a good example of the Congress's arbitrary treatment of various peoples in its rearrangement of the map of Europe; but Norway had no national tradition, and anyway she was to retain her own government and army; her alliance with Sweden was to work until 1905.

8   Poland was 'liberated', but with the foreseeable result that it fell under Russian influence. Here in effect, if not in intention, was the Congress's greatest frustration of nationality.

9   Conclusion: the Congress of Vienna was moved more by pragmatism than by principle; so, though it did often flout the ideals of nationality (as of Liberalism), this was hardly a conscious decision. The main principle followed was legitimacy (e.g. the Bourbon restoration, Austrian rule in Italy), but far more important was a pragmatic concern for the balance of power.

Question bank

1   Document question (The Congress of Vienna): study extracts I and II below and then answer the subsequent questions (a) to (g):

Extract I

'Among these four powers, Austria found herself in the most <u>awkward position</u>. She could no longer regard the Emperor Alexander…as other than a declared <u>enemy</u>, and Prussia, carried along by <u>her own greed and her own ambition</u>, as the inseparable ally of this enemy. She was nervous of too close a 'rapprochement' with France…for fear of offending public opinion by aligning herself openly with a power who had recently been the common enemy of Europe…. Another factor also restrained Austria. <u>Though she agreed completely with France in her views on the affairs of Poland and of Germany she held different views on the affairs of Italy…</u>. There remained therefore only England as Austria's sole support; but <u>England wanted peace, peace above all</u>, peace…at any price and on nearly any conditions.'
(Metternich's Memoirs concerning the Congress of Vienna)

Extract II

'…There were three particular interests which were vital to British security and which must at all costs be safeguarded. The first was <u>British maritime rights</u> or a solution in our favour of the freedom of the seas. The second was the creation in the Low Countries of a unitary State, closely allied to Great Britain, and capable of forming a barrier against any further French aggression. And the Third was the exclusion, so far as was possible, of French influence from the Iberian Peninsula….'
(Harold Nicolson, *The Congress of Vienna*)

(a) What ambitions had the Emperor Alexander revealed at Vienna which led Metternich to regard him as an 'enemy'?   (3)
(b) Regarding which territories did Prussia, at the Congress, show 'greed and ambition'? How far was this ambition satisfied?   (4)
(c) Explain for what reasons and with what results Austria and France agreed completely…on the affairs of Germany.   (4)
(d) Why did the French and Austrians have 'different views on the affairs of Italy'?
                                                                           (4)
(e) To which 'British maritime rights' in particular had neutral nations objected during the Revolutionary and Napoleonic Wars?   (3)
(f) How far does an examination of the second and third British 'interests' mentioned in Extract II support the view expressed by Metternich in Extract I that 'England wanted peace, peace above all'?   (5)
(g) Discuss whether, despite Metternich's complaints about Austria's 'awkward position', the Congress of Vienna can be regarded as having produced a settlement of Europe which was satisfactory to Austria.   (8)

2   What was more important in the conduct of international relations 1815–48, the shared values of the rulers or the territorial interests of their states?
(NISEAC, June 1990)

3 'He never tried to make things happen, only to prevent them happening. 'Is this a fair comment on Metternich between 1815 and 1948?

(Oxford, Summer 1991)

4 Why were the Bourbons overthrown in France in 1830?(WJEC, June 1991)

5 'The Congress System failed because the leaders of Europe were terrified of revolution'. Discuss. (Oxford and Cambridge, June 1992)

READING LIST

Standard textbook reading

Agatha Ramm, *Europe in the Nineteenth Century 1789–1905* (Longman, 1984), chapters 8 and 9.

David Thomson, *Europe since Napoleon* (Penguin, 1977), chapters 1-6.

Anthony Wood, *Europe 1815–1945* (Longman, 1975), chapters 4–8.

L. W. Cowie and R. Wolfson, *Years of Nationalism, European History 1815-1890* (Edward Arnold, 1985), chapters I and II.

Robert Gildea, *Barricades and Borders, Europe 1800-1914* (OUP, 1987), chapter 3.

Further suggested reading

R. Albrecht-Carrié, *The Concert of Europe* (Harper and Row, 1968).

F.B. Artz, *Reaction and Revolution 1814-32* (Harper and Row, 1963).

F. Bridge and R. Bullen, *The Great Powers and the European State System 1815–1914* (Longman, 1980).

C. Church, *Europe in 1830* (Allen & Unwin, 1983).

C.W. Crawley, *The New Cambridge Modern History 1793-1830*, volume IX (CUP, 1974), chapter 25.

Henry A. Kissinger, *A World Restored: Metternich, Castlereagh and the Problems of Peace 1815-22* (Gollancz, 1973).

J. McManners, *Lectures on European History 1789–1914* (Blackwell, 1974).

G. die Bertier die Sauvigny, *Metternich and his Times* (Darton, Longman and Todd, 1962).

L.C.B. Seaman, *From Vienna to Versailles* (Methuen, 1972).

A. Sked, *The Decline and Fall of the Habsburg Empire* (Longman, 1989).

A. Sked (ed.), *Europe's Balance of Power* (Macmillan, 1979).

Mack Walker (ed.), *Metternich's Europe* (Harper and Row, 1968).

CHAPTER 2

LIBERALISM, NATIONALISM AND 1848

Units in this chapter

Chapter objectives

❶ The idea of Liberalism; its political and economic aspects, both based on individualism; usually a middle-class doctrine, useful for attacking traditional vested interests. The basic belief in progress through free institutions, toleration and natural rights (the freedoms of speech, movement, assembly, press and worship); also the freedom of trade. Often associated with ideas of democracy, but many liberals were distrustful of full universal suffrage.

❷ Nationalism; its debt to the French Revolution; Napoleon stimulated it in Italy and provoked it (against himself) in Prussia and Spain; especially strong in areas of Habsburg rule; often associated with, but sometimes incompatible with, Liberalism (as in the German liberals' attitude to the Polish question).

❸ The intellectual strain of Nationalism, stressing linguistic tradition and culture; poets, philologists, historians; examples of Greece and Serbia.

❹ Businessman's nationalism, seeking efficiency through centralisation. Customs unions and economic consolidation as preludes to Nationalism; Nationalism and the middle class.

❺ The economic and social causes of the 1848 revolutions.

❻ The role of Liberalism in the 1848 revolutions, especially in Germany; the Frankfurt Parliament; Mazzini and democratic-republican Liberalism in Italy; Thiers and the Liberal opposition in France; the Viennese Liberals; the attack on the Carlsbad Decrees; demands for citizen militias to replace standing armies.

❼ The role of Nationalism in 1848; Poles, Italians, Magyars, Czechs, Danes; many German liberals were also expansionist nationalists with Grossdeutsch ambitions; the Panslav Congress; the conflict of nationalisms. Nationalism was not fulfilled in 1848 but the year was extremely influential in its development and it gained martyrs.

⑧ Liberalism and Nationalism were especially strong among intellectuals; 1848 as 'the revolution of the intellectuals'; note the existence of large numbers of lawyers, teachers and journalists without adequate prospects of employment.

⑨ Other factors causing revolution; the rise of Anarchism and Socialism among new proletariats or 'classes dangereuses'; the power of Paris to influence events in the rest of Europe, e.g. the *Journal des Débats* read by students as far afield as those in Moldavia and Wallachia; improved transport speeded the movement of ideas.

⑩ The suppression of revolutions and the reasons for failure; Liberalism and Nationalism were only able to unite disparate classes in the face of common enemies, like Metternich; once successful, the revolutionaries became sharply divided among themselves. Note, too, the *positive achievements* of the revolutions e.g. abolition of the *Robot* in the Habsburg Empire. Also its significance for the subsequent unification of Italy and Germany.

In 1848 revolution spread across the European continent from Sicily to Denmark and from France to Hungary. The background to these upheavals was one of severe economic crisis, of disastrous harvests, commercial failure and very high unemployment. This was combined, though, with considerable political unrest.

The dominant political ideas of the revolutionaries were Liberalism and Nationalism. These ideas had been closely identified with each other in the first half of the nineteenth century in the agitations against the political order upheld by the Vienna Settlement, and epitomised in the Carlsbad Decrees.

'Metternich's Europe', which had been shaken in 1830, now faced major revolutions in France, Italy, Germany and Central Europe, and in the last three Nationalism played a very major part. There were, however, very marked divisions between the moderate liberal and the radical revolutionaries – between those who wanted constitutional changes and those who envisaged a new order of society.

In spite of the failure of the revolutions to achieve such objectives as the unification of Germany, they had considerable achievements to their credit – for instance, the abolition of serfdom in the Habsburg Empire. The year 1848, which has been described as the 'seedplot of modern history', also had a very considerable influence on subsequent social and political developments.

2.1 LIBERALISM

Nineteenth-century Liberalism had its origin in the French and American revolutions.

It was associated with human rights and liberties: the right to property, freedom of speech, of the press, worship and political assembly. It involved the demand for free institutions in society and equality before the law.

During the French Revolution the principle of the sovereignty of the people had been put forward. The underlying notion here was that the only legitimate foundation for a government were the interests and consent of the people it governed.

The term 'Liberal' only became a widespread political description after the Spanish liberal revolt of 1820. It was an expression of the resistance to autocratic and absolutist (non-representative) governments and rulers and of the movement in favour of constitutions and free institutions. It became the battlecry for the opponents of the post-Napoleonic order and Metternich's 'System'.

Another important aspect of this period was the growth of *economic liberalism*: the demand that industry, trade and agriculture be freed from government regulation and supervision. This was a principle that could be traced in the immediate past to the

French economic philosophers of the eighteenth century and to Adam Smith, author of *The Wealth of Nations*.

Liberalism developed as an international movement of ideas, transcending the boundaries of the European states. At the same time, during the period 1815–48 the liberal ideal and ideas of national independence and identity were closely linked.

2.2 NATIONALISM

Nineteenth-century nationalism was particularly encouraged by the influence of the French Revolution. It was the revolutionaries in 1792 who had first clearly formulated the principle of the nation's 'natural frontiers' within which the 'sovereignty of the people' should be exercised.

The two most striking examples of Nationalism during the century were the creation of a united Italy and a united Germany. Diplomacy, war, economic developments and revolution were all to assist in this process. But there was a strong underlying movement of ideas: the emergence of the notion of the *Nation-State*.

This was that a people speaking the same language, of the same race and with the same customs should correspond to an independent state in an identifiable territorial unit.

A clearly defined geographical area, as with the Italian peninsula, was only one criterion. The strongest element in the early nineteenth century was *linguistic* nationalism – the common identity of a people speaking the same language. A common religion was another factor, but it was by no means to be found in all nationalist movements – e.g. Germany was divided between Catholic and Protestant confessions.

The term 'Nationalism' came into current usage in the 1830s. The most influential nationalist of this period was the Italian Giuseppe Mazzini, founder of 'Young Italy' and 'Young Europe'.

His ideas united Nationalism and Liberalism. He eloquently supported the aims of all nationalist groups in Europe. He believed that the popular desire for national independence and freedom was the motive force of nineteenth-century history. He was also convinced that free nations would not go to war with one another and looked forward to the evolution of a united Europe.

At the same time there was another strand of Nationalism, strongly exemplified, for instance, in later German policies, which was anti-liberal in essence. It tended to glorify the individual nation's traditions and demands at the expense of neighbouring peoples. This was to lead to the demand for the suppression of the nationhood of other peoples.

In the period up to 1848 Nationalism was closely allied with Liberalism. The enemies of individual rights and of the freedom of nations were seen to be the same: the conservative order of the Vienna Settlement, the Holy Alliance, autocratic monarchs, the separate governments of the German and Italian states.

2.3 THE REVOLUTIONS OF 1848

The background and causes

Though there were common political aims among the revolutionaries in 1848, there were also specific demands. The first outbreak, for instance, which was in Palermo, was essentially a Sicilian move for independence from Naples.

The fall of King Louis-Philippe in France, which precipitated the spread of revolutions throughout Germany and Central Europe, had as its immediate cause the demand for the extension of the suffrage.

There were moderate demands, such as for liberal constitutions, and far more radical ones, such as the Communist manifesto of Marx and Engels. There were demands for, and concessions of, liberal constitutional reform throughout Europe in 1846–7. These included Chartism in Britain, the amnesties and reforms of Pope Pius IX, the reform banquets in France, the summoning of parliaments in Prussia, Saxony and Wuerttemberg and restiveness in the lands under Habsburg rule.

The economic situation These political demands would not have attracted widespread support among the masses but for the grave economic situation and social hardship at this time.

Since 1845 Europe – everywhere from Poland to Ireland – had suffered a series of poor, and sometimes catastrophically bad, harvests. High food prices resulted and these in turn reduced the demand for manufactured goods, leading to high unemployment in the towns and cities. The situation was aggravated by poor communications, panic buying of agricultural produce and speculation.

In the urban centres there was often marked overcrowding. The rapid growth of towns and cities is one of the great social characteristics of this period. These populations were highly vulnerable to agricultural shortages. In a Europe which was still predominantly rural and in which only Britain and Belgium were really advanced in industrialisation, it was almost inevitable that there should be marked tensions between peasantry and the urban populations. Though not universally, the peasantry were to prove very largely a conservative force in the revolutions of 1848, voting for non-revolutionary candidates in elections, as in France, and participating as conscripts in the suppression of the revolutions.

The revolutions of 1848 were essentially *urban* affairs. To some extent they began as large-scale riots. There had already in the immediately previous period been a number of food riots – for instance in Berlin in 1847.

The support for revolution Many of the most militant supporters of the revolutions came from among the skilled workers, displaced in increasing numbers by the growth of power-driven machinery. There was widespread machine-breaking.

In 1848 the large-scale modern factory employing hundreds and thousands, rather than tens of workers was very much the exception and factory workers were not a large proportion of the urban population.

The social distress of these years is emphasised by the marked increase of emigration from Europe. The various crises were linked and this explains the extent of upheaval and discontent: in 1847 the agricultural crisis was followed by a financial crisis which checked investment and made credit hard to come by. This was accompanied by a major industrial depression.

The peasantry Over large areas of Europe the decayed feudal order in the countryside had not been abolished. In the Habsburg Empire the situation was acute. There the peasants were determined in 1848 to sweep away the surviving feudal burdens and jurisdictions. The restriction of landed property to the nobility, the limitation of personal rights, the maintenance of tithes and forced labour services encouraged grave discontents among the peasantry of Central Europe. Their emancipation by the Habsburgs in 1848 was to be one of the great achievements of that year.

The course of the revolutions

Though the first outbreak of revolution in 1848 was at Palermo in Sicily, it was the campaign of political banquets in Paris in favour of the extension of the suffrage and against the government of M. Guizot which precipitated both the events in France and the revolts which spread throughout Germany and Central Europe. In France the Second Republic was instituted. Manhood suffrage was introduced and slavery abolished in the French colonies.

By mid-March 1848 Metternich was forced to flee from Vienna; Frederick William IV, faced with civilian commotion, had withdrawn his soldiers to barracks in Berlin. In Italy the independent or semi-independent states, the Papal States, Tuscany, Piedmont and Naples were forced to grant liberal constitutions and there were successful risings against Austrian rule in Venice and Milan.

The revolutionary demands The new governments which came into existence in the year of revolutions were above all interested in political reform, constitutional liberties, parliamentary assemblies and bills of rights.

More particularly in Italy and Germany and the Habsburg lands the revolutionaries sought national unity as well. So in Germany, for instance, the revolutions aimed at political reforms within the states and also produced a parliament at Frankfurt committed to national unification. The parliament soon faced numerous problems. It was without an army, bureaucracy or financial resources and the majority of its members came from the small university-educated middle class. In order to have the vote one had to be economically independent and a citizen of the State in which one voted. Both the poor and migrant workers were disfranchised. In Italy the risings within states coincided with a Piedmontese war of liberation against Austria.

The Habsburg Empire The events in the Habsburg Empire are particularly complex. There were four dominant 'master' nationalities within it. These were the Germans, Hungarians (Magyars), Poles and Italians. Their upper and middle classes also covered the territories of the subject races, the Czechs, Slovaks, Yugoslavs, Rumanians and Ruthenes.

The four 'master' races demanded a united Germany, Italy, an independent Hungary and a reunited Poland, including between them all the territories of the subject races.

There was a clash between the various nationalities and a historic divide between the subject and master races. Nationalism threatened the Habsburg dynasty with complete disruption.

In essence, during the 1848–9 upheaval the subject races supported the Habsburgs against the master races. The major challenges to the Habsburg Empire came from the Czech uprising in Prague, the revolution in Vienna and the nationalist revolts in Hungary, Lombardy and Venetia.

The divisions and failure of the revolutions

In their attacks on the established order there was no real harmony between the objectives of the urban populations and the peasantry. This became particularly apparent after the abolition of forced peasant labour by the Emancipation Act of 7 September 1848.

In the cities there was also a conflict of purpose between the hard-pressed artisans, who wanted government assistance, and the middle classes, who wanted an end to economic restrictions. Moderate revolutionary governments moved quickly to quell more radical uprisings.

Different programmes were put forward for national unification in Italy and Germany. It was disputed whether or not a united Germany could incorporate Austria. The nationalities came into conflict.

Further, in many parts of Europe, as in Italy, the revolts were more inspired by local loyalties than national patriotism. In the last resort, the Romans were fighting for Rome and the Venetians for Venice. Sicily rejected Naples and Prussia refused to merge into Germany.

The two ideas, Liberalism and Nationalism, which had seemed inseparably linked in the pre-1848 period, were now effectively in conflict.

By and large in Germany and the Habsburg Empire, liberals – when faced with a challenge to their national group – jettisoned their liberal principles. In Vienna the German revolutionaries bitterly rejected Czech demands for autonomy. In the Frankfurt Assembly, many Germans came to recognise that their nationalist objective might well have to be achieved by illiberal means and with the support, or at least acceptance of the least liberal institution in German life – the Prussian army.

There was a fundamental division between the moderate advocates of limited political reforms and the radical supporters of major social upheaval and transformation. In Italy, for instance, some nationalists came to fear democratic republicanism more than they feared the domination of Austria.

Objectively, radical republicanism had no chance in the France of 1848 and certainly none elsewhere in a continent which was still so very largely agrarian and in which military power lay in the hands of conservative monarchs.

The revolutions failed to gain lasting mass support, not least because the economic situation improved. By the spring of 1849 the revolutionary impetus had largely exhausted itself. The most important exception was Hungary. And there, Russia, afraid of the influence of Magyar success on Poland, intervened to put down the revolution.

The achievements of 1848

The Europe that emerged from 1848–9 was very considerably changed. In many respects 1848 did for Europe what 1789 had done for France.

The abolition of serfdom and of all checks on personal freedom enabled worker and peasant to move about at will. One of the consequences was greatly increased emigration.

Some of the most obvious constitutional gains were in countries such as the Netherlands which had not undergone revolutions. The impact of 1848 was nowhere forgotten.

In France universal suffrage and the principle of popular sovereignty were established; in Italy encouragement was given to the process of the Risorgimento; in Germany the national movement drew the conclusion that unification would be achieved by other than liberal parliamentary means. The social influence of these events was also very significant. The 'June Days', for instance, confronted people in a very dramatic way with the major problems of an urbanised society. While it encouraged the liberalisation of society, it also signified the future greater political consciousness and activity of the masses.

At the same time, though, the defeat of the revolutions ensured that a conservative political and social order survived in Europe, at least until the First World War. The Paris Commune of 1871 and the Russian Revolution of 1905 were exceptions to this stabilisation, but they came in the aftermath of serious military defeat. It was not until the unprecedented upheavals of 1914–18 and the Russian Revolution of 1917 that the fear and fact of revolution came again to exercise a determining influence on governments.

2.4 CHRONOLOGY

France

1848	27 January	De Tocqueville warned the Chamber of Deputies of impending social and political revolution.
	22 February	THE OUTBREAK OF REVOLUTION IN PARIS.
	23	Dismissal of M. Guizot.
	24	Flight of King Louis-Philippe; LAMARTINE secured the approval of a provisional government.
	25	DECLARATION OF THE RIGHT TO WORK.
	26	Declaration of the setting up of NATIONAL WORKSHOPS (Ateliers Nationaux).
	28	Blanqui founded the Central Republican Committee on release from prison; the National Workshops and the LUXEMBOURG COMMISSION set up.
	2 March	INTRODUCTION OF UNIVERSAL MANHOOD SUFFRAGE; reduction of working day in Paris to ten hours and in the provinces to twelve.
	4	LAMARTINE'S MANIFESTO TO EUROPE.

	23 April	Elections held for National Assembly; defeat for the radical revolutionaries.
	9 May	Institution of the Commission of Executive Power.
	24	DECISION TO CLOSE THE NATIONAL WORKSHOPS.
	23 June	THE 'JUNE DAYS' in Paris began.
	24	GENERAL CAVAIGNAC opened offensive against the insurrection.
	26	Defeat of the Paris revolt.
	4 November	Adoption of a new constitution by the National Assembly.
	10 December	LOUIS NAPOLEON ELECTED PRESIDENT OF THE REPUBLIC. (See Chapter 5: Napoleon III and the Second Empire).
1851	15 March	THE FALLOUX LAW.
	31 May	New electoral law reducing electorate from 9.5 million to 6 million.
	2 December	COUP D'ETAT OF LOUIS NAPOLEON.

Italy

1848	2 January	'Cigar riots' in Milan.
	12	Revolt in Sicily and declaration of independent government.
	10 February	Constitution proclaimed in Naples by Ferdinand II.
	14	Pius IX created a Commission of Reform.
	17	Constitution announced in Florence.
	4 March	CHARLES ALBERT proclaimed constitution in Piedmont.
	14	Piux IX granted constitution in Rome.
	17	Daniele Manin led revolution in Venice.
	18	'THE FIVE DAYS' – uprising in Milan; Radetzky evacuated city.
	20	Revolt in Parma.
	22	Republic proclaimed in Venice.
	24	Sardinia declared war on Austria.
	8 April	Piedmontese troops defeated Austrians at Goito.
	13	Sicily declared independence from Naples.
	25	Papacy joined war against Austria.
	29	Pius IX withdrew support from the nationalist movement and condemned the Italian war.
	15 May	Collapse of the Naples revolt.
	29	Battle of Curtatone; Austrians defeated Tuscany.
	3 July	Venice supported Charles Albert.
	25	BATTLE OF CUSTOZZA. Major victory for Radetzky. Sardinian troops driven from Milan and the remainder of Lombardy.
	9 August	Armistice of Vigevano between Austria and Sardinia.
	11	Sardinian troops expelled from Venice.
	15 November	Assassination of Count Rossi, Prime Minister of the Papal States.
	24	Pius IX escaped to Gaeta.
1849	8 February	Proclamation of the Tuscan Republic.
	9	MAZZINI PROCLAIMED REPUBLIC IN ROME.
	12 March	Sardinia ended truce with Austria.
	23	BATTLE OF NOVARA; major Austrian victory. Abdication of Charles Albert; accession of VICTOR EMMANUEL II.
	25 April	French troops landed in Papal States.
	15 May	Neapolitan troops occupied Palermo.
	4 July	French troops entered Rome; Piux IX restored.
	6 August	PEACE OF MILAN concluded Austro-Sardinian conflict.
	28	Venice finally surrendered to Austrians.

Germany

1848	18 March	UPRISING IN BERLIN; FREDERICK WILLIAM IV GRANTED CONSTITUTION.
	31	The VORPARLAMENT met at Frankfurt.

	2 May	Prussia invaded Denmark over the SCHLESWIG-HOLSTEIN QUESTION
	18	GERMAN NATIONAL ASSEMBLY MET AT FRANKFURT.
	22	Berlin meeting of Prussian National Assembly.
	14 June	Frankfurt: the First Democratic Congress.
	29	Archduke John of Austria elected REICHSVERWESER at Frankfurt.
	16 August	Berlin: the JUNKERPARLAMENT.
	23	Berlin: The Congress of Workers' Associations.
	26	TREATY OF MALMÖ between Denmark and Prussia.
	16 September	Frankfurt Parliament ratified the Malmö armistice.
	18	Republican riot and state of siege in Frankfurt.
	5 December	Dissolution of Prussian National Assembly.
1849	23 January	PRUSSIA ADVOCATED UNION OF GERMANY WITHOUT AUSTRIA.
	15 February	Frankfurt: formation of the GROSSDEUTSCHLAND group.
	17	Frankfurt: formation of the KLEINDEUTSCHLAND group.
	27 March	GERMAN NATIONAL ASSEMBLY OFFERED THE TITLE 'EMPEROR OF THE GERMANS' TO AN UNWILLING FREDERICK WILLIAM IV.
	5 April	The Vienna government recalled the Austrian deputies from Frankfurt.
	28	FREDERICK WILLIAM REFUSED THE IMPERIAL CROWN.
	10 May	Heinrich von Gagern resigned.
	14	Frederick William annulled the mandates of the Prussian deputies at Frankfurt.
	30	THE PARLIAMENT LEFT FRANKFURT; in Berlin the edict of the three estates was promulgated.
	6 June	The National Assembly moved to Stuttgart.
	18	Troops dissolved the Stuttgart Assembly.
	23 July	Baden rebels surrendered to Prussia.
1850	31 January	A LIBERAL CONSTITUTION GRANTED IN PRUSSIA.
	20 March	German Parliament summoned to Erfurt by Frederick William.
	29 April	Erfurt Parliament opened.
	2 July	Peace of Berlin between Prussia and Denmark.
	28 November	CONVENTION OF OLMÜTZ; Prussia subordinated to Austria and recognised the Frankfurt Diet

The Habsburg Empire

1848	12 March	OUTBREAK OF REVOLUTION IN VIENNA.
	13	Resignation of Metternich.
	15	The Hungarian Diet accepted the reforms of March 1847.
	8 April	BOHEMIAN CHARTER.
	11	SANCTION OF THE HUNGARIAN CONSTITUTIONAL LAWS; ABOLITION OF THE SEIGNORIAL REGIME.
	25	Constitution, including responsible government, granted to Austria.
	15 May	Second rising in Vienna.
	17	The Emperor Ferdinand fled from Vienna to Innsbruck.
	2 June	THE PAN-SLAV CONGRESS met in Prague.
	10	Vienna confirmed the integrity of the Kingdom of Hungary.
	12	Prague riot and the end of the Czech movement.
	17	Czech rising suppressed by the Austrians.
	28	DISSOLUTION OF THE PRAGUE CONGRESS.
	22 July	Vienna: the opening of the Reichstag Constituent Assembly.
	12 August	The Emperor Ferdinand returned to Vienna
	23 August	Vienna: the workers' insurrection
	7 September	ABOLITION OF SERFDOM IN AUSTRIA.
	24	KOSSUTH proclaimed President of the Committee for the National Defence of Hungary.
	6 October	Third rising in Vienna: assassination of Latour.
	31	GOVERNMENT IN FULL CONTROL AGAIN; VICTORY OF WINDISCHGRATZ.
	9 November	Vienna: execution of Robert Blum.

	21	SCHWARZENBERG appointed Prime Minister and Minister of Foreign Affairs.
	27	AUSTRIAN DECLARATION ON THE 'STATE UNITY OF THE EMPIRE'.
	2 December	Abdication of Ferdinand; accession of Franz Joseph.
1849	5 January	Windischgrätz occupied Pest.
	26	Defeat of the Hungarians of Kapolna.
	4 March	PROCLAMATION OF AUSTRIAN CONSTITUTION.
	7	Dissolution of the Reichstag at Kremsier and the concession of a centralised constitution to the Empire.
	9	Austria proposed the formation of a Central European Federation.
	14	Austria confirmed the abolition of seignorial dues.
	14 April	Hungarian Diet proclaimed independence, with Kossuth as leader.
	13 August	BATTLE OF VILAGÒS: Hungarians defeated by the Austrians who were aided by the Russians.
1851	31 December	Austrian constitution abolished.

Illustrative questions and answers

1 Explain why there were so many revolutions in 1848.

Tutorial note

This is not a question on the causes of *all* the revolutions of 1848. It asks rather which causes were *common* to most or all of those revolutions, and what factors there were which encouraged the spread of revolution.

You need to know about

The causes of the revolutions of 1848 and the general history of Europe in the previous 30 years.

Suggested answer plan

1   Make the point that *Nationalism*, which received a great boost in the events of 1848 (gaining martyrs), has coloured subsequent views of the events of that year. Because of the strength of nationalism *since* then, it is easy to forget how integrated (i.e. supranational) upper-class Europe was in the first half of the century. Ukrainian nobles had more in common with, say, Spanish grandees than either had with their own peasants.

2   The 'old order' therefore had a unity. In attacking it, revolutionaries in different countries often thought of themselves as attacking the same thing: the 'system' symbolised by Metternich.

3   Moreover, revolutionary ideologies developed an international flavour; *Communist Manifesto* for workers of the world to unite; Liberalism, Socialism and Anarchism all had an international flavour. Paris was especially influential in this.

4   The example of Paris was all the greater because of the growth of communications; telegraphs and railways (though the latter also helped to move troops and so to repress revolutions).

5   Economic factors common throughout Europe; beginnings of industrial revolution break up old monopolistic methods of economic regulation (guilds, etc.); only in Britain and Belgium, however, (where revolutionary discontent was limited) was the economy sufficiently advanced to guarantee employment in mass-producer industries.

6   There was an economic crisis throughout Europe during 1845–6, with deflation causing severe unemployment in 1847–8, especially among the artisan handicraft classes (e.g. the hand-weavers of Silesia and Britain).

7 There was agricultural failure, especially in the Balkans, Habsburg lands, Poland and Ireland. Note the impact of the dramatic rise in food prices.

8 So there was no need to blame, as contemporaries liked to do, international conspiracies. Apart from the common problems facing different countries, the nature of the pre-1848 regime throughout Europe was such that the revolution was bound to be contagious.

2 'France was bored': is this a sufficient explanation of the downfall of Louis-Philippe?

Tutorial note

This is a fairly straightforward question on the causes of the French revolution of 1848. It pushes you in the direction of explanation along the lines of mass psychology, but this should not prevent discussion of all other factors behind the revolution.

You need to know about

Louis-Philippe's policies and political system generally. Opposition movements. The condition of French society in 1848. The influence of the French historical tradition and the intellectual life of Paris.

Suggested answer plan

1 The meaning of Lamartine's criticism and of the allegation that 'France was bored'; the growth of European anarchist movements centred on Paris; the influence of the French revolutionary tradition.

2 Louis-Philippe personally could not measure up to the glamour of French history; the regime with its pragmatism and expediency, after the extremism of the legitimist Charles X, seemed unequal to the pageant of French traditions.

3 Louis-Philippe tried to tap the Napoleonic legend by the expedition to Algeria and by bringing Napoleon's bones home to Les Invalides. But it remained obvious that the regime's only real ideology was the materialism of 'enrichissez-vous', of great increase of personal fortunes, of economic competition and of private enterprise; note de Tocqueville's view that the government was a joint-stock organisation for the profit of its members.

4 Boredom stemmed from restrictions on political participation: there were brilliant debates in the Chambre, but only a narrow franchise; only ¼ million had the vote in a population of 32½ million; as 92% of the voters were landed, so urban political participation was even lower; the lesser bourgeoisie were also disfranchised, including schoolteachers, for instance, who helped to influence youth against the regime. Note French diplomatic defeat in the second Mehemet Ali crisis.

5 There was boredom also with a humiliating foreign policy; the acquisition of Algiers, for example, did not compensate for Palmerston's public contempt for France.

6 Other explanations of revolution: Republican opposition (especially by Thiers) was frustrated by Guizot's success in consolidating the Centre-Right government after 1840; Thiers prepared to stir up revolutionary feeling against the regime, simply because he was unable to gain office within the system.

7 There were economic difficulties; the deflationary crisis of 1845–6, social problems and growth of working-class consciousness; there was an absence of social legislation, except the 1841 Labour Law. Note failure to come to terms with the problems posed by rapid urbanisation.

8 Corruption: there was a narrow oligarchy in control of the regime. A number of public scandals alienated public opinion.

9 The immediate causes of revolution were: the role of the press, the Banquet campaign for the extension of the franchise and the row over the fortifications of Paris.

10 Conclusions: a regime which has no fixed body of support depends on public opinion ultimately; but a regime of compromises finds it hard to satisfy opinion in a country like France prone to extremism. Boredom did not cause the revolution, but it helps to explain why few bothered to rally round Louis-Philippe when he was in trouble.

3 To what extent should the revolutions of 1848 be explained in social rather than political terms?

Tutorial note
This is almost a straight question on the causes of the 1848 revolutions. Go through these causes one by one, grouping them under the headings 'political' and 'social and economic'. It is probably best to deal with the revolutions as a group rather than country by country, but as you discuss each cause do not forget to point out the differences between countries.

You need to know about
The causes of revolution in France, Spain, the Habsburg Empire, Italy, Poland, and perhaps Ireland. The social and economic conditions in the 1840s. The political effects of liberal and nationalist movements.

Suggested answer plan
1   A brief survey of the revolutionary outbreaks, the rapidity of their spread across Europe.
2   Distinguish between the instigators and leaders of revolution, and the masses whose support alone makes revolution possible. The leaders were mainly motivated by political aims, their inarticulate followers motivated more by social pressures.
3   Liberalism as a political explanation: the middle classes aspired to political power after the British 1832 example; frustration with the narrowness of the franchise under Louis-Philippe; concern for economic opportunities, the promotion of railways; the desire for basic human freedoms (speech, conscience, etc.), especially strong in the German states; the ideas of Mazzini.
4   Nationalism as a political explanation; various national movements in Europe. Distinguish the cultural, linguistic, romantic nationalism from middle-class economic and bureaucratic nationalism.
5   The alienation of the intellectuals: the expansion of education and of professional training (as in law and medicine), without a corresponding expansion of employment opportunities for professionals, provides another *political* explanation.
6   Also 1848 saw the birth of political anarchism and the cult of violence. This led the middle classes to desert the revolution.
7   As Marx realised, 1848 was also a social phenomenon, e.g. 'The June Days'. Explain the causes of this upheaval.
8   But the main support for revolution comes from those classes beginning to be left behind by industrial development, and unable to compete with factory operatives; Louis Blanc and 'the right to work'; handloom weavers of Silesia; the Artisan Congress demanded the restoration of guild controls over production; a clear clash between these social interests and those of the political revolutionaries of Frankfurt who desired free trade.
9   The peasants as a social factor; the state of serfdom in Europe; the failure of the potato crop in the 1840s causes starvation and suffering, (e.g. in Ireland and Galicia).
10   The economic depression throughout Europe in 1847; the recovery in 1848 undermined the revolution; this suggests that while *politics* provided a focus, the social condition of the people mainly explains what happened and accounts for the initial force of the revolutions.

Question bank

1 Document question (Prussia and the 1848 revolutions): study the extract below and then answer the questions (a) to (g):

Extract

'To my Beloved Berliners...By my patent of convocation this day, you have received the pledge of <u>the faithful sentiments</u> of your King towards you and towards the whole of the German nation. The shout of joy which greeted me from unnumbered faithful hearts still resounded in my ears, when a <u>crowd of peace-breakers</u> mingled with the loyal throng, making <u>seditious and bold demands</u>, and augmenting in numbers as the well-disposed withdrew.

'As their impetuous intrusion extended to the very portals of the Palace...and insults were offered to my valiant and faithful soldiers, the courtyard was cleared by the cavalry <u>at walking pace and with their weapons sheathed</u>; and two guns of the infantry went off of themselves, without, thanks be to God!, causing any injury. A band of wicked men, chiefly consisting of foreigners...have converted this circumstance into a palpable untruth, and have filled the excited minds of my faithful and beloved Berliners with thoughts of vengeance for supposed bloodshed; and thus have they become the fearful authors of bloodshed themselves. My troops, your brothers and fellow-countrymen, did not make use of their weapons until forced to do so by several shots fired at them from the Königsstrasse. The victorious advance of the troops was the necessary consequence.

'It is now yours, inhabitants of my beloved native city, to avert a fearful evil. Acknowledge your fatal error; your King, your trusting friend, enjoins you, by all that is most sacred, to acknowledge your fatal error. Return to peace; remove the barricades which are still standing: and send to me men filled with the genuine ancient spirit of Berlin, speaking words which are seemly to your King; and I pledge you my royal truth that all the streets and squares shall be instantaneously cleared of the troops, and the military garrisons shall be confined solely to the most important buildings – to the Castle, the Arsenal and a few others and even here only for a brief space of time. Listen to the paternal voice of your King, ye inhabitants of my true and beautiful Berlin; and forget the past, as I shall forget it, for the sake of that <u>great future</u> which, under the peace-giving blessing of God, is <u>dawning upon Prussia, and through Prussia, upon all Germany...</u>'

Written during the night of 18/19 March 1848.

(Frederick William IV addresses the Berliners)

(a) What events of the previous day in Berlin led to the writing of this letter? (3)

(b) What were 'the faithful sentiments' which the King pledged 'towards you' (i.e. the Prussians) 'and towards the whole of the German nation'? (4)

(c) Why were such pledges insufficient to reassure the 'crowd of peace-breakers' who made such seditious and bold demands'? (3)

(d) How do you explain the King's conciliatory tone in the second paragraph of this letter, and his insistence that his cavalry had acted 'at walking pace and with their weapons sheathed'? (4)

(e) What significance may be attached to the King's appearance, shortly after the date of this letter, wearing the black, red and gold sash of the former Holy Roman Empire? (3)

(f) In which German city at this time did the hopes of the liberal nationalists chiefly centre? Discuss the suggestion that the efforts in that city to promote the cause of unification in 1848–9 were too narrowly based. (6)

(g) In what ways did the events of the next three years run contrary to the royal prediction that a 'great future' was 'dawning upon Prussia, and through Prussia upon all Germany', and how do you account for these events? (8)

2 How far was Liberalism or Nationalism or Socialism a distinctive movement in the period before 1848? ˊ (NISEAC, June 1990)

3 'Liberalism was only for the middle classes'. Is this a sufficient explanation for the failure of the 1848 revolutions? (Oxford and Cambridge, June 1991)

4 What were the effects of the Napoleonic wars upon Europe after 1815? (Oxford and Cambridge, June 1990)

5 'A government of many virtues, yet one which was little mourned'. Examine this comment on the Orleanist Monarchy. (Cambridge, Summer 1986)

READING LIST

Standard textbook reading

L. W. Cowie and R. Wolfson, *Years of Nationalism, European History 1815–1890* (Edward Arnold, 1985), chapters II and III.

Robert Gildea, *Barricades and Borders, Europe 1800–1914* (OUP, 1987), chapter 4.

J. A. S. Grenville, *Europe Reshaped 1848–78* (Fontana, 1976), Part 1.

Agatha Ramm, *Europe in the Nineteenth Century 1789–1905* (Longman, 1984), chapters 10–13.

David Thomson, *Europe since Napoleon* (Penguin, 1977), chapters 9–11.

Anthony Wood, *Europe 1815–1945* (Longman, 1975), chapters 9–13.

Further suggested reading

M. Algulhon, *The Republican Experiment 1848–5* (CUP, 1980).

M. S. Anderson, *The Ascendency of Europe* (Longman, 1972).

J. P. T. Bury (ed), *The New Cambridge Modern History 1830–70*, volume X (CUP, 1964), chapters 9 and 15.

H. Hearder, *Italy in the Age of the Risorgimento* (Longman, 1983).

E. J. Hobsbawm, *The Age of Revolution, Europe 1789–1848* (Sphere, 1977).

E. J. Hobsbawm, *The Age of Capital 1848–1875* (Abacus, 1977).

P. Jones, *The 1848 Revolutions* (Longman, 1982).

H. Kohn, *Nationalism: Its Meaning and History* (Anvil, 1965).

W. L. Langer, *Political and Social Upheaval 1832–52* (Harper and Row, 1972).

K. Marx and F. Engels (ed. D. Fernbach), *The Revolutions of 1848* (Penguin, 1973).

L. B. Namier, *1848 – The Revolution of The Intellectuals* (OUP, 1962).

Roger Price (ed.), *1848 in France* (Thames and Hudson, 1975).

L. C. B. Seaman, *From Vienna to Versailles* (Methuen, 1972).

P. N. Stearns, *The Revolutions of 1848* (Weidenfeld and Nicolson, 1974).

J. L. Talmon, *Romanticism and Revolt* (Thames and Hudson, 1967).

CHAPTER 3

THE EASTERN QUESTION TO 1856

Units in this chapter

Chapter objectives

❶ The origins of the Eastern Question in the late eighteenth century and the basic elements of the problem: Christians' rights and Balkan unrest; the growing weakness of the Sultan's authority; Russian involvement; the attitude of Britain, France and Austria; British and Austrian agreement to shore up 'the sick man of Europe'.

❷ A clear grasp of the geography of the Near East with an appreciation of the various nationalities in the Ottoman Empire (Moldavia, Wallachia, Serbia, Bulgaria, Greece, Egypt, etc.).

❸ An analysis of the delicate balance of power in Europe after 1815 and of the ways in which the Eastern Question threatened to disrupt it.

❹ The causes of the Greek Revolt (1820–30) and the involvement of Egypt, Russia, Britain, Austria and France.

❺ The reorientation of Russian policy under Nicholas I between 1829 and 1840; his cooperation with Metternich to sustain the Ottoman Empire and secure a peaceful extension of influence there on the basis of the Treaty of Unkiar-Skelessi (July 1833).

❻ Mehemet Ali and the Egyptian revolt against the Sultan (1831–40); Palmerston's intervention and French protestations; British encouragement of Syrian rebellion against Egypt; the decline of Egyptian power and the terms of the Straits Convention of July 1841.

❼ The causes of the Crimean War; disputes concerning the Holy Places and the protection of the Christians; the role of diplomats on the spot such as Lord Stratford de Redcliffe, public opinion in Britain and France and the xenophobic hatred of Russia; the reasons for Tsar Nicholas's stand on the question of the Sultan's Christian subjects; his occupation of the Principalities in July 1853; circumstances leading to the declaration of war.

❽ The course of the war, including the long siege and eventual fall of Sebastopol; the tactics and technology employed; the condition of the troops.

❾ The outcome of the war; the terms of the Treaty of Paris.

⑩ The longer-term consequences and developments: failure of Turkey to reform; persistence of unrest and rebel movements within the empire; Russia's repudiation of the Black Sea clauses in 1871. The impact of the war on the domestic politics of the participants. The results for the international standing of Piedmont and Austria's position among the Powers.

The Eastern Question was the dominant diplomatic issue among the major European Powers in the nineteenth century. It had political, strategic, economic, religious and cultural implications. The Ottoman Empire, whose growing weakness had long encouraged Russian expansion southwards, continued to decay. The Serbian rising of 1804 had posed the threat of Balkan nationalism, but it was the Greek struggle for independence which created the major confrontation. It underlined the conflict of interest between the Powers in this area, particularly the British, French and Austrian apprehensions over Russian aims.

The establishment of Greek independence was followed by the Mehemet Ali crises. The crucial strategic balance of power question of the Straits was dealt with in the Treaty of Unkiar-Skelessi and the Straits Convention. Subsequently, Napoleon III's interest in the holy places and Tsar Nicholas I's claim to the right of protection over the Orthodox minorities precipitated the Crimean War between Russia and the Western Powers in support of Turkey. This was the first conflict among the major European Powers for 40 years. The war, and the Treaty of Paris which concluded it, had far-reaching effects on European diplomatic relations.

3.1 BACKGROUND TO THE EASTERN QUESTION

More than any other single issue in international affairs during the nineteenth century, the Eastern Question was a continual preoccupation of the Powers.

In essence it resulted from the progressive decline of the Turkish Empire. As the control of the Sultan of Constantinople over his territories, subject peoples, and local governors weakened, the Empire became increasingly an object of anxious speculation and rivalry among the Powers.

The balance of power

During the later eighteenth century the spread of Russian influence in the area had aroused growing apprehension among the Western Powers (Britain and France and Austria).

Particularly at issue were the fate of Constantinople and the Straits and the future of the Balkan territories. What happened here would affect the balance of power in Central Europe and the Mediterranean. It could have even wider consequences: the growth of Russian influence in the Near East was regarded by the British as posing a distinct threat to their imperial position in India.

Constant factors

Constant factors in the Eastern Question were: (1) the repeated failure of the Turkish Empire to be effectively reformed; (2) the existence of a very large Christian Greek Orthodox minority under Mohammedan rule (approximately two out of five of the Sultan's subjects were Christian); and (3) increasing restlessness of the Balkan peoples and a tendency to fight among themselves the more they liberated themselves from the common enemy, Turkey.

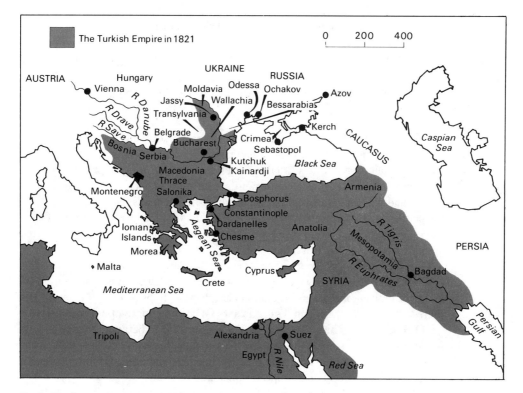

Fig.1 The Eastern Question to 1856. The geography of the Near East showing the extent of the Ottoman Empire in 1821

3.2 THE GREEK QUESTION

In April 1821 the Orthodox Archbishop Germanos openly rejected Turkish rule over the Greeks. Popular unrest erupted into a long war of independence.

Turkish control of South-Eastern Europe had been under increasingly sharp attack since the turn of the nineteenth century. There were various reasons for this: (1) the growing awareness of individual nationhood which was to develop into strong nationalist movements; (2) the influence of the example of the French Revolution; and (3) a surge of foreign sympathy for the Greek cause, both for the Christian Orthodox and, because of the spread of Philhellenism, the veneration for the Greek contribution to civilisation and culture.

Philiké Hetairia

Greeks were being made aware of their own ancient literature and traditions and the demand for independence was combined with a strong cultural revival. In 1814 the 'Philiké Hetairia' was founded to press for the liberation of Greece. This movement gained influence in many cities and attempted to enlist the support of Tsar Alexander I whose foreign minister, Capodistrias, was a Greek.

Philhellenic societies all over Europe collected arms and supplies to support Greeks, who were pictured in the West as the defenders of civilisation. Their ambition was to reconstruct the Byzantine Empire with Constantinople as its capital.

The intervention of the Powers

The rebels were soon weakened by factional differences among themselves and the growing resistance of the Turks. In 1825 the Sultan appealed to the Pasha of Egypt, Mehemet Ali, for help, promising him Syria and Crete as a reward. By 1827 it appeared that the Greek struggle was lost.

The European Powers intervened at this point to prevent the outbreak of a wider struggle and to safeguard their own interests. These were Russia, Great Britain, France and Austria and they had conflicting objectives.

Russia For obvious strategic and commercial reasons the dominant Russian aim was the freedom of her ships to pass the Straits and gain access to the Mediterranean. Some advisers to the Tsar called for the outright seizure of Constantinople.

Other significant considerations in the Russian view were that the major part of the Balkan peoples belonged to the Eastern Orthodox Church while many of them were also, as the Russians were, of Slav race. In the Treaty of Kutchuk-Kainardji of 1774 the Russian monarchy had sought to secure certain privileges for itself as protector of the Christian Orthodox in the Turkish Empire.

Great Britain The Napoleonic period had alerted Great Britain to the major strategic significance for her of the Eastern Mediterranean. As a maritime and imperial power she had secured Malta and the protectorate of the Ionian islands at the Treaty of Vienna. Control of this area by another Power could easily threaten her imperial possessions, particularly India. She was therefore opposed both to Russian and French ambitions in the Near East. The exclusion of these Powers from a controlling position in the area became a fixed aim of British policy in the nineteenth century.

France The French interest in the Levant was long-standing. The French monarchy had traditionally enjoyed a position as protector of the interests of the Catholic Christians in the Near East. France already had an established interest in the area when Napoleon led his expedition to Egypt. This interest was well illustrated during the Mehemet Ali Crisis, in which she pursued an independent policy, and in the subsequent French colonisation of the Mediterranean area.

Austria Austria was opposed to any extension of Russian influence in the Balkans. The close kinship between the Russian people and the Balkan Slavs, later to be emphasised by the Panslav movement, was already posing a long-term threat to the multi-national Habsburg Empire. At the same time, Austria had a strong interest in the free navigation of the Danube and the Principalities, Moldavia and Wallachia.

The Russo-Turkish War

In July 1827 Russia, Great Britain and France signed a treaty to enforce an armistice and to make Turkey agree to the establishment of an autonomous Greece. The allies destroyed the Egyptian fleet at Navarino and in April 1828 the Russians declared war against Turkey. In September 1829 Turkey was forced to concede the independence of Greece and greater autonomy for the Principalities in the Treaty of Adrianople. With the accession to the Greek throne of Otto of Bavaria, Greece became the first independent Christian Balkan kingdom in the nineteenth century.

The Greek revolt and the status quo

Throughout the Greek crisis one should bear in mind not simply the course of events and conflict of interest among the Powers but also the way in which it was related in the minds of statesmen to the question of order within states.

International opinion came to support the national and constitutional demands of the Greek rebels. Metternich, on the other hand, regarded the revolt as a possible threat to the status quo generally. And much as Tsar Alexander might sympathise with the Christian Greeks, he recoiled from the implications of supporting revolution against the principles of the Holy Alliance.

3.3　THE CRIMEAN WAR

The Crimean War originated in 1853 with a Russian attempt to protect the rights and privileges of the Orthodox communities in Turkey. It brought to a head the underlying conflict of interests. Russia occupied Moldavia and Wallachia, which were already protectorates and, after the Russian Black Sea fleet destroyed a Turkish fleet at Sinope, Britain and France came to Turkey's help. The entry of the British and French fleets into the Black Sea amounted to their claiming predominance in the area.

The attitudes of the Powers

Great Britain saw herself as acting to protect the Straits and Constantinople from Russian control. Public opinion in Britain was incensed at Russian actions and credited Russia, among other things, with a desire to destroy Great Britain's influence in the Near East. Liberals and Radicals in particular saw the war more as an issue of principle with Russia than a defence of the Turkish Empire. For them it assumed the character of an ideological struggle, a battle between the ideas of autocratic government and constitutional authority based on popular representation.

Napoleon III's claims on the Sultan over the Holy Places were interpreted by Tsar Nicholas I as an attempt to replace Russian influence with French.

In the eyes of Russian nationalists, the Western Powers came to the help of the 'infidel' Turk out of a deep-seated distrust of Russia and her desire to 'liberate' the Christian Balkan peoples.

Tsar Nicholas feared the revival of Bonapartist sentiment in France and that Napoleon's actions would spread revolution throughout Europe and destroy the 1815 settlement.

Russia demanded that the Turks respect not only the religious rights of the Orthodox but that the Sultan accept the Tsar as protecting *all other rights* that he might feel properly belonged to the Christian Orthodox. This was a claim unjustified by the terms of the Treaty of Kutchuk-Kainardji.

The consequences

The main battleground was the Crimean Peninsula. The war revealed the general backwardness of Russia and the military unpreparedness of the Western Powers. The British forces in particular suffered more from the effects of disease than from battle.

In Britain, Palmerston, among others, favoured exploiting the opportunity of war with the support of the French navy to inflict a defeat on Russia which would not simply contain her expansion, but cripple her potential as a power for a generation or more. The war with Russia was also waged in the Baltic. By 1856 preparations were laid for the 'Great Armament' for the capture of the naval base of Kronstadt. After the fall of Sebastapol the defending general, Todleben, had been recalled to work on the Baltic naval base. Rather than face further defeat, Russia accepted Allied terms. By this time, there was the threat that Sweden would join in against her, while Prussia was pressing Russia to capitulate at the same time.

Nicholas had mistakenly counted on Austrian support. The Austrians mobilised part of their army to protect the mouth of the Danube but stayed neutral. After the fall of the fortress of Sebastopol in September 1855, peace negotiations started in Paris.

The significance of the peace terms

Turkey Turkey was admitted as a member of the Concert of Europe and the Powers undertook to respect Turkish independence. The Sultan promised to improve the conditions of his subjects without discrimination of race or creed.

Russia Not until the end of the First World War was any state forced to submit to such an obvious and humiliating limitation of its freedom of action as Russia in the settlement of 1856.

Russia lost the right of sending her Black Sea Fleet into the Mediterranean. She also lost control of the mouth of the Danube. The Straits were closed to all foreign warships when Turkey was at peace and the Principalities were no longer a Russian Protectorate. They were to have 'an independent and national' administration. The foundation was laid at the Paris Congress for the future independent state of Rumania (recognised officially in 1878).

The significance of the clauses neutralising the Black Sea was that Russia was neither allowed to construct a navy nor support its operations there. On the other hand, if Russia in any way infringed the terms of the Treaty, the British and French navies could enter the Black Sea at will. The nullification of these clauses was Russia's primary ambition over the next 15 years.

Wider considerations

The Crimean War put an end to the Holy Alliance. Russia gave up her eternal mission of defending the Vienna Settlement and preserving Europe from revolution. It forced her to abandon her dominant influence in Central Europe.

She now concentrated on her great expansion in Central Asia and took an increasing interest in the problems of the Balkan Slavs – an interest which was to be of the utmost significance for the later evolution of the Eastern Question.

Alexander II, Tsar from 1855-81, was prompted by the revelation of Russia's weakness in the war to give priority to reforms within Russia, most notably the emancipation of the serfs. The same Crown Council meeting that accepted the Allied tems agreed in principle to the emancipation of the serfs (see Chapter 7).

Austria found her position relatively weakened. Without Russian support she became increasingly isolated as a Power. Indirectly, the Crimean War helped to make possible the emergence of the united nation-states of Italy and Germany, both achieved at Austria's expense.

3.4 CHRONOLOGY

1774	July	THE TREATY OF KUTCHUK KAINARDJI: Russia received territory in the Crimea and obtained the right of free navigation for trading vessels in Turkish waters. Turkey recognised the right of Russia to make representations on behalf of Christian subjects in the Ottoman Empire. This was used as justification for later Russian involvement in Ottoman affairs.
1783		Russia incorporated the Crimea. Sebastopol became a Russian naval base.
1812	May	THE TREATY OF BUCHAREST: following a six-year Russo-Turkish war. Turkey surrendered the province of Bessarabia to Russia. Limited autonomy was granted to Serbia.
1814		PHILIKÉ HETAIRIA: founded at Odessa with the blessing of the Russian government. Led by Alexander Hypsilanti, a member of a Greek family from Moldavia and an officer in the Russian army.
1815		THE VIENNA SETTLEMENT: British protectorate over the Ionian islands and the possession of Malta.
1820		Britain assumed defensive responsibilities in Persia and the Persian Gulf.
1821	February–March	OUTBREAK OF THE GREEK REVOLT in the Danubian Principalities and the Morea.
1825	February	EGYPTIAN INTERVENTION IN GREECE: Ibrahim, son of PASHA MEHEMET ALI, landed in the Morea and subdued the revolt in the peninsula
1826	April	THE ST PETERSBURG PROTOCOL: signed by Britain and Russia. The two Powers agreed to mediate between Greece and Turkey on the basis of autonomy for Greece under Turkish suzerainty.
1827	July	THE TREATY OF LONDON: Britain, France and Russia agreed that if the Turks refused an armistice the three Powers would threaten to support the Greeks.
	October	THE BATTLE OF NAVARINO: destruction of the Egyptian fleet by British, French and Russian squadrons.

1828	April	OUTBREAK OF THE RUSSO-TURKISH WAR.
1829	March	THE LONDON PROTOCOL: Greek autonomy guaranteed by the Powers.
	September	THE TREATY OF ADRIANOPLE between Russia and Turkey: the Russians abandoned their conquests in Europe; Russia to occupy the Danubian Principalities pending the payment of an indemnity; the Turks accepted the London Protocol
1830	February	New three-Power protocol provided for Greek independence.
1831	November	MEHEMET ALI DECLARED WAR ON THE SULTAN, having demanded Syria as a reward for his help against the Greeks.
1832	March	OTTO OF BAVARIA appointed King of Greece.
	July	Turkey finally accepted Greek independence
	December	The battle of Konieh. Ibrahim completely routed the main Turkish army.
1833	February	The Sultan requested Russian protection against Mehemet Ali – the Muraviev mission.
	May	Russian intervention forced the Egyptians to make peace.
	July	THE TREATY OF UNKIAR SKELESSI: this was between Russia and Turkey for a term of eight years. Each party was to come to the other's aid in event of attack. A secret clause excused the Turks from fulfilling this obligation provided they closed the Dardanelles to foreign warships. This represented the height of Russian influence at Constantinople. Britain and France interpreted the treaty to mean that the Bosphorus was to remain open to Russian warships and that Turkey was to be at the mercy of Russia.
	September	THE MÜNCHENGRÄTZ AGREEMENT: the Tsar agreed with Austria to maintain the Ottoman Empire; if partition became inevitable, action would only be taken after consultation between the two Powers.
1839	April	The Sultan declared war on Mehemet Ali with the invasion of Syria.
	June	Egyptian victory at Nizib.
1840	July	THE TREATY OF LONDON: Britain, Russia, Austria and Prussia agreed to force a settlement on the Egyptians. Mehemet Ali rejected the demand to give up Crete, northern Syria, Mecca and Medina, hoping for French support for his ambitions.
	November	Mehemet Ali makes peace.
1841	June	THE STRAITS CONVENTION: signed by the five great Powers. The Straits were to be closed to all foreign warships in time of peace.
1844	June	TSAR NICHOLAS I visited Britain. He proposed to Lord Aberdeen that Britain and Russia should consult together in the event of the collapse of the Ottoman Empire.
	September	THE NESSELRODE MEMORANDUM: The Russian foreign minister summed up the supposed Anglo-Russian agreement.
1848	September	Russian troops suppressed revolt in Moldavia and Wallachia.
1849	May	Russian troops defeated the Hungarian revolution.
	October	Crisis over Hungarian Kossuth's presence in Turkey and Russian and Austrian demands that the revolutionaries be extradited. British and French naval demonstration at Besika Bay.
1850–52		DISPUTE OVER THE HOLY PLACES: the Sultan yielded to pressure from Napoleon III to grant privileges to Roman Catholic monks. Quarrel with the Greek Orthodox supported by the Tsar.
1853	January	TSAR NICHOLAS'S CONVERSATIONS WITH LORD SEYMOUR, the British ambassador. The Tsar predicted the collapse of the Ottoman Empire and made a bid for British agreement. He stated that while Russia would not take Constantinople, he would not allow any other power to occupy it.
	February–May	THE MENSHIKOV MISSION TO CONSTANTINOPLE: Prince Menshikov attempted to gain Turkish concessions over the Holy Places and to secure a treaty recognising a Russian protectorate over Orthodox churches in Constantinople. ARRIVAL OF LORD STRATFORD DE REDCLIFFE (British Ambassador to Turkey), who advised the Turks to reject the wider demands of Menshikov. Russians decided to occupy the Principalities.
	June	British and French fleets went to Besika Bay.
	July	RUSSIAN TROOPS INVADED MOLDAVIA AND WALLACHIA. THE VIENNA NOTE.
	October	The Turks declared war on Russia.

	November	THE BATTLE OF SINOPE between the Russian and Turkish fleets. Outburst of anti-Russian indignation in Britain.
1854	January	BRITISH AND FRENCH FLEETS ENTERED THE BLACK SEA to protect the Turkish coasts and transports. Russians rejected request to evacuate Moldavia and Wallachia.
	March	ALLIANCE OF BRITAIN AND FRANCE WITH TURKEY AND DECLARATION OF WAR ON RUSSIA.
	August	THE VIENNA FOUR POINTS: the suggested conditions of peace were to be (1) a collective guarantee of the position of the Principalities and Serbia; (2) free passage of the mouth of the Danube; (3) a revision of the Straits Convention in the interest of the balance of power; (4) Russian abandonment of claims to a protectorate over the Sultan's subjects. Russians rejected these demands. Russians evacuated Moldavia and Wallachia.
	September	LANDINGS IN THE CRIMEA BY THE BRITISH AND FRENCH. The battle of Alma and the siege of Sebastopol.
	October	The battle of Balaclava.
	November	The battle of Inkerman.
1855	March	Accession of TSAR ALEXANDER II.
	September	The Russians evacuated Sebastopol.
	November	Austrian alliance with Britain and France. Austria mobilised all her forces and issued an ultimatum to Russia but did not engage in hostilities.
1856	February–March	PEACE AGREED AT CONGRESS OF PARIS.
		Joint declaration by the British, French and Austrian governments that they regarded any infringement of Turkish independence and integrity as a 'casus belli'.
		The Turkish reform edict, the HATTI-HUMAYUN: the most significant Turkish reform edict of the nineteenth century, offering Christian subjects security of life, honour and property. Civil offices thrown open to all subjects of the Sultan.

Illustrative questions and answers

1 Explain why the Eastern Question loomed so large in European affairs between 1815 and 1841.

Tutorial note

Consider not only the instability of the Near East and the problems faced by the Sultan, but the reasons why the Great Powers became involved. The question is as much about the balance of power as about developments within the Turkish Empire.

You need to know about

The various national movements against the Sultan and the internal weaknesses of the Empire. Economic, religious and territorial reasons for Great Power involvement in Turkish affairs. General diplomatic history 1815–41. The course of Greek and Egyptian revolts. The details of European attitudes and intervention.

Suggested answer plan

1 The state of Europe after the Napoleonic War; emphasise war-weariness, both economic and psychological; consequent attempts to maintain peace at all costs by congress and cooperation; the Eastern Question as the main threat to peace after 1815, finally shattering it in 1854.

2 The main reasons for this were to be found in the internal political weakness of the Ottoman Empire, and also in the rise of Balkan nationalisms; discuss the latter, beginning with the Serbian revolt of 1804–12 and append a sketch map.

3 The interest of the Great Powers in the fate of Turkey; Russian and French involvement as rival protectors of the Sultan's Christian subjects, and Russia's territorial ambitions in the Balkans; Britain's commercial interests in the Near

East and her concern to maintain the freedom of the Straits and the route to India; France's conquest and settlement of Algeria (1830) and North African ambitions generally, as a means of offsetting her loss of power inside Europe; Austria's own historic role as protector of Europe against the Turks and her anxiety to prevent an extension of Russian power in the Balkans.

4   A brief narrative of the Greek national revolt 1820–30; attitudes of Alexander and Nicholas, and also of Metternich, Canning and Polignac.

5   A brief account of the Egyptian revolt under Mehemet Ali and Ibrahim Pasha; attitudes and involvement of the Powers, leading to the Straits Convention and settlement of 1841.

6   Show that, whereas the Greek episode had ultimately encouraged cooperation among the Powers, the Egyptian affair led to a division of Europe into opposing camps. The problem was that Russia and Britain, the two main victors against Napoleon, the one with her great territorial empire, the other with her immense commercial preponderance, were bound to dispute over the spoils of the crumbling Turkish empire; realistic, Nicholas recognised this by offering Greece to Britain in 1844, if only he could have Constantinople.

Meanwhile, France supported Britain, but was anxious to maintain her own say in the matter; just as Austria supported Russia, but more to check her influence over the Porte than to encourage it. The outcome was the Straits Convention and 12 years of uneasy and unusual quietness on the Eastern Question.

2   Do you consider that the policy of Tsar Nicholas I towards Turkey led inevitably to the Crimean War?

Tutorial note

This is a straight question on the causes of the Crimean War, slightly disguised. You will need to sort out the short-term and immediate factors leading to the outbreak of war from the longer-term factors which made a conflict inevitable sooner or later. Emphasis in both cases should be on Nicholas's role, but you should also set the answer in the context of the responsibility of other participant countries, especially France and Britain.

You need to know about

The background to the Eastern Question. Its development 1815–53. Russian attitudes and policy under Nicholas I. The attitude of the Great Powers. Diplomatic manoeuvres preceding the war.

Suggested answer plan

1   The internal situation in Turkey since the late eighteenth century; Balkan nationalism and the plight of Christian peoples.

2   The development of Russian policy since Catherine the Great; Moscow's status as the 'Third Rome' and protector of Christians in Constantinople; Russia's territorial ambitions towards the feeble Turkish Empire.

3   The accession of Nicholas I; his and Nesselrode's Near-Eastern policy; cooperation with Britain and France against the Turkish navy at Navarino; Unkiar-Skelessi and the reorientation of policy to secure the peaceful penetration and exploitation of Turkey; Mehemet Ali and the Egyptian crisis; the strong hostility of Britain (especially Palmerston) to Russian policy, and her fear that it would lead to separate French and Russian 'spheres of influence' in the Near East; the 1841 Straits Convention established the Eastern Question as a European 'problem'.

4   The immediate build-up to the war; Nicholas's extreme demands in the dispute with France over the Holy Places; Russia's occupation of Moldavia and Wallachia; a brief account of diplomatic manoeuvres leading to the Turkish declaration of war and the engagement of the the Powers.

5 The view that Napoleon III was more to blame than Nicholas; Napoleon used the dispute over the Holy Places as an excuse for the exercise of 'la gloire' and to attack the Vienna Settlement of 1815; against this, Napoleon was dependent on Catholic support – i.e. on French Catholic opinion that France should protect the Latins in the Holy Places.

6 The view that Britain was mainly to blame for the Crimean War; economic interests' desire to penetrate Turkish markets; the roles of Stratford de Redcliffe and Palmerston; hostility of British public opinion to Russia, its impact on the government.

7 Conclusion: it is sometimes said that the Crimean War was an 'accident'; on the other hand, Russia and Turkey had fought about every 20 years for the previous two centuries; the war in 1854 was different because the fear of Russian aggrandisement led Britain and France to back Turkey. In western eyes, Russia, the greatest Slav nation, represented all that was barbaric; war became inevitable when even Francis Joseph of Austria, whom Nicholas had rescued in 1849 when he put down the Hungarian revolution, refused to support Russia.

3 Examine whether the Crimean War had greater consequences for Western Europe than for Eastern Europe.

Tutorial note

'Consequences' here infer not simply the direct and immediate, but also the indirect and long-term results. You should be ready to comment on any significant influence of the war on domestic developments in the countries concerned, as well as on the more obvious international consequences. Eastern Europe may be defined as (1) the Russian sphere of influence and (2) the Balkans.

You need to know about

The results of the Crimean War: the Paris Congress, especially its territorial and strategic implications; the effects on the Ottoman Empire; its long-term implications for relations between the Powers and developments within them.

Suggested answer plan

1 The Congress of Paris: the conclusion of peace terms and the imposition of a European solution on the Turks; emphasise that the participants in the Congress had aims of their own: Britain wished to weaken Russia strategically in every way; France was anxious to treat Russia leniently; Austria wished to strengthen her hold on the Principalities.

2 The terms affecting Russia and the Balkans; the clause regarded as most significant by the victorious Powers was the neutralisation of the Black Sea; but Britain and France could enter the Black Sea at will should Russia attack Turkey or otherwise infringe the terms of the treaty; there was a vulnerability, therefore, to the South Russian coastline.

3 Navigation of the Danube was freed from Russian influence; Serbian rights were guaranteed; the emergence of an independent Rumania (formally recognised by the Powers at the Congress of Berlin). Stress the growth of Balkan nationalism; by denying both Russia and Austria an extension of influence in the Balkans, conditions came about which permitted the creation of independent states from the declining Ottoman Empire.

4 The collapse of the Ottoman Empire, which Nicholas I had predicted, was postponed; some genuine efforts at internal reform were made; the Sultan announced the *Hatti-humayun*, proclaiming religious equality throughout the Empire, economic reforms and abolition of bribery and tax-farming; but progress towards reform was too slow and incomplete.

5   Wider consequences of the Crimean War: Russia became a revisionist Power; the war ended the period during which the conservative solidarity of governments and the maintenance of the status quo were emphasised; the final blow to the Holy Alliance. Russia now concentrated on expansion in Central Asia and on a policy of general support for the Slavs; the reforms under Alexander II were a direct result of the exposure of Russian weakness by the war.

6   The diplomatic impact on Western Europe of the war: Austria found herself isolated; the war alienated Russia; it was not the revolutions of 1848 but the Crimean War which finally destroyed the balance of the Metternich era, only after the Crimean War did those political upheavals become possible which the Austrian minister worked so hard to postpone; the subsequent successes of Cavour and Bismarck were helped by the weakening of the Habsburg Empire after the Crimean War.

7   Conclusion: the consequences of the war were of major significance in both Eastern and Western Europe, though, on balance, the impact on developments in the West was probably even greater – more particularly in indirectly encouraging the emergence of a united Italy and a united Germany; the results for Russia and the Balkans should also be given full weight.

Question bank

1   Document question (The Great Powers and the Greek problem): study the extract below and then answer the subsequent questions (a) to (g):

Extract

'In the Name of the Holy and undivided Trinity.

His Majesty the King of the United Kingdom of Great Britain and Ireland; His Majesty the King of France and Navarre, and His Majesty the Emperor of all the Russias, penetrated with the necessity of putting an end to the sanguinary contest which, by delivering up the Greek provinces and the isles of the Archipelago to all the disorders of anarchy, produces daily fresh impediment to the commerce of the European States, and gives occasion to piracies, which not only expose the subjects of the High Contracting Parties to considerable losses, but besides render necessary burdensome measures of protection and repression; (the Kings of the United Kingdom and France) having besides received, on the part of the Greeks, a pressing request to interpose their mediation with the Ottoman Porte, and being as well as His Majesty the Emperor of all the Russias, animated by the desire of stopping the effusion of blood, and of arresting the evils of all kinds which might arise from the continuance of such a state of things, have resolved to unite their efforts and to regulate the operation thereof by a formal treaty, with the view of re-establishing peace between the contending parties by means of an arrangement which is called for as much by humanity as by the interest of the repose of Europe....

'1. The Contracting Powers will offer to the Ottoman Porte their mediation with a view to bringing about a reconciliation between it and the Greeks. This offer of mediation shall be made to this Power immediately after the ratification of the Treaty, by means of a collective declaration signed by the Plenipotentiaries of the allied Courts at Constantinople: and there shall be made, at the same time, to the two contending parties, a demand of an immediate armistice between them, as a preliminary condition indispensable to the opening of any negotiation.

'2. The arrangement to be proposed to the Ottoman Porte shall rest on the following bases: the Greeks shall hold of the Sultan as their suzerain; and in consequence of his suzerainty they shall pay to the Ottoman Empire an annual tribute, the amount of which shall be fixed, once for all by a common agreement. They shall be governed by the authorities whom they shall themselves choose and nominate, but in the nomination of whom the Porte shall have a determinate voice.'

(*Treaty of London for the Pacification of Greece*, 6 July, 1827)

(a) What caused the Greeks to send to the British and French 'a pressing request to interpose their mediation' at this time? (3)

(b) What, in the area affected by the Greek revolts, were the special interests of *each* of 'His Majesty the King of the United Kingdom of Great Britain and Ireland, His Majesty the King of France and Navarre, and His Majesty the Emperor of all the Russias'? (6)

(c) How had Russian policy been affected by the accession of Nicholas I as 'the Emperor of all the Russias'? (4)

(d) Why was it that Britain, Russia and France 'resolved to unite their efforts'? (5)

(e) What were the dangers for the future in the London decision that the Greeks should 'hold of the Sultan as their suzerain'? (2)

(f) How, and with what results, did 'the Contracting Powers' try to enforce 'an immediate armistice'? (4)

(g) How successfully was the Greek problem settled by 1832, and what did Russia and Britain respectively contribute to the settlement? (7)

2 Examine the view that the outcome of the Crimean War (1854–56 'marked a watershed in European diplomacy'. (London, June 1991)

3 'The Eastern Question was essentially about the balance of power.' Consider this view in relation to the period from 1815–1841.
(Cambridge, Summer 1986)

4 'The significance for Russia of its defeat in the Crimea lay more in its domestic than in its international repercussions.' (Oxford and Cambridge, June 1992)

5 'The Sick Man of Europe'. What did the survival of the Ottoman Empire between 1840 and 1878 owe to European support?
(Oxford and Cambridge, June 1991)

READING LIST

Standard textbook reading

L. W. Cowie and R. Wolfson, *Years of Nationalism, European History 1815-1890* (Edward Arnold, 1985), chapter II (4).

J.A.S. Grenville, *Europe Reshaped 1848–78* (Fontana, 1976), chapters 10 and 11.

Agatha Ramm, *Europe in the Nineteenth Century 1789–1905* (Longman, 1984), chapter 14.

David Thomson, *Europe since Napoleon* (Penguin, 1977), chapter 12.

Anthony Wood, *Europe 1815–1945* (Longman, 1975), chapter 15.

Further suggested reading

M.S. Anderson, *The Eastern Question 1774–1923* (Macmillan, 1966)

J.P.T. Bury (ed), *The New Cambridge Modern History 1830–70*, volume IX (CUP, 1964), chapter 10.

M.E. Chamberlain, *British Foreign Policy in the Age of Palmerston*, (Longman, 1980).

D. Clayton, *Britain and the Eastern Question from Missolonghi to Gallipoli* (University of London, 1971).

C.W. Crawley (ed), *The New Cambridge Modern History 1793–1830*, volume IX, (CUP, 1974), chapter 19.

D. Dakin, *The Greek Struggle for Independence, 1821–33*, (Batsford, 1973)

D. Gillard, *The Struggle for Asia 1828-1914*, (Methuen, 1977).

W.E. Mosse, *The Rise and Fall of the Crimean System 1855–71* (Macmillan, 1963).

L.C.B. Seaman, *From Vienna to Versailles* (Methuen, 1972).

A.J.P. Taylor, *The Struggle for Mastery in Europe* (OUP, 1971).

Sir C. Webster, *The Foreign Policy of Palmerston 1830–41* (Bell, 1951).

D. Weigall, *Britain and the World 1815–1986: A Dictionary of International Relations* (Batsford, 1987).

THE RISORGIMENTO

Units in this chapter

Chapter objectives

❶ The impact of the French Revolution and Napoleonic rule on Italian nationalist feelings and on the government and administration of the Italian states.

❷ Italy in 1815: the effect of the Congress of Vienna; the restoration of Austrian, Bourbon and Papal rule; the nature of this government.

❸ The Risorgimento proper, or the romantic phase of Italian nationalism; the Carbonari, the literati and the 1820–21 revolutions; the republican and democratic nationalism of Mazzini and 'Young Italy'; the risings of the 1830s.

❹ The two rulers who briefly took up the cause of Italian nationalism: Pius IX and Charles Albert of Piedmont; the influence of the neo-Guelph writers (Gioberti, Farini, Balbo); the Piedmontese war against Austria and the 'Constitution' of 1848.

❺ The 1848 revolutions in the peninsula and their suppression by Radetzky; an analysis of support for nationalism in Naples, Tuscany and Milan.

❻ Piedmont and the businessman's phase of Italian nationalism; the abandonment of the democratic revolutionary approach of Mazzini; the desire for an Italian Zollverein, or customs union with a common tariff and communications system, uniform weights and measures; frustrations with the economic restrictions of Austrian rule; the National Society.

❼ The restoration of the credibility of the Piedmontese monarchy after the defeat of the 1848 revolutions by D'Azeglio; his replacement by Cavour; Cavour's financial and administrative reforms, economic expansion and the development of the bourgeois liberal state; his anticlerical measures (the Siccardi Laws); his admiration for Britain and France; his relations with Victor Emmanuel, who forced him to engage in the Crimean War.

❽ Cavour's announcement of Piedmont's claims at the Treaty of Paris; his decision to secure unification through diplomacy; the attitude of the Powers to Italy; the secret diplomacy with Napoleon (Plombieres) and provocation of the war with Austria; the French motives for supporting Piedmont; the reasons for Napoleon's disengagement from the war and Villafranca.

❾ The plebiscites of 1859, completing the first stage of Italian nationalism.

⑩ The political and social background of the Two Sicilies; Mazzini, the revolution and Garibaldi's adventure; his republicanism and distaste for Piedmont; the attitude of Britain and France; Cavour's skill in exploiting the situation; the intervention of the Piedmontese army; the incorporation of the Two Sicilies in the Kingdom of Italy.

⑪ The diplomatic and military manoeuvres leading to the incorporation of Venice and Rome; the attitude of the Powers, especially France, to these events.

⑫ The nature of the new Italian state; its bureaucratic and centralised structure, which alienated many patriots; the domination of North over South; Piedmont's free trade competition ruins the South's precarious economy; the estrangement between the Papacy and the new Italian state.

The Vienna Settlement replaced the Napoleonic rule of Italy by establishing the Habsburg Empire as the dominant power in occupation of Lombardy and Venetia. During the years after 1815, Italian nationalist sentiments found expression in conspiratorial societies, such as the Carbonari, in a general cultural reawakening and, in the 1830s and 1840s, in specific political programmes for the unification of the peninsula. The best-known romantic revolutionary and nationalist of this period in Europe was Mazzini, founder of 'Young Italy'.

After the failure of the 1848 revolutions and the discrediting, in nationalist eyes, of Pope Pius IX there was growing recognition that Italy could not, unaided, liberate herself. In the event, the unification was brought about under the leadership of Piedmont and her Prime Minister, Count Cavour.

In 1859, following his secret meeting with Cavour at Plombieres, Napoleon III assisted Piedmont in defeating Austria and gaining Lombardy from the Habsburgs. This was followed by the incorporation of the central Italian principalities. In 1860 Garibaldi and his volunteer troops landed in Sicily and then, crossing to the mainland, proceeded to capture most of the Kingdom of Naples. Cavour forestalled his march on Rome and Garibaldi surrendered his conquests to King Victor Emmanuel.

The new Kingdom of Italy was proclaimed in March, 1861. Venetia was gained as a result of the Austro-Prussian War and Rome, which had been garrisoned by the French, followed after the Prussian defeat of France. The Pope, deprived of his temporal power, refused to recognise the new Italian state. The Piedmontese administrative system was extended to the rest of Italy. The new kingdom was weakened by deep divisions and deeply disappointed many nationalists, like Mazzini.

4.1 THE RISORGIMENTO

The term 'risorgimento' – in the sense of a movement of national rebirth or resurgence – was first used in the eighteenth century.

It is used to describe the general movement of growing national consciousness and revival from that period, but more particularly from 1815 onwards. Very frequently it is employed more comprehensively to include the actual process of territorial unification through war and diplomacy between 1859 and 1870.

Very many Italians during the nineteenth century neither comprehended nor sympathised with the idea of a united Italy, and many after the unification opposed it.

During the first part of the century there seemed to be almost insuperable barriers to unity which included: (I) the division into seven separate states; (2) strong regional loyalties; (3) economic backwardness and divisions; (4) mass illiteracy; (5) the institution of the Papacy, a primarily international institution, whose territories cut

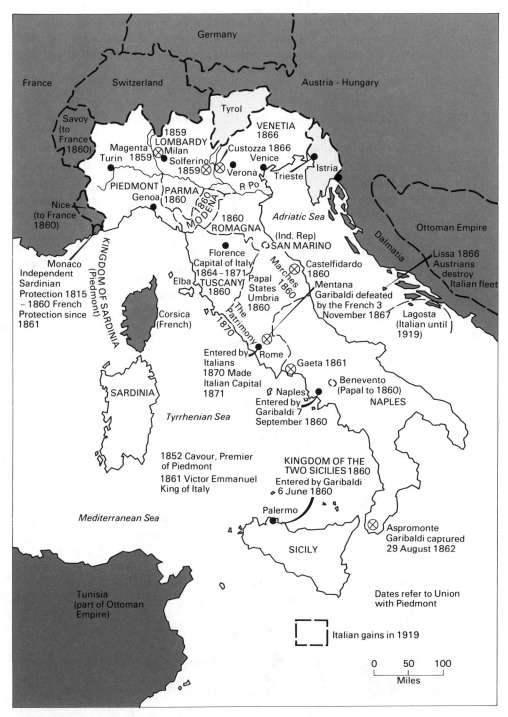

Fig. 2 The stages of Italian unification 1859–70, including the gains of 1919

the peninsula in two; (6) the domination of Italy either directly or indirectly following the Vienna Settlement. (Metternich described Italy as a 'geographical expression'.)

Napoleon I and Italy

The revolutionary conquests of Napoleon did much to destroy the old regime in Italy. His imperial rule strengthened the idea of national unification in two ways:

❶ it aroused the intense opposition of Italians to foreign domination – this expressed itself after 1815 against the Austrians; and

❷ the idea of the nation-state propagated by the French Revolution and the introduction of administrative modernisation and reforms under the Emperor encouraged the breakdown of the traditional Italian system of separate states. It accustomed the educated classes in particular to a greater degree of unity and efficiency.

The Restoration

After 1815, when Italy came under Austrian domination, patriots and reformers became increasingly insistent on the need for independence and at least some degree of unification. This was the period of the secret societies, such as the Carbonari, or Charcoal Burners, and of revolts in Naples, Sicily and Piedmont. But among many of the opponents of the restored governments the unification of Italy was in no sense a priority. They were more concerned with reforms and constitutionalism.

It was only in the 1830s and 1840s that clear and positive alternatives were put forward for the future of the peninsula.

The alternative programmes for unification

The basic choices which emerged were these: (a) was Italy to be a fully unified and centralised state or was it to be a federation? (b) Was it to be a monarchy or a republic?

Three major alternatives were put forward:

❶ The achievement of a single unified republic through popular insurrection. This democratic idea of unification was put forward by the most influential prophet of the Risorgimento and the leading exponent of early nineteenth-century nationalism, Giuseppe Mazzini, founder of 'Young Italy'.

❷ A confederation of states under the leadership of the Pope. This solution was proposed by Vincenzo Gioberti, who wrote *Of the Moral and Civil Primacy of the Italians* (1843). In this he argued that the Papacy and Roman Catholicism were the glories of Italy and must lead the national revival.

❸ The unification of Italy under the King of Piedmont.

All of these ideas found supporters during the revolutions of 1848, but following the rejection by Pope Pius IX of Gioberti's role for him, the second alternative was very largely discredited. In the event it was the Piedmontese solution which was to succeed.

4.2   PIEDMONT AND CAVOUR

After the 1848 revolutions, Piedmont was alone among the Italian states in preserving her constitution.

Her government remained free of Austrian domination and during the 1850s she underwent important reforms and modernisation.

Cavour, with the reputation of being a moderate liberal and supporter of parliamentary institutions, established himself as the leading Piedmontese politician. By 1852 he had become Prime Minister. As a believer in free trade and constitutionalism he achieved much during the 1850s. In this period Piedmontese trade trebled and she became the leading, as well as the most liberal, state in Italy.

Italian independence

Though he had little experience of foreign affairs when he came to power, Cavour hoped for the achievement of Italian independence.

As a skilled practical politician he was very conscious of the reasons for the failure of the 1848 revolutions, when it had optimistically been assumed by many of the revolutionaries that an Italy that was divided, and in many areas backward, could liberate itself.

He recognised that it was only when one or more of the Powers developed a serious interest in helping Italy would it become a possibility – and he looked to France for that support.

The Peace Congress of Paris

Cavour had contributed Piedmontese troops to the allied side against Russia in the Crimean War. This war, in turn, had helped to make possible the unification of Italy by transforming the relations between the Powers.

The Vienna Settlement had been shaken: Russia was no longer committed, as in the earlier period, to upholding the established order in Europe. Austria had been weakened and isolated. It became possible for Napoleon III, who considered support for Italian freedom to be part of the hereditary policy of his dynasty and who had been involved in his youth in the revolt of 1831 in the Romagna, to ally with Piedmont against Austria.

The Plombières Agreement

In 1858 an Italian nationalist revolutionary, Felice Orsini, made an attempt to assassinate Napoleon III as a dramatic gesture in favour of Italian liberation. Orsini regarded Napoleon as a traitor to the Italian cause, with which he had earlier been associated, and the destroyer of the Roman Republic as President of the French Second Republic. Napoleon allowed Orsini to be executed but authorised the publication of Orsini's appeal to him to free Italy.

Six months later Napoleon met Cavour at Plombieres and laid down the basis for the future alliance and reorganisation of the peninsula. The essential terms of this were:

❶ that, with French help, Piedmont would annex Italy above the Apennines (Lombardy and Venetia);

❷ Savoy and Nice were to be given to France;

❸ the territories of Central Italy, except Rome and the surrounding area, would constitute a separate kingdom;

❹ Southern Italy would conserve its unity and frontiers, though the ruling dynasty would be changed.

At this stage it seems clear that neither Cavour nor Napoleon anticipated the unification of *all* Italy, nor even desired it.

The war with Austria

Austria allowed herself to be provoked into a declaration of war by demanding that Piedmont disarm. The conflict lasted from April to July 1859, with the French and Piedmontese capturing most of Lombardy following the battles of Magenta and Solferino. Simultaneously, revolts broke out in the states of Parma, Tuscany, Modena and the Romagna. The rulers of the Duchies left their states, and Piedmontese authorities moved in to run provisional governments. This went beyond the arrangements agreed at Plombieres.

Villafranca

In July 1859 Napoleon made a truce with the Austrian Emperor, Francis Joseph, at Villafranca.

Two major reasons for his halting the war after Solferino were his fear of Prussian mobilisation against France and his distrust of Cavour's activities in the Duchies, especially Tuscany which, according to Plombières, was not to be part of the enlarged Piedmont.

Villafranca arranged that only Lombardy should be ceded to Piedmont. Venetia was not included and the future of central Italy was left uncertain. The agreement of Plombieres, therefore, was only partly fulfilled and Cavour, who was excluded from the negotiations, resigned.

The annexation of central Italy

Cavour's supporters and the nationalist group, the 'National Society', worked very actively in central Italy, campaigning for annexation to Piedmont. Increasingly, ideas of reform and Liberalism, characteristic of the period up to 1848, were giving way in risorgimentist circles to aggressive Nationalism and militarism.

In January 1860 Cavour returned to power and negotiated this annexation. Plebiscites were held and pronounced in favour of unification. In March 1860 the Romagna, Tuscany, Modena and Parma became incorporated in the North Italian Kingdom. Savoy and Nice were handed over to France, though the agreement at Plombières had specified that this would be in return for liberating Italy to the Adriatic (i.e. Lombardy *and* Venetia).

4.3 GARIBALDI AND THE 'THOUSAND'

Up to this point the political initiative was in the hands of Cavour. In the next phase of unification he found himself challenged by Mazzini and the democratic programme of complete unification.

Mazzini had formed the idea of an expedition to the South which would work its way up to Rome and Venetia. In April 1860 Garibaldi's volunteer army of the 'Thousand' left Genoa for Sicily, conquering first the island and then Naples. He appeared determined to march on Rome, where a French garrison had been stationed since 1849.

Both Cavour and Napoleon were extremely opposed to anything like a Mazzinian republican movement gaining control in Italy.

Secondly, if Garibaldi were allowed to march on Rome this would almost certainly involve French intervention to protect the Pope.

Cavour was also aware of the problems, social and economic, that the annexation of the southern territories would bring to the government of a united Italy.

In September 1860 Cavour forestalled Garibaldi by advancing along the Adriatic coast and taking the rest of the Papal State except the area immediately around Rome. Piedmontese troops then linked up with Garibaldi, who surrendered his conquests to the Piedmontese King, Victor Emmanuel. Plebiscites ratified the annexations and the Kingdom of Italy (excluding Rome and Venetia) was proclaimed in March 1861.

Some underlying considerations

Cavour employed the force of Italian patriotism which Mazzini had done so much to encourage. He linked it with the traditional desire of Piedmont to expand in northern Italy. By enlisting Napoleon's help he was able to exploit the balance of power and create a Kingdom of Italy.

The essential condition for this was that Austria, defeated in 1859, was unwilling to resume the war. Napoleon recognised that the other Powers would not allow France to extend her influence on a large scale in Italy.

In the actual form which the unification took, the preparatory work of the 'National Society' was of considerable significance. Its supporters argued that it was essential for the national movement to rally round Piedmont and her monarchy. They set themselves against Mazzini's democratic and republican ideas. Their propaganda for Italian unity laid particular emphasis on the economic benefits which would come from it.

In Sicily Garibaldi's achievement was largely due to the revolt of the peasants. When he reached the island it was already out of the control of the government. To start with he allied himself with the peasantry, abolished the hated milling tax and promised land redistribution. Later he suppressed peasant uprisings. In the event it was not surprising that the land-owning class came to the conclusion that the re-establishment of order in the countryside would be better entrusted to the Piedmontese monarchy and its army.

4.4 THE CONSTITUTION OF THE NEW ITALY

The government of the new Kingdom of Italy after 1861 was based on a very restricted franchise (approximately 2% of the population). It was supported by an elite.

The work of the Risorgimento came to be seen not, as Mazzini had hoped, as an achievement of 'the people of Italy', but of an upper and upper-middle-class minority.

The Piedmontese constitution (Il Statuto) was extended to the rest of Italy together with the legal system and bureaucracy. A rigidly centralised system of administration was adopted. This and the process of integration were costly and imposed a heavy burden of taxation which was much resented.

In the South the relationship of the classes remained semi-feudal. The social and economic predicament of the South was to loom very large in the history of the new Italy. The failure of politicians to understand – or, if they did understand, to act effectively towards meeting the problem of the South, helps to account for its continuing backwardness and for the serious civil war which broke out in the 1860s.

4.5 THE COMPLETION OF UNIFICATION AND THE PAPACY

The completion of unification came with:
➊ the gain of Venetia in 1866 as a result of the Austro-Prussian War, and
➋ the acquisition of Rome in 1870 during the Franco-Prussian War, when the French garrison withdrew.

The second involved the destruction of the temporal power of the Pope. In the 'Syllabus of Errors' the Pope had already declared an out-and-out opposition to such liberal and secular ideas as those on which the new Italian state was based.

By the Law of Guarantees the Italian Government unilaterally settled the Pope's affairs. He was to remain in possession of the Vatican and to draw a pension from the Italian State. He ignored the Law, refused to take his allowance and presented himself to the world as the 'prisoner of the Vatican'. This division remained a grave weakness for the Italian State until the Concordat between the Vatican and Fascist Italy in 1929.

Historians have drawn attention to the deep divisions in the new Italy, the gulf between the new administration structure, the 'legal' Italy and the 'real' Italy. But the history of the unification process makes this hardly a surprise. As Denis Mack Smith has pointed out, 'every war of the Risorgimento was a civil war.' For instance, one-third of Radetzky's army in 1848 were Italians. Both in 1848 and 1860 the uprising started in Sicily and the Sicilians were in revolt not for the unification of Italy, but autonomy. Cavour intervened in the Papal States in 1860, with the primary motive of halting Garibaldi. Nor would the unification have been possible without the support of France for Piedmont, Britain's benevolent neutrality, Prussian support in 1866 and the steady decline of the Austrian Empire, diplomatically isolated after the Crimean War.

4.6 CHRONOLOGY

1851–61		COUNT CAMILLO BENSO DI CAVOUR: entered the government at Piedmont under D'Azeglio as Minister of Agriculture and Commerce.
1852	November	CAVOUR PRIME MINISTER OF PIEDMONT. His government was a coalition of the Right-Centre and Left- Centre; the 'Connubio' Programme of modernisation: finances reorganised; tariffs revised; new commercial treaties negotiated; rapidly accelerated railway construction; modernisation of the Piedmontese army.
1855–56		Piedmont entered the Crimean War on the Franco-British side. Cavour attended the Congress of Paris and pressed the grievances of Italy.
1856		FOUNDATION OF THE NATIONAL SOCIETY: this argued for the unification of Italy under Piedmont. It had the encouragement of Cavour. Though its policy conflicted with the ideas of Mazzinian republicanism, it also gained backing from numbers of Mazzinians.
1858	January	THE ATTEMPTED ASSASSINATION OF NAPOLEON III AND THE EMPRESS EUGENIE BY FELICE ORSINI. Orsini appealed to Napoleon from his death cell to liberate Italy.
	July	THE SECRET MEETING OF NAPOLEON AND CAVOUR AT PLOMBIERES; Napoleon agreed to join Piedmont in a war on Austria provided it could be provoked in a manner to justify it in the eyes of French and European opinion. Austrians were to be expelled from northern Italy and Lombardy and Venetia were to be incorporated by Piedmont. France was to be rewarded with Savoy and Nice. An independent kingdom of central Italy was to be set up.
	December	The formal treaty of alliance signed by France and Piedmont.
1859	March	Piedmontese reserves called up.
	April	Mobilisation of Austrian army. AUSTRIAN ULTIMATUM TO PIEDMONT; directed her to demobilise in three days. This supplied Cavour with the provocation which he and Napoleon needed. The ultimatum was rejected and the war began.
	May	Revolutions in Parma, Modena and Tuscany encouraged by the National Society.
	June	THE BATTLE OF MAGENTA. Insurrections in Bologna, Ferrara, Ravenna and the Papal Legations. BATTLE OF SOLFERINO.
	July	PEACE OF VILLAFRANCA: Lombardy was to be granted to France with the exception of Mantua and Peschiera. Napoleon was to cede this to Piedmont. Venetia was to remain under Austrian control. Italian princes were to be restored. Resignation of Cavour.
	August–September	Representative assemblies in Parma, Modena, Tuscany and the Romagna declared for unification with Piedmont.
	November	Treaty of Zürich finalised the agreement of Villafranca.
1860	January	CAVOUR RETURNED TO POWER, NEGOTIATED THE ANNEXATION BY PIEDMONT OF THE CENTRAL STATES IN RETURN FOR THE CESSION OF NICE AND SAVOY.
	March	PLEBISCITES IN PARMA, MODENA, TUSCANY AND THE ROMAGNA VOTED FOR ANNEXATION TO PIEDMONT. Treaty of Turin: Piedmont ceded Savoy and Nice to France after a plebiscite.
	April	Unsuccessful rising in Sicily against the Bourbons.
	May	GIUSEPPE GARIBALDI AND HIS 'THOUSAND' SAILED FROM GENOA TO SICILY. Garibaldi defeated the Neapolitans at Catalfimi, captured Palermo and set up a provisional government.
	August	Garibaldi crossed to the mainland.
	September	GARIBALDI TOOK NAPLES, PLANNING TO MARCH ON ROME AND TO PROCEED TO THE CONQUEST OF VENETIA. Cavour, fearing French intervention on behalf of the Pope, intervened. The Papal forces defeated at Castelfidardo. Piedmontese forces advanced into Neopolitan territory and joined forces with Garibaldi.
	October	Naples and Sicily voted by plebiscite for union with Piedmont.
1861	February	The siege of Gaeta

	March	THE KINGDOM OF ITALY PROCLAIMED BY THE FIRST ITALIAN PARLIAMENT WITH VICTOR EMMANUEL AS KING. The government was based on the Piedmontese constitution of 1848, the 'Statuto'.
	June	Death of Cavour.
1862	August	The battle of Aspromonte: Garibaldi and his volunteers were defeated by government troops.
1864	September	THE SEPTEMBER CONVENTION: Napoleon finally agreed to evacuate Rome within two years in return for an Italian promise to move the capital of Italy from Turin to Florence. Napoleon regarded this as a renunciation of Rome.
1866	May	Alliance of Italy and Prussia encouraged by Napoleon.
	June	ITALY DECLARED WAR ON AUSTRIA. ITALY DEFEATED AT THE SECOND BATTLE OF CUSTOZZA.
	July	VENETIA CEDED TO ITALY.
1867	November	THE BATTLE OF MENTANA. Garibaldi defeated by Papal troops supported by the French. The Roman question continued to be an open dispute in relations between France and the new Italy and to prevent an alliance.
1870	August	WITHDRAWAL OF FRENCH TROOPS FROM ROME IN THE FRANCO-PRUSSIAN WAR.
	October	Rome was annexed to Italy after a plebiscite and became the capital.
1871	May	THE LAW OF GUARANTEES: defined the relations between the Italian government and the Papacy. The Pope was granted full religious liberty and the Vatican was given the rights of an independent territory. He was offered an annual income from the Italian treasury. This law was not accepted by the Pope (Pius IX) who asserted that he was 'the prisoner of the Vatican.' The relations between the Papacy and the new State of Italy were not regularised until the Lateran Concordat of 1929.

Illustrative questions and answers

1 Consider the view that Italy was unified by improvisation rather than by calculation.

Tutorial note

First you need to consider how far the great calculator, Cavour, really planned his moves ahead and how far he merely seized at opportunities as they presented themselves. Then you must assess the relative contributions of Cavour and the improviser *par excellence*, Garibaldi. You may also weigh up other factors, such as the long-term social, economic and geopolitical forces making unification inevitable, and largely independent of political or military intervention.

You need to know about

The details of the unification process from 1852 to 1870. The careers of Cavour and Garibaldi. The economic and diplomatic background to the unification.

Suggested answer plan

1 Brief survey of the course of the unification 1852–70; domestic development of Piedmont – secret diplomacy – war – plebiscites – Sicilian revolution and Garibaldi's Redshirts – intervention of Piedmont and its annexation – incorporation of Venice and Rome.
2 Evidence of forethought and planning on Cavour's part; his realisation that unification was impossible without European diplomatic and even military assistance; sees how to develop the state on West European, liberal free-trade lines.

3   It was once thought that Cavour had calculatingly engaged Piedmont in the Crimean War in order to put his Italian ambitions at the forefront of European attention; now we know that Victor Emmanuel pushed a reluctant Cavour into the war in order to divert attention in Piedmont away from domestic problems. So Cavour's actions at the Congress of Paris were more opportunist than calculated.

4   Diplomatic calculation was shown at Plombieres and in engineering the Austrian attack on Piedmont. Note, however, that the policy was nearly disastrous for Italian unity; the outcome of the war was far from satisfactory. Only the decisions of Parma, Modena and Tuscany to join Piedmont (thanks to Ricasoli and Farini, not Cavour) made Cavour's diplomacy seem successful.

5   Garibaldi, his background and attitudes; has more fixity of purpose and is more single-minded than Cavour: 'Unity in one fell swoop – to get Rome and all will follow'. But Garibaldi's methods were those of an adventurer; his Redshirts created a situation for Cavour to exploit, and enabled Cavour to incorporate Naples within Italy; Garibaldi's march on Rome (1860); Cavour improvised on Garibaldi's improvisations. (Note also that Cavour was largely motivated by hatred of Garibaldi, and by a desire to thwart him, as much as by a desire to affix Naples to Italy; he played on the spectre of republicanism to prevent Garibaldi's solution.)

6   Did Cavour plan unification? Even if he did, it would never have begun without Napoleon III and without Garibaldi it would never have been completed.

7   Besides, there are long-term economic and geopolitical factors to be considered. The need for economic consolidation and administrative centralisation pushed both Germany and Italy unwittingly towards unification; the decline of Austria also created a political vacuum in both areas. Calculation and improvisation therefore affected the timing of unification more than the fact of it.

2   Compare the nationalism of Mazzini with that of Cavour.

Tutorial note

This is a straightforward question whose meaning is clear. It is important to avoid treating Mazzini and Cavour in isolation, or lapsing into a narrative about their respective roles in the story of unification. It will help here if you measure both men against some yardstick of what nineteenth-century Nationalism was about.

You need to know about

The careers and philosophies of Mazzini and Cavour. A working knowledge of Nationalism as a force in Italy and Europe generally.

Suggested answer plan

1   Define what is meant by Nationalism in the nineteenth century; explain the impact of the French Revolution and Napoleon and relate Nationalism to the romantic movement in literature.

2   Discuss the connection of Nationalism with Liberalism in both its political (democratic) and economic (free trade) aspects; examine the widespread identification of Liberalism and Nationalism as twin forces of revolution against legitimist and authoritarian governments. Often, as in pre-1848 Germany, Diets were the only forums for the expression of nationalist feelings; this made Nationalism seem to be liberal.

3   Consider the illiberal and anti-individualist aspects of nineteenth-century nationalism; the idea of the 'General Will', the state or 'Volk'. Nationalism also often encouraged centralisation, bureaucratic conformity and the suppression of individual liberties.

4   Relate Mazzini and Cavour to the above discussion: the former a democratic nationalist, the latter making use of democracy (plebiscites) but more of a businessman's and bureaucrat's nationalist; the former preferring *political* to economic liberalism; the latter encouraging economic liberalism in his bid to build Piedmont into an efficient, western industrial power.

5   Amplify this view of Mazzini with details of his life and activities: his contempt for the Carbonari; his linguistic and republican forms of Nationalism; his belief in individual liberty; he formed *Young Italy* and then *Young Europe*, with their doctrines of 'sacred nationality' and equality.

6   Do likewise for Cavour, his aims and policies, both domestic and foreign: his concern for economic efficiency and expansion, and his admiration of the West; his success in 'achieving' unification and his influence on the form of the new Italian state.

7   Explain why Cavour's type of nationalism 'won'; Mazzini's refusal to compromise; his disgust with the monarchical middle-class state established in Italy.

3   In what ways did the internal unification of Italy remain incomplete in 1870?

Tutorial note

The word 'internal' may appear perplexing, for Italy was subjected to a high degree of administrative centralisation after unification. It is best to interpret the word in the widest sense, emphasising the distinction between the real and legal Italies (as explained below). Put another way, the question asks: what divisions still existed (and were felt to exist) in Italy in the year in which the territorial unification was completed?

You need to know about

The background: the Risorgimento and the process of unification. The constitution and nature of the new Kingdom of Italy. The internal opposition to the new state. The political, economic, social and religious divisions in Italy in 1870.

Suggested answer plan

1   Quote Massimo D'Azeglio, in conversation with King Victor Emmanuel: 'Sir we have made Italy, now we must make Italians'. A very large proportion of the population had little or no comprehension of the reality of the new Italian state called *Italy*. Loyalty was still overwhelmingly to the locality and region and there were wide regional cultural and economic differences. Even the elite who had been most influential in the Risorgimento had often been less inspired by Italian national consciousness than by a hatred of petty oppression and of Austrian domination.

2   The process of unification had been achieved by a series of annexations to Piedmont of the various Italian states. Cavour had pushed ahead in the end to forestall Garibaldi. The new state developed from the start as an expansion of the old Piedmont rather than as the totally new political creation Mazzini and Garibaldi had hoped for. With the unification, the Piedmontese constitution and administrative system were extended over the rest of the peninsula.

3   Cavour had given Neapolitan and Sicilian leaders to believe that there would be a good degree of regional autonomy. In fact rigid centralisation on the French model was instituted.

4   *However*, the new Italy, though legally and administratively one, did not embrace either the political support of the masses or their involvement. The solution of unification by Piedmont was imposed from above. Italy was not built by 'the people' on new foundations.

5   The parliament was elected on an extremely narrow franchise, the property qualification enfranchising only 600,000 in a population of 27 millions. The people of the Mezzogiorno (the south) were particularly under-represented; in some parts the vote was only enjoyed by a few notabilities. There was, from the start, a great divide between the rulers and the ruled.

6 Economic divisions: there was a very marked gap between the commercially and industrially developing north of Italy and the backward south. In one crucial respect the governments of the new Italy *widened* this division. They refused to discriminate in favour of the south and instead, with very damaging effects, exposed the struggling commerce of the south to free-trade competition from the rest of Italy.

7 The peasants still constituted the majority of the population but, with the exception of Sicily, they had played only a little role in the unification. They remained alienated in the new state. The sale of church lands which followed the unification benefited the 'latifundists' (large-scale landowners), who also frequently in these years misappropriated common lands. The land question generated bitter class hatred; there was widespread brigandage, particularly in the south, and revolts against heavy government taxation – e.g. the 'macinato' (a tax payable on the grinding of corn). There was mass resentment of the new state, whose principal personifications seemed to be the army recruiter and the taxman.

8 The question of Church and State: with the loss of temporal power, Pope Pius IX declared out-and-out hostility towards the new state. The 'Roman Question' bedevilled Church-state relations until the Lateran pact under Mussolini in 1929. The Church encouraged the enemies of the new state (e.g. the Bourbons) and called on Catholics to boycott political life – i.e. neither to vote nor offer themselves as candidates. This was accompanied by papal denunciations of the liberal spirit in modern society, as manifested by the state.

9 The newly united Italy, therefore, contained very deep divisions – some of which were aggravated by the unification process under Piedmont. The refusal of successive governments to decentralise emphasised both this and their particular fear of social instability and revolt in the south.

Question bank

1 Document question (Italy 1815–49): study extracts I, II and III below and then answer questions (a) to (f) which follow:

Extract I

'Austria…cuts Italy in half and is its actual mistress…By the re-establishment of the entire temporal domain of the Pope, two and a half millions of Italians have been plunged afresh into a state of absolute nullity, and the King of Naples, relegated to the end of the peninsula, has no longer any means of contributing to the defence of Italy, while on the other hand Austria threatens the King of Piedmont on his flank…

'Examples ranging over several centuries prove that there will always be blood to shed until Italy is left alone with all foreigners alike excluded. Neither France nor Austria will ever consent to yield to the other – as long as this rivalry exists Europe can hope for no real peace. The only means of extinguishing it would seem to be the establishment in the north of Italy of a state strong enough to defend the Alps and bar the gates of Italy to all foreigners.

'…Each part of northern Italy is at exactly the same stage of civilisation; there is a general consensus of opinion and a community of interests; in fact in many ways the inhabitants resemble one another far more than they do those of Tuscany, Rome or Naples. Northern Italy would have a population of seven or eight millions. A state of that size could not give rise to jealousy. Situated between two great Powers…it would hardly be able to maintain its independence without the help of Russia.'

(Memorandum by the Piedmontese ambassador to the Tsar Alexander, March 1818)

Extract II

'(These experiences) all confirmed me in the conviction that *carbonarism* was in fact dead...and that it would be better...to seek to found a new edifice upon a new basis...I conceived the plan of the association of *Young Italy*...I was led to prefix unity and the Republic, as the aim of the association...I saw regenerate Italy becoming at one bound the missionary of a religion of progress and fraternity, far grander and vaster than that she gave to humanity in the past.... Why should not a new Rome, the Rome of the Italian people, arise?'

(From *The Life and Writings of Mazzini*, London, 1864)

Extract III

'Italy contains within herself, above all through religion, all the conditions required for her...*risorgimento*...she has no need of revolutions within and still less of foreign invasions or foreign exemplars...

'The real principle of Italian unity...the Papacy, is supremely ours.... It is concrete, living, real – not an abstraction or a chimera, but an institution, an oracle and a person....

'The benefits Italy would gain from a political confederation under the moderating authority of the Pontiff are beyond enumeration....

'(It) would increase the strength of various princes without damaging their independence...place Italy again in the first rank of the Powers...provide opportunities to resume expeditions and the establishment of colonies in various parts of the globe...eliminate, or at least reduce, the difference in weights, measures, currencies, customs duties and systems of ceremonial and civil administration which...divide the various provinces.

(V. Gioberti, *On the Moral and Civil Primacy of the Italians*, 1843)

(a) Explain briefly what the writer in Extract I meant by each of the following statements: 'Austria cuts Italy in half and is its actual mistress'; 'two and a half millions of Italians have been plunged afresh into a state of absolute nullity'; 'Austria threatens the King of Piedmont on his flank'. (6)

(b) Show what you understand by each of the following terms: 'carbonarism'; 'Young Italy'; 'Risorgimento'. (3)

(c) Which of the arguments put forward in Extract I for a unified kingdom of northern Italy were likely to appeal to the Tsar? (3)

(d) How does the plan proposed in Extract II differ from the plan envisaged in Extract I in (i) content, and (ii) tone? (4)

(e) Quote sections of Extract III which suggest that Gioberti's arguments were designed to appeal to *each* of the following: nationalists; the middle classes; the monarchists. (6)

(f) Explain how the events of 1848–49 in Italy revealed weakness in *each* of the plans outlined in the three extracts. (9)

2 Analyse the obstacles to political change in Italy between 1815 and 1870.
(AEB, June 1989)

3 Why did the movement for republicanism in Italy fail in the period 1848–61?
(Oxford, Summer 1991)

4 How important was the part played by Italians themselves in bringing about the unification of their country? (London, June 1991)

5 Compare and contrast the progress towards unification achieved in Germany and Italy by 1850. (Oxford and Cambridge, June 1990)

READING LIST

Standard textbook reading

L. W. Cowie and R. Wolfson, *Years of Nationalism, European History, 1815–90* (Edward Arnold, 1985), chapters III (4) and IV (4).

Robert Gildea *Barricades and Borders, Europe 1800–1914*, (OUP, 1987) chapter 7.

J. A. S. Grenville, *Europe Reshaped 1848–78* (Fontana, 1976), chapter 12.

David Thomson, *Europe since Napoleon* (Penguin, 1977), chapter 14.

Anthony Wood, *Europe 1815–1945* (Longman, 1975), chapter 12.

Further suggested reading

D. Beales, *The Risorgimento and the Unification of Italy* (Longman, 1982).

J. P. T. Bury (ed), *The New Cambridge Modern History 1830–70*, volume X (CUP, 1964), chapter 21.

O. Chadwick, *The Popes and the European Revolution* (OUP, 1981).

J. Gooch, *The Unification of Italy*, (Methuen, 1985).

H. Hearder, *Italy in the Age of Risorgimento 1790–1870* (Longman, 1983).

Edgar Holt, *The Risorgimento: the Making of Italy 1815–70* (Macmillan, 1970).

J. McManners, *Lectures on European History 1789–1914* (Blackwell, 1974)

D. Mack Smith, *Cavour* (Weidenfield and Nicolson, 1985).

D. Mack Smith, *The Making of Italy 1796–1870* (Harper and Row, 1968).

G. Procacci, *A History of the Italian People* (Penguin, 1973).

A. Ramm, *The Risorgimento* (Historical Association, 1967).

Jasper Ridley, *Garibaldi* (Constable, 1974).

L. C. B. Seaman, *From Vienna to Versailles* (Methuen, 1972).

C. Seton-Watson, *Italy from Liberalism to Fascism* (Methuen, 1967), Prologue.

CHAPTER 5

NAPOLEON III AND THE SECOND EMPIRE

Units in this chapter

Chapter objectives

❶ The rise of Louis Napoleon; his personality, sense of historical mission; his early attempted coups against the Orleanist regime of Louis-Philippe. His writings: *Napoleonic Ideas* and *The Extinction of Pauperism*.

❷ The reasons for his election as President of the French Republic in December 1848 on the platform of stability and law and order.

❸ The coup of 2 December and the establishment of the Second Empire.

❹ The constitution of the Empire during the 1850s. Napoleon's ability to work through administrators and to keep the new liberal ministers (Morny, Persigny) relatively powerless. The organisation of bureaucratic rule through prefects, maires, etc.; the limitation of the Assembly's powers; the shrewd exploitation of plebiscites and universal suffrage; the control of elections through the use of official candidates; the control of public opinion by press controls, restriction on meetings and the superintendence of education.

❺ Expansionist economic policy: deficit financing, public works (canals and railways), free trade, large-scale mobilisation of funds amassed under the Orleanist through the Banque de France, Crédits Mobilier and Foncier; a state-directed industrial revolution, fulfilling Napoleon's dreams of a technological future (influence of Saint-Simon).

❻ Paternalist social policy: benevolent attempts at the redistribution of wealth and the protection of the working classes; permission for workers to strike and form cooperatives.

❼ The court and social life; the Empress and the 'gilded beauties of the Second Empire'; Haussmann and the reconstruction of Paris.

❽ Foreign policy; Napoleon's overriding desire to disrupt the humiliating Vienna Settlement of 1815; his role in the unification of Italy; his domestic and foreign policy motives in his dealings with Cavour; the annexation of Savoy and Nice; the Mexican adventure and the problems posed for France by the rise of Prussia in the 1860s.

❾ Analysis of the reasons for the support of the Second Empire by: peasants, army, clergy, nouveaux riches, haute bourgeoisie (industrialists, merchants, stockholders).

⑩ The opposition to the regime, as reflected in the 1863 and 1869 elections: the hard core of opposition from the Republicans of Paris, Lyons, Marseilles, led by Thiers and Simon; also the Bourbons and Orleanist legitimist opposition and the contempt of figures like Victor Hugo; the disappointment after Napoleon's withdrawal from the Piedmontese/Austrian War; army resentment at foreign policy reverses; the dislike by protectionists of Cobden/Chevalier Treaty.

⑪ The liberal reforms of the constitution after 1867 in response to growing unpopularity, leading to the proclamation of the Liberal Empire under Ollivier in 1870.

⑫ Foreign policy disasters: the Hohenzollern candidature and Bismarck's success in involving Napoleon in war; the course of the Franco-Prussian War; the overthrow of the Empire; the siege of Paris and the Commune; surviving remnants of Bonapartism as an occasional force in Third Republic politics.

Louis Napoleon, nephew of the great Emperor, who had previously made two failed attempts against the July Monarchy, was elected president of the French Republic in 1848. He benefited from the growing appeal of the 'Napoleonic legend', and appeared to offer order and stability after a period of frightening upheaval. He worked hard to establish his popularity with the mass of the French people, not least the Catholic middle classes.

Re-election of the President was prohibited by the constitution and, on 2 December, 1851, he mounted a coup d'état, extending his presidential authority, and then, a year later, took the title of Emperor. He appealed directly to the people over the heads of the politicians by means of the plebiscite and received their overwhelming support.

His ambition was to reconcile order with progress and he greatly strengthened the executive presidential power at the expense of the legislature. He imposed authoritarian controls, such as censorship, but after 1859 there was progressive liberalisation of the regime, culminating in the ministry of Emile Ollivier – though this did not mean full parliamentary rule on the British model. His rule spanned a period of considerable economic expansion and rising prosperity.

In his foreign policy Napoleon set out to undo the Vienna Settlement. He appealed to French nationalism both by seeking additional territory and by espousing the idea of a Europe reorganised on national principles. Success against Russia in the Crimean War was followed by his intervention in Italy in 1859 and the expulsion of Austria from Lombardy. His relations with the new Italian state, however, were complicated by the Roman Question. The regime suffered humiliation over Mexico.

By 1865 Napoleon was in poor health – he gravely miscalculated over the Austro-Prussian War and was brought to defeat, following the Hohenzollern candidature to the Spanish throne, in the Franco-Prussian War of 1870.

5.1   PRINCE LOUIS NAPOLEON

Prince Louis Napoleon was heir to the Napoleonic tradition. As an exile under the law of 1816 which banned the House of Bonaparte from France, he had made two unsuccessful attempts to seize power as pretender at Strasbourg in 1836 and at Boulogne in 1840. Sentenced to life imprisonment in 1840, he had escaped from the fortress of Ham and taken refuge in England where he remained until the outbreak of the 1848 revolution. He had written two books which were significant for his subsequent political career: *Napoleonic Ideas* and *The Extinction of Pauperism*. 'The Napoleonic idea,' he wrote, 'is not an idea of war, but a social, industrial, commercial idea – an idea of humanity'. The *Extinction of Pauperism* served to associate Bonapartism in the public mind with the need for social reform.

The President of the Second Republic

In 1848 Louis Napoleon could rely on the support of the Napoleonic legend, which had established the emperor as the champion of progress and the defender of religion and society. His campaign for the Presidency laid the basis for his subsequent power and was cleverly conceived. He posed as a man above class or party who would put an end to revolutionary agitation, maintain order, restore prosperity and revive French glory. In *The Extinction of Pauperism* he had argued that in future it would only be possible to govern with the support of the masses.

He did not openly recommend a restoration of the empire, but declared his approval of a republic based on universal suffrage. In the majority of the Départements he received 80% of the votes.

Various factors explain his success:

❶ the fame of his family name among a largely illiterate and politically unaware electorate;

❷ the general desire for stability and order after the upheavals of 1848;

❸ the unpopularity of the republic;

❹ the mutual dislike of royalists and republicans;

❺ his well-advertised interest in the 'social question'.

All these helped to secure his victory over General Cavaignac, the 'butcher' of the 'June Days', by a massive majority. He was only elected for a term of four years, however. He soon made it clear that he had no intention of being simply the figurehead President which many of the members of the Assembly wanted him to be.

The coup d'état

On December 2nd 1851, the anniversary of the coronation of Napoleon I and the battle of Austerlitz, he took the law into his own hands. With a carefully planned coup he seized power, changed the constitution and gave the Presidency overwhelming authority and a ten-year term of office.

He presented himself as the people's champion by reintroducing the universal suffrage which the assembly had refused to restore the previous summer. He had taken the solemn oath to uphold the Republic. Now he appealed to 'the solemn judgement of the only sovereign whom I recognise in France – the people'.

This was confirmed by a plebiscite in which 91% of those voting expressed approval of his actions. By an administrative order special tribunals were instituted in January 1852, the 'mixed commissions' to take action against opponents of the new order. About 10,000 were transported to Algeria.

Napoleon's political appeal through the device of the plebiscite or referendum was directly to the people over the heads of the politicians. A country which had never really reconciled itself to the Second Republic welcomed the rule of a man whose name signified something to all men and who promised the restoration of order, the return of national confidence and the recovery of business.

The restoration of the Empire

In November 1852 another plebiscite approved the end of the Second Republic and the proclamation of the Second Empire. The promise of revived national glory, empire without war, and of stability outweighed the attraction of those political liberties which were suppressed in the new order.

Significantly, he had by this time won the strong support of the Roman Catholic vote, both through his defeat of the Roman Republic of Mazzini in 1849 and through the Falloux Law which had consolidated Church power over education. He had succeeded where Louis-Philippe had failed in winning over the clericals from their allegiance to the House of Bourbon.

His aim was to reconcile order and progress, by offering a rule above the factions. In the first period until 1859 he was to maintain an authoritarian rule, establish close relations between the government and the Church and give vigorous aid to business enterprise.

5.2 THE CONSTITUTION

The constitution of the Second Empire was based on that of 1800. The powers of the lower house, or Corps Législatif, were greatly reduced. The Senate acted as the guardian of the constitution and its members were, in practice, Napoleon's nominees.

The lower house could only meet for three months in the year and its membership numbered only a third of the old assembly. Their debates were not allowed to be reported in the press and ministers were not permitted to be questioned by deputies. It could discuss but not amend bills initiated by the emperor.

Everything was done to strengthen the executive power, the Emperor and his ministers. Only the Council of State, dominated by Napoleon, was allowed to introduce laws. Napoleon appointed to all offices, was Commander-in-Chief of the forces and had the right of declaring war and making treaties. He described his political system as a pyramid which former rulers had tried to balance upon its apex and which he now set on its base – that is the consent of the masses.

Centralised administration and control

The system of the Second Empire relied on the powers of centralised administration. Under the guidance of the Minister of the Interior, the prefects in the Départements, (or administrative provinces of France), exercised greater powers than ever before, though many of them were inherited from the July Monarchy.

Strict censorship of the press throughout France was effectively established by the requirement that no newspaper in Paris or in the provinces could be published without government authority. Any newspaper could be suspended after three warnings had been given to it by the prefects or Minister of the Interior.

At the same time, political clubs were suppressed. There was interference in education. The National Guard was disbanded except in Paris. Official candidates were nominated for elections and not a single republican deputy was elected until 1857.

Economic developments

The Second Empire was a period of considerable financial, commercial and industrial development. In 1852 Napoleon gave a charter to a joint-stock investment bank, the Crédit Mobilier, which channelled capital into numerous enterprises, particularly railways and mining.

There was a rapid development of land and sea transport associated with a boom in the metallurgical and mining industries. Foreign investment rose sixfold. Though it did not promote anything like a revolution in agriculture, the period saw the steady relative decline of the rural population in favour of the towns. The Crédit Foncier engaged in large investments in urban real estate.

To the great majority of Frenchmen Napoleon appears to have offered what they wished for, a guarantee of stability and order and a marked increase in prosperity. He was aware of the political importance of providing for the material welfare of the masses. He sought through public works another means to help the peasant and the urban worker; he was anxious to create conditions of full employment.

One of the most marked features was the rapid development of communications. In 1848 only 1,800 kilometres of railway line existed. By the end of the Second Empire a network of 17,500 kilometres had been laid. A larger, more unified market stimulated production. This was also a period of major building construction – most notably the transformation of central Paris by Baron Haussmann.

5.3 FOREIGN POLICY

Before the Empire had been in existence for two years it was involved in a major war with Russia. Napoleon's involvement in the Crimean War resulted partly from his desire to rally Catholic support at home through championing Catholic interests in the Near East and also from his keenness for an alliance with England. He was particularly anxious to avoid what he regarded as his uncle's grave error of enmity with Great Britain.

By the Quadruple Alliance of 1815 the Allies had agreed to look upon the return to France of Napoleon or any of his relatives as tantamount to a French declaration of war on the rest of Europe. He went out of his way to disclaim any aggressive purpose with his statement 'the Empire means peace'. He was nevertheless clearly intent on taking any opportunity to challenge the status quo of the Vienna Settlement and was sympathetic to nationalist ideas. Just as he wanted to restore harmony within France, he was anxious to assert her diplomatic pre-eminence in Europe. The Peace Congress of Paris in 1856, which concluded the Crimean War, seemed to confirm France's revived position on the Continent.

France and Italy

As a young exile in Rome in 1831 Napoleon had supported the Italian revolution against the Pope. After Orsini's attempt to assassinate him, he reached a second agreement with Cavour, Prime Minister of Piedmont, at Plombières; this led to the war against Austria in 1859 (see 4.2).

The Napoleonic tradition pointed to Italy as a French sphere of interest. By destroying Austrian predominance in Italy, Napoleon would be able to reverse the Vienna Settlement while at the same time being seen to 'do something for Italy' and give support to the principle of nationality.

He did not wish to create a wholly united Italy but sought – while helping to reorganise it – to keep it still divided and looking to France for support. He did not want to stir up popular nationalism and was deeply opposed to the republicanism of Mazzini.

Napoleon III's Italian policy also had a domestic political significance. Throughout his reign he attempted to reconcile two conflicting traditions of French history – that of the Catholic monarchy of Louis XIV and that of the revolution of 1789. In the Italian question this led to an impossible paradox. On the one hand he was spurring on the process of unification by his support for Piedmont. On the other, he was giving the Pope military aid against the emerging Italian kingdom.

The 'Liberal Empire'

In November 1860 Napoleon announced that he would 'give the great bodies of the state a more direct part in the formation of the general policy of our government'. The second half of his reign saw striking constitutional reforms at home which have led to the period from 1860 being described as the 'Liberal Empire'. Already in 1859 he had issued a general amnesty to his political opponents. This was followed by more moderate laws and an increase in the powers of the lower chamber – for instance, the right to scrutinise the budget. He also attempted to woo the workers, allowing them limited rights of association and the right to strike. In 1868 they were allowed to form unions.

In 1860 the French government signed the Cobden-Chevalier treaty encouraging freedom of commerce with Great Britain; and in subsequent years concluded agreements along similar lines with Belgium, the Netherlands, the Zollverein, Sweden, Switzerland, Italy and Spain.

Emile Ollivier

The elections of 1857 had brought into the Corps Législatif five deputies, including Emile Ollivier and Jules Favre, who were to become a nucleus of republican opposition. The elections of 1863 and 1869 saw successive increases in the numbers of republicans returned to the lower house, while Thiers, who returned to active political life in 1863, undertook to organise a conservative opposition, known as the 'Third Party'.

The election of 1869 showed strong support for liberal constitutional reform. Those who were out-and-out opponents of the Empire, the 'irreconcilables', remained a small minority. But a large number of deputies were returned who wished to combine support for the Empire with constitutional reform. They wanted a ministry which was dependent on the consent of the legislature.

In January 1870 Emile Ollivier formed a new ministry. The emperor now appointed a cabinet which enjoyed the support of the chamber. The 'Liberal Empire' fell far short, however, of the idea that the executive should be solely responsible to the majority in the chamber; it did not mean a full parliamentary regime on the British model.

The revised constitution was essentially a compromise between autocratic rule and parliamentary sovereignty, and Napoleon retained considerable powers. He could, for instance, propose a revision of the constitution, which would require a plebiscite but not the sanction of parliament. He reserved sufficient power to be able to restore his personal rule.

This new constitution was overwhelmingly approved by the French people in May 1870. Napoleon's electoral support was only 10% less than that secured in 1851.

5.4 THE COLLAPSE OF THE SECOND EMPIRE

While Napoleon greatly extended French influence overseas, for instance in West Africa, China and Indochina, the apparent foreign policy successes of the first 10 years of his rule gave way in the second decade to grave errors. His record was badly damaged by the following:

❶ the Prussian success in consolidating their power in North Germany after Sadowa;

❷ his failure to secure 'compensation' (e.g. Luxemburg) after the Austro-Prussian War;

❸ the collapse of the Mexican adventure; and

❹ the failure of his diplomacy to strengthen the French position before the Franco-Prussian War.

The Mexican adventure was a particularly spectacular disaster. By giving help to conservatives who were eager to overthrow the Mexican regime, France would be seen as serving the Catholic Church by saving it from the menace of republican anti-clerical policies. France could also present herself as the guardian of the Catholic and Latin peoples of the New World against the Anglo-Saxon and Protestant influence of the US. At all events, what started out as an attempt to build a liberal catholic empire had ended by 1867 with the withdrawal of French troops and the execution of Maximilian by the Mexican revolutionaries.

After 1867 there was no real possibility of friendly Franco-Prussian cooperation, but Napoleon did not wholeheartedly pursue any alternative policy. The continued presence of French troops in Rome protecting the Pope prevented the creation of an alliance with Italy.

The Franco-Prussian War was the final act of the Second Empire (see Chapter 6 for its origins). The war started on 1 August 1870, and on 3 September news reached

Paris of the surrender at Sedan and the capture of the emperor. On receipt of this news, the republican opposition in the Corps Législatif proclaimed the overthrow of the Empire and the establishment of a Republican Government of National Defence.

5.5 CHRONOLOGY

		Prince Charles Louis Napoleon Bonaparte (1808–73): nephew of Napoleon I; made two failed attempts as Bonapartist pretender against the July Monarchy of Louis-Philippe at Strasbourg (1836) and Boulogne (1840).
1848	December	ELECTED PRESIDENT OF THE SECOND REPUBLIC with the support of over 5 million votes. Swore 'to remain faithful to the democratic Republic and to defend the Constitution.'
1849	April–June	French intervention against the Roman Republic.
1850	March	THE FALLOUX LAW considerably extended the influence of the Roman Catholic Church in French education.
1851	2 December	The COUP D'ÉTAT: dissolution of the Assembly: restoration of universal suffrage and the convening of a plebiscite for revision of the constitution. Staged on the anniversary of Napoleon I's coronation and the battle of Austerlitz. THE PLEBISCITE: the President secured 7.5 million against 640,000 votes.
1852	January	THE NEW CONSTITUTION: the Chief of State declared 'responsible to the nation' but given 'free and unfettered authority'. A Council of State, Senate and Legislative Assembly set up.
	February	Repressive measures introduced; control of the press through a system of warnings to editors. Establishment of joint stock banks issuing long-term credit: Crédit Foncier and Crédit Mobilier. Programme of public works. (From 1854 the rebuilding of Paris by Baron Haussman.)
	2 December	THE RE-ESTABLISHMENT OF THE EMPIRE: Napoleon took the title of Napoleon III in accordance with the imperial tradition which recognised the Duke of Reichstadt as Napoleon II although he had never been crowned. The powers of the Emperor were extended by a 'Senatus-consultum': he was given authority to conclude treaties of commerce, the budget of every ministry was voted by the Legislative Assembly, but the subdivision of sums granted was to be settled by imperial decree.
1853	January	Napoleon married EUGÉNIE DE MONTIJO.
1854	March	French declaration of war on Russia (see Chapter 3).
1855	May–November	The Paris International Exhibition.
1856	February–April	THE PEACE CONGRESS AT PARIS: end of the Crimean War.
1858	January	Attempt of Felice Orsini to assassinate Napoleon and the Empress (see Chapter 4).
	July	COMPACT OF PLOMBIÈRES.
1859	May	GENERAL AMNESTY: those who had been exiled in 1851 allowed to return to France. War of France and Piedmont against Austria.
	July	PEACE OF VILLAFRANCA.
1860	January	THE COBDEN-CHEVALIER TREATY WITH GREAT BRITAIN: France revoked the general prohibition on the import of British goods and reduced the duties upon imported coal, iron, machinery and raw textiles, while Britain reduced the duties upon French wines and spirits.
	March	French annexation of Savoy and Nice.
	November	Powers of the legislature extended: the decrees empowered the Senate and Legislative Assembly to move and discuss freely a reply to the address from the throne; parliamentary debates to be fully reported.
1861	November	The financial powers of the legislature extended. Napoleon renounced the right to borrow money while the legislature was not in session and agreed that the budget should be voted by sections.

1861–7		THE MEXICAN EXPEDITION; owing to the refusal of the revolutionary Juarez government to meet its debts, France, Britain and Spain decided to force fulfilment of these obligations. The British and Spanish withdrew when they recognised Napoleon's plans to establish a Catholic Latin Empire in Mexico while the US was involved in the Civil War. French troops captured Mexico City (June 1863) and proclaimed the Habsburg Archduke Maximilian Emperor. By 1866 the US was demanding the withdrawal of the French, and Napoleon – because of his European involvements – was forced to desert Maximilian, who was captured and executed by the Mexicans (June 1867).
1864		THE SEPTEMBER CONVENTION: Reversing his attitude on the Roman question, Napoleon agreed to withdraw his troops from Rome within two years in return for a promise from the Italian government not to attack Papal territory. This move outraged French Catholics. The Pope issued the encyclical QUANTA CURA and THE SYLLABUS OF ERRORS.
1866	March	Emergence of the THIRD PARTY: this wished to support the Empire but favoured the development of political liberties and the establishment of a Ministry responsible to the legislature, which was to control the general policy of the government.
	July	Prussian defeat of Austrians at SADOWA (see Chapter 6). The failure of Napoleon to secure 'compensation' was widely regarded by French public opinion as a national humiliation.
1867	January	The right of interpellation granted (the right to question the Government on policy and its actions).
	March	The Senate was given the right to examine projected laws in detail.
1868	May	LIBERAL PRESS LAWS: the abolition of the power of government to warn, suspend or suppress newspapers.
	June	Limited right of public meeting: public meetings allowed to be held subject to police supervision.
1869	May	Parliamentary elections resulted in an Assembly including 30 republicans.
	June	The Third Party demanded the creation of a responsible Ministry.
	July	THE NEW LIBERAL REGIME: by decree of the Senate the Legislative Assembly was given the right to propose laws, criticise and vote the budget and to choose its own officers. The Senate became a deliberating body with public sessions and had the right to discuss laws voted by the Assembly and send them back for consideration.
	December	EMILE OLLIVIER was entrusted with the formation of a Cabinet representative of the majority of the Legislative Assembly.
1870	April	The Senate was made an upper house, sharing legislative power with the Assembly; constituent authority was taken from the Senate and given to the people.
	May	PLEBISCITE ON THE LIBERAL REFORMS: by a majority of 7.3 million to 1.5 million, gave approval of the liberal reforms since 1860 and ratification of the 'Senatus-consultum' of April 1870. A sweeping victory for Napoleon.
	July	French declaration of war on Prussia (see Chapter 6).
	September	Napoleon and the Army capitulated at SEDAN. FRENCH THIRD REPUBLIC PROCLAIMED.
1871	May	THE PEACE OF FRANKFURT: end of the Franco-Prussian War: France agreed to cede Alsace-Lorraine except Belfort, but including Metz, and to pay an indemnity of 5 million francs. North-eastern France remained under occupation until the indemnity was paid in 1873.

Illustrative questions and answers

1 'A showman and a sham dictator.' Examine this view of Napoleon III.

Tutorial Notes

The proposition is that Napoleon's policies were based mainly on fantasies (such as his longing to emulate his great uncle) and images (such as his lavish court life and the transformation of Paris by Haussmann). You are entitled to disagree, and to argue, if you wish, that he was a hard-headed and ruthless realist intent on consolidating his own power. A balanced answer would survey the evidence for each viewpoint.

You need to know about

Napoleon's personality. His domestic and foreign policies. The strength of the revolutionary and counter-revolutionary traditions. The power of slogans and images – which made the French so susceptible to a 'politician of appearances' like Napoleon.

Suggested answer plan

1   Napoleon's early life and personality; Bonapartist fantasies; plots and coups against the Orleanist regime.
2   Summary of his foreign policy, emphasising his fondness for empty gestures and secret diplomacy; encouraged Cavour but was not prepared to carry through his support for Italian unity; the Mexican adventure; Bismarck revealed Napoleon's lack of realism and caution in the secret diplomacy of the later 1860s.
3   Summary of his domestic policies, showing his emphasis on the regime's image: Eugénie and the sumptuous court life; the transformation of Paris.
4   On the other hand, Napoleon showed keen awareness of shifts of public opinion, and a pragmatic sense of what he could get away with; he shrewdly exploited plebiscites and for a time was successful in controlling elections; his diplomatic gestures seemed empty, but were made with a careful eye to conciliating sections of opinion at home. He could be ruthless in persecuting subversives and shrewd in handling ministers.
5   Which view do you think best fits the evidence? Perhaps his decision to abandon the Piedmont/Austria War after Solferino illustrates the problem. Do you think he did it because, being humane, he could not stand the sight of blood on the battlefield? Or did he pull out because Prussia was mobilising, and because Piedmont's success could threaten the Papacy and alienate Catholic opinion at home?
6   Many people called him a mountebank and adventurer; Bismarck said he was 'a sphinx without a riddle, a great unfathomed incapacity'. Note how much the French had responded since 1789 to gestures and images and how Louis-Philippe had been lacking in successful 'showmanship'. Note, too, that Napoleon's rule lasted longer than average in nineteenth century France and only ended because of external disasters.

2   Explain why the Second Republic was so soon replaced by a Second Empire.

Tutorial notes

In order to explain why the Republic was short-lived, you need to consider both Louis Napoleon's personal political ambitions and the instability of the constitution established in December 1848. You may conclude that the word 'replaced' is slightly misleading, and that the Empire was a logical and likely outcome of the previous constitutional compromise.

You need to know about

The causes, occasion and course of the February revolution. Louis Napoleon's life, ideas, aims; the circumstances of his election as President. The various political parties and ideas in France and why, at the time, his campaign divided Frenchmen least. The domestic policies of the Republic (especially on education). Foreign policy (with particular reference to Rome). Opposition to Louis Napoleon's Presidency. The circumstances of his coup d'état and his confirmation as Emperor.

Suggested answer plan

1   Explain the origins of the Second Republic, starting with the causes of the February Revolution; explain divisions in the new provisional government between middle-class republicans (Lamartine) and full-blooded socialists (Louis

Blanc); show how the National Assembly's attack on Blanc's national work-shops scheme led to bloody insurrection and its suppression during 'the June Days'. Note how this created fear among nearly all Frenchmen except the proletarians of Paris, Lyons and Marseilles.

2   The National Assembly decided to create a Republic with a president to be elected (for four years without the possibility of re-election) by universal suffrage. Analyse the candidates. Introduce Louis Napoleon – his ancestry, character, ideas (e.g. 'idées napoleoniennes'), and previous attempts at a coup d'état, imprisonment and forced exile. Point out that he was almost totally unknown, except among a few score henchmen, on his arrival in France in 1848.

3   Explain his enormous success in the presidential elections; his perception that the vast majority of Frenchmen desired stability after the turmoil of the 'June Days'; fear of Socialism among the middle class and peasants; provincial France's desire for revenge on Paris which had single-handedly made the February revolution; the glamour of Louis Napoleon's name and associations contrasted with the drab boredom of Louis-Philippe; even conservative monarchists supported him, owing to division in their ranks between Orleanists and Bourbons; even workers preferred him to Lamartine and Cavaignac, their June oppressors.

4   Show how Louis Napoleon was able to convert this goodwill into support for – or at least tolerance of – the Empire; his own ambitions and desire to imitate his uncle.

5   Show how Louis Napoleon, by carefully fostering conservative support through the expedition to Rome and the Loi Falloux (education law), *almost* succeeded in achieving his ambition by constitutional means; the important role of the clergy in moving public opinion towards him.

6   The coup of 2 December and the controlled use of force and repression; the plebiscite of 1852 confirmed Napoleon as emperor; his skilful management and reasons for lack of opposition.

7   Conclusion: short-lived nature of the Republic is no surprise; that its President should have survived it is more surprising and due mainly to his political skill and sympathy with the aspirations of ordinary Frenchmen. The basic problem was constitutional: Napoleon never solved the problem of the relationship between the executive and the legislature; moreover the constitution was so inflexible that there was no means to alter it – except by force.

3   Do you agree that Napoleon III's domestic policy was 'authoritarian but paternal'?

Tutorial notes

This is largely a straight question on domestic policy; the difficulty lies in the definitions contained in the question. By definition, all paternal governments are authoritarian; it could be held that all authoritarian government must be paternal. The fact that the quotation is 'authoritarian but paternal' implies that the word 'paternal' is used here, not merely to mean 'fatherlike' (which would include authoritarianism) but 'kindly', 'caring', 'anxious to please one's subjects'. In other words, here is a moral judgement for you to assess – 'Napoleon was dictatorial but had his people's welfare at heart'.

You need to know about

All aspects of Napoleon's domestic policies (political, constitutional, social, economic) as well as an ability to discuss the concepts 'paternal' and 'authoritarian' – with perhaps some comparative references, perhaps to Napoleon I or the Enlightened Despots.

Suggested answer plan

1   Analyse the meaning of the two terms with *brief* references to eighteenth-century enlightened despotism and Napoleon I.

2   Discuss Louis Napoleon's character and early political ideas, his strong impulse to govern dictatorially but also to do what most people wanted and to be popular. Consider the view that he manufactured public opinion and then followed it; you may prefer the view that, though egocentric, he was also soft-hearted and genuinely sought to please and to find out what people did want.

3   Analyse the authoritarian nature of the regime, sometimes called a 'benign police state': the limitation of the powers of the Legislative Assembly; the use of prefects, mayors, etc. to control elections and influence public opinion; the cunning exploitation of plebiscites, and increased clerical control of education; press censorship and restrictions on thought – the latter mainly unsuccessful.

4   Note also the relaxation of the constitution in the 1860s, leading to the Liberal Empire of 1870, based on parliamentary democracy. Admittedly this was partly defensive, a panic response to growing opposition; but it was partly genuine – Napoleon's conscience never quite recovered from the events of 2 December, 1851, and its aftermath.

5   The paternalism of the regime was little more than sentiment. There was some protection for striking workers, some small redistribution of wealth by fiscal methods; Napoleon had some Saint-Simonian ideas, but had more ideas of a technological future than socialist ones.

6   The main direction of his economic policy was away from paternalism and protection and towards free trade and the release of capital. His regime encouraged the release of private enterprise through commercial trade treaties and a new banking system. Public enterprise was considerable but essentially to complement private economic activity. Competition, not paternalism, was the main aim.

7   Possible conclusions: persistent opposition suggests that his regime, thought corrupt and repressive, was neither successfully authoritarian nor paternal.

Question bank

1   Document question (Louis Napoleon): Study extracts I and II below and then answer questions (a) to (g) which follow:

Extract I

'I do not think that any of us doubted that he (Louis Napoleon) would try to become Emperor…. We thought that once we had made use of the popularity of his name to overthrow <u>the revolutionary usurpers of February 1848</u> and restabilise the bases of a disturbed society, we should retain the influence to prevent him….

'It is probable that it would have been a very simple matter if the President Prince had been such as his <u>exploits at Boulogne and Strasburg</u> had led us to suppose, and such as he had been judged…on the benches of the Constituent Assembly, an adventurer who was both mad and incapable, with <u>the confidence of a visionary in his imperial star</u>, but lacking experience, knowledge or reliable resources of character and intelligence….

'<u>Once he had reached the end of his mandate</u> and attempted to prolong it illegally, he would not have found any support in the sane and sensible section of the population…. (But) far from being weakened during his three years presidency, on the contrary…there were now added to the blind votes of the crowd the support of all <u>the commercial and industrial interests</u>….

'We realised that an army of four hundred thousand men, and all the resources which the administration in France provides for the man in power, joined to immense popularity, made of this candidate for Empire a very redoubtable adversary for those who remained faithful to liberal and constitutional principles.'

(From the *Mémoires du Duc die Broglie*, published in 1938)

Extract II

'In the year 1851, France passed through a kind of minor trade crisis.... The French bourgeoisie attributed this stagnation to purely political causes, to the struggle between parliament and the executive power, to the precariousness of a merely provisional form of state.... But this influence of the political conditions was only local and inconsiderable.

'The apparent crisis of 1851 was nothing else but the halt which over-production and over-speculation invariably makes in describing the industrial cycle before they...rush feverishly through the final phase of this cycle and arrive once more at their starting point, the general trade crisis.

'Now picture to yourself the French bourgeois, how in the throes of this business panic his trade-sick brain is tortured...by rumours of coups d'état and the restoration of universal suffrage, by the struggle between parliament and the executive power, by the Fronde war between Orleanists and Legitimists.... You will comprehend why the bourgeois madly snorts at his parliamentary republic: "Rather an end with terror than terror without end!" Bonaparte understood this cry.'

(Karl Marx, 1852)

(a) Explain the reference to 'the revolutionary usurpers of February 1848'. (3)
(b) What were Louis Napoleon's 'exploits at Boulogne and Strasburg' and what had been their effect on his reputation? (4)
(c) Explain what is meant by (i) 'the confidence of a visionary in his imperial star', and (ii) 'once he had reached the end of his mandate'. (4)
(d) In what ways did the fears expressed in the last paragraph of Extract I come true, both in 1851 and in later years? (6)
(e) What do you understand by 'Orleanists and Legitimists'? (2)
(f) Describe briefly why, according to the writer of Extract II, 'the French bourgeoisie' supported Louis Napoleon and explain what mistake the writer thought that they had made. (5)
(g) How far does an examination of the subsequent history of France (1852–70) suggest that 'the commercial and industrial interests' had been wise to support Louis Napoleon? (7)

2 How far did the regime of Napoleon III represent a 'popular dictatorship'?
(Cambridge, June 1991)

3 To what extent was the continuance and stability of the Second Empire in France dependent on a successful foreign policy? (Cambridge, Summer 1986)

4 Why could neither the Second Republic nor the Second Empire command the lasting support of Frenchmen? (Oxford and Cambridge, June 1991)

5 Assess the achievements of Louis Napoleon.
(Oxford and Cambridge, (June 1992)

READING LIST

Standard textbook reading
L. W. Cowie and R. Wolfson, *Years of Nationalism, European History 1815–1890* (Edward Arnold, 1985), chapter IV (2).
J. A. S. Grenville, *Europe Reshaped 1848–78* (Fontana, 1976), chapters 9,16, 17.

Agatha Ramm, *Europe in the Nineteenth Century 1789–1905* (Longman, 1984), chapters 10 and 16.
David Thomson, *Europe Since Napoleon* (Penguin, 1977), chapter 13.
Anthony Wood, *Europe 1815–1945* (Longman, 1975), chapter 15

Further suggested reading

M. Agulhon, *The Republican Experiment 1848–52* (CUP, 1980).

J. P. T. Bury, *France 1815–1940* (Methuen, 1969).

Alfred Cobban, *History of Modern France, volume 2 1799–1871* (Penguin, 1970).

A. Horne, *The Fall of Paris: the Siege and the Commune* (Macmillan, 1965).

M. Howard, *The Franco-Prussian War* (Hart-Davis, 1961).

R. Magraw, *France 1815–1914: the Bourgeois Century* (Fontana, 1992).

J. McManners, *Lectures on European History 1789–1914* (Blackwell, 1974).

A. Plessis, *The Rise and Fall of the Second Empire 1852–71* (trans. J. Mandelbaum) (CUP, 1985).

L. C. B. Seaman, *From Vienna to Versailles* (Methuen, 1972).

J. M. Thomson, *Louis Napoleon and The Second Empire* (Blackwell, 1954).

CHAPTER 6

THE UNIFICATION OF GERMANY

Units in this chapter

Chapter objectives

❶ As background: the rearrangement of Germany into 39 states in 1815; the increased influence of Prussia and Austria; the constitution of the new Germanic Confederation – the Bund.

❷ Nationalist movements in Germany, 1815–48, and the social classes and groups supporting them; the intellectual and literary traditions of Nationalism in Prussia; the influence of the 'War of Liberation'.

❸ Economic expansion and integration, 1815–48; the Zollverein; the ideas of Friedrich List.

❹ The 1848 revolutions (see Chapter 2); the Frankfurt Parliament and the rival Artisan Congress; pressing respectively for free trade and guild controls; the Kleindeutsch versus the Grossdeutsch ideas of unity; Frederick William IV's refusal of the Crown of a united Germany; the reasons for the failure of the revolutions.

❺ The 1850s: political disappointments for Prussia and economic disappointments for Austria; Prussia's 'humiliation' at Olmütz; the badly-handled mobilisation of the Prussian Army during the Italian War of Independence; on the other hand, Austria failed to break into the Zollverein and suffered badly from the Vienna financial crash of 1856–7.

❻ Otto von Bismarck: his Junker background, personality and political ideas; his reactions to Prussia's 'humiliations' which he was in the Bundestag at Frankfurt; his devotion to established Prussian political and social order; the debate as to whether he planned the unification of Germany or merely seized opportunities later claiming that he planned it.

❼ Bismarck's appointment as Prime Minister-President of Prussia in 1862; Roon, Manteuffel and the Army budget crisis; the liberal wish for a Landwehr instead of the aristocratically controlled regular Army; Bismarck's solution, by-passing the Chamber and collecting taxes directly; the constitutional significance of the crisis.

⑧ The first stage of unification: the Polish and Schleswig-Holstein crises.

⑨ The second stage of unification: the Austro-Prussian War; the militarisation of Prussia, Moltke and the General Staff seeking to exert Army control over the politicians; improvements in weaponry and communications; the international significance of the battle of Sadowa; the extent and constitution of the North German Confederation; the domestic implications, e.g. the Indemnity Bill.

⑩ The final stage of unification: relations with France 1867–70; the Hohenzollern candidature crisis; the Franco–Prussian War and its results.

⑪ The constitution of the new German Empire, 1871; the influence of Prussia within it, and the attitude of the South German states towards it.

⑫ The industrial development of Germany in the 1850s and 1860s: the extent to which Germany was united by 'coal and iron' rather than by 'blood and iron'.

The 1815 settlement created a Germanic Confederation in which Austrian influence was dominant. In the subsequent period of Romantic Nationalism there was growing agitation against the disunity of Germany, particularly among the student clubs, the Burschenschaften, in the universities. The largest step in the direction of German unification in these early years, however, was the creation of the Prussian-dominated customs union, the Zollverein, from which Austria was excluded.

During the revolutions of 1848 conflicting programmes for a united Germany were advanced in the Frankfurt Assembly and were rejected by the Austrian and Prussian monarchs. In the event, the actual process of unification owed more to diplomatic rivalry and war than to nationalist sentiment.

A major constitutional crisis between William I of Prussia and the Prussian House of Representatives over Army reform brought Otto von Bismarck to power as Minister-President in 1862. He was determined to uphold Prussian interests and the existing conservative monarchical order and he proceeded to finance an expanded Army without parliamentary authorisation.

With a well-equipped Army and a rapidly developing industrial economy to support it, Prussia went to war against Denmark over the old issue of the Danish possession of Schleswig-Holstein, territories with a partly German population. Joint occupation of the Duchies with Austria enabled Bismarck to provoke the Seven Weeks' War against Austria. This, which led to the Austrian defeat at the battle of Sadowa, brought all of the German states north of the river Main into the North German Confederation – a new entity under Prussian leadership.

Deterioration of relations with Napoleon III and, in 1870, the issue of the Hohenzollern candidature to the Spanish throne precipitated the Franco–Prussian War. This completed the unification of Germany, which now incorporated the South German states, Alsace and most of Lorraine. The new German Empire was declared in the Palace of Versailles in January, 1871.

6.1 THE IMPETUS TO UNIFICATION

The transformation of Germany from the 39 separate states of the Confederation (Bund), as it was in 1815, into the German Empire of 1871 was a process which comprised several different elements. It is important to analyse them and see how they relate to one another.

❶ First, on one level, it was a resolution of the long-standing rivalry between the dynasties of Prussia and Austria over the German states that lay between them.

- **Austria** with its extensive Slav, Italian and Hungarian dependencies, was primarily a non-German Power. From the Congress of Vienna, however, it had maintained a controlling influence in German affairs in the Bund. This dominance was re-established after the 1848 revolutions, at Olmütz (1850).

- **Prussia**, on the other hand, after the acquisition of the Rhineland in 1815, gradually consolidated her position as a German Power, particularly in the economic sphere. Between 1866 and 1870, through three wars, she dramatically extended her authority over the rest of Germany and excluded Austria.

❷ The process of unification also reflected the strong force of popular *German nationalism* which had been so evident during the revolutions of 1848. This emphasised the unity of Germany and allegiance to the nation as a whole rather than its particular states. It was both a political and a cultural force. Towards the end of the century this was to find an even wider expression in German imperialism. While, to begin with, it appeared that Prussia had annexed Germany, in the end Germany and German nationalism were to absorb Prussia.

❸ There was the powerful economic impetus of rapid industrial growth, of improved communications, particularly railways, and of the commercial integration of the various parts of the country. This was particularly encouraged by the *Zollverein*, or customs union, of 1834 which continuously strengthened the Prussian position throughout this period.

6.2 'GROSSDEUTSCH' AND 'KLEINDEUTSCH'

As the events of 1848–9 very clearly showed, German nationalists were divided among themselves over both the extent and the constitution of a united Germany. At this time local and regional ties still dominated in Germany political life. So, too, there were partisan divisions among the groups which championed the nationalist cause.

The 'Grossdeutsch' or 'greater German' solution looked to Austria for leadership. To incorporate Austria in a German national state was impossible, however, so long as the Habsburgs insisted on retaining – as they did – their non-German territories and peoples. Increasingly, therefore, German patriots turned to Prussia for the achievement of unification: the 'Kleindeutsch' or 'lesser German' solution which excluded Austria.

While the growth of nationalist feeling was contributing to a sense of common German identity, it was also undermining the multinational Habsburg Empire. The force of Nationalism, which was the dominant political development of the nineteenth century, was later – in the wake of the First World War – to bring about the Empire's collapse.

The example of the Italian War of Independence did a good deal to reawaken national ambitions in Germany and, in 1859, a national society was formed which campaigned for a parliamentary regime in a united Germany under Prussian leadership which soon had 20,000 members. Another society, the Reformverein, was also created. In 1859 the mobilisation of France against Austria in Italy also aroused fear of French expansionism against the German confederation.

Otto von Bismarck

The determination of the Prussian monarchy to assert itself in Germany had a long history. Bismarck, who played a unique role in the process of unification, saw himself as upholding this tradition of strengthening Prussia and conserving its institutions.

He had become involved in politics as a representative of the Junkers (landed gentry) in Berlin in 1847 and was noted for his extremely conservative views. He showed himself to be passionately opposed to German liberalism and the Frankfurt Parliament of 1848. In 1851 he was chosen to serve as Prussia's ambassador to the revived German

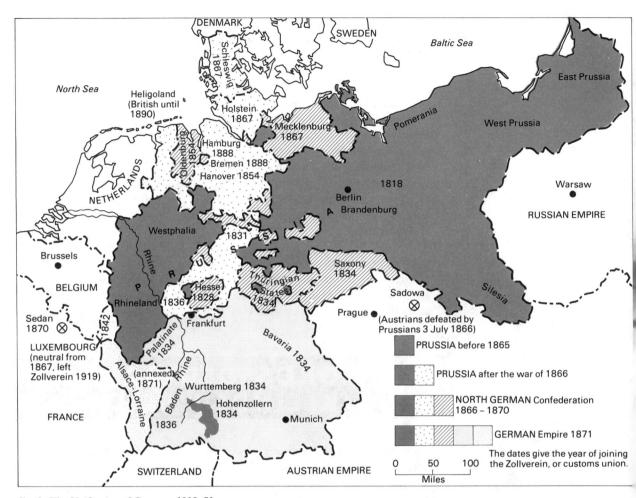

Fig 3. The Unification of Germany 1818–71

Diet. In 1857 he was sent as ambassador to St. Petersburg. In 1862 he was transferred to Paris and then invited back to Berlin in September of that year to push through the violently disputed army reforms in the face of Liberal opposition.

6.3 THE ARMY REFORMS AND CONSTITUTIONAL CRISIS

In 1860 the Prussian Landtag was presented with a Bill for army reforms. Though the population of Prussia had doubled since 1815 the number of recruits had not risen.

The Bill proposed to increase annual recruitment by more than a half, to raise the period of active service to three years (rather than two) and to integrate the Landwehr, the semi-civilian reserve force, with the regular army.

The Liberal majority passed the budget for increased expenditure for a year but refused to accept the principle of military reform. They insisted that the two-year term of service should be retained and rejected the forcing of the militia out of the field army.

This precipitated a major constitutional crisis and the Prussian King, William I, threatened abdication. In his view the army must remain a strong and reliable instrument in the hand of the monarch. It must strengthen the traditional position of the Crown, not the people. A new political party, the Progressive Party, was founded in 1861 to fight what was a constitutional battle of Liberal parliamentarians against the established order of Junkerdom and entrenched institutions.

Bismarck assumed ministerial power to resolve this conflict in the King's favour. For four years (1862–6) he conducted the government of Prussia without a constitutionally sanctioned budget. He waged two wars (against Denmark and Austria) without any grant of money from the representative assembly. He imposed press controls, dismissed numerous officials and intervened in elections to force through the royal policy.

Prussian leadership in Germany

It is important to consider Bismarck's contribution to unification of Germany in context. His role, particularly as diplomatist, was extremely important – indeed, crucial. But there are other factors – besides this and the modernisation of the Prussian army – which would have favoured Prussian dominance, whoever had been Chief Minister at Berlin:

❶ The Zollverein had already made most of Germany an economic unit and the industrialisation of North Germany was already well under way by 1862. The starting point for this was the financial reforms of Maassen in 1818. In order to unite the scattered provinces of Prussia, he created a new tariff system which abolished all internal customs and established free trade throughout Prussia.

❷ The German population was increasing with great rapidity, notably more, for instance, than that of France.

❸ A good railway network had been constructed.

❹ The acquisition of the Rhineland in 1815.

❺ An extremely efficient civil service at the disposal of the Prussian monarch.

❻ The relative weakening of the Habsburg Empire due to economic factors, the unresolved problems of the nationalities and of internal rivalries, and Prussia's growing diplomatic isolation.

6.4 THE SCHLESWIG-HOLSTEIN QUESTION

As Prussian ambassador to the revived Germanic Diet at Frankfurt, Bismarck had first-hand experience of the Austro-German rivalry. The first step to Prussia's renewed rise to power, as he saw it, would be to make her master north of the river Main.

In a memorandum to William I, Bismarck explained that the more Prussia was bound by German federal arrangements, the less her real power would be because Austria could always organise the other members of the Bund against her.

In January, 1864, he induced the Austrians to sign an alliance with Prussia against Denmark on the grounds that the new King of Denmark, Christian IX, had infringed the London agreement of 1852 over the duchies of Schleswig and Holstein.

This complex issue of competing national claims was then manipulated by Bismarck to bring about war with Austria after the Convention of Gastein. The dispute with Austria was both over Schleswig-Holstein and over rival proposals for a constitution for Germany to replace or reform the constitution of the Confederation. Beneath this there was the perennial rivalry of the two major German Powers.

The diplomatic background

The war of Austria and Prussia against Denmark convinced Bismarck that Britain and Russia were unlikely to intervene in an Austro-Prussian conflict. The diplomatic scene favoured Prussia in three main ways:

❶ Russian relations with Austria had been cool since the neutrality of the Habsburgs in the Crimean War; while Bismarck had moved quickly to offer Russia support at the time of the Polish uprising in 1863.

❷ In October, 1865, he had met Napoleon III at Biarritz and prepared the way for French neutrality in the event of a struggle with Austria. (By February 1866, Bismarck was declaring that such a conflict had now become only a matter of time.)

❸ In April 1866 a secret alliance was concluded between Prussia and Italy. Article 2 provided that, if Prussia's plans for reforming the German Confederation failed and Prussia took up arms, Italy would follow Prussia in declaring war on Austria. As a reward Venetia was to be ceded to Italy.

6.5 THE OUTBREAK OF WAR WITH AUSTRIA

Bismarck's weapon against the Austrian-dominated German Confederation, which was an alliance of sovereigns, was to threaten to place German's future in the hands of a German parliament elected on the basis of universal suffrage.

His clear aim, as the Austrians saw it, was to exclude them from any say in German affairs. Prussia, by force of her size and her economic and military power, would then be able to dominate the 'lesser Germany'.

They broke off negotiations over Schleswig-Holstein and proposed to the German Diet that all the German States, except Prussia, should be mobilised.

Sadowa

The 'Seven Weeks' War' was arguably the central event in nineteenth-century German history. The battle of Sadowa finally resolved the long Austro-Prussian rivalry and assured the victory of the 'Kleindeutschland' solution.

Austria was excluded from the future development of German affairs and North Germany was consolidated under Prussian leadership.

At the same time, the triumph of the Prussian army – through superior planning, efficiency and mobilisation – destroyed the possibility that Prussia might become a parliamentary state on the British model: it was also a domestic victory of established institutions over the Liberal opposition.

The desire for a strong Germany under Prussian leadership in the event proved stronger than the wish for a liberal Germany. The Indemnity Bill emphasised this shift of opinion. The majority of the Liberals became government supporters and for more than a decade the National Liberal and Free Conservative parties gave Bismarck the support he needed to consolidate the foundations of the German Empire.

6.6 THE TREATY OF PRAGUE

Bismarck imposed a moderate peace. The Habsburgs were not required to sacrifice any territory. Prussia annexed Hanover, Schleswig-Holstein, part of Hesse-Darmstadt and the City of Frankfurt; the independence of the remaining North German states was lost except for a measure of local autonomy in the North German Confederation.

In this, central authority was exercised by the Bundesrat, the Federal Council, in which Prussia could always secure majority. The King of Prussia assumed the title of President of the Bund and the function of Commander-in-Chief. He appointed, and could dismiss, the Federal Chancellor. Officially he controlled foreign policy and could declare war and make peace.

The constitution also provided for the election of a representative assembly, the *Reichstag*, on the basis of universal manhood suffrage. But this was only allowed a limited role. It did not, for instance, have control over the military budget, which comprised the major part of the Confederation's taxation.

6.7 BISMARCK AND NAPOLEON III

Before the Treaty of Prague the French Emperor had won the assurance that France would not face a united Germany that included the territories to the south of the Main. Behind Napoleon's back, however, Bismarck concluded secret alliances with the Southern States. In return for Prussia not insisting on large indemnities from them, it was agreed that – if Prussia found herself in a war endangering her territory – the Southern States would place their armies under the command of the King of Prussia.

There has been much historical debate over Bismarck's precise intentions after 1867. Did he, for example, see a war with France as necessary and inevitable?

In fact, the North German Confederation already included two-thirds of the whole of Germany. It was obvious from the start that the remaining states would find it very difficult to enjoy the 'independent sovereign existence' as laid down in the Treaty of Prague.

In this period Bismarck proposed elections throughout all the German states for a gathering of a 'Zollparlament', or customs parliament, with a view to this assembly extending its jurisdiction over non-commercial questions.

At the same time he refused to 'compensate' Napoleon for French neutrality during the Austro-Prussian War. He rejected the 'hotel-keeper's bill', as he called it. Among other things he stirred up German national feeling against the idea of ceding Luxemburg to France.

The Hohenzollern candidature

This diplomatic crisis which led to the Franco–Prussian War originated in September, 1868, when a revolution in Spain drove the reigning Queen out of the country. The idea of approaching a Hohenzollern prince for the Spanish throne came from the leading minister of the revolutionary government.

Bismarck's assertion that he had nothing to do with the affair until the full crisis broke in July 1870 is false. In March 1870 he had already sent a memorandum to William I arguing the case for the candidature and he subsequently sent agents to Spain.

The French government argued that a German prince on the Spanish throne would mean the 'encirclement' of France. The French played into Bismarck's hands by demanding that King William not simply repudiate the candidature but also offer an assurance that he would not authorise a renewal of it.

William's refusal to meet the second of these demands, which was emphasised by the Ems telegram, left Napoleon and his ministers with only two ways out of the situation which they had created – either to climb down or to fight.

By the time of the declaration of war Bismarck had contrived to make it appear that all the blame for the war was French. This allowed him to bring into force the military alliances between Prussia and the South German States. He presented it as a patriotic war in defence of the Fatherland.

6.8 THE RESULTS OF THE FRANCO–PRUSSIAN WAR

The French lost Alsace, most of Lorraine and the fortresses of Strasbourg and Metz – a cause of lasting grievance for France. She was also forced to pay an indemnity of five billion francs and a German army of occupation was to remain in northern France until it was paid.

With the proclamation of William I as German Emperor in January, 1871, Germany emerged as the dominant continental state, a role which France had enjoyed since the seventeenth century. The Empire, which incorporated the Southern States, was a federal rather than a unitary state.

Two other incidental but significant results of the Franco–Prussian War were:

❶ that Russia stated, and the Powers accepted, that she would no longer be bound by the Black Sea clauses of the Treaty of Paris (1856), and;

❷ following the withdrawal of the French garrison, Rome was incorporated as the capital of Italy.

6.9 CHRONOLOGY

1850	November	THE PUNCTUATION OF OLMÜTZ: the re-establishment of the Germanic Diet at Frankfurt.
1853		Brunswick, Hanover and Oldenburg joined the ZOLLVEREIN (formed 1834), bringing the whole of non-Austrian Germany into the customs union.
1858		WILLIAM I appointed Regent (King of Prussia from 1861).
1859–62		GENERAL VON ROON appointed Minister of War to reform the army; VON MOLTKE becomes the Chief of the General Staff. THE STRUGGLE BETWEEN THE LIBERAL MAJORITY IN PARLIAMENT AND THE MONARCHY OVER ARMY REFORM; PRUSSIAN CONSTITUTIONAL CRISIS; WILLIAM I THREATENED ABDICATION.
1862		OTTO VON BISMARCK became Minister-President of Prussia, later Chancellor. Carried on the constitutional struggle with the Prussian parliament for the next four years.
1863	February	THE POLISH REVOLT: Bismarck sent von Alvensleben to offer Prussian support to Russia against the rebels.
	July	The Diet of the Germanic Confederation demanded that the two Duchies be taken from Denmark and submitted to the rule of the German Duke of Augustenburg, son of one of the claimants to the succession.
	August	Congress of Princes, summoned by the Austrian Emperor, Francis Joseph, to reform the German Confederation. Bismarck refused to allow William I to attend. THE SCHLESWIG-HOLSTEIN QUESTION: Proclamation of King Frederick VII of Denmark in March 1863 announced the annexation to Denmark of the Duchy of Schleswig. This breached the London Protocol of 1852.
	October	The Diet voted for action against Denmark.
	November	Death of Frederick; succeeded by Christian IX, who signed a new constitution indicating his intention to incorporate Schleswig.
	December	Federal troops entered Holstein.
1864	January	Austria joins Prussia in alliance.
	February	Austrian and Prussian troops invaded Schleswig.
	April	Capture of Düppel forts; German invasion of Denmark.
	April–June	THE LONDON CONFERENCE. War renewed at end of June, resulting in defeat of the Danes. Surrender of the Duchies of Schleswig, Holstein and Lauenburg to Austria and Prussia.
	October	The Peace of Vienna.

1865	August	THE CONVENTION OF GASTEIN: Joint sovereignty of Prussia and Austria over the Duchies. Austria to administer Holstein and Prussia Schleswig. (Lauenburg ceded to Prussia in return for a money payment to Austria.)
	October	BISMARCK MET NAPOLEON AT BIARRITZ; a vague offer of 'compensation' for France in return for a promise of French neutrality in the event of an Austro-Prussian war.
1866	April	BISMARCK, SUPPORTED BY NAPOLEON, CONCLUDED AN OFFENSIVE AND DEFENSIVE ALLIANCE WITH ITALY: Italy to join Prussia if war broke out between Austria and Prussia within three months, with Venetia as the reward for Italy. Bismarck introduced a motion for federal reform into the Frankfurt Diet with the intention that Austria reject it and precipitate a conflict. Prussia and Austria started to mobilise. Austria signed a secret treaty with Napoleon III. In return for French neutrality Austria promised to cede Venetia to Napoleon who was then to give it to Italy. The Frankfurt Diet voted against Prussia for violating Holstein territory. The majority of the German States, including Bavaria, Saxony and Holstein, sided with Austria against Prussia.
	June	The Austrian governor of Holstein summoned the Holstein Diet in order to discuss the future of the Duchy. Bismarck denounced this as a violation of the Gastein Convention and ordered Prussian troops into the Duchy.
	June–August	THE SEVEN WEEKS' WAR: complete victory for the Prussians at the battle of SADOWA (Königgrätz) in Bohemia. Napoleon offered to mediate; Bismarck accepted this only on condition that the peace terms should be determined before the armistice was completed.
		THE PEACE PRELIMINARIES OF NIKOLSBURG: the states of Hesse, Frankfurt, Nassau and Hanover to be incorporated in Prussia. Austria excluded from Germany. German states north of the river Main were to form a North German Confederation under Prussian leadership. The South German States were to remain independent and to be allowed to form a separate confederation. Bismarck took advantage of the fears aroused by French demands for compensation to persuade the South German States (Bavaria, Baden and Würtemberg) to conclude secret military alliances with Prussia, operative in the event of a French attack.
	August	TREATY OF PRAGUE: the Germanic Confederation, established in 1815 was dissolved; Austria was excluded from participation in German affairs.
	September	THE BILL OF INDEMNITY: gave retrospective assent to Bismarck's expenditure without the consent of parliament during the constitutional crisis. The majority of the Liberals now rallied to Bismarck, in spite of their previous bitter opposition, because of his achievement of national objectives.
1867	April	The CREATION OF THE NORTH GERMAN CONFEDERATION. The Luxemburg crisis.
	July	Bismarck brought the four South German States into the Zollverein and established the ZOLLPARLAMENT, customs parliament.
1868–70		THE HOHENZOLLERN CANDIDATURE FOR THE SPANISH THRONE.
1870	June	Leopold of Hohenzollern-Sigmaringen accepted the offer of the Spanish throne.
	6 July	The French foreign minister Gramont made a speech to the French Chamber indicating France would go to war unless the Prussian government withdrew the candidacy.
	9–11	The French ambassador to Berlin, Count Benedetti requested William I to order Leopold to withdraw.
	12	Prince Charles Anthony, father of Leopold, withdrew the candidacy on behalf of his son. Not content with this diplomatic victory, the French government proceeded to demand guarantees from William I that he should both disavow the candidacy AND promise that it would never be renewed.
	13	THE EMS INTERVIEW: the Prussian king rejected Benedetti's demand; Bismarck amended the EMS TELEGRAM.
	19	French declaration of war on Prussia.
1870–71		THE FRANCO-PRUSSIAN WAR: Bismarck and the armed support of the South German States. Britain secured the neutrality of Belgium. THE BATTLE OF SEDAN (1 September, 1870); THE CAPITULATION OF METZ (27 October); THE FALL OF PARIS (28 January, 1871).
1871	18 January	THE FOUNDATION OF THE GERMAN EMPIRE: As a result of the war the new Reich consisted of 25 states. Germany acquired Alsace and eastern Lorraine, including Metz and Strasbourg, and incorporated the States south of the Main in the North German Confederation.

Illustrative questions and answers

1 Is it true to say that diplomacy was more important than war in the process of German unification between 1862 and 1871?

Tutorial note

You may point out that the question implies a highly debatable assumption. Whereas it is reasonable to ask whether, say, economic factors were more important than military factors, it most arguably the case that war and diplomacy are not alternatives, but that war is in fact diplomacy by other means; it is often very difficult to distinguish between them and you should tell the examiner so.

You need to know about

Bismarck's career and the military and diplomatic events between 1862 and 1871.

Suggested answer plan

1 Rather than opposites, war and diplomacy may be seen as separable parts of a nation's dealings with other states; no foreign minister can know when or whether his diplomatic bluffs will be called and may lead to war; this was most certainly the case with Bismarck.

2 Narrative of the first stage of the process of unification: the Polish Revolt and Bismarck's defiance of Prussian liberals in pledging support for the Tsar; the Schleswig-Holstein Question; 1848 dispute and the 1852 Treaty of London, and the cession of Christian IX of Denmark; Prussia and Austria invaded the Duchies on behalf of the German Confederation and military victory gave Schleswig to Prussia and Holstein to Austria.

3 Narrative of the second stage: Bismarck negotiated with Italy and met Napoleon at Biarritz (1865); Bismarck, Moltke and Roon engineered a dispute with Austria over the administration of the Duchies after the Convention of Gastein, partly to score domestic political points against the Prussian liberals; the Austro–Prussian War and the unexpectedly speedy and easy Russian victory; Prussian military improvements (e.g. the Roon Army reforms) and the reasons for her superiority.

4 The establishment of the North German Confederation under Prussia (and Bismarck's) thumb (1867); its constitution was the nucleus of the Empire to be founded in 1871; the gradual accommodation between the South German states and the confederation; Bismarck's secret alliances with these states.

5 The domestic rising in Spain and the abdication of Isabella; Bismarck suggested a Hohenzollern candidate for the Spanish throne; French objections to German 'encirclement'; the Ems telegram and the Franco–Prussian War; the easy Prussian victory and the reasons for it (weaponry, logistics, tactics); the foundation of the German Empire.

6 By far the most active diplomacy in all these events occurred immediately before the 1866 and 1870–1 wars, and was directed successfully towards preventing them. As for Bismarck's own diplomacy, clearly this could not have brought about unification own, but it was an important enabling factor. Especially it secured the neutrality of Russia (in alleged gratitude for Bismarck's support in 1863); and of Italy and France in 1866. Also, by deliberately not humiliating Austria after the 1866 war, Bismarck's diplomacy may, perhaps, have prevented a Habsburg campaign of revenge in 1870.

7 But undoubtedly it was the events on the battlefield which created German unity; diplomacy played only a secondary role.

2 How clear was it before Bismarck's assumption of office in 1862 that Germany would be united under Prussia?

Tutorial note

This question begs a more fundamental one: how clear was it before 1862 that German unification would be achieved at all? If the answer to this is that it *was* clear, then probably it was also clear that it would be achieved under Prussian leadership.

You need to know about

The internal histories of Prussia and Austria, c. 1848–71; Bismarck and the course of German unification during 1863-71.

Suggested answer plan

1   Bismarck after the event claimed to have had a clear intention of uniting Germany from the time of his appointment as Minister-President in 1862, and also a clear view of how to do it. This seems unlikely; Bismarck was an opportunist rather than a long-term calculator.

2   The only thing that was clear by 1862 was that Germany would not be united under Austria; the Grossdeutsch solution had been ruled out by Prussia's objection to the invasion of Austria's Slav lands; Austria would not accept a Kleindeutsch solution; Austria's severe economic weakness further undermined her power in Germany; Austria's last real attempt at dominance was her 1862–3 scheme for a German federal union under Austrian, Prussian and Bavarian leadership; despite the approval of King William of Prussia, Bismarck managed to thwart the proposal, and any lingering hopes of an Austrian 'solution'.

3   Since no institutions existed for the 'popular' unification of Germany, it was therefore clear by 1862 that *if* Germany were to be united it could only be under Prussian leadership. Prussia was economically a very strong state, thanks partly to the Zollverein, and this in turn was to enable her to strengthen her military capacity (though not fully before 1862). What she lacked was confidence – the 'humiliation' of Olmütz still rankled – and this is what the leadership of Bismarck supplied.

4   But by 1862 it was still far from clear that Germany would be united; the success of the Zollverein perhaps illustrated that formal political union was not economically essential; national sentiment of a cultural sort was in the doldrums at this time – it was far less apparent than in, say, Italy or Poland – and was to be a product rather than a cause of the process of unification; the Liberal Nationalism of the intellectuals and lawyers of 1848 seemed to be in marked decline after the Frankfurt Parliament of 1848; none of the European Powers wanted German unification and the series of wars which created it could hardly have been foreseen in 1862, even by Bismarck.

5   The motive for unification was there in 1862; subsequent successes enabled Bismarck to reconcile the liberal middle classes (or at least a large proportion of them) to the existing political system in Prussia. Austria, on the other hand, could only suffer from German unification. If it was to come, therefore, it was obviously going to be under Prussian direction.

3   What were the consequences for Germany of the Zollverein?

Tutorial note

You need to consider the economic and political development of the German states c. 1830–70, and decide how far they were prompted or retarded by the Zollverein.

You need to know about

The creation of the Zollverein and its policies. The economic development of both those states which made up the Zollverein and those excluded from it. The effects of such economic development on the internal politics of the states and on the German unification movement.

Suggested answer plan

1   It is sometimes said that Germany was united by 'coal and iron' not by 'blood and iron'; this view assigns a central role to the Zollverein in the process of unification; note though, that there have been many examples of the tendency towards economic concentration and integration during the last two centuries, but these have not always led on to political unification.
2   The territorial settlement of Germany in 1815; the events leading to the creation of the Zollverein: Prussia abolished internal customs barriers in 1818 in response to pressure from Rhineland industrialists; Prussia concluded several bilateral tariff negotiations with other German states during the 1820s; this increased her status in Germany at a time when Austria was causing annoyance by interfering in the internal police and censorship regulations of the smaller states.
3   In 1834 these bilateral agreements were merged to form the multilateral Zollverein; Metternich attempted to frustrate it but Saxony and Bavaria joined it; note that the states' motives for acceding to it were *economic* and not political; the Southern States would not have joined if they could have foreseen its political consequences; most of them were still loyal to Austria culturally and politically.
4   The economic development of the Zollverein to c. 1850; railway building, begun in 1834, had achieved 5,000 miles by 1850; commercial treaties and a large reduction in tariffs in 1845 led to a big increase in trade and manufacturing, especially in Prussia, whose industrial magnates, e.g. the Krupps, came to dominate the Zollverein.
5   The attempts of Brunswick, Hanover and Oldenburg and the Hansa towns to remain outside as a rival trade bloc collapsed with the accession of the first three to the Zollverein in 1844, 1851 and 1852 respectively. By this time Prussia's dominance was developing *political* implications. There was the growing imbalance between Prussia and Austria which was accelerated by the financial collapse of 1856-7; it became ever less likely that Austria – whose industries needed protection – could join the Zollverein, whose policies were increasingly free-trade. In 1862 Prussia replaced Austria as France's 'most favoured trading nation', symbolising the turn-around in fortunes.
6   Industrial leaders from the Ruhr and Rhineland, like Camphausen and Hansemann joined the Liberal Party inside Prussia; this was seen to pose a threat to the old Prussian nobility and the traditional governing class. In the process of unification and subsequent consolidation of Germany, Bismarck made economic concessions to this new group.
7   The Zollverein contributed a great deal to the unification of Germany and to the dominance of Prussia in the new nationstate; at the same time it helped to make the new middle classes a very powerful element in Prussia; to a certain extent Bismarck diverted attention to national German affairs in order to resist the pretension to political power of the new industrial and financial middle class.

Question bank

1   Document question (the Austro-Prussian War): study the extract below and answer questions (a) to (f) which follow:

Extract

'We had to avoid wounding Austria too severely: we had to avoid leaving behind in her any unnecessary bitterness of feeling or desire for revenge; we ought rather to reserve the possibility of becoming friends again with our adversary of the moment, and in any case to regard the Austrian state as a piece on the European chessboard and the renewal of friendly relations with her as a move open to us. If

Austria were severely injured she would become <u>the ally of France and of every other opponent of ours:</u> she would even sacrifice her <u>anti-Russian interests</u> for the sake of revenge on Prussia.

'On the other hand, I could see no future acceptable to us, for the countries constituting the Austrian monarchy, in case the latter were split up by risings of the Hungarians and Slavs or made permanently dependent on these peoples... . German Austria we could neither wholly nor partly make use of. The acquisition of provinces like Austrian Silesia and portions of Bohemia could not strengthen the Prussian State; it would not lead to an amalgamation of German Austria with Prussia, and Vienna could not be governed from Berlin as a mere dependency....

'The resistance I was obliged, in accordance with these convictions, to offer to the King's views with regard to the following up of the <u>military successes</u>, and to his inclination <u>to continue the victorious advance</u>, excited him to such a degree that a prolongation of the discussion became impossible; and under the impression that my opinion was rejected, I left the room with the idea of begging the King to allow me, in my capacity as an officer, to rejoin my regiment.'

(Bismarck's record of his advice to the King of Prussia at Nikolsburg, 1866.)

(a) What did Bismarck mean by 'wounding Austria too severely'? (2)
(b) 'The ally of France and of every other opponent of ours'. Why did Bismarck consider France as an opponent of Prussia at this time? (4)
(c) Explain Austria's 'anti-Russian interests'. In what ways might Austria need to sacrifice them to obtain revenge on Prussia for a harsh peace treaty? (6)
(d) What were 'the military successes' and why was the King so anxious 'to continue the victorious advance'? (5)
(e) In the peace treaty eventually made between Austria and Prussia, did the wishes of the King or of Bismarck prevail? What, for the Austrian monarchy, was the constitutional result of the war and the peace? (6)
(f) What light is shed by this passage, especially the second paragraph on Bismarck's long-term aims for the future of Germany? Did the settlement of 1871 conform to these aims? (8)

2 Why did the other Great Powers fail to prevent Prussian domination of Germany in 1871? (AS Level, AEB, June 1989)

3 To what extent was the unification of Germany or of Italy based on a compromise? (NISEAC, June 1991)

4 What did German unification between 1861 and 1871 owe to Prussian militarism? (Oxford and Cambridge, June 1991)

5 Why did Prussia rather than Austria take the lead in German unification after 1848? (Oxford and Cambridge, June 1992)

READING LIST

Standard textbook reading

L. W. Cowie and R. Wolfson, *Years of Nationalism, European History 1815–1890* (Edward Arnold, 1985) chapter IV (3).

Robert Gildea, *Barricades and Borders, Europe 1800–1914* (OUP, 1987), chapter 7.

J. A. S. Grenville, *Europe Reshaped 1848-78* (Fontana, 1976), chapters 7, 8, 14, 15, 17.

Agatha Ramm, *Europe in the Nineteenth Century 1789–1905* (Longman, 1984), chapters 17 and 18.

David Thomson, *Europe since Napoleon* (Penguin, 1977), chapter 14.

Anthony Wood, *Europe 1815–1945* (Longman, 1975), chapters 17–19.

Further suggested reading

H. Böhme, *The Foundation of the German Empire* (Oxford, 1971).

J. P. T. Bury (ed), *The New Cambridge Modern History 1830–70*, volume X (CUP, 1964), chapters 19, 22.

W. Carr, *A History of Germany 1815–1990* (4th edn. Arnold, 1991).

L. Gall, *Bismarck – The White Revolutionary* (trans. J. A. Underwood) (Allen & Unwin, 1986).

M. Howard, *The Franco–Prussian War* (Hart-Davis, 1961).

W. N. Medlicott, *Bismarck and Modern Germany* (English Universities Press, 1965).

O. Pfnanze, *Bismarck and the Development of Germany 1848–1871* (Princeton University Press, 1963).

A. Ramm, *Germany 1789–1919* (Methuen, 1967).

W.M. Simon (ed.), *Germany in the Age of Bismarck* (Allen & Unwin, 1968).

F. Stern, *Gold and Iron, Bismarck, Bleichröder and the Building of the German Empire* (Allen & Unwin, 1977).

A. J. P. Taylor, *Bismarck* (New English Library, 1974); and *The Struggle for Mastery in Europe* (OUP, 1971).

B. Waller, *Bismarck* (OUP, 1985).

D.G. Williamson, *Bismarck and Germany 1862–1890* (Longman, 1986).

7

RUSSIA, 1855–1917

Units in this chapter

Chapter objectives

❶ The nature of Russian society at the accession of Tsar Alexander II: its backwardness as revealed by the defeat in the Crimean War; the problems facing the autocracy – indebtedness, and the need for modernisation and reform.

❷ The Emancipation Edict: the background to and reasons for this reform (particularly the Tsar's motives): its terms for serfs and landowners; its failure to solve the question of the land – the continuance of the 'mir' (commune) and burdensome redemption payments for the peasants.

❸ The other reforms of Alexander II: the Zemstvo Law, the reform of the judiciary, of municipal government, of the Army and of education; the disappointing reaction of Russian society to the reforms – obstruction by a bureaucracy increasingly staffed with conservative noblemen; Populism; the growth of terrorism – 'Land and Liberty', 'The Will of the People'.

❹ The reasons why Alexander's 'revolution from above' was only, at the very most, a half-revolution; his unwillingness to provide a proper liberal regime with a representative parliament – i.e. his refusal to introduce a national asembly; the problem of applying Western liberal ideas in Russian society.

❺ The impact of the assassination of Alexander II and the reaction under Tsar Alexander III; Pobedonostsev's influence: bureaucratic paternalism and a strenuous upholding of the principles of Russian nationalism, autocracy and of the Orthodox religion – censorship, Russification, pogroms against the Jews; the banning of opposition political groups, curbs on education; the Land Captains.

❻ Economic development and industrialisation: Sergei Witte and 'state capitalism', funded through foreign loans paid for by heavy taxation; the emphasis on heavy industry, capital goods and the development of the railway system; the social consequences of this programme of forced industrialisation.

❼ The growth of political opposition to the tsarist order under Nicholas II: the Social Revolutionaries, Liberals and Social Democrats; the growth of Marxist ideas in Russia, with special reference to the early career of Lenin and his ideas on revolution; the significance of the 1903 split of the Social Democratic Party into Mensheviks and Bolsheviks.

⑧ The Russo–Japanese War and its impact on the Russian government. Note, as background, the great imperial expansion of Russia into Central Asia, Siberia and Manchuria.

⑨ The causes, course of events and consequences of the 1905 revolution, noting particularly the role in it of the peasants, industrial workers and the national minorities; the massacre of 'Bloody Sunday', the October Manifesto, the soviets and the Fundamental Laws.

⑩ The constitution, scope and significance of the Dumas; the electoral law of 1907; the career and reforms of Stolypin, particularly his encouragement of private peasant ownership; the reasons for his unpopularity both in reactionary and liberal political circles.

⑪ Russia at war, 1914–17: the way in which it exposed the underlying weaknesses of the tsarist order; the land problem; inflation; administrative chaos; the personal role of the Tsar and of court circles; the consideration as to whether – without the impact of a disastrous war – Russia might have evolved along the path of evolutionary reform rather than collapsed.

On his accession in 1855, Alexander II was faced with the need to modernise and reform a backward peasant society if Russia was to maintain her status as a great Power, something which was called in question by the defeat in the Crimean War. He introduced a wide range of reforms, of which the most important was the Emancipation Edict. These reforms were intended to strengthen, not weaken, the tsarist autocracy and he refused to create a parliamentary assembly along Western liberal lines.

After his assassination, his successors, Alexander III and Nicholas II, combined very conservative political and social policies with a programme of rapid state-led industrialisation.

The failure to solve the land question at a time of very sharply increasing population and the social changes brought about by rapid industrialisation contributed to the outbreak of revolution in 1905, which followed Russia's humiliation in the war against Japan. This was succeeded by the period of the State Dumas and further reforms, notably those sponsored by Stolypin.

Final disenchantment with the regime came in 1917 when the failures of the government, plus seemingly insoluble economic problems, all combined with military defeat and insurrection to bring down the tsarist order.

7.1 TSAR ALEXANDER II

Russian society and the state in 1855

Russian society Russia was in 1855 still very much a pre-industrial society. The vast majority of Russians were either landowners' serfs or 'state peasants' (that is 'owned' by the State). These peasants were governed by the nobility and a very small bureaucracy. The tsarist autocracy depended for its power on the nobles' control of the serfs through the *commune*. This institution was the typical village government in Russia and the means whereby land was periodically redistributed to meet the varying needs of the commune's families.

All services to the lord by either labour service or money, or produce rent, were paid communally, as was the poll tax. Furthermore, the serfs *thought* communally as well – eg. the famous phrase: 'We are yours, but the land is *ours*.'

This system discouraged the incentive of individual peasant families, because it offered no guarantee of possession of land from one generation to another. Thus Russian agriculture in 1855 was not increasing greatly in productivity.

This stagnation of agriculture, coupled with poor means of transportation in Russia, meant that Russian grain could not compete in its traditional European markets against the new, highly productive agriculture being introduced in the West. The result was that the income of the landed nobility declined sharply. Indebtedness to the state had reached crisis proportions by 1855 and it appeared to many that serfdom was not providing the benefits to the ruling class which were its justification.

The State The tsarist regime was also suffering from competition in the provision of raw materials in which, in the eighteenth century, it had had a virtual monopoly, in parallel to its official monopoly within Russia – e.g. timber, gold and flax. It experienced severe financial crises in the early nineteenth century. The agrarian economy was not able to sustain the expenditure nor to provide the new technology necessary to maintain Great Power status in an age of industrialisation. As a result, Russia experienced humiliating defeat in the Crimean War and incurred a huge public debt.

By 1855 the economic bases of the traditional autocracy were disappearing. A new system had to be found if the tsarist regime was to preserve its internal political and international standing. The wish for Great Power status was a constant element in tsarist policy.

The experiment with Liberalism

In the West the political accompaniment of capitalistic economic growth was Liberalism. This had two forms: (a) economic 'laissez-faire' and (b) parliamentarism and representative government. Both, however, were in direct opposition to the tsarist autocracy.

Since the time of Peter the Great, however, Russia had tended to look to the West for answers to Russia's problems: the nobility often spoke French better than Russian and were often educated along Western lines. It was not surprising that the regime should try again after 1855 to use Western methods of modernisation.

7.2 THE REFORMS OF ALEXANDER II

The accession of a new tsar, Alexander II (1855–81) brought an expectation of change to the system in the direction of progressive Liberalism.

The Statute of Emancipation

It had been axiomatic in Russia that serfdom was a 'necessary evil'. Even Tsar Nicholas I condemned it in principle. Given the economic situation and bearing in mind that he had received a liberal education, Alexander decided in 1857 that emancipation of the serfs was due in the interests of the power as well as the moral prestige of the state and its nobility. The 1861 Statute of Emancipation gave the peasants legal emancipation and also the right to own their own land. But there were notable drawbacks:

❶ The peasants were forced to make very large redemption payments for any land other than their own personal allotments; this was in the interest of the debtor nobility.

❷ The new administrative system, the 'volost' courts, etc., was still dominated by the land-holding nobility and was not integrated with the national judicial system.

③ The system of land tenure remained communal. Thus the most serious obstacle to a liberal/capitalist agricultural system was retained in the new order. This was because the regime would only reform *partly* and not compromise the basis of its tax system and the traditional peasant society – the commune. The result was the continued backwardness of agriculture.

④ The effect of the Emancipation was further weakened by the counter-attack of the conservatives in the government. After 1861 the agrarian experiment was effectively in the hands of its opponents.

⑤ The post-Emancipation peasantry continued to be subjected to widely resented legal and civil disabilities. In addition, more than half of the peasantry belonged to underprivileged and oppressed ethnic and/or religious minorities, who increasingly asserted their separate identities, aspirations and demands from the 1890s onwards.

The other reforms

The Emancipation was followed by a series of measures to provide a new state system along liberal lines:

* In 1864 the Zemstvos (locally elected assemblies) were set up on an unequal franchise to provide local government services at provincial and county levels.

* A liberal system of justice was introduced with a jury system and on the principle of the 'rule of law'. The peasant 'volost' courts were excluded from this system. The police were also reformed.

* Education policy was relatively liberalised, universities were made autonomous and censorship was somewhat relaxed. Secondary and elementary schooling was expanded slightly. Education was still seen as socially dangerous, and likely to undermine popular acceptance of the existing order of society.

* The Defence Minister, Milyutin, provided the Army with real, in-depth, liberal reforms, preparing it for success in the 1877–8 Russo-Turkish War.

* Attempts were made to encourage enterprise by providing credit institutions, such as the State Bank, and by removing barriers to trade, e.g. the reduction of exports and import duties after 1863.

The impact of the reforms

From 1861, and especially from 1866 with the attempt on Alexander's life, the liberals began to lose credibility and power. This was for several reasons:

① The Tsar and the regime were anomalous *as liberals*, because Liberalism called for a parliamentary assembly, which the autocracy denied.

② The series of measures after 1861, hailed as 'a revolution from above', really only amounted to half-measures, because Liberalism could not accomplish the task of bolstering up the tsarist regime while modernising society; and Russian society reacted poorly to the reforms, or at least many of them. For instance, the increase in political terrorism *after* the reforms dimmed liberal prospects.

③ The experience of Russian agriculture after Emancipation was varied. In the Ukraine, and in the east, the Emancipation – combined with easier transport – did lead to increased grain production on capitalist lines, which meant that grain exports went up steeply (31% of exports in 1861–5, 47% in 1891–5). But generally speaking, agriculture remained backward, tied down by the communal system and the lack of capitalist enterprise amongst the nobility. The result was the continued impoverishment of a growing peasant population coupled with the bankruptcy of the landed nobility who gave up the land in droves and became officials in the vastly expanded bureaucracy, which increased from 2,000 to 10,000 in the 1870s.

Thus the liberals, such as they were, were swamped by this gentry bureaucracy.

7.3 RUSSIA, 1881–1905

The poor results of the liberal programme, as far as tsarist power and prestige were concerned, meant that – even before Tsar Alexander II's assassination in 1881 – Liberalism was in many respects a spent force. It is true Loris-Melikov had, in the last year, been used by Alexander to try and provide the necessary reforms and there was even talk of a constitution. But Alexander's death scotched this faint possibility and instead the regimes of Alexander III and Nicholas II embarked on a combination of the repression of political opposition, conservative social policy and a state-led, forced industrialisation.

The reaction

The bureaucracy became jealous of any power base but itself:

- The Zemstvos came under attack. In 1889 their contact with the peasants, the Justices of the Peace, were abolished and replaced by a Land Commandant who had to be a noble.
- The universities were brought under the control of inspectors once more (1884). Censorship was increased.
- All other nationalities in the tsarist empire were subjected to Russification. The first pogrom was in 1881.
- All political parties in opposition to the regime were banned.

   The regime, especially the Ministry of the Interior, followed a very paternalist path in the interests of preserving the traditional social hierarchy:

- No attempt was made to abolish communal tenure, in spite of arguments from the Ministry of Finance, because Tolstoy at the Ministry of the Interior felt it was a major agent for social peace and, thus, loyalty to the regime among the peasants.
- Education: similar arguments justified the refusal to institute a classless educational system. In secondary education the raising of fees to keep out lower-class pupils in 1887 had the result that there were fewer pupils at this level in 1895 than there had been in 1882. At the elementary level, education was left to the Church. By 1900 only a quarter of the population was literate.

State capitalism

The Ministry of Finance, particularly under Sergei Witte between 1892 and 1903, remained a bastion of Liberalism, of a sort. As in the West, however, development was to be achieved by protectionism and led by the state. Industry was protected by high import duties and encouraged by government demand for the new state railway system, which expanded greatly in the 1890s.

State expenditure and capital investment was paid for partly by a large inflow of foreign loans, made easier after 1897 by putting the Rouble on the Gold Standard. These loans were serviced by revenue from tariffs, but also from the heavy indirect taxes on the urban poor and the peasants, which provided the foreign-currency earner of grain exports.

This hothouse economic programme produced a dramatic expansion of 8% per annum in the 1890s. But it did not stimulate the international market. Demand was state-led and dependent on taking money from the peasants. Thus grain exports were coupled with famines, because the conservative social policy, viz. the communes, meant that the agrarian economy could not respond to, or even accommodate, Witte's programme. Therefore from 1900–05 the economy stagnated, as the state ran into financial difficulties. State capitalism left Russia with a much more advanced economic structure, but also with a financially oppressed peasantry and a discontented urban proletariat, the product of a continuing population increase among the peasantry. It was clear by 1905 that something had to change.

7.4 THE REVOLUTION OF 1905

Opposition to the autocracy

The growing social turmoil caused by the effects of the modernisation programme found expression in the formation of three, illegal, political parties:

❶ the Social Revolutionaries (1901), who represented a new sort of populism, and had redistribution of the land to the peasants as their first priority;

❷ the Liberals (1903), whose main aim was to try to create a liberal democratic constitutional government which could match Russia's newly emerging society;

❸ the Social Democrats (1903), who voiced the growing frustration of the new urban proletariat through the language of Marxism.

Therefore most sectors of Russian society were in opposition to the state: only the noble bureaucrats, the state-dependent industrialists and the Army supported the regime. And even before the Russo-Japanese War broke out in January, 1904, the regime was in a very poor situation. When war resulted in abject defeat, Russia experienced a massive upheaval.

The elements in the 1905 revolution

There were really four uprisings involved:

❶ the rising of the national minorities against Russification, especially in Poland and the Baltic provinces, coupled with demands for political and economic reforms;

❷ the seizure by the peasants of what they saw as their land – i.e. the nobles', Church's and state lands – due to the pressures of overpopulation;

❸ the rising of the urban proletariat – through illegal strikes and demonstrations – against their employers and the autocracy; and

❹ a campaign by the Union of Liberation based on the French banquet campaign of 1848 to force the regime to liberalise.

The events of 1905

On the 9 January workers demonstrating against conditions were fired on by troops outside the Winter Palace. 'Bloody Sunday' was a tremendous blow to the Tsar's prestige and uprisings spread. In February, decrees were issued by Nicholas II to try to quell opposition: they promised 'participation' by the people in government. In October there was a general strike by the railwaymen. The regime was now paralysed.

Witte returned from the peace negotiations and took over the government. On 17 October the Tsar issued the 'October Manifesto' which promised an elected Duma with legislative powers and civil liberties. This did not immediately break the opposition, but it did produce a split in the Liberals between the 'Octobrists' and 'Kadets', the former accepting the October Manifesto in good faith, the latter wanting more.

Soviets (workers' councils) were formed in St. Petersburg and Moscow. During October–November there were large-scale peasant riots but workers in St. Petersburg and Moscow alienated their liberal allies by continuing actions against their employers. In December the St. Petersburg Soviet was dispersed and Moscow street risings were put down by the regime's forces (by this time, troops were returning from the Far East).

With the issue of the Franchise Law in December, 1905, and the subsequent Fundamental Laws, the government indicated that it had reasserted its control over the situation.

7.5 THE PERIOD OF THE DUMAS

The effect of the 1905 revolution was to create a constitution in Russia and a parliamentary body in the Duma. It also brought about a rethinking of economic and social policy under the ministry of Stolypin. However, the renewed attempt at westernisation through Liberalism again experienced fatal problems so that, under the pressure of another war, the newly renovated regime again failed.

Constitutional politics

Parliamentarism When the First Duma met in April, 1906 the weakness of the regime had been remedied. The Fundamental Laws already pointed towards a trimming of the Duma's power.

Its radical composition – 30% workers or peasants – ensured its early dissolution. The Second Duma was, however, equally radical; meeting in February, 1907, it was dissolved in June. Only with the Third Duma was there a body which would cooperate with the tsarist order. However, this was based on a restrictive franchise and followed a new bout of repression of opposition.

In practice the Third and Fourth Dumas became only another agency of the huge, sprawling bureaucracy; Russia, by the eve of war in 1914 justified Witte's claim that it was 'ungovernable'. The bureaucracy, the Army, the Council of State, the Duma and the Zemstvos were all competing for power.

Democracy The Electoral Law of 1907 effectively disfranchised the vast bulk of Russians and meant that they remained outside of political decision-making. Government policy towards strikes, etc. remained harsh, as seen in the aftermath of the Lena goldmine strike in 1912. Moreover, the Duma was sometimes more reactionary than the government, as in the continued pursuit of Russification.

The lack of social cohesion before 1914 meant that if the government were in difficulties it could not count on the alienated masses for support. By 1917 even the majority of the Duma, the 'Progressive Front', was calling for radical change.

Economic and social policy

Stolypin's reforms, 1906–11 Stolypin, chairman of the Council of Ministers from 1906, decided that the peasants must be freed from the commune if the 'sober and strong' were to provide the capitalist agriculture and internal market, the absence of which he saw as the main impediment to development. He was probably right.

However, his famous reforms between 1906–11, encouraging peasants to leave the communes, were very disappointing in their results. It now looks as though most peasants were content to continue the communal system and were more intent on increasing their communal landholdings by purchase or by seizure. By 1917 the peasants owned roughly 90% of the land – due to the retreat of the nobility and the need to provide for an ever-increasing peasant population. In many areas the amount of large-scale capitalist production of grain actually decreased as landlords gave up.

Therefore, although the period after 1906 saw a more prosperous peasantry (helped by the state through loans, etc.), the central problems remained unresolved. Thus, during the war, peasant farmers retreated from the market and fed their grain to their livestock.

Industry Russia experienced an economic boom from 1906–17 comparable with that of the 1890s. The State again played a leading role with an increased military budget, especially after 1914. Also its inflationary monetary policy to finance the war fuelled the boom in its later stages. The expansion was characterised by ever larger foreign loans. The period saw the rise of huge cartels on the German model. The labour force, not given the same kindly treatment as the peasants, from 1910 became more radical, thus culminating in the St. Petersburg strike of 1914

7.6 RUSSIA IN 1917

The war entered in 1914 was the end towards which tsarist economic policy had prepared since the defeat of the Crimean War. At first it caused the nation to unite behind their Tsar. With the stalemate of 1914–16 came disenchantment with the regime, especially given the Rasputin scandal and the terrible financial and bureaucratic mismanagement, itself a result of the ramshackle, anarchic nature of a government apparatus which had never been fully rationalised. This caused overwhelming political pressure from all sides.

Furthermore, the unsolved problem of Russian agriculture crippled the home front in 1917. Due to the chaos caused by war requisitioning and inflation (due to the lack of adequate revenues) and official grain prices, internal transport and trade collapsed and the peasants refused to sell on the black market. The effect of this was the starving masses of St. Petersburg in February, 1917. When the troops, themselves mostly peasants and demoralised by the mismanagement of the war, joined them, the attempt by the tsarist regime to force Russians to maintain its great power status in the new industrial era had come to a close.

7.7 CHRONOLOGY

1855–81		Reign of Tsar Alexander II; the 'Tsar Liberator'.
1861	March	THE EMANCIPATION EDICT: all serfs were given personal freedom, together with allotments of land for which the original owners were paid by the State in treasury bonds. The peasants were to repay the bonds over a 49-year period. The land was given to the 'mir', village commune, for distribution.
1863–4		THE SECOND POLISH REVOLUTION: this spread into White Russia and Lithuania. Suppressed in May, 1864. Polish autonomy was abolished and Russian administration re-established.
1864		THE ZEMSTVO LAW: the establishment of a system of local self-government. Local boards, Zemstvos – on which the nobility, townsmen and peasants were represented – were empowered to levy taxes for such purposes as primary education and public health. THE REFORM OF THE JUDICIARY: the old system of class courts was abolished and modernised procedures substituted. The separation of judicial authority from the administrative.
1870		REFORM OF MUNICIPAL GOVERNMENT: the towns given self-government under a council elected by the propertied classes.
1874		ARMY REFORM: the introduction of the principle of universal military liability in place of the former system of taking recruits only from the lower classes.
1875–8		THE EASTERN CRISIS.
1876		The secret society, 'Land and Liberty', spearhead of the Populist movement founded.
1879		Organisation of the society 'Will of the People'.
1881	March	Assassination of Tsar Alexander II.
1881–94		TSAR ALEXANDER III: the autocratic system affirmed; the influence of the Metropolitan Pobedonostsev. Persecution of religious dissenters and discrimination against the national minorities. Sergei Witte. The industrialisation of Russia.

1881		CONCLUSION OF THE ALLIANCE OF THE THREE EMPERORS BETWEEN GERMANY, RUSSIA AND AUSTRIA: renewed in 1884, but in 1887 was replaced by a separate pact between Germany and Russia, the REINSURANCE TREATY.
1891–94		CONCLUSION OF THE FRANCO-RUSSIAN ALLIANCE.
1894–1917		Reign of TSAR NICHOLAS II.
1898		Formation of the SOCIAL DEMOCRATIC PARTY among the industrial workers. Marxism had been introduced into Russia by PLEKHANOV. His moderate programme was challenged by the radical wing under LENIN.
1901		Organisation of the SOCIAL REVOLUTIONARY PARTY.
1901–1903		SPLIT IN THE SOCIAL DEMOCRATIC PARTY AT THE PARTY CONGRESS in London: MENSHEVIKS and BOLSHEVIKS. Formation of the Union of Liberation, calling for a liberal constitution.
1904–5		THE RUSSO-JAPANESE WAR, a result of Russian expansion in the Far East. Outbreak of hostilities. 8 February, 1904; fall of Port Arthur, January 1905; the battle of Mukden, 23 February–10 March; naval disaster at Tsushima.
1904	July	Assassination of the Minister of the Interior, Plehve.
	November	Zemstvo Congress met at St Petersburg and demanded the convocation of a representative assembly and the granting of civil liberties.
1905	January	BLOODY SUNDAY: the emergence of workers as a factor in the protest movement. A procession of workers led by Father Gapon fired on. Outbreak of strikes.
	March	The Tsar announced his intention to convoke a consultative assembly.
	May	THE UNION OF UNIONS: this brought together the liberal groups in a demand for universal suffrage and parliamentary government.
	June–August	Strikes, agrarian outbreaks, national movements in the border provinces, mutinies in the army and navy. The POTEMKIN incident.
	August	THE TSAR ISSUED A MANIFESTO CREATING THE IMPERIAL DUMA: this assembly to be elected on a restricted franchise with only deliberative powers. The failure of this concession to satisfy popular demands.
	20–30 October	THE GENERAL STRIKE: a spontaneous movement across the country.
	26	The St Petersburg workers formed the first SOVIET to direct the strike.
	30	THE OCTOBER MANIFESTO: granted Russia a constitution. The Duma to have legislative power; Witte was appointed Prime Minister. The liberal group divided into the CONSTITUTIONAL DEMOCRATIC PARTY and the OCTOBRIST PARTY.
	December	Members of the St Petersburg Soviet arrested. Insurrection of workers in Moscow. Punitive repression; the 'Black Hundreds'.
1906	May	Dismissal of Witte. THE FUNDAMENTAL LAWS issued. The Tsar retained complete control over the executive and armed forces. The legislative power to be divided between the Duma and Imperial Council. The government reserved the right to legislate by decree when the Duma was not in session. THE MEETING OF THE FIRST DUMA: The Constitutional Democrats (the Kadets) formed the largest party. Criticism of the government.
	July	THE DUMA DISSOLVED: Kadet leaders issued the VIBORG MANIFESTO calling upon the country to refuse to pay taxes.
	November	The agrarian reform of STOLYPIN.
1907	March–June	THE SECOND DUMA: reactionary groups pressed for a return to the autocratic system forcing the dissolution of the Duma. New electoral law, greatly increasing the representation of the propertied classes.
1907–1912		THE THIRD DUMA: returned a conservative majority; the suppression of revolutionary disorders. Reforms local administration, justice and health insurance for workers.
1907	August	CONCLUSION OF THE ANGLO-RUSSIAN ENTENTE.

1908–9		THE CRISIS WITH AUSTRIA OVER BOSNIA AND HERZEGOVINA.
1911	September	The assassination of Stolypin.
1912–16		THE FOURTH DUMA suspended by the Tsar for much of the war. A clear warning of impending revolution given to the Tsar in November 1916.
1912–13		THE BALKAN WARS.
1914	1 August	GERMAN DECLARATION OF WAR ON RUSSIA.

Illustrative questions and answers

1 'A disappointing liberal, an inefficient autocrat'. Examine this assessment of Alexander II.

Tutorial note

The question is about Alexander II and the myth of the 'Tsar Liberator'. It asks you to examine the traditional view expressed in the title. In doing so one must say if it describes Alexander adequately. In addition, one should examine the assumptions behind the question, especially concerning Liberalism in the Russian context, to assess whether or not the judgement in it is fair.

You need to know about

The economic and social structure of Russia in the mid-nineteenth century. Political events from c. 1850–1881. Alexander's personality and policies, especially details of the Great Reforms.

Suggested answer plan

1 The traditional view of Alexander II. as the 'Tsar Liberator', 'Russia's White Hope': his reign seen as starting purposefully, losing impetus, then going forward again, only to be cut short by assassination before progress and Liberalism had really begun. The period presented as a chance missed for Russia to enter the modern world; hence the 'Tsar Liberator' becomes 'an inefficient autocrat' and also a 'disappointing liberal'.
2 Examine Alexander's attitude to his own authority: autocratic power must be used to reform the state when necessary – he adopts liberal policies to preserve the Russian autocracy. The state and nobility must be seen to lead, hence the reforms. He justified the emancipation of the serfs by claiming, among other things, that it benefits the nobility. Liberalism was a means to an end, the shoring-up of the power and the prestige of the autocracy (which is identified in Alexander's view with the interests of Russia itself). When unrest continues, Alexander retreats and the liberals are disappointed. But Alexander is not really a Liberal.
3 The connection of 'autocracy' and 'Liberalism' in Russia; the progressive bureaucracy was western educated; the belief in benevolent absolutism; hence the emancipation and other reforms. But Liberalism in the fullest sense is not just about administrative measures, but also about the *form* of the administration – i.e. the parliamentary representative form of government. This was rejected by Alexander, who refused, for instance, to contemplate a national assembly. In fact in the circumstances a Russian national assembly would not have been 'liberal' in outlook but a collection of reactionary nobles!

4   A brief comment on the social background: Russia was *not* a capitalist country; the peasants' organisation was communal and remained so after the emancipation of the serfs; there was debate about this, but the peasants were not treated as individual farmers; the retention of the commune as an institution meant that modernising capitalist enterprise was held back.

5   The reaction during the latter part of his reign must be seen in the context of: *(a)* the failure of many of the liberal reforms to increase state power or prestige (for example the adverse reaction to the 1861 emancipation proposals, the acquitting of terrorists by the new juries); *(b)* the increasing conservatism of the bureaucracy in the 1870s; and *(c)* increasing revolutionary activity; note that Russian populism was anti-liberal.

6   At the very end Alexander did try to prevent unrest by structural liberal changes, i.e. the Loris-Melikov proposals, but these were not very liberal and not 'constitutional' in the western sense. Moreover, Loris-Melikov found himself alone against the nobles in the bureaucracy.

7   Conclusion: Alexander II was *not* a Liberal but an autocrat; he gave the appearance of inefficiency, but he achieved a considerable amount. To some extent he gave Tsarism a new lease of life. In the last resort his reign was disappointing because the liberal policies he adopted only increased opposition and did not achieve the modernisation of Russian society. It is questionable, in the circumstances, whether this was possible; one must balance Alexander's 'failure' against the inappropriateness of Liberalism in the Russian setting.

2   How successful was Tsar Alexander II in solving the problems facing Russia during his reign?

Tutorial note

You should discuss the problems of Alexander II's reign; then assess how far they were solved during his reign, and what effect his policies had after 1881.

You need to know about

Russia's economic and social structure in the nineteenth century. Alexander's personality and policies. A general knowledge of historical developments in Russia before and after Alexander's reign.

Suggested answer plan

1   The reign of Alexander II, the 'Tsar Liberator', is commonly seen as a progressive period in which Russia *almost* broke out of its medieval backwardness and developed into a modernising liberal society. He is presented as half-successful; he introduced major reforms in the 1860s, but these were flawed by the reaction of the 1870s. This traditional view needs some qualification There were the problems as the tsarist regime perceived them *and* the deep-rooted obstacles to any easy transition from a feudal to an industrial society.

2   The major problems facing the regime were bankruptcy of the nobles who governed the serfs; serfdom was no longer profitable and Russian agriculture was unable to compete with the 'new lands' (e.g. America) in the grain markets; the bankruptcy of the regime; the general backwardness of Russian society revealed in the defeat of the Crimean War, which itself led to more debts. Alexander II saw a threat to the authority of the Tsar if he did not renovate the Russian state through 'reform from above'.

3   Alexander's solution: the Emancipation; liberalisation of the law, education and the economy; the building of railways which, apart from providing improved communications, helped to increase trade and hence revenue; the Zemstvo reforms; the reform of the Army by Milyutin, which led to victory in the Russo-Turkish War.

3   In fact, though, these reforms were flawed: at a deeper level there were problems which went unanswered; the autocratic basis of government remained; the nobility dominated the bureaucracy and resisted radical proposals for reform; in important respects the economic structure of society was little changed – for social and administrative reasons the commune remained and so peasants tended to continue to be subsistence farmers.

4   In the short term Alexander's reforms appeared quite successful in meeting the *perceived* problems, but disappointment during the reign and the crisis of terrorism at the end can be explained by underlying problems which were ignored. Note the poor reaction to the reforms: revolts by the peasantry were more numerous after the Emancipation than before. Liberalism did not really work unless certain crucial Russian institutions were swept aside. This was the lesson of the period and such radical reform was beyond both the power and the intention of the regime.

5   It could be argued that Alexander II managed to preserve the regime a while longer through reform, but did not really solve the underlying problems. In the longer term the new course he had set would conflict disastrously with Russian traditions and lead to the eventual demise of the tsarist order in 1917.

3   How far may the period 1881–1914 be regarded as 'wasted years' in the solution of Russia's internal problems?

Tutorial note

You need to assess the effectiveness of the tsarist regime's policies in trying to bring about the modernisation of Russian society and its economy. Further, you should be able to discuss alternative policies and their likelihood of success in the Russian setting and to judge whether there was any alternative which would have been less wasteful.

You need to know about

Tsarist policies 1881–1914. The economic and social structure of Russia during the same period. A general idea of notions of progress and economic development in Europe c. 1900.

Suggested answer plan

1   Russia embarked during the second half of the nineteenth century on a conscious policy of economic development led by the state, which has been described as 'state capitalism'. But this was under an oppressive regime, whose inadequacies were to lead to defeat and revolution in 1917. Much has been written about what could have happened if the regime had been more liberal and progressive. However, these years can only be called 'wasted' if there was a *viable* alternative – given the situation in 1881.

2   Comment briefly on the policies pursued after 1881, particularly Witte's strategy for industrialisation, noting that the political order remained autocratic and bureaucratic.

3   The result was that, when Russia went to war and was beaten by Japan in 1904–5, there was a severe political crisis, rebellions among the minority nationalities, peasant riots, upheavals in the capital; this was a direct result of the tsarist policies: an inefficient bureaucracy and Army, starving peasants, an exploited working class, indignant Poles and a revolutionary intelligentsia.

4   However, it can be argued that the alternatives proposed during this period are either impracticable or harmful:
    (a) It was too late to revert to a non-developed society.
    (b) Russian Populism had been discredited by the apathy of the peasantry.
    (c) A Marxist revolutionary solution looked highly implausible in a society which was 80% peasant; in any case both Marx and Lenin thought in terms of an accompanying Western European revolution.

(d) The only acceptable alternative to tsarist repression seemed to be Liberal-ism, the guarantee of individual and institutional liberties, the guarantee of property and representative government.

5 Note the failure to follow up Alexander II's reforms in the succeeding period to 1905; e.g. agriculture was still left under communal control; there was the failure to provide a constitution to regulate government; the Zemstvos were not given adequate authority; there was only 21% literacy in Russia in 1900.

6 Improvements were enacted, though, by the government under Stolypin *after* the 1905 revolution:

(a) the 1906 Land Reform Act;

(b) educational opportunities were greatly increased; and

(c) there was the Duma, a new representative assembly. *However,* Russia remained an autocracy and the new liberal policies can be seen in a number of respects to be very superficial. The Duma was largely ignored by the Tsar after the October Manifesto. The franchise was reduced to produce a more manageable assembly. The fact is that Liberalism had *no real power base* in Russian society: by 1914 only a small percentage of the land had been transferred from communal to individual tenure.

7 Russia had major problems in its economy and society which it could not easily solve. The government policy after 1881 probably made things worse by over-straining the economy. But given their aim of restoring Russia to the status of a Great Power, there was arguably no truly viable alternative in the Russian context. In that sense it was unrealistic to class the years 1881–1914 as 'wasted'. It would be more appropriate to observe the tragedy of a county of such potential being unable to shed the shackles of a bygone age before 1881.

Question bank

1 Document question (Russia – 1905 and after): study extracts I and II below and then answer questions (a) to (g) which follow:

Extract I (concerning the events of 1905)

'After 9 January (Bloody Sunday) the revolution showed that it controlled the consciousness of the working masses. On 14 June, by the rising on board the Potemkin Tavrichesky, the revolution showed that it could become a material force. By the October strike it showed that it could disorganise the enemy, paralyse his will, and reduce him to complete humiliation. Finally by organising workers' Soviets throughout the country, the revolution showed that it was able to create organs of power.

'...After 17 October, when the conditions for the constitutional deal were already written down, and it seemed that all that was left was to put them into effect, the revolution's further work obviously undermined the very possibility of such a deal between the liberals and the authorities. From then on the proletarian masses, united by the October strike and organised within themselves, put the liberals against the revolution by the very fact of their existence.'

(Trotsky, *1905*)

Extract II (concerning developments of 1906–1908)

'Driven into a historical cul-de-sac by the irreconcilable attitudes of the nobility and the bureaucracy, who once more emerged as the unlimited masters of the situation, the bourgeois parties are once more looking for a way out of the economic and political contradictions of their position – in imperialism... .

'The so-called "annexation" of Bosnia and Herzegovina was greeted in St. Petersburg and Moscow with the deafening clatter of all the old ironware of patriotism. And the Kadet party, which, of all the bourgeois parties, claimed to be the most opposed to the old order, now stands at the head of <u>militant 'neo-Slavism'</u>... .

'...The same government that buried the reputation of its strength in the waters of <u>Tsushima</u> and the battlefields of <u>Mukden</u>; the same government that suffered the terrible sequel of its adventurist policies, now unexpectedly finds itself patriotically trusted by the nation's representatives...it receives the Duma's support for its new adventures in the Far East. More than that: by Right and Left, by <u>the Black Hundreds</u> and the Kadets, it is actually reproached because its foreign policy is not active enough.'

(Trotsky, *1905*)

(a) State briefly what happened on 'Bloody Sunday'.　　　　　(3)
(b) What did Trotsky mean by 'the revolution showed that it could become a material force'?　　　　　(2)
(c) Identify each of the following: 'Soviets'; 'the Kadet Party'; 'the Black Hundreds'.　　　　　(3)
(d) Explain what is meant by
　　　(i)　'the deafening clatter of all the old ironware of patriotism', and
　　　(ii)　'militant neo-Slavism'.　　　　　(4)
(e) Explain Trotsky's references to 'Tsushima' and 'Mukden'.　　　　　(4)
(f) Discuss the nature of the 'constitutional deal' and explain what, according to Extract I, were the main difficulties facing 'the proletarian masses' after October, 1905.　　　　　(6)
(g) How adequate is Trotsky's view in Extract II of the results in Russia (during the years 1906–8) of the 1905 revolution?　　　　　(9)

2　How extensive and how effective in promoting change was the opposition to the Tsarist system in Russia from 1881–1914?　　(AEB, June 1989)

3　'Twenty momentous years for Russia.' Comment on this view of the period 1894–1914.　　(JMB, June 1988)

4　Did the 1905 Revolution demonstrate the strength of the Tsarist regime, or point the way to its destruction?　　(Oxford, June 1991)

5　Evaluate the importance of the First World War as a factor in bringing about the downfall of the Tsarist regime in Russia.　　(Cambridge, June 1991)

READING LIST

Standard textbook reading

L. W. Cowie and R. Wolfson, *Years of Nationalism, European History 1815–1890* (Edward Arnold, 1985) chapters IV(1) and V(4).

Robert Gildea, *Barricades and Borders, Europe 1800–1914* (OUP, 1987) chapters 8, 15.

J. A. S. Grenville, *Europe Reshaped 1848–78* (Fontana, 1976), chapter 13.

Norman Stone, *Europe Transformed 1879–1919* (Fontana, 1983), III 3.

David Thomson, *Europe since Napoleon* (Penguin, 1977), chapters 15–17.

Anthony Wood, *Europe 1815–1945* (Longman, 1975), chapters 18, 22.

Further suggested reading

J. P. T. Bury (ed), *The New Cambridge Modern History 1830–70*, volume X (CUP, 1964), chapter 14.

R. Charques, *The Twilight of Imperial Russia* (OUP, 1965).

M. T. Florinsky, *Russia, a History and an Interpretation*, volume II (Macmillan, 1969); and *The End of the Russian Empire* (Collier Books, 1961).

P. Gatrell, *The Tsarist Economy 1850–1917* (Batsford, 1986)

L. Kochan, *The Making of Modern Russia* (Penguin, 1970).

W. E. Mosse, *Alexander II and the Modernisation of Russia* (English Universities Press, 1958).

H. Rogger, *Russia in the Age of Modernisation and Revolution 1881–1917* (Longman, 1983).

Hugh Seton-Watson, *The Russian Empire 1801–1917* (OUP, 1967).

A. Ulam, *Russia's Failed Revolutions* (Weidenfeld and Nicolson, 1981).

J. N. Westwood, *Endurance and Endeavour, Russian History 1812–1986* (OUP, 1987)

CHAPTER 8

THE ORIGINS OF THE FIRST WORLD WAR

Units in this chapter

Chapter objectives

❶ The distinction between the long-term and underlying causes of general conflict in 1914 and the immediate occasion of war.

❷ The alliance system: as background, Bismarck's network of alliances and its objectives, noting particularly the Dual Alliance and the Reinsurance Treaty; the origins and development of the Triple Alliance and the Triple Entente; an assessment of the individual foreign policy aims of Britain, France, Russia, Italy and Austria-Hungary and of the rivalries of these Powers.

❸ German foreign policy from 1890: 'Weltpolitik' (World Policy), the demand for a 'place in the sun' and for colonies, for preponderance in Central and Eastern Europe ('Mitteleuropa'), and for influence in the Near East; the influence of the Kaiser, Bülow, Holstein, Kiderlen-Wächter and Bethmann-Hollweg on the conduct of German policy; the underlying domestic factors of the rapid growth of population and industrial might.

❹ The major prewar crises, 1914: the First Moroccan Crisis; the Bosnian Crisis; the Second Moroccan Crisis; the Balkan Wars.

❺ An understanding of the underlying conflict of interest over the Balkans: the development of nation states and their rivalries; the growth of Pan-slavism and Pan-germanism; the attitude of the Habsburg Empire to the threat of Slav nationalism, particularly Serbian ambitions; the confrontation of Russia on the one hand of Austria-Hungary and Germany on the other over this area.

❻ The naval rivalry between Britain and Germany: Tirpitz and the Navy Laws; Fisher and the Dreadnought programme; the impact of this on public opinion in the two countries.

❼Military preparations: the application of science and technology to warfare after 1870; planning and time-tabling, involving the growth of permanent general staff; the plans for mobilisation and their influence on governments; an examination in particular of the way in which military thinking in Europe was dominated by the implications of the Schlieffen Plan and how the urgent need of both France and Germany for rapid mobilisation and for an early offensive by their eastern allies accelerated the tempo of the crisis in 1914.

❽The prewar mood of public opinion towards the prospect, or possibility, of war; the way in which domestic social and economic pressures (particularly in Germany) intensified international tensions.

❾The Sarajevo assassination and the July crisis: a detailed grasp of the events leading to war and the way in which a local conflict became a general war; particular attention to be paid to the German 'blank cheque' to Austria, the Austrian ultimatum to Serbia, Russian mobilisation; the role of Britain and France and the question of Belgian neutrality.

❿The 'war guilt debate' – the historical controversy over the respective responsibilities of the Powers for the outbreak of war in 1914.

The alliance system created by the German Chancellor Bismarck after the Congress of Berlin in 1878 was intended to forestall the possibility of a war on two fronts against the new German Empire. After his fall from power there was a gradual realignment of the Powers which brought Britain, France and Russia together and, in 1914, to war with the Central Powers.

After 1871 Germany was unquestionably the dominant continental Power; under Kaiser William II she increasingly demanded recognition as a world Power. German expansion and influence, particularly the construction of a large Navy under the guidance of Admiral Tirpitz, led to the growing rivalry of the Powers which characterised the years before the First World War and was illustrated, for instance, in the two Moroccan crises.

The immediate cause of the war, however, lay in the conflict between Slav nationalist aspirations, especially of Serbia, and the Austro-Hungarian Empire. As could be seen in the Bosnian crisis of 1908, the Balkan area was increasingly drawing the Habsburgs and Germany into rivalry and confrontation with Russia.

The assassination of Archduke Francis Ferdinand at Sarajevo on 28 June led to the conflict. The French decision to support Russia and the 'blank cheque' pledge of Germany to Austria-Hungary transformed a local Balkan conflict into a European war.

The question of the responsibility for the outbreak of war continues to be a major debate among historians – a debate in which the role of public opinion, domestic political problems and considerations of military planning have all, in recent years, been given particularly detailed attention.

8.1 THE 'NIGHTMARE COALITION'

Bismarck's system of alliances was intended to preserve peace in Europe and, more particularly, to prevent a war against Germany on two fronts. Such a 'nightmare coalition' of Russia and France would, as he saw it, prove fatal to the new German Empire.

It was just such a war which faced Germany in August 1914. A clear appreciation of its origins must take account of how Europe became divided into the Triple Alliance (Germany, Austria-Hungary and Italy) and the Triple Entente (Great Britain, France and Russia). In the event, from 1915, Italy was to side with the Entente.

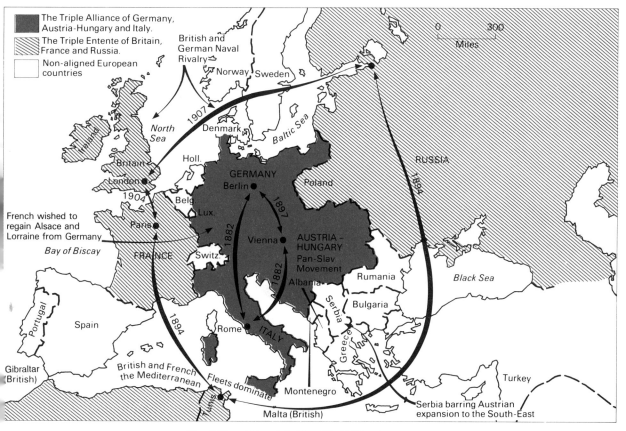

Fig. 4 The origins of the First World War. It is important to understand the reasons for and implications of the emergence of two rival armed camps prior to 1914

The collapse of Bismarck's system

Bismarck's essential objectives had been (a) to isolate France, and (b) to prevent any military conflict, between Austria and Russia over the unsettled countries of the Balkans, such as would force Germany to choose between the Powers.

His complicated system achieved the diplomatic isolation of France, an understanding with Russia (as in the **Dreikaiserbund** and the **Reinsurance Treaty**) and the maintenance of European peace. At the same time, this period of the 'armed peace' was one of unprecedented growth in military and naval power and increasing imperial rivalry.

The network of alliances started to disintegrate after Bismarck's fall from power in March 1890. In that year Kaiser William II allowed the Reinsurance Treaty to lapse. The cornerstone of Bismarck's construction was gone. In 1891 an entente, or understanding, was signed between France and Russia. This was followed by a military convention in which the two partners promised to give each other assistance in the event of an attack by Germany.

The diplomatic revolution

In 1904 the Entente Cordiale was established between France and Great Britain, to be followed by the Anglo-Russian understanding of 1907. These were settlements of outstanding colonial rivalries and brought to an end a period in which Anglo–French rivalry (as in the Fashoda crisis of 1898) and Anglo–Russian friction were dominant factors in international affairs. They were now replaced by a growing fear of the dramatic increase of German power and its imperial demands.

The principal step in the Entente Cordiale was the exchange of French recognition of British dominance in Egypt in return for a French sphere of influence in Morocco. From 1906 onwards this was followed by military discussions between the British and French authorities.

The Anglo-Russian Convention reached agreement over Afghanistan, Tibet and the division of influence of the Powers in Persia.

The emergence of Europe into two rival and increasingly hostile camps reduced much of the flexibility of the old balance of power and made it that much harder for statesmen to preserve the peace. In itself this did not make war with Germany inevitable. But it made it more likely. This was particularly well illustrated in the Moroccan crises of 1905 and 1911, which strengthened the resolve of the other Powers to resist German expansion and demands. The first of these coincided significantly with the weakening of Russia following the Russo-Japanese War.

8.2 GERMAN WORLD POLICY

The unification of a majority of Germans under the leadership of Prussia had helped to make Germany into the greatest concentration of power on the continent. Rapid industrialisation, concentrated military power, a young and dramatically increasing population (43% increase between 1880 and 1910) had raised it into a position of potential domination over Europe. With an expanding economy and overseas colonisation, she now started to demand recognition as a world power.

The term **Weltpolitik**, or world policy, was first used by Kaiser William in 1896 as a description for the German version of an imperialism which was shared by the other Powers. It was summed up in his statement that 'nothing must henceforth be settled in the world without the intervention of Germany and the German Emperor'.

This concept of expansion found expression in the construction of the Baghdad railway, the launching of a large navy and the quest for colonies. (Already, in the 1880s, Britain and Germany had come into conflict over African and Pacific territories.) Through their naval and colonial ambitions they were seen to menace British imperial interests. By assuming the role of protector of Turkey, Germany was felt to be thwarting the traditional aims of Russia in Asia Minor and in the Balkans.

The naval race

The major instrument for an increasing world role was the construction of a strong navy and this led to growing rivalry with Britain. This was at a time when German economic power was developing, relatively, at the expense of Britain and there was mounting apprehension over Germany's commercial potential.

Admiral von Tirpitz used political persuasion, propaganda and the support in particular of industrialists to gain approval for a German fleet large enough to deter any hostile British action.

At the same time, the British were determined to maintain their wide margin of superiority on which traditionally their supremacy had rested. From 1898 to 1912 successive Navy Laws underwrote this competition, which was seen primarily in terms of the heavy-gun battleship.

This mutual suspicion was underlined when the Haldane Mission of 1912 attempted to reach an understanding with Germany: the German government was willing to offer minor modifications of its naval building programme, but it demanded in return wide colonial concessions and an assurance of British neutrality in the event of war.

Such a promise of neutrality would have meant the destruction of the Anglo-French Entente of 1904 and was quite unacceptable to Great Britain.

8.3 THE BALKANS

Though the changed diplomatic scene operated to bring the Great Powers to war in August 1914, the crisis from which the war immediately originated did not lie in that system itself, in the military and naval competition or in the clash of colonial and economic interests. The immediate cause sprang from the tension in the Balkans and the conflict between Slav nationalist aspirations and the Austro-Hungarian Empire.

It was the combination of intense nationalist unrest and instability in the Balkans with the conflicting interests of the Powers, particularly Russia and Austria-Hungary, which made the situation there so explosive.

- Austria believed that the recognition of South Slav demands would bring about the collapse of the Empire.
- Austria and Russia were the main rivals, though Germany was showing an increasing interest in the Balkans and the Near East (see, for instance, her involvement in Turkey).
- Austria-Hungary had a definite interest in preventing the spread of Russian influence through the area, both in those parts immediately affecting her interests, like Serbia, and at Constantinople and the Straits.
- Russian nationalists, on the other hand, emphasised their Pan-slav affinities with the Balkan peoples and stated their determination that the Slavs should not be humiliated by the Austro-Hungarian Empire.
- At the same time, Russia wished to preserve access to the Mediterranean and, for her own strategic reasons, was anxious to resist any expansion of Austro-Hungarian influence which might make this difficult.

Bosnia and Herzegovina

A major step towards conflict came when Austria annexed Bosnia and Herzegovina in 1908, territory which it had previously only administered.

The Austrian Foreign Minister, Aerenthal, believed that the Empire was close to collapse and that only a policy of annexation could restore Habsburg fortunes. He particularly wanted to humiliate Serbia, which was encouraging Slav nationalism. He had promised to allow Russia a sphere of influence in the Straits in return for this annexation. But this expansion of Russian influence was blocked by the other Powers.

The issue represented a major diplomatic reverse for Russia, which she was determined not to allow to be repeated. In May 1909 Germany issued a note to Russia calling upon her to abandon support for the Serbs and to recognise the annexation.

The Balkan Wars

Following Italy's attack on the Turkish Empire for the acquisition of Tripoli, the First Balkan War broke out. Serbia, Greece, Montenegro and Bulgaria formed a Balkan League to attack Turkey (1912). All wanted parts of Macedonia, but Serbia had wider ambitions. She wanted to provoke a war between Austria-Hungary and Russia which would allow her to incorporate Austria's South Slav provinces.

The Second Balkan War followed in 1913, when Bulgaria attacked Serbia and Greece for refusing to hand over the bulk of Macedonia. Rumania and Turkey seized the opportunity to declare war on Bulgaria.

In the Treaty of Bucharest of August, 1913, Serbia and Greece acquired most of Macedonia. Rumania also gained territory while Turkey recovered part of Thrace. Bulgaria was left with small areas of Thrace and Macedonia.

Sarajevo

The main loser from the Balkan wars was the Habsburg Empire. Serbia was strengthened and had Great Power support: when the Serbs re-entered Albania, both France and Russia backed them.

With this challenge of militant Slav nationalism to the status quo, the Powers moved to defend their own interests. As the Austrian Chief-of-Staff, Conrad, saw it, the loss of the South Slav provinces would reduce the Empire to the status of a small Power. He hoped to save it by a preventive war against Serbia.

The assassination of the Archduke Francis Ferdinand by Gavrilo Princip, a Bosnian living in Serbia, on 28 June 1914, led to the culmination of a long-term and mounting conflict of interest between Slav nationalism and the Empire.

8.4 THE EUROPEAN CRISIS

The Austrian decision to settle scores with Serbia once and for all was the act that set the European crisis in motion. In contrast with 1908 and 1913, Russia this time stood firmly behind Serbia.

The French decision to back Russia and the unconditional pledge of Germany to Austria, the 'blank cheque', brought the network of alliances and obligations into play. They transformed a local conflict into a European war.

The Austrian decision to proceed against Serbia was made transparently clear in the ultimatum of 23 July, which the British Foreign Secretary, Sir Edward Grey, described as 'the most formidable document I have ever seen addressed by one State to another that was independent'.

Germany felt herself to be increasingly isolated and 'encircled' by the Entente and particularly fearful of the growing strength of Russia. There was a mood among the German High Command of 'now or never'. Germany was unclear whether Britain would go to war.

Her strength, military preparedness and challenge to the interests of the other powers were linked by the summer of 1914 with the determination of her only reliable ally, Austria-Hungary, to arrest her own rapid deterioration as a Power.

The war guilt clause (Article 231) of the Treaty of Versailles attributed responsibility for its outbreak to Germany and her allies. From the start this provoked violent controversy and resentment. It was immediately used to discredit the Versailles settlement and its reparations demands.

- Many historians continue to see the conflict as overwhelmingly the result of German ambitions and actions.
- Others would support the view put forward by the British Prime Minister, Lloyd George, that the Powers stumbled into war.
- Still others lay special emphasis on wider factors such as imperial rivalry, pressure of population, the development of military technology or a 'general will to war'.
- Most do not lay sole blame on any one of the Powers. France, Great Britain, Russia, Austria-Hungary and Serbia have all been apportioned responsibility. (For example, Britain's failure to make it absolutely clear to Germany that she would support France.)

All governments made miscalculations and suffered from misconceptions. During the later stages there was also the crucial consideration of military momentum as a result of advance planning, e.g. the German Schlieffen Plan and a desire not to lose the race of mobilisation which statesmen found impossible to resist.

Over the last thirty years the debate on the origins of the war has centred on the arguments of the German historian Fritz Fischer who claimed that the German government deliberately tried in 1914 to achieve expansionist territorial and power-political aims which had been developed in the preceding years.

His critics deny that Germany seized on the Sarajavo assassination to force a major war, and that her initial wish was only to encourage Austria to achieve a localised victory against the Serbs. They argue that it was only when it was obvious that Russia could not be kept out of an Austro–Serbian quarrel that the German military pressed for a major war.

In this debate considerable attention has been paid to the role of the German Chancellor Bethmann Hollweg's motivation. Was he less concerned with avoiding war than with achieving the optimum international conditions for waging it? Or did he have no alternative but to back the Habsburg Monarchy once Russia had declared her hand? Either way it is true, as John Lowe points out, that 'it is difficult to find a single constructive move that Germany made throughout the July Crisis'.

8.5 CHRONOLOGY

1890	March	Dismissal of Bismarck.
	June	REINSURANCE TREATY not renewed.
1891	August	FRANCO-RUSSIAN ENTENTE agreement to consult in the event of threat of aggression to one of the Powers.
1892	August	Franco-Russian Military Convention.
1893	January	FRANCO-RUSSIAN ALLIANCE SIGNED.
1895	January	The Kaiser sent a telegram to Kruger, President of the Transvaal congratulating him on the defeat of the Jameson raid. Indignation of British public opinion.
1897	June	ADMIRAL TIRPITZ nominated State Secretary for the Navy.
1898	April	The Reichstag ratified THE FIRST NAVY LAW: German decision to build a battle fleet powerful enough to deter the strongest naval power from attacking. THE GERMAN NAVY LEAGUE founded.
	September–November	THE FASHODA CRISIS on the Nile between Kitchener and Major Marchand. The most acute confrontation between Britain and France in the prewar period, threatening all-out conflict.
1899	May–July	FIRST HAGUE PEACE CONFERENCE called at the instigation of Tsar Nicholas. A permanent court of arbitration provided.
	October	Start of the Boer War.
1900	June	Reichstag ratified SECOND NAVY LAW: fleet of 38 battleships to be built in 20 years.
	June–August	The Boxer Rising in China.
1901	October–December	Collapse of Anglo-German alliance negotiations.
1902	January	ANGLO-JAPANESE ALLIANCE formed the end of 'splendid isolation'.
1904	February	RUSSO-JAPANESE WAR BEGAN.
	April	ENTENTE CORDIALE BETWEEN FRANCE AND BRITAIN: settlement of colonial differences between the powers, particularly over Egypt and Morocco.
	October	THE DOGGER BANK INCIDENT: acute Anglo-Russian crisis after sinking of a British trawler by the Russian fleet.
	November	Russo-German alliance negotiations broke down.
1905	March	KAISER VISITED TANGIER: THE FIRST MOROCCAN CRISIS, testing the strength of the Entente.
	April	Anglo-French military conversations.
	May	Japanese defeat of the Russians at Tsushima.

	July	TREATY OF BJÖRKÖ between William II and the Tsar.
	October	DREADNOUGHT constructed.
1906	January–April	ALGECIRAS CONFERENCE: France supported by all the Powers except Germany and Austria. France to have major control in Morocco.
1906	June	THE THIRD NAVY LAW – the Novelle – ratified by the Reichstag.
1907	January	Eyre Crowe's memorandum warning on German foreign policy.
	June	SECOND HAGUE PEACE CONFERENCE BEGAN: British efforts to secure arms limitation thwarted by opposition of other Powers. Germany rejected proposals for compulsory arbitration.
	August	ANGLO-RUSSIAN ENTENTE: settlement of imperial conflicts between the Powers, particularly over Persia, Afghanistan and Tibet.
1908	June	THE FOURTH NAVY LAW.
	October	AUSTRIA-HUNGARY ANNEXED BOSNIA AND HERZEGOVINA: Germany supported Austria-Hungary. Anger of Russian nationalists.
		THE DAILY TELEGRAPH published interview with the Kaiser in which he pictured the German people as hostage to Britain.
1909	February	FRANCO-GERMAN AGREEMENT OVER MOROCCO: Germany recognised France's special political interests in Morocco.
	March	British Navy Bill passed.
1911	May	French occupied Fez in spite of warnings from Germany that they were infringing the Algeciras Act.
	July	THE SECOND MOROCCAN CRISIS.
		THE GERMAN GUNBOAT 'PANTHER' SENT TO AGADIR: Germany demanded the whole of the French Congo in compensation for their Moroccan rights.
		LLOYD GEORGE WARNED GERMANY IN MANSION HOUSE SPEECH.
	September	The Tripoli War between Italy and Turkey.
	November	THE MOROCCO AGREEMENT SIGNED: Germany agreed to leave France a free hand in Morocco in return for the grant of part of the French Congo.
1912	February	The Kaiser announced major Army and Navy Bills.
		THE HALDANE MISSION TO BERLIN: Germany unwilling to make naval concessions without a promise of British neutrality in the event of war.
	March	THE BALKAN LEAGUE between Serbia and Bulgaria formed.
	October	THE FIRST BALKAN WAR BEGAN: between Bulgaria, Serbia and Greece on the one hand and Turkey on the other.
1913	March	Winston Churchill proposed 'Naval Holiday'.
	June	SECOND BALKAN WAR BEGAN: Bulgaria attacked Serbia and Greece; Rumania and Turkey joined to defeat Bulgaria.
		German Army Bill passed.
		French Army Bill ratified.
	August–October	PEACE OF BUCHAREST – end of the Second Balkan War.
	December	ARRIVAL OF LIMAN VON SANDERS IN CONSTANTINOPLE: Russian protest at German mission.
1914	28 June	ASSASSINATION OF FRANCIS FERDINAND AND HIS WIFE AT SARAJEVO.
		Mission of Count Hoyos, Chief of Cabinet in the Austro-Hungarian Foreign Ministry; the Kaiser issued 'blank cheque'.
	8 July	Ultimatum to Serbia prepared.
	15 July	Poincaré the French president and Viviani, Prime Minister and Foreign Minister, left for St. Petersburg.
	19 July	Austro-Hungarian Ministerial Council approved an ultimatum to be passed to Serbia on 23 July.
	20 July	Poincaré and Viviani arrived in St. Petersburg.
	21 July	Francis Joseph approved ultimatum.
		Text of ultimatum sent to Berlin.
	23 July	ULTIMATUM SENT TO SERBIA.
	24 July	Austria-Hungary informed France-Russia and Britain of the ultimatum.
		German ambassadors transmitted note in Paris, London and St. Petersburg recommending that the conflict be localised.

	Cambon, French Ambassador in Berlin, proposed a conference.
	Grey, British Foreign Secretary, suggested mediation.
	Russian Council of Ministers considered partial mobilisation.
25 July	SERBIA REPLIED TO ULTIMATUM.
	Vienna broke off diplomatic relations with Belgrade.
	The Kaiser ordered the return of the Fleet.
	Russian Crown Council approved resolutions of the Ministerial Council.
	Tsar ordered that preparations be made for mobilisation.
26 July	Russia asked Germany to exert a moderating influence on Austria-Hungary.
	Grey proposed that a four-Power conference of ambassadors be held in London.
	Austria mobilised on the Russian frontier.
	France took precautionary military measures.
27 July	Austria-Hungary *decided* to declare war on Serbia.
	France accepted Grey's proposals.
	Bethmann-Hollweg, the German Chancellor, rejected the idea of a four-Power conference.
28 July	AUSTRIA-HUNGARY DECLARED WAR ON SERBIA AND SHELLED BELGRADE.
	The Kaiser issued an appeal call to Austria to 'halt in Belgrade'.
	The Kaiser appealed to the Tsar's spirit of monarchical solidarity.
	Russia ordered the mobilisation of four of her western military districts.
29 July	Vienna refused to enter into negotiations with Belgrade. Tschirschky, German Ambassador in Vienna, presented the Kaiser's 'halt in Belgrade' proposal.
	Germany informed of Russian partial mobilisation.
	Germany warned Russia.
	Moltke, German Chief of Staff, demanded general mobilisation.
	Bethmann-Hollweg made move to keep Britain neutral.
	Grey informed Lichnowsky, German Ambassador in London, that Britain could not remain neutral in the event of a continental war.
	Russian general mobilisation ordered, but revoked by the Tsar.
30 July	Austria-Hungary agreed to negotiations with Russia, but refused to delay operations against Serbia.
	Moltke pressed for general mobilisation.
	Austria-Hungary ordered general mobilisation for 31 July.
	Russian general mobilisation ordered for 31 July.
31 July	Vienna rejected an international conference and ordered general mobilisation.
	Russian general mobilisation becomes known in Berlin at noon. Kaiser proclaimed 'state of imminent war' an hour later.
	Germany refused to mediate and issued an ultimatum to Russia.
	French Ministerial Council decided to order mobilisation for August 1.
1 August	GERMAN ULTIMATUM TO RUSSIA EXPIRED, SHE DECLARED WAR ON RUSSIA AND MOBILISED. STILL HOPE IN BERLIN THAT BRITAIN MIGHT REMAIN NEUTRAL.
2 August	GERMAN TROOPS OCCUPIED LUXEMBOURG.
	Berlin sent ultimatum to Belgium.
3 August	Germany declared war on France.
	Belgium rejected German demands.
	Italy remained neutral.
	German-Turkish treaty concluded.
	BRITAIN MOBILISED ARMY. CABINET DECIDED TO ISSUE ULTIMATUM TO GERMANY.
4 August	GERMAN TROOPS INVADED BELGIUM.
	British ultimatum transmitted to Berlin.
	ULTIMATUM EXPIRED AT MIDNIGHT. BRITAIN AND GERMANY AT WAR.

Illustrative questions and answers

1 Assess the significance of the Moroccan crises of 1905 and 1911.

Tutorial note

It is essential for you to clarify, above all, the *international* significance of these crises. You must be prepared to describe the effect of the Kaiser's visit to Tangier in 1905 and of the 1911 Agadir incident and their consequences on the relations in particular between Germany, France and Great Britain. The word 'significance' in the question indicates that you should be willing to set these events in the wider context of pre-First World War diplomacy. You may also wish to consider the influence of these crises on public opinion within these countries.

You need to know about

The course of international relations from c. 1890–1914. The Moroccan crises of 1905 and 1911. The immediate outcome of these crises and their longer-term significance.

Suggested answer plan

1   The diplomatic background. These crises should be considered against the background of the Entente Cordiale of 1904, which agreed to terminate Anglo-French colonial rivalries. The French acceded to the British control of Egypt and the British allowed the French to take over Morocco.

2   *The 1905 crisis.* Note that the Kaiser's announcement that he would aid the Moroccans was made at a time when the power of Russia was severely eclipsed by her defeat in the Russo-Japanese War and when she was hardly in a position to offer France effective support. He hoped to expose the weakness of British support for France – all the evidence shows that his intervention had little to do with German economic interests and a great deal to do with the Entente. At the subsequent Algeciras Conference, though, all the Powers, except Austria, rallied to France's side and the British were so antagonised that they promptly entered into defensive military arrangements with France. J. M. Roberts describes this crisis as marking 'the real end of isolation for England'.

3   *The Agadir incident of 1911.* The arrival of the 'Panther' was seen by Britain and France as a further German challenge to the Entente. Britain also viewed apprehensively the possibility of Germany constructing a naval base close to Gibraltar. The gravity of the crisis was conveyed in the Mansion House speech of the British Chancellor of the Exchequer, David Lloyd George, in which he stated that Britain was not to be treated 'as if she were of no account in the Cabinet of Nations…peace at that price would be a humiliation intolerable for a great country like ours to endure.' This carried particular weight in Berlin since Lloyd George had hitherto shown himself more well-disposed towards Germany than many of his colleagues. In November 1911, Germany recognised the French position in Morocco in return for the French Congolese territory.

4   The result of both crises was a strengthening of Anglo-French relations, and the second crisis revealed in full the peculiar state of Anglo-German relations in the period of rivalry which preceded the First World War. There was talk of war on both sides but there was nothing concrete at issue to fight about. Germany wanted a spectacular diplomatic victory. Britain, on the other hand, was convinced that if French interests were not supported the European balance of power would be destroyed and British security endangered. Both sides assumed that a North African colonial squabble would involve the European balance of power.

5   Though the Moroccan problem itself was solved, the crises left a legacy of intensified Anglo-German suspicion and hostility. The Agadir crisis wrecked any hope of improved Franco-German relations. Note the effect of these crises on public opinion within Germany – for instance, the Pan-German League and Tirpitz were able to manipulate the national sense of humiliation to press for a larger fleet. The Second Moroccan crisis also encouraged Italy to seek 'compensation' for French gains in Morocco. Italy declared war on Turkey in September 1911, landing troops in Tripoli. This further assault on Turkish rule encouraged the outbreak of the First Balkan War.

2   Do you consider that the outbreak of a general war was inevitable after the assassination of Archduke Franz Ferdinand?

This question queries the inevitability of a *general* war *after* the assassination. It is a specific question and should not be taken simply as an invitation to say whether or not you believe a general war was inevitable, or to enter into a discussion of the forces and rivalries making such a war probable. You should take care to distinguish between the localised Balkan issue and the reasons for the wider involvement of the major Powers in a European conflict, and be clear as to how the one led to the other after Sarajevo.

You need to know about

The diplomatic background to the First World War. The Balkan problem. The military preparations of the Powers. A detailed grasp of the course of events between the Sarajevo assassination and the outbreak of the First World War.

Suggested answer plan

1   In the view of A. J. P. Taylor, 'It would be wrong to exaggerate the rigidity of the system of alliances or to regard the European war as inevitable. No war is inevitable until it breaks out.' To an extent this is fair comment but it deserves qualification. While the armaments race, Great-Power rivalries and demands for 'preventive war' characterise the prewar years, one can on the other hand point to widespread anti-war sentiment, the spread of international agencies and a willingness to resolve issues through arbitration. There was no general assumption of the inevitability of a major war, nor was this the reaction of the Powers on receipt of the news of the Sarajevo assassination.

2   The traditional machinery of diplomacy, which had preserved peace in the past and prevented major conflict since the Congress of Berlin (1878), had localised war as recently as during the Balkan Wars. Even if the assassination made an Austro-Serbian war inevitable (and this was not so until the issue of the ultimatum to Serbia), this does not mean that a general war was inevitable.

3   There was, of course, increasing urgency in Vienna that the Slav problem (the threat posed to Habsburg interests by Slav nationalism) be 'solved'. There was also strong evidence that Russia would not accept another humiliation in the Balkans, such as that over Bosnia-Herzegovina in 1908 and that she would not allow the Serbs to be crushed by Austria-Hungary.

4   The extremely severe Austrian ultimatum to Serbia produced a marked Russian reaction and Russia confirmed that she would not allow Serbia to be destroyed. This meant that the Austro-Serbian conflict now threatened a more dangerous Austro-Russian one which, because of the rivalry of the Triple Entente and Triple Alliance, presented a very real *possibility* of a general war.

5   But note that a situation of this sort was by no means unprecedented. War was not inevitable. Britain put forward the suggestion of an international conference to localise the dispute. The German response to this was unfavourable and, on 28 July, Austria formally declared war on Serbia. This step was not irretrievable, for the Austrian forces were not fully prepared for action. Nevertheless, with the crucial 'blank cheque' from the Kaiser, Austria had the guarantee of support for her actions and the German willingness to go to war was the dominant factor in the July crisis. Even this, though, did not make general war inevitable at this stage. The Kaiser favoured the 'halt in Belgrade' scheme: Austria would occupy Belgrade but hold operations there, thus giving a final chance to diplomacy.

6   The question of mobilisation: this was a massive and complex operation that, once launched, was very hard to stop. Inescapably it meant that priority was given to military factors. As Professor Michael Howard comments: 'The lesson of 1870 was burnt into the mind of every staff officer in Europe: the nation which loses the mobilisation race is likely to lose the war'. He adds: 'In no country could the elaborate plans of the military be substantially modified to meet political requirements.'

7   It was only German mobilisation, however, which *inevitably* involved war, because the Schlieffen Plan demanded the rapid invasion of France via a surprise advance through Belgium. Professor L. C. F. Turner has identified the night of 29–30 July as the crucial point. The German Chancellor, Bethmann-Hollweg, had heard that Britain would almost certainly intervene in the war if Germany came into conflict with France. He was, therefore, trying to reverse the trend of German policy and now *restrain* Austria. However, when the German Chief of Staff, von Moltke, heard that Austria was only going to mobilise in the Balkans, he recognised that, unless she launched an offensive in Poland against Russia, the German Army in East Prussia would be overwhelmed by the Russians and the Schlieffen strategy gravely compromised. At this point he pressed Austria for immediate mobilisation against Russia, promising unqualified German support in a European war. In this manner, because of strategic considerations, Germany pushed forward to make the war inevitable.

8   It is clear that the outbreak of a general war was neither inevitable nor considered to be so as a result of the Sarajevo assassination. However, as the July crisis deepened it became progressively more likely. The *inevitability* of the Austro-Serbian dispute turning into a general European war is much more easily argued in the context of the inflexibility of the mobilisation plans and preparations for war, more particularly the German Schlieffen Plan. Once priority was given to military factors the momentum towards war seemed irresistible.

3   'Unfriendly and provocative.' To what extent is this an accurate summary of Germany's policies towards the European Powers between 1890 and 1914?

Tutorial note

It is obvious that other European Powers – particularly Britain, France and Russia – came to see Germany's policies as 'unfriendly and provocative'. You should attempt to separate German motives and intentions from the impression her policies created, and assess the extent to which this impression was justified. Note that the two descriptions are not necessarily inseparable – you may for instance, find her policies 'provocative' but not essentially 'unfriendly'. You should certainly *not* take this question as simply an opportunity to discuss German responsibility for the outbreak of the First World War.

You need to know about

German policies towards the European Powers and their interests 1890–1914. European diplomatic relations in this period and the attitudes of the other Powers to Germany. The influence of German domestic policy and of her internal problems on her foreign policy.

Suggested answer plan

1   The basic difference between German foreign policy under Bismarck and under William II and his ministers: Bismarck's purpose was to establish Germany as the diplomatic arbiter of Europe – but it was limited, circumscribed and essentially peaceful in character. He had little sympathy with Pan-German ambitions and, for most of his term of office, was markedly unenthusiastic about colonies. Under William II the role of dominant continental Power was no longer enough for Germany. She aspired to the 'place in the sun' of world politics. With 'Weltpolitik', Germany advanced ambitions for recognition as a world Power, with colonies and a large Navy.

2   The 'New Course' in German diplomacy reflected the growth in the power of a nation that had consolidated its position on the Continent and was seeking new outlets for its nationalist and expansionist energies; note the very considerable growth of German industrial potential. However, German

imperial ambitions reached their height in the late period of nineteenth-century imperialism when there was little territory left for distribution among the Powers. Seen from one angle, the German leaders simply applied to their own situation imperialistic ideas and ambitions that existed everywhere. Other countries had long been world Powers and were used to rounding off their territories in a suitable way.

3   German demands were accompanied, though, by particularly swashbuckling statements and propaganda, e.g. General Bernhardi's book *World Power or Destruction*; and the Pan-German League, which argued that Germany would draw to itself all German-speaking peoples in Europe and emphasised the 'world horizon'. Those Powers which were already established resented what they saw as the reckless and threatening assertion of German power: there was rivalry with Britain, particularly over naval policy; Alsace-Lorraine and Morocco soured Franco-German relations, while Germany's claim to influence in the Near East aroused strong Russian apprehensions.

4   When the actual *content* of German ambitions is examined, they turn out to be lacking in precision. There was a disproportion between the vastness of potential menace, as seen by Britain, France and Russia, and the actual German pursuit of concrete objectives – e.g. Germany was throughout this period acquiring major financial interests in the Near East (at this time her share of the Turkish debt rose from 5%–20%). But wild talk from the Kaiser, declaring himself the friend of 300 million Moslems, and the arrival of German military experts in Constantinople gave legitimate interests a flavour of reckless aggression, which was plainly provocative.

5   Over Morocco the Kaiser was anxious to prove that no serious issue in world politics could be decided without him. This was a recurring pattern. In each case there was *something* to be said for German demands. For instance, what gain had Germany to compare with the most recent French acquisitions of Tunis and Morocco? The misfortune of the German situation was that she was in a position where she could not expand without destroying the existing order – that is, expand in line with her growing power, population and economic potential. Her position, therefore, forced her to appear consistently unfriendly in her ambitions. Her presentation of her demands and policies, particularly the interventions of the Kaiser, were diplomatic catastrophes and plainly extremely provocative.

6   Relations with Britain: When Britain launched the Dreadnought in 1906 all previous battleships were rendered obsolete and the navy race became desperate. While for Germany the fleet was a luxury, the British regarded their own fleet as essential for their survival as an imperial world Power. Tirpitz's 'risk theory' amounted to diplomatic blackmail. The effect was inevitably to bring Britain closer to both France and Russia, whereas she might have been a natural ally of Germany. It was not simply with this (and such provocations as the support for Austria during the Bosnian Crisis) that Germany lost the sympathy of the Powers – it appeared to them that she was quite indifferent to their attitude.

7   Note the domestic background to German policy: 'Weltpolitik' represented in part a systematic attempt to mobilise the forces of conservatism in Germany. What Tirpitz called 'this great overseas policy' was intended to silence internal criticism and rally support for the Kaiser and the Reich.

8   There were grounds on which each of the main elements of 'Weltpolitik' might be justified – these elements being the naval expansion, the development of empire in Africa and the commercial and financial penetration of the Near East. It can be argued, though, that for Germany to pursue all three courses at the same time was the worst possible policy. It kept alive the suspicion of the Entente Powers and made them more anxious than ever to stick together.

9   The success of the Triple Entente's policy of containment and rearmament increasingly limited the scope of German policy and gave rise to increasing fears of 'encirclement'. In the end, the Reich stood alone in 1914 with Austria-Hungary as the only reliable ally. But the outbreak of war was not so much the

result of reckless German imperialism as of her desire to have complete security in the face of the other Powers. While her policies from 1890 onwards were undoubtedly ill-judged, tactless and provocative, it is harder to substantiate that they were consistently unfriendly. There were threats but there was also considerable vacillation.

Question bank

1   Document question (The Outbreak of the First World War): study extracts I and II below and then answer questions (a) to (f) which follow:

Extract I

'The shots of death must ring as a fearful warning in the ears of the Austro-Hungarian government. Franz Ferdinand fell as the victim of his country's Balkan and national policy. He was the defender of clericalism and the mightiest representative of reaction and of so-called Austrian imperialism. He kept Serbia from her goal...the open road to the Adriatic, and so her hate rose as against an enemy. Franz Ferdinand is the victim of a false system which has outlived its time; but however loud may be the death shots of Sarajevo, they will hardly be heard by those who should hear them.

'That alliance (with Austria-Hungary) is not a source of strength but of weakness; the problem of Austria is ever and ever a greater danger to European peace. If we do not wish this danger to be realised in all its hideous reality, we must strive with all our power to bring about friendly relations with France and England.'

(*Vorwärts*, a German Socialist newspaper, July, 1914)

Extract II

'The Austro-Hungarian note was so drawn up as to make war inevitable; the Austro-Hungarian government are fully resolved to have a war with Serbia, and its postponement or prevention would undoubtedly be a great disappointment.'

(*The British Ambassador in Vienna to Sir Edward Grey, 27 July, 1914*)

(a)   'The defender of clericalism and the mightiest representative of reaction'. What do you learn of Franz Ferdinand from this description of him?   (4)

(b)   How had Serbia been kept 'from her goal...the open road to the Adriatic'?   (5)

(c)   What was 'that alliance' and why might it be regarded as 'a source...of weakness'?   (5)

(d)   What truth is there in the statement that 'Franz Ferdinand fell as the victim of his country's Balkan and national policy'?   (5)

(e)   To what 'Austro-Hungarian note' does the Ambassador refer? How far do you agree that it 'was so drawn up as to make war inevitable'?   (5)

(f)   What evidence is contained in these extracts of German and British attitudes to the prospect of war? To what extent may these extracts be considered reliable sources of information about public opinion at that time?   (7)

2   Should we stress short-term or long-term factors in an explanation of the outbreak of the First World War?   (NISEAC, June 1990)

3   Why did events in the Balkans in 1914 develop into a general European war?   (Cambridge, June 1991)

4   'The First World War was caused by a deadlock in international relations which it appeared could be resolved only by recourse to war; it developed into a military deadlock which was resolved by developments in technology.' Discuss.   (London, June 1990)

5 'Military and naval preparations for war served to heighten tension between the European powers, they did not of themselves occasion the resort to war in August 1914.' Discuss this statement. (JMB, June 1989)

READING LIST

Standard textbook reading

Robert Gildea, *Barricades and Borders, Europe 1800–1914* (OUP, 1987) chapter 15.

J. M. Roberts, *Europe 1880–1945* (Longman, 1967), chapters 4, 6, 8.

Norman Stone, *Europe Transformed 1879–1919* (Fontana, 1983), III 1–6 and IV 1.

David Thomson, *Europe since Napoleon* (Penguin, 1977), chapters 19–22.

Anthony Wood, *Europe 1815–1945* (Longman, 1975), chapter 24.

Further suggested reading

Michael Balfour, *The Kaiser and his Times* (Penguin, 1975).

V. Berghahn, *Germany and the Approach of War in 1914* (Macmillan, 1973).

F. Bridge and R. Bullen, *The Great Powers and the European States System* (Longman, 1980).

G. A. Craig, *Germany 1866–1945* (OUP, 1978).

Fritz Fischer, *War of Illusions: German Policies 1911–14* (Chatto, 1975).

I. Geiss, *July 1914: The Outbreak of the First World War* (Batsford, 1967).

O.J. Hale, *The Great Illusion 1900–14* (Harper and Row, 1971).

F. H. Hinsley, *Power and Pursuit of Peace* (CUP, 1963).

E. J. Hobsbawm, *The Age of Empire 1875–1914* (Weidenfeld and Nicolson, 1887).

James Joll, *The Origins of the First World War* (Longman, 1984).

L. Lafore, *The Long Fuse* (Weidenfeld and Nicolson, 1965).

R. Langhorne, *The Collapse of the Concert of Europe* (Macmillan, 1981).

John Lowe, *Rivalry and Accord – International Relations 1870–1914* (Hodder and Stoughton, 1988).

Z. Steiner, *Britain and the Origins of the First World War* (Macmillan, 1987).

A. J. P. Taylor, *The Struggle for Mastery in Europe 1848–1918* (OUP, 1971).

L. C. F. Turner, *The Origins of the First World War* (Edward Arnold, 1976).

CHAPTER 9

THE PEACE TREATIES AND RESETTLEMENT OF EUROPE

Units in this chapter

Chapter objectives

❶ A comparison of the European frontiers of 1914 with those of 1919: particular attention to be paid to Germany and the territories of the Habsburg Empire; a clear grasp of the territorial consequences of the treaties of Versailles, St. Germain, Neuilly, Trianon and the earlier Treaty of Brest-Litovsk.

❷ The Turkish settlement: the treaties of Sèvres and Lausanne.

❸ The differing approaches of Britain, France, the United States and Italy to the settlement. The individual objectives of the major figures, Lloyd George, Clemenceau and President Woodrow Wilson; the extent to which these influenced the outcome, for example in the questions of the Rhineland and the Italian frontier.

❹ The factors which helped to influence the settlement: (a) the pacifist mood of public opinion in the aftermath of war; and the desire for retribution; (b) the commitments entered into by the Powers during the war (for instance, the Treaty of London, 1915); (c) the composition of the Peace Conference, noting particularly the absence of Germany and Russia; and (d) the impact of the Russian Revolution of 1917.

❺ The underlying principles which helped to shape the treaties. The most important of these were: (a) the determination of the Allies to ensure against the possibility of future German aggression and the demands of French security; (b) the principles of President Woodrow Wilson – the Fourteen Points, especially national self-determination and the general association of states in the League of Nations; (c) the compensation for war losses, reparations; (d) the need for the military defence of the Successor States of Central and Eastern Europe (e.g. the incorporation of the Sudetenland into Czechoslovakia); (e) the need for economic outlets (e.g. Danzig and the Polish Corridor).

❻ Those aspects of the Versailles settlement which were seen by the

Germans and others (for instance, J. M. Keynes, *The Economic Consequences of the Peace*) as severe and unjust: the scope of such criticisms and the extent to which they were justified.

⑦ The Covenant of the League of Nations: the work of the League and its agencies and the attempts made to strengthen it during these years; its weakness as a peacekeeping body.

⑧ The differing approaches of Britain and France to the question of Germany: their mutual distrust; the Ruhr invasion of 1923.

⑨ An understanding of the questions of war debts and reparations; the Balfour Note, the Dawes Plan and the Young Report; the attitudes of the various powers to these questions.

⑩ The Treaty of Locarno and its consequences.

The problems facing the representatives of the victorious Allies, who met in Paris in 1919 to decide the fate of Germany and its defeated partners, were of an unprecedented scale. Not least, four empires – the German, Habsburg, Russian and Ottoman – had collapsed.

Already, before the end of the war, President Woodrow Wilson had issued his celebrated Fourteen Points. His main emphases were on the right of self-determination and the need for a league, later the League of Nations, to preserve peace. He and the other two major figures at the peace conference, Clemenceau and Lloyd George, approached the settlement often from conflicting viewpoints. For instance, Clemenceau wanted to end Germany's status as a Great Power, while Britain required the revival of the German economy to ease her own unemployment.

In Eastern Europe a dangerous power vacuum – of unstable successor states situated between two resentful giants, Germany and the Soviet Union – was confirmed. The settlement in Eastern Europe automatically created grievances. In the Near East the Turks refused to be bound by the Treaty of Sèvres.

The German settlement was the most controversial and aroused widespread criticism for its alleged injustice and severity – the 'war guilt clause', reparations, territorial clauses, loss of her colonies and the drastic reduction in her forces.

Following the invasion of the Ruhr by France and Belgium in 1923, the reparations payments were moderated according to the Dawes Plan, and in 1925 the Locarno Treaties ushered in a period of relative international stability. But the resentments of the revisionist Powers – Germany, Italy and Russia – remained, and were to lead to war in the following decade.

9.1 GERMAN RESPONSE TO THE TREATY OF VERSAILLES

The First World War had proved that Germany was strong enough to defy a coalition of Great Britain, France, Russia and Italy. She had imposed a humiliating settlement on Russia in the Treaty of Brest-Litovsk and only the intervention of the US in 1917 had swung the balance of superior force against her.

The lesson of 1918, in spite of her defeat, was Germany's strength – not her weakness. In population and economic potential she remained the dominant continental Power. It was highly probable that the restrictions imposed upon her by the Treaty of Versailles would, sooner or later, be contested.

The 'Diktat'

There was overwhelming German resentment against the terms of the settlement, which was denounced as a 'Diktat', or dictated arrangement. It was contrary to their expectation that it would be based on President Woodrow Wilson's Fourteen Points. Criticism was above all directed against the following:

❶ Article 231 – the war guilt clause;
❷ reparations;
❸ the disarmament clauses;
❹ the prohibition of German-Austrian unification;
❺ the territorial settlement; and
❻ the disposal of the German colonies.

Self-determination

In fact the principle of self-determination – the right of peoples to their own self-government and national independence, and which was one of the cardinal points in President Wilson's programme – was applied *against* Germany. This was so, for instance, in the creation of the Polish Corridor.

At the same time, the peace treaty with Austria prohibited the unification of this small state, now shorn of the Habsburg Empire, with Germany. This unification, however, was later achieved by force when Hitler invaded Austria in the Anschluss of 1938.

9.2 THE WIDER UNPOPULARITY OF THE SETTLEMENT

The unpopularity of the settlement for its territorial and economic clauses was echoed abroad. One of the bitterest and most influential denunciations was *The Economic Consequences of the Peace* (1919) by the British Treasury official and economist, J. M. Keynes. He attacked it on both economic and moral grounds and warned of its likely political effects. He was particularly concerned with the likely impact of the reparations payments which were demanded. Though this was disputed, particularly by France, there was soon a fairly widespread view that the settlement was unjust and required modification.

Eastern and Central Europe

A major weakness of the settlement was the situation in Eastern and Central Europe. The collapse of the Habsburg Empire at the end of the war had left behind new successor states. The British Prime Minister, Lloyd George, pointed out very clearly in his Fontainebleau Memorandum the likely consequences for these states and European peace. They would be extremely vulnerable in the event of a revival of either German or Russian power.

Though the principle of self-determination was allowed to operate, this created new and serious tensions and difficulties. The basic reason for this was that the successor states contained dissatisfied ethnic minorities. For example: Germans and Poles came under Czechoslovak rule and Germans came under Polish rule.

From the start there was instability and rivalry. To give only two instances: Czechoslovakia and Poland were hostile to one another; and Hungary, which had lost substantial territories at the end of the war, was anxious to win them back from the Little Entente States, Yugoslavia, Rumania and Czechoslovakia.

The background to the treaties

It is important to set the peace treaties and their shortcomings in the context of the immense problems which faced the statesmen of 1918. No peace treaties of modern times have come under such criticism and abuse.

Fig. 5 European frontier changes after 1918

Woodrow Wilson, Lloyd George, Clemenceau and Orlando were faced with the collapse of four empires, the German, the Habsburg, the Russian and the Turkish. The Paris Peace Conference met against a European background of revolution, chaos and famine. The balance of power had been destroyed. Russia was in the throes of civil war and the US was about to withdraw from political involvement in Europe. Self-determination, whatever the problems it raised – and these were many – was a reality and its consequences had to be confronted.

Criticisms of the settlement should take account of these facts: the problems of 1918 were on an altogether larger scale than those, for instance, of 1815 and the Vienna Settlement, with which Versailles is frequently and unfavourably compared.

The Decline of Europe

At the same time, Europe was increasingly being challenged overseas. The First World War had speeded up this process. From being the major overseas investors of capital, Britain, France and Germany had become major debtors to the US. The whole tangle of reparations and war debts is a very important aspect of the history of this period.

The US were now, in a very large way, moving into European, colonial and other overseas markets. Simultaneously, the war accelerated the rise of nationalist movements against European colonial rule.

In spite of the terms of the settlement, however, Germany had been less weakened by the war than her European enemies. Unlike devastated France, Belgium, Poland and Serbia, she emerged from Versailles not only physically undamaged but strategically much advantaged. The adoption of self-determination created a situation in Central and Eastern Europe which was to be an open invitation to German expansionism.

Britain and France, under economic pressure yet determined to preserve their empires, were to find themselves forced increasingly to make compromises in the face of revived German power.

The Rhineland and the Ruhr invasion

French military leaders at the end of the war had insisted on control of the left bank of the Rhine as a guarantee of security against a future German attack. In the event, France abandoned this in return for the offer of an Anglo-American Treaty of Guarantee against aggression. This fell through when the US failed to ratify the Versailles Treaty.

France was the leading military power in Europe after 1918, but she had a very much smaller population than Germany and she was without powerful allies, as (a) Britain had refused to renew her wartime alliance, and (b) France's eastern allies, Poland, Czechoslovakia, Rumania and Yugoslavia were weak and divided.

The limitations of French power were very clearly demonstrated when she and Belgium occupied the industrial Ruhr area of Germany to enforce the payments of reparations. Britain and America were extremely hostile to this move. The invasion was almost entirely counterproductive and in Germany was met by passive resistance. France was subsequently forced to accept considerable revision of the reparations agreement in the Dawes Plan. These were later to be modified further in Germany's favour in the Young Plan.

Anglo-French relations

The Ruhr episode was only one of a number in which Britain and France revealed a mutual suspicion and division of view which was (a) to prevent a proper understanding between the Powers; (b) to assist Germany in challenging the Versailles system. The British authorities were wary of French ambitions and anxious to avoid needless entanglement in European affairs.

Secondly, there was a fundamental difference of view over Germany. The major priority of British government in this period was the revival of trade. And postwar unemployment seemed to confirm the argument of Keynes that the recovery of the European economy depended on Germany's revival as a trading partner.

Britain was anxious to see the Versailles Treaty revised in Germany's favour if this would help to preserve peace and encourage prosperity. France, for whom the arguments of national defence were paramount, argued that her security depended on upholding the Treaty as it stood.

9.3   THE LEAGUE OF NATIONS

The desire of public opinion to avoid a future war was a very strong one during the interwar years in the democracies. Many people held traditional power politics, alliances and secret diplomacy to have been largely responsible for the outbreak of war in 1914.

The League of Nations was an attempt to respond to this mood and to provide an international peace-keeping machinery. As an organisation it always attracted more trust from public opinion at large than from governments.

From the start it had serious shortcomings: Germany was excluded from it (until 1926); Russia was absent and the US failed to ratify the Treaty of Versailles, of which it was a part.

Germany saw it as a club of the victorious powers, helping to enforce an unpopular and unjust settlement on her. This association of the League with the controversial treaty was a hindrance to its international acceptance as an impartial peacemaker.

Other major weaknesses were (a) the fact that the League had no peace-keeping force at its disposal and (b) the rule that policy decisions of the League Council and Assembly needed the unanimous consent of all states represented. Mussolini's attack on Corfù was an early indication of the League's – later much more apparent – ineffectiveness as a preserver of peace.

One should at the same time bear in mind its successes in dealing with such disputes as Danzig, the Aaland Islands and the welfare work – for instance, among refugees – performed by its agencies.

Locarno

France accepted the international guarantees offered in the Locarno agreements of October 1925. By these, Germany, France and Belgium agreed to recognise their existing frontiers as permanent, including the demilitarised zone of the Rhineland.

Britain and Italy guaranteed this arrangement and the Treaty provided for the settlement of all disputes through the League of Nations. Locarno offered a temporary illusion of lasting peace and stability, but it had major shortcomings. It is significant that no such guarantees were offered to Eastern Europe – as France very much wanted.

Germany was admitted to the League, but Locarno did not answer the problem of the revival of German power. To what extent was this compatible with the preservation of peace?

If anything, détente in the later 1920s increased German impatience with Versailles. Behind the scenes Stresemann was pressing not simply for evacuation of the Rhineland and the return of colonies but also for revision of the frontiers with Poland and Czechoslovakia, the incorporation of Austria and even the recovery of Alsace-Lorraine. It ended the possibility of military discussions between Britain and France.

Though it inaugurated a period of relative stability, the Locarno settlement meant very different things to the powers concerned:

❶ to the French it offered some guarantee of security;

❷ to the German Foreign Minister, Gustav Stresemann, it was envisaged as a first step towards revision of the treaties; and

❸ to the British it meant a minimum guarantee to France without involving Britain in wider obligations, such as in Eastern Europe.

At this time, in collusion with the Soviet Union, Germany was already evading the disarmament clauses of the Versailles Settlement. One should remember that the disarmament clauses had, in any case, enabled the German Government to recruit a small professional army of the highest calibre. The last detachments of Allied troops evacuated the Rhineland in 1930. Locarno was swept aside when Hitler invaded the Rhineland in 1936.

9.4 CHRONOLOGY

1918	January	PRESIDENT WOODROW WILSON'S FOURTEEN POINTS: outlining the peace programme, on the basis of which Germany and Austria sought armistices.
	March	THE TREATY OF BREST-LITOVSK between Russia and the Central Powers. The Russians surrendered the Baltic provinces; the Ukraine, Finland, the Caucasus, White Russia and Poland. THE GERMAN ARMISTICE (11 November 1918) invalidated the treaty.
1919	January	THE PARIS PEACE CONFERENCE began: dominated by the 'Big Four', Clemenceau, Woodrow Wilson, Lloyd George and Orlando. A congress of 'allied and associated powers' to determine the peace settlement.
	February	LEAGUE OF NATIONS COVENANT APPROVED: the League was an organisation set up to preserve peace and settle disputes by arbitration. President Wilson had called for such a body in his Fourteen Points.
	March	THE COMINTERN FOUNDED at Moscow and the Third International established by the Bolsheviks to promote revolutionary Marxism abroad. THE COUNCIL OF FOUR BEGAN.
	June	THE VERSAILLES TREATY SIGNED: the settlement with Germany; Germany signed under protest and the US refused to ratify the treaty.
	September	THE TREATY OF ST GERMAIN-EN-LAYE: between the Allies and the Austrian Republic. The independence of Czechoslovakia, Poland, Hungary and Yugoslavia was recognised. Amongst other clauses, Austria was forbidden to unite with Germany and was deprived of about one-third of her German-speaking population.
	November	THE TREATY OF NEUILLY WITH BULGARIA: Western Thrace was ceded to Greece and other areas to Yugoslavia.
1920	January	The Treaty of Versailles came into force.
	March	Final US Senate rejection of the Versailles Treaty.
	April	The San Remo Conference: the main lines of the Turkish agreement drawn up. Polish offensive against Russia.
	June	THE TREATY OF TRIANON WITH HUNGARY: old Hungary lost three-quarters of its territory and two-thirds of its inhabitants.
	July	THE SPA PROTOCOL: Germans arranged reparations payments.
	August	THE TREATY OF SÈVRES: the Sultan's government renounced all claims to non-Turkish territory; the Straits were internationalised. The Poles defeated the Russians at Warsaw.
1921	March	The Russo-Polish Treaty of Riga. Plebiscite in Upper Silesia.
	May	The London Schedule of Reparations Payments.
	November	THE WASHINGTON CONFERENCE BEGAN: discussion of naval limitation and the question of the Pacific and Far East.
1922	February	The Permanent Court of International Arbitration established at the Hague.
	April	THE RAPALLO TREATY: the German and Soviet governments re-established diplomatic relations and pledged cooperation. Both Powers renounced reparations. THE GENOA CONFERENCE: called to consider the Russian problem and general economic questions. It broke down on the insistence by France that Russia recognise its prewar debts.
	August	THE BALFOUR NOTE on war debts: offered to abandon all further claims to reparations, provided a general settlement of debts could be arrived at. The US rejected this on the grounds that reparations and inter-allied debts were not connected problems.
1923	January	OCCUPATION OF THE RUHR BY FRANCE AND BELGIUM: followed the German failure to fulfil reparations obligations. Led to passive resistance of German workers and to British and American condemnation.
	July	THE TREATY OF LAUSANNE: final peace treaty with Turkey following the refusal of Turkish nationalists to be bound by the Treaty of Sèvres and following their victories against the Greeks in Asia Minor. Turkey gave up claims to any territory formerly in the Ottoman Empire occupied by non-Turks.
	August	THE CORFÙ INCIDENT: Greek appeal to the League of Nations against the attack on Corfù by Italy. Greece was made to accept most of the Italian demands.

	September	German passive resistance in the Ruhr ended.
1924	February	Britain recognised the Soviet government.
	April	THE DAWES PLAN: proposed revision of the reparations agreement with Germany; provided for loan to be granted to stabilise the German currency; the plan would help her to meet her treaty obligations in the period 1924–9.
	July	Britain rejected the Draft Treaty for Mutual Assistance. The London reparations conference ADOPTED THE DAWES PLAN.
	October	THE GENEVA PROTOCOL FOR PACIFIC SETTLEMENTS OF INTERNATIONAL DISPUTES: provided for the compulsory arbitration of all disputes and defined the aggressor as the nation unwilling to submit its case to arbitration. The decisive factor in the rejection of this attempt to strengthen the League was the opposition of the British Dominions. (Rejected finally in March 1925).
1925	October	THE LOCARNO CONFERENCE AND TREATIES: this most significant treaty confirmed the inviolability of the Franco-German and Belgo-German frontiers and the demilitarised zone of the Rhineland. (This was violated in 1936 with Hitler's reoccupation of the Rhineland.)
1926	September	Germany entered the League of Nations.
	May	The World Economic Conference at Geneva. Britain broke off relations with the Soviet Union.
	June	The Geneva Naval Conference: Great Britain, the US and Japan.
1928	August	THE KELLOGG-BRIAND PACT: convention formally renouncing war as an instrument of national policy and providing for the peaceful settlement of disputes.
1929	June	THE YOUNG REPORT: proposed a reduction of German reparations by 75% and that payments should be made in the form of annuities. Proposals abandoned, though accepted by Germany, because of the world economic crisis. Hitler declared his opposition to paying any further reparations.
	September	The Briand proposal for a European federal union.
	October	THE WALL ST. CRASH: heralded the economic slump.

Illustrative questions and answers

1   'This is not peace. It is an armistice for 20 years.' Why do you think Marshal Foch so described the Versailles Settlement?

Tutorial note
Foch criticised the Treaty of Versailles in this way because he believed it did not adequately safeguard France against German attack. But you should not regard this question as being specifically about Foch: rather it invites you to consider the Versailles Settlement as an 'armistice' or truce, and to discuss whether its deficiencies were in any way responsible for the renewal of war in 1939.

You need to know about
The main provisions of the Treaty of Versailles and the part played by these provisions in the diplomacy of the 1920s and, especially, of the 1930s.

Suggested answer plan
1   The Treaty of Versailles (signed between Germany and the Western Powers in 1919) resembled an 'armistice' in two respects: (a) its short duration (much of it was overthrown even before 1939 – contrast this with the settlements of 1815, 1871 or with that after 1945) and (b) when war resumed in 1939–41, Britain, France, the US and the Soviet Union were again pitted against Germany, and, even though Italy and Japan changed sides, the two World Wars can be seen as successive phases of a single conflict.

2   Is it possible to go a step further than this and argue that the Treaty of Versailles in some way *caused* the Second World War? The Treaty has been criticised on two, contradictory, grounds: (a) it was not severe enough to prevent Germany from recovering as a military Power – in particular, it did not attempt to undo Bismarck's unification of the country; and (b) it was not conciliatory enough to resolve the differences between Germany and the Western governments. Instead, arguments about the Treaty terms poisoned relations between Britain, France and Germany throughout the 1920s and 1930s, and eventually caused a renewal of war.

3   It would be fairer to the peacemakers of 1919 to acknowledge that the Treaty was a compromise between the school of thought based on coercion and that based on conciliation. It was also a compromise between rival French, British and American views. Can it, nonetheless, be argued that the Treaty of Versailles fell between two stools and managed *neither* to coerce Germany *nor* to grant it conditions that it could accept voluntarily?

4   The first of these charges will not stand up. The Treaty in its territorial, financial and, especially, military clauses *was* strong enough to make Germany powerless to wage war. But, under pressure first from Weimar Germany and then from Hitler, the Allies had by 1936 allowed the most important of these clauses to lapse. In particular:

(a)   reparations payments were reduced under the Dawes and Young Plans (1924 and 1929) and ended in 1931–2, allowing Germany to expand its heavy industrial capacity in the 1920s with the aid of American loans;

(b)   the Allies evacuated the Rhineland by 1930 and permitted Hitler to remilitarise it (in violation of the Treaty) in 1936;

(c)   in the 1920s Germany began secretly to rearm, and accelerated this after 1933. In 1935 Hitler announced the reintroduction of conscription and of a German air force, again in violation of the Treaty.

5   Germany, therefore, regained the power to wage war as a result of the *failure to enforce* the Treaty. But what about the second argument? It appears that Germany nearly went to war with Britain and France in 1938 over its treaty frontier with Czechoslovakia, and actually went to war in 1939 over its treaty frontier with Poland. This, however, confuses the *occasion* of war with its deeper causes. The issue in 1939 was not in itself the Versailles Settlement as it affected Danzig and Poland, but the determination of Britain and France to prevent a further growth of German power in Europe. Conflict between Hitler and the West would have been likely even if the Treaty of Versailles had placed all the German-inhabited areas of Eastern Europe within Germany's frontiers.

6   The links between the Treaty of Versailles and the outbreak of war in 1939 were, therefore, only very indirect.

2   Why did the Locarno Pact of 1925 fail to live up to the high hopes of its signatories?

Tutorial note

You must be able to assess why Locarno was regarded as such a hopeful settlement for the preservation of peace, what the expectations of the individual signatories were and why these were disappointed by subsequent events.

You need to know about

The Versailles Settlement, more particularly as it affected Western Europe. Franco-German and Anglo-German relations after 1918, especially the significance of the Ruhr crisis of 1923. The terms of the Locarno Pact and the motivation of the Powers in signing it, noting especially the policy of the German Foreign Minister, Gustav Stresemann. The weaknesses of the Pact and its subsequent collapse.

Suggested answer plan

1   Begin with the postwar tensions arising from the Versailles Settlement: the failure to meet reparations payments led to the Franco-Belgian occupation of the Ruhr and to the revival of the French plan for the separation of the Rhineland from Germany; the French desire for security; the need to achieve reconciliation in the interests of general peace.

2   An assessment of the initiatives to reduce land armaments (the Washington Naval Treaty allowed for limited naval armaments); the French insistence that this disarmament could only follow a security system; the British refusal to accept wide ranging commitments for universal peace-keeping (e.g. the Geneva Protocol); the Locarno Pact was welcomed by Austen Chamberlain as a much more limited (regional as against universal) agreement.

3   The terms of the Locarno Pact: an international guarantee of Western frontiers, with Britain and Italy underwriting this arrangement; provision for the settlement of disputes through the League of Nations.

4   The differing objectives of the Powers: to the French, Locarno was some guarantee of security against Germany; to the German Foreign Minister it was a step towards the revision of Versailles; to the British, a guarantee to France not involving them in wider obligations, particularly to Eastern Europe.

5   The weaknesses of the Pact: it failed to extend guarantees, as France wanted, to Eastern Europe (an 'Eastern Locarno'); it ended the justification for bilateral military discussions between Britain and France, but did not resolve the problem of French security in the face of the revival of German power.

6   The Locarno Pact did not appear under threat in the period of prosperity between 1925 and 1929; but this changed with the economic collapse, the death of Stresemann and the rapid growth of political extremism, particularly of the Nazi Party. Hitler: his desire to reverse the Versailles Settlement in both the East and the West; his reoccupation of the Rhineland in 1936 (which was his first territorial step to the revision of Versailles) marked the destruction of Locarno.

3   Do you consider that the peace treaties which ended the First World War embodied any general principles?

Tutorial note

You should take care here not to confuse general principles with what were simply prior commitments – for instance, the Treaty of London (1915). You must identify the underlying principles, such as that of self-determination, and explain the extent to which the peace treaties reflected them. Note that the question is not confined to the Treaty of Versailles, and that the scope of your answer should cover the other peace settlements as well.

You need to know about

The terms of the Treaties. Woodrow Wilson's Fourteen Points. The differing priorities of the peace makers. The extent to which public opinion influenced the peace treaties.

Suggested answer plan

1   Introduction: initially President Woodrow Wilson's Fourteen Points seemed to offer a set of general principles which might form the basis of a reasonable and acceptable overall settlement. In the peace discussions and hard bargaining that followed the war, these were often found to conflict with other principles and to contradict the commitments or interests of the other Powers; the particular difficulty of applying general principles to the situation in Central and Eastern Europe.

2   The principle of self-determination: the new postwar states, such as Yugoslavia and Poland, were based upon this principle; but the frontiers which this would require were in turn modified by other considerations and overriding concerns, such as defence and economic viability; the Sudetenland, and the Polish Corridor; the contradiction of the principle of self-determination in the ban on Austro-German unification.

3   The preservation of peace: President Woodrow Wilson's concept of a general association of states built into the peace treaties; the concept of collective security embodied in the League of Nations was weakened by the exclusion of Germany and the Soviet Union and by the refusal of the American Senate to ratify the agreement; in spite of the League and the sentiments of public opinion in favour of collective security, the discussions and bargaining at Versailles reflected very clearly the preoccupation of statesmen with their individual national interests.

4   French objectives at Versailles: Clemenceau's primary concern was to protect France against future German aggression. He proposed an independent Rhineland, but this idea ran contrary to the principle of national self-determination; instead France obtained the demilitarisation of the Rhineland, and its occupation for 15 years and also acquired the Saar coal mines. Note the criticism of French demands; final terms were a diplomatic defeat for France.

5   National ambitions versus the general principle in the Treaty of Sèvres: Greece was compensated for her participation in the war by being given the right to set up a colony at Smyrna on the Turkish mainland (a conflict here with the principle of nationality); Arab lands were transferred from Turkey to Britain and France; Italy was given islands in the Aegean.

6   The general principles advanced at the time of the peace treaties were very considerably modified by power-political and other practical considerations (such as in the refusal to allow Austria to unite with Germany). From the start, Britain and France had showed scepticism over the Fourteen Points; at the same time, the complexity of the situation in Central and Eastern Europe after the collapse of four empires was such as to defy the possibility of the successful application of the principle of national self-determination; though guarantees were given to national minorities, these aroused hostility and led to instability.

Question bank

1   Document question (The Treaty of Versailles): study extracts I and II below and then answer questions (a) to (f) which follow:

Extract I

'(We are) a government and people seeking no selfish and predatory aims of any kind, pursuing with one mind and one unchanging purpose: <u>to obtain justice for</u> others. We desire neither to destroy Germany nor diminish her boundaries: we seek <u>neither to exalt ourselves nor to enlarge our Empire.</u>'

(D. Lloyd George, 5 January 1918)

Extract II

'It is comparatively easy to patch up a peace which will last for thirty years. What is difficult is to draw up a peace which will not provoke a fresh struggle when those who have had a <u>practical experience of what war means</u> have passed away.... <u>You</u> <u>may strip</u> Germany of her colonies, reduce her armaments to a mere police force and her navy to that of a fifth-rate power; all the same <u>if she feels she has been</u> <u>unjustly treated</u>... she will find <u>means of exacting retribution from her conquerors.</u>'

(D. Lloyd George memorandum, 1919)

(a) To what is Lloyd George referring when he claims to be seeking 'to obtain justice for others'? (4)

(b) How far is Lloyd George's assertion that 'we seek neither to exalt ourselves nor enlarge our Empire' borne out by the terms of the Versailles Treaty? (3)

(c) Explain, with reference to the Versailles Treaty, what Lloyd George is referring to by 'You may strip Germany of her colonies, reduce her armaments to a mere police force and her navy to that of a fifth-rate power.' (5)

(d) Why, at the peace conference, was the point of view expressed by Lloyd George in Extract II not generally adopted? (5)

(e) Discuss whether Germany had cause to 'feel she has been unjustly treated'. (6)

(f) Do you consider Lloyd George right in thinking that 'practical experience of what war means' influenced statesmen to try to preserve the peace settlement during the next 20 years? (8)

2 'The peace settlement at the end of the First World War left far too many dissatisfied powers in Europe to have much prospect of survival.' How far would you agree? (NISEAC, June 1991)

3 'Its provisions for territorial adjustment, demilitarisation and economic compensation to the victorious Allies were harsh, vindictive and unrealistic.' Discuss this judgement on the Versailles Settlement of 1919. (JMB, June 1989)

4 'Neither a peace of iron nor a peace of reconciliation'. Was this the fatal flaw in the Treaty of Versailles, 1919? (Cambridge, Summer 1986)

5 Was Woodrow Wilson's attempt to apply the principle of self-determination in 1919 a hopeless ambition? (Oxford and Cambridge, June 1991)

READING LIST

Standard textbook reading
J. M. Roberts, *Europe 1880–1945* (Longman, 1967), chapters 9–11.
David Thomson, *Europe since Napoleon* (Penguin, 1977), chapters 24–25.
Anthony Wood, *Europe 1815–1945* (Longman, 1975), chapters 27–29.

Further suggested reading
C. J. Bartlett, *The Global Conflict, 1880–1970* (Longman, 1984).
J. Joll, *Europe since 1970* (Weidenfeld and Nicolson, 1973).
S. Marks, *The Illusion of Peace: International Relations in Europe 1918–1933* (Macmillan, 1976).
C. L. Mowat (ed), *The New Cambridge Modern History 1898–1945*, volume XII (CUP, 1968), chapter 8.
A. J. Nicholls, *Weimar and the Rise of Hitler* (Macmillan, 1979).
H. Nicolson, *Peacemaking 1919* (Methuen, 1964).
A. Sharp, *The Versailles Settlement* (Macmillan, 1991).
R. Sontag, *A Broken World 1919–39* (Harper and Row, 1971).
E. Wiskemann, *Europe of the Dictators* (Fontana, 1973).

RUSSIA, 1917–41

Units in this chapter

Chapter objectives

❶ The failure of Russia during the First World War: the economic and political breakdown in Petrograd; the February Revolution; the reasons for the fall of the Tsar.

❷ The Provisional Government: its positive achievements – for instance the eight-hour working day, the freeing of political prisoners, Polish independence; the resistance to the Provisional Government and the reasons for this – for example, the continuation of the war and failure to transfer land to the peasants; the July rising, the influence of Lenin and of Bolshevik propaganda, the Petrograd Soviet, the Kornilov coup.

❸ The November Revolution: explanation of the weakness of the Provisional Government; the role of the Petrograd Soviet; the contribution of Trotsky; the Land and Peace decrees.

❹ Lenin's contribution: his earlier career as a revolutionary and the development of his ideas; the transfer of political and economic power from the traditional classes to the Bolsheviks; note the position of the Bolsheviks as a minority party and Lenin's decision to disband the Constituent Assembly; a comparison of Bolshevik objectives with the programmes of the other political parties.

❺ The Civil War: the terms of the Treaty of Brest-Litovsk and the reasons for its acceptance; the causes of the Allied intervention and its consequences; the aims of the White armies and their leaders; the Red Army and its organisation by Trotsky; the explanation of its success; the murder of the Tsar and his family.

❻ War Communism and the New Economic Policy (NEP): how, as a party of urban workers, the Bolsheviks attempted to win over the peasantry; the NEP as a recognition of the failure of Bolshevik agrarian policy; the reorganisation of industry and agriculture; opposition; the significance of the Kronstadt Mutiny; the suppression of resistance, the Cheka.

❼ The battle for the succession to Lenin; the contrasting ideas of the contestants; the methods used by Stalin to gain power, his role in the Communist Party as General Secretary, his membership of the triumvirate of the Politburo; the extent to which, in organisational powers and ideas, Stalin was the direct successor to Lenin.

⑧ The first Five-Year Plan and its successors (a) as a means of establishing a heavy industrial base for the Soviet Union; (b) as 'the second agrarian revolution', a further attempt to do what War Communism had failed to do – to eradicate the Kulaks and establish state or collective farms as the norm of the Russian agrarian economy; and (c) the problems of industrial and agrarian discipline; Stakhanovism.

⑨ An understanding of the policy of 'Socialism in One Country' and the conflict between Stalin and Trotsky's revolutionary programmes.

⑩ The ways in which divergence and debate in the earlier Soviet system gave way to rigid uniformity where deviation would be punishable by dismissal or death; the liquidation of the Kulaks; the growth of the Stalinist system of dictatorship; the labour camps; the show trials of the 1930s; the judicial murder of the Old Bolsheviks and the army leaders; the degree of control achieved by Stalin over Russian political, economic and cultural life by the end of the 1930s.

⑪ The preoccupations of Soviet foreign policy in this period; the 'siege mentality' and the attitude towards the Western democracies; relations with Germany: Rapallo; the reaction to the rise of Nazism and Hitler's policies; the reasons for the Molotov-Ribbentrop Pact.

The revolutions in Russia in 1917 resulted from grave economic and social problems and military failure in the First World War. After the March revolution and the downfall of the Tsar, Nicholas II, the Provisional Government attempted to rule Russia but was obliged to share power with the Soviets (workers' councils). In November, 1917 Lenin and the Bolsheviks seized power, issuing decrees on the paramount issues of land and peace. After elections which only gave the Bolsheviks a minority of the seats, Lenin ordered the closure of the Constituent Assembly and proceeded to consolidate power on the basis of a single-party totalitarian dictatorship.

From the period of the Civil War, in which the Whites were defeated by the Red Army organised by Trotsky, the new Communist order became more and more identified with Russian nationalism. Following the period of 'War Communism', the New Economic Policy and the collapse of revolutionary hopes in Western and Central Europe, Stalin emerged as the dominant figure. He announced the slogan of 'Socialism in One Country'. He pressed ahead with the collectivisation of agriculture and the massive industrialisation of the five-year plans. While there was rapid economic development, these programmes were only accomplished with the grossest inhumanity.

Meanwhile, Stalin consolidated his personal power by defeating both the Left and Right Opposition. The murder of Kirov provided him with an excuse for mounting a bloody purge, accompanied by show trials, of the Communist Party, which carried away the Old Bolsheviks and a high proportion of the military command. In foreign policy, tentative moves towards a common front against Germany from the mid-30s were terminated by the Molotov-Ribbentrop Pact. In 1941 Hitler launched his invasion of Russia.

10.1 THE MARCH REVOLUTION

The revolutionary situation in Russia in 1917 resulted from the bankruptcy of the tsarist regime and the grave impact of three years of war. Russia was the first Great Power to suffer real military disaster in the struggle with Germany and its failures led to Nicholas II's downfall. It is questionable in any event, however, how long tsarism as it existed in 1914 could have survived. Military defeat hastened what was most likely to be an inevitable collapse. The war-weariness of the Russian people and the widespread distrust of the pro-German faction in the Imperial Court combined with economic deprivation to produce a series of riots and strikes in Petrograd, leading to a mutiny of the troops garrisoning the capital.

When the revolution broke out in March, 1917, the Bolshevik leaders, who were for the most part at this time in exile, were taken more by surprise than the government itself. An emergency committee of the Duma and the newly created 'Soviet (Council) of Workers' and Soldiers' Deputies' in Petrograd set up the provisional government under Prince Lvov. This was followed by the abdication of the Tsar and his brother.

The March revolution was not an unwelcome event to the Western Allies to start with. They tended to interpret it as a vote of no confidence in the tsarist management of the war effort. Further, the Provisional Government appeared to share most of the political ideas of the Western Powers – was it not possible to envisage Russia evolving towards a constitutional and democratic order on the Western model? The major significance of 1917 and what followed is that Russia did not follow this path. The Soviet Union developed in a radically different direction.

The Provisional Government and the Soviets

For eight months the Provisional Government attempted to rule Russia. What power it had it was obliged to share with the Soviets and at the end of this period it was overthrown by the Bolsheviks.

In April, 1917, the Germans, knowing that the Bolshevik leaders would undermine the war effort, offered Lenin a safe passage from his revolutionary's exile in Switzerland to Russia in a sealed train: On his return Lenin at once set about exploiting the difficulties of the Provisional Government to his advantage.

In the famous 'April Theses' he announced a political programme which called for peace, the nationalisation of the land and the granting of power to the soviets. He underlined what were increasingly seen by the Russian people as the major failures of the Provisional Government – the failure to solve the land question and their continuation of the war with Germany.

The Soviets were the great institutional innovation of the Russian revolution. While the unrepresentative Duma did not appeal to the masses as the basis of a new government, a Soviet was elected in Petrograd in March, and in June a National Congress of Soviets was convened. 'Order Number 1' required the election of a committee in each military and naval unit, which was to have charge of arms and which was in effect to decide which orders were to be obeyed. Lenin justifiably spoke of a 'dual power', a sharing of government between government and Soviets. Indeed, shortly after the March revolution the Petrograd Soviet began to act as a shadow government, challenging the acts of the Provisional Government. Within the Soviets at this time the Bolsheviks were only a minority. Both the Social Revolutionaries and the Mensheviks were more numerous. The urban population in Russia at this time was in any case only about a sixth of the total. Russia was still overwhelmingly a peasant economy.

Lenin and the Provisional Government

Lenin judged that if the Bolsheviks offered a programme with sufficient revolutionary appeal they could gain control over the Soviets. While the Provisional Government, which did not have a clear or incisive line of policy, muddled along, discovering increasingly that it could not sustain both war and revolution at the same time, Lenin proceeded to outflank the other parties. He stole popularity from the Social Revolutionaries with his programme of land for the peasants and showed himself more radical than the Mensheviks (who argued that Russia was not ready for a socialist revolution) by calling for an immediate proletarian upheaval. He declared quite unhesitatingly for peace and with this demand he attacked the Provisional Government at its weakest point.

With the last failed military offensive by Russia on the Galician front in July, 1917, the Provisional Government, now under the leadership of the Socialist Revolutionary

Alexander Kerensky, began very quickly to lose credibility. In the same month the Bolsheviks made their first, abortive, coup. Meanwhile Kerensky's government showed that it could reach no agreed solution on the central question of land reform. A move by the Right wing – the Kornilov coup – forced him to turn to the Bolsheviks for support. By October the Russian armies were breaking up and the soldiers drifting home; the peasants were taking matters into their own hands across the country and seizing the land. At the same time, the Bolsheviks, strengthened by the defeat of the Kornilov coup, had by now managed to achieve a majority in the Petrograd Soviet. Confusion and administrative chaos had gone too far for the situation to be saved for the Provisional Government.

10.2 THE BOLSHEVIK REVOLUTION

The Bolsheviks seized power on the night of 6 November, 1917. The coup was timed to coincide with the All-Russian Congress of Soviets. This received full power from the Petrograd Soviet, which it in turn delegated to the local Soviets. The main agents of the revolution were the Petrograd Soviet, units of the Army and Navy and the Party organisation itself.

The programme formulated by Lenin was fourfold:
➊ land to the peasants;
➋ distribution of food to the starving;
➌ power to the Soviets; and
➍ peace with Germany.

The first of these was already spontaneously happening with the peasant seizure of land and the last was brought about by the Treaty of Brest-Litovsk, which involved massive losses of Russian territory and of productive capacity. The second and third were achieved together in that food was distributed only to those willing to grant power to the Soviets.

Soviets sprang up all over Russia, especially in the factories and Army units under the auspices of the Party. The two decrees on land and peace consolidated the revolution at this early stage, winning the initial support of the peasantry for what had started as an urban insurrection. The Congress appointed a Council of People's Commissars to govern the state.

In this new situation power was wielded by the highly disciplined and organised Party which Lenin had been forging since 1903. In theory Lenin had done what he had promised: he had won all power for the Soviets. In practice the Bolshevik leaders had seized power for themselves, and the concentration of power at the centre – which Soviet Communism involved – was later to be fully revealed in the period of Stalin's rule.

The Consolidation of Power

Though they had won a majority in the Petrograd Soviet, in the local provincial Soviets the Bolsheviks were still outnumbered. The elections for the Constituent Assembly produced in fact a clear majority for the Social Revolutionaries (the Bolsheviks obtained fewer than a quarter of the seats). The Bolshevik military command acted immediately, closing down the assembly. The third All Russian Congress of Soviets, which the Bolsheviks were now able to dominate, assumed the functions of the Constituent Assembly.

There was now, quite clearly for all to see, a sharp distinction between what the Bolsheviks were doing and the model of Western parliamentarism and democracy. The Bolsheviks showed themselves willing to seize and consolidate power in defiance of democratic legality, as expressed in the election to the Constituent Assembly.

The authority of the Bolsheviks was further consolidated by the creation of **Cheka**

('The Extraordinary All Russian Commission of Struggle against Counter-Revolution, Speculation and Sabotage'), and a month later in January, 1918, the Red Army was founded by Trotsky. Lenin proceeded to lay the basis of a single-party, totalitarian dictatorship principally through the four instruments of the Party (designated 'the Communist Party' in March, 1918), the Soviets, the secret police and the Red Army.

10.3 THE RUSSIAN CIVIL WAR

The subsequent developments of the Russian revolution (in spite of opposition to this drift of affairs by Trotsky and others) moved increasingly towards identifying Communism with Russian national interests. The period of foreign intervention – the civil war – served particularly to strengthen the power of the Communist government as a national government. It forged the Red Army into a more efficient fighting force for national defence and its triumph over the mixed forces of the counter-revolutionaries, which included British, French, US and Japanese contingents, left the Party and its instruments without serious armed opposition. On the home front the Cheka launched a reign of terror against all elements of 'bourgeois reaction' and eliminated all rivals to the Bolsheviks among the other revolutionary movements.

During the period of 'War Communism', urban workers were subjected to a militarisation policy and were enrolled in labour battalions; the peasantry had to submit to forced requisitioning of their produce. Only by such drastic means were the Bolsheviks able to keep the economy functioning at all and to provide the cities and the Red Army with basic rations. By 1920 industrial production had fallen to only 16% of its 1912 level. In this crisis, workers' control gave way to strict factory discipline imposed by state-dominated trade unions.

The victory of the Red Army over the Whites in the Civil War was due primarily to the following:

❶ the creation of the Red Army, formed as a volunteer force out of virtually nothing by Trotsky;

❷ a marked lack of coordination among the anti-Bolshevik forces;

❸ the Reds' possession of the strategic advantage of internal lines of communication;

❹ the crucial asset of appearing to be on the Russian people's side – the White armies were associated with reaction and the restoration of the old order;

❺ the conviction amongst the peasantry that a White victory would mean the abrogation of the revolutionary land settlement;

❻ the White generals' association with the intervention by foreign Powers which made the Bolsheviks more and more appear to be the patriotic defenders of the Motherland.

One should remember in this also the very important nationalities question: the Red victory had an additional significance of being a triumph of the Great Russian over the minor nationalities.

The 'New Economic Policy'

Lenin's revolutionary expectation that the Bolshevik seizure of power would lead to successful upheavals throughout Western Europe was not fulfilled. Furthermore, following the naval mutiny at Kronstadt in March, 1921, Lenin found himself obliged by the seriousness of the economic situation to beat a tactical retreat. He introduced the 'New Economic Policy', which made extensive concessions to private enterprise.

The major aim was to give inducements to get the economy moving again. Conciliation with the peasantry was essential: in Lenin's words, 'only agreement with the peasantry can save the socialist revolution in Russia'. By the 'Fundamental Law' of May 1922, the peasants were given security in land tenure; they were further permitted to sell or lease their land and to hire labour to work it. In industry small private enterprise was allowed an equal freedom.

The critics of this policy, which included Trotsky, pointed to the return of 'bourgeois' habits, the emergence of a class of 'new rich'. But it is important to note that the 'commanding heights' of the economy – heavy industry, foreign trade and the transport system – remained in state hands.

10.4 STALIN AND 'SOCIALISM IN ONE COUNTRY'

After the final failure of Communism in Germany after the First World War, in 1923, the Russian regime reconciled itself to the fact that revolution would not spread throughout Europe in the easily foreseeable future. In the autumn of 1924, Stalin launched the slogan of 'Socialism in One Country'. Russia, he argued, could create Socialism on its own, without relying on foreign help. His policy in fact was to be a mixture of Trotsky's demand for intensive industrialisation and his opponents' strategy of subordinating international revolution (which had not taken place) to the national needs of Russia.

This linking of Communism with the historic sentiments of Russian nationalism was to be consolidated by the achievements of the five-year plans, by the cult of Stalin as the great national hero and by the experience of sustained patriotic resistance to the German invasion after 1941.

The collectivisation of agriculture

From the mid-1920s the Soviet Union faced a chronic and growing crisis in feeding its urban population. Stalin embarked on a massive and brutal programme to collectivise agriculture against the stubborn resistance of the peasants, more particularly the richer peasants, the Kulaks, whom the New Economic Policy had notably advantaged. Class warfare was encouraged in the countryside. The poorer peasants who had something to gain from collectivisation were incited against the richer ones, who had everything to lose from it. By the outbreak of the Second World War about 95% of the Soviet Union's farms had been collectivised.

Apart from the economic aim – the urgent need to achieve greater productivity from the land – there was in Stalin's mind a clear political objective. The conquest and consolidation of political power in a backward country whose peasants clung to private ownership, dictated collectivisation. Lenin had hoped that the peasantry might gradually come to accept the modernisation of agriculture. But when this expectation failed, and when the NEP did not resolve the crisis of food shortages, Stalin pressed full speed ahead with collectivisation, regardless of the human consequences.

The five-year plans and industrialisation

Lenin's successor also proceeded after 1928 with plans to equip Russia with heavy industry and better transport and to develop new sources of power and industry beyond the Urals. Lenin had not envisaged detailed economic planning in 1917, but under Stalin it became and remained a permanent characteristic of the Communist order. The effect was to produce a highly integrated economy. By 1939, four-fifths of Russian industrial production came from plants built during the previous ten years and, as many of these were situated east of the Urals, they carried modern industrialisation into the heart of Asia.

This rigorous drive to transform Russia into a first-class industrial power made necessary a high degree of political centralisation. The transition from Marxism to Leninism and from Leninism to Stalinism was brought about by a self-constituted bureaucratic elite which had become independent of the masses in whose name it was supposed to rule. The re-constitution of the familiar Russian tradition of autocratic domination and state control was made possible by the institution of a single-party monopoly.

Stalin's policies involved gross inhumanity – slaughter, deportation, imprisonment and famine on a massive scale. At the same time there was rapid economic progress. It is estimated that in the decade after 1929 the Russian gross national product grew by just under 12% a year. The greatest single failure (as today) was to be found in Russian agriculture. But even there, by paying the collectives far less than the market price and absorbing the difference, the state forced agriculture to swell the accumulation of capital which powered the industrial programme. While the price of collectivisation was extremely high and while historians question whether Stalin's brutality was necessary to achieve the pace of Soviet development, collectivisation and grain surpluses made it possible to pursue the aims of the five-year plans. Collectivisation caused bitter disaffection, not only among the peasantry.

The period of the purges

The assassination of a popular leading Leningrad Communist, Kirov, in 1934 provided Stalin with an excuse for what was to be a bloody purge of the Communist Party. In 1935 Zinoviev and the other Old Bolsheviks were brought to trial and condemned. In the years that followed hundreds of thousands of Party officials and administrators were shot, deported or simply replaced. Half the officer corps of the Army was also removed.

These purges had the evident purpose of, on the one hand, removing all Stalin's earlier rivals and adversaries, and, on the other, of forestalling any potential future opposition. They must be set against the background of the rise of Nazi Germany. Abroad, the well-advertised show trials confirmed conservative-minded statesmen and politicians in their hatred and suspicion of the Soviet Union and of Communist totalitarianism. At the same time the dramatic purge of the Red Army made military leaders in France and Germany sceptical about Russia's value as a possible ally against Germany.

At the same time, sympathisers with the Soviet system in other countries mistakenly saw in the new Soviet Constitution of 1936 an apparently liberal and democratic creation. In fact, though this provided excellent propaganda material for Stalinism abroad, it simply disguised the real totalitarian police-state nature of the regime.

The real significance of the Constitution was that it ended conclusively the era of improvisations. It emphasised the fact that Soviet rule had hardened into its final form. The abolition of the distinctions that had denied full rights to the former possessing classes most clearly demonstrated that they no longer represented any sort of threat to the new Stalinist order, that the power of these classes had been broken.

10.5 THE SOVIET UNION AND THE WESTERN POWERS

The attitude of the European Powers to the new phenomenon of Bolshevik Russia passed through various phases. At first the revolution and the terror provoked a violent reaction of fear. Then Russia made her first formal agreement with Germany at the Treaty of Rapallo (1922). During the next decade the Soviet Union made trade agreements with other Western countries and in 1934 she was admitted to the League of Nations.

Her relations with the West were periodically disturbed by the activities of the Comintern (founded in 1919). On the one hand, Stalin seemed intent on 'building Socialism' in Russia alone; on the other, Soviet propaganda continued to argue that world revolution was the inevitable goal of Communism and that no opportunity should be missed to promote that end. Distrust and hostility continued, therefore, to characterise relations with the West.

The years 1936–8, the major years of the purges, were also marked by a new direction in Soviet foreign policy. It seemed unlikely to Stalin that the Western Powers, which had acquiesced in Hitler's invasion of the Rhineland, would be willing to resist German expansion at Russia's expense. This lesson seemed to be underlined by the Spanish Civil War and the Munich Conference. At the same time Stalin was only agreeable to participating in effective collective security against Germany if the Soviet Union was allowed access across Poland, the Baltic states and Rumania. This was something Western governments would not contemplate since it meant the establishment of Russian military domination over Eastern Europe. This was the background to the Nazi-Soviet Non-Aggression Pact of August, 1939.

At the end of December, 1940, Hitler finally took the decision which was essential for his objective of 'Lebensraum' (living space) in the East and he issued his orders for the preparation of the attack on Russia. On 22 June, 1941, German troops attacked the Soviet Union in Operation Barbarossa on a broad front from the Baltic to Rumania.

10.6 CHRONOLOGY

1917	March	Outbreak of riots in St Petersburg. The Duma refused to obey an imperial decree ordering its dissolution. Abdication of the Tsar Nicholas II; establishing of the PROVISIONAL GOVERNMENT UNDER PRINCE LVOV. Power struggle between the Provisional Government and the PETROGRAD (St Petersburg) SOVIET. Issue of Order No 1 by the Soviet.
	April	LENIN ARRIVED AT PETROGRAD. His programme: 1 the transfer of power to the Soviets; 2 the cessation of war; 3 the seizure of land by the peasants; 4 the control of industry by committees of workers.
	July	Bolshevik attempt to seize power in Petrograd; Trotsky arrested; Lenin went into hiding. KERENSKY succeeded Prince Lvov.
	September	KORNILOV attacked the government; in defeating him, Kerensky came under the domination of his Bolshevik allies.
	6 November	THE BOLSHEVIK REVOLUTION: the Bolsheviks led by the military revolutionary committee, the soldiers of the Petrograd garrison and the Red Guards seized key government offices, stormed the Winter Palace and arrested members of the Provisional Government.
	7	THE SECOND ALL-RUSSIAN CONGRESS OF SOVIETS: the new government assumed the name of the Council of Peoples Commissars; headed by Lenin and including TROTSKY, as Commissar for Foreign Affairs and STALIN, Commissar for National Minorities. THE LAND DECREE: ordered the immediate distribution of the land among the peasants. Nationalisation of the banks; the repudiation of the national debt. Workmen given control over the factories, confiscation of church property.
	25	The elections to the Constituent Assembly returned 420 Social Revolutionaries as against only 225 Bolsheviks. When the Assembly met in Petrograd (January 1918) it was dispersed at once by the Red troops.
1918	March	THE TREATY OF BREST-LITOVSK: between Russia and the Central Powers. The Russians surrendered the Baltic provinces; the Ukraine, Finland, the Caucasus, White Russia and Poland. The government moved the capital from Petrograd to Moscow. Independent governments formed all along the Russian frontier.
1918–20		THE CIVIL WAR: the war with the Cossacks; the struggle for the Ukraine; the war in White Russia and the Baltic region. Allied intervention in northern Russia; the campaigns of Denikin and Wrangel in the Caucasus and southern Russia; the war in Siberia and eastern Russia.
1918	July	PROMULGATION OF THE SOVIET CONSTITUTION. MURDER OF NICHOLAS II AND HIS FAMILY.

	August	An attempt by a Social Revolutionary to assassinate Lenin inaugurated a systematic reign of terror by the Bolsheviks.
1919	March	COMINTERN FOUNDED: for the propagation of revolutionary Marxism abroad.
1920	April–October	The Russo-Polish War.
1921	March	The Treaty of Riga, defining the frontier between Russia and Poland. THE KRONSTADT MUTINY. THE NEW ECONOMIC POLICY (NEP): a partial restoration of freedom of trade and other changes declared to be a 'temporary retreat' from communism.
1922	April December	THE TREATY OF RAPALLO between Germany and Soviet Russia. THE UNION OF SOVIET SOCIALIST REPUBLICS.
1924	January	The death of Lenin; followed by a power struggle between Stalin and Trotsky.
1926	July–October	The victory of Stalin over the Leftist opposition bloc led by Trotsky which called for the discontinuation of the NEP and the speeding-up of world revolution.
1927	December	Definitive victory of the Stalin faction over the Trotsky group; the 15th All Union Congress of the Communist Party condemned all 'deviation from the general Party line'. (Trotsky expelled from Russia in January 1929).
1928		NEW SOCIALIST POLICIES; SPEEDY INDUSTRIALISATION, THE FIVE YEAR PLANS, THE COLLECTIVISATION OF AGRICULTURE.
1929	November	Expulsion from the Party of Bukharin and other members of the Rightist opposition.
1933		PURGE OF THE COMMUNIST PARTY: about one-third of its members expelled.
1934	September December	The Soviet Union joined the League of Nations, which it had previously denounced. Started to work for collective security and supported France in the scheme for an eastern European pact. Assassination of Kirov, followed by purges and the trials of many of the older leaders of the Party.
1935	May August	Conclusion of the Franco-Russian alliance. Alliance between Russia and Czechoslovakia which obliged the Russians to come to the assistance of Czechoslovakia in the event of an attack, provided France decided to act. Decision at a meeting of the Comintern that Soviet Russia should throw its weight on the side of the democracies against Fascism.
1936	August December	Zinoviev, Kamenev and others put on trial and executed for alleged plotting with enemy Powers against the regime of Stalin. Adoption of a new 'democratic' constitution.
1939	August	Trade pact concluded with Germany. THE MOLOTOV-RIBBENTROP NON-AGGRESSION PACT: included pledges to maintain neutrality if either country was at war. Secret clauses gave Lithuania and western Poland to Germany and eastern Poland, Estonia, Latvia, Finland and Bessarabia to the Soviet Union.
1941	22 June	Operation Barbarossa launched by Hitler against the Soviet Union.

Illustrative questions and answers

1   Consider how far Stalin had closed the gap between the Soviet Union and the more advanced countries by 1941.

Tutorial note

This is basically a question on the economic achievements of the Soviet Union before the German invasion. You should consider the problems of economic development in Russia as a backward country and Stalin's solution for them. Given the terminal date, an assessment of Russia's preparedness for war would be appropriate – as would wider considerations of the social gap between Russia and the advanced countries (which may be taken to be the US and those of Western Europe).

You need to know about

A general understanding of the structure and history of the Russian economy and society since the 1880s. A detailed grasp of Stalin's policies, particularly the collectivisation of agriculture and the five-year plans, and the levels of agricultural and industrial achievement. The level of development in the West.

Suggested answer plan

1   The fact that the Soviet Union was able to withstand and finally to defeat the very highly industrialised Nazi Germany is an indication of the level of industrial achievement that Stalin's rule and policies had encouraged. However, although the catching-up process was dramatic, it was not complete, and we can still see serious weaknesses in the Russian economy.

2   When Stalin came to power Russia was still a few islands of advanced economy in a sea of backwardness. A *brief* explanation of the collectivisation of agriculture, of the five-year plans and of the relationship between them.

3   Industrial achievements: by 1941 Russia was a very major producer in some fields (third in the world league of steel production); coal output had increased fourfold since 1913; in petroleum, Russia was second only to the US; there was great investment in steel plants, dams, electricity, etc.

4   In agriculture the areas cultivated had increased by one-third since 1913; the grain and beet crops had gone up threefold; milk and meat production had nearly doubled; Russian town dwellers were now considerably better fed, particularly as the growth of industry had reduced the need to export agricultural crops in exchange for machinery. Nevertheless, note the failure of the collective farms to produce sufficient food for the population in a rapidly developing economy.

5   By 1941 the Soviet Union had, in material terms, made a huge stride forward in basic heavy industry, which was the basis for military strength; but to some extent Stalin's totalitarian grasp, the mistakes made by centralised planning and the discouragement of individuality reduced the scale of advance.

6   Consumer goods were in very short supply – in personal consumption and standard of living of the populations there was still a wide divide between the Soviet Union and the West.

7   While the economic gap had appreciably narrowed, it had greatly widened in terms of personal freedom. A new constitution in 1936 had *theoretically* widened the boundaries of freedom: in fact, with the purges and the terror, the drive to uniformity in every sphere, including the cultural, was overwhelming.

8   The invasion of 1941 and the subsequent war effort encouraged a further very considerable development of Soviet industrial might, supported by intense Russian patriotism and investment of American capital. Even so, it is still clear today in its legacy that the Stalinist achievement was a partial one and the narrowing of the gap with the West was also partial: there was the persistent agricultural problem, continuing low levels of consumption and the need for totalitarian controls.

2   Why were there two revolutions in Russia in 1917?

Tutorial note

The question requires you to examine why the March Revolution happened in the first place; but further, why it failed to solve Russia's crisis. You must also be able to explain how a tiny minority radical group, the Bolsheviks, came to dominate the

Russian state in the second revolution, with the support of the urban proletariat.

You need to know about

The structure and history of Russia's economy and society from c. 1880 to 1917, particularly the agricultural problem. The history of radical revolutionary politics in Russia, especially the Mensheviks and the Bolsheviks. The effects of the First World War on Russia. The period of the Provisional Government.

Suggested answer plan

1   Marxist ideology in the early 20th century argued that a society had to go through *two* revolutions – a liberal bourgeois one, followed much later, at the full development of capitalism, by a socialist revolution led and controlled by 'the dictatorship of the proletariat'. In Russia both revolutions happened in the same year and this fact can only be understood through an analysis of Russian society in the early twentieth century.

2   The contrasts in Russian society: her need to develop the economy in order to be a Great Power; state capitalism and industrialisation; the contribution of Sergei Witte; conversely, the problem of the land and the peasantry – capitalist-run estates were the exception; rapid, but localised, industrial development was taking place m a society where the majority of the population were largely self-sufficient peasants. The social structure meant the lack of a strong liberal middle class such as exists in the Western European states; the Tsarist autocracy had stifled the growth of political consciousness along western lines and the social structure seemed not to be capable of producing effective 'reformist' politics.

3   The only real political opposition was in the cities among a Socialist/Populist intelligentsia; their ideas were intellectual and radical, and Lenin's ideas were essentially anti-western and anti-liberal; the contrast between the Bolshevik and Menshevik approaches; the Mensheviks attempting to retain the orthodox Marxist view of the two revolutions, in spite of the realities of Russian society.

4   The effects of the First World War: a huge economic boom, but the Government and administration were not flexible enough to cope; the Government broke down under the strains of war in 1917; the failure to feed the towns; financial chaos; the distrust of Tsarist circles; the mismanagement of the war effort; desertion of troops.

5   The March Revolution: a liberal revolution bringing the Provisional Government to power; this had fundamentally no effective new approaches to the problems of Russian society; it did nothing to reclaim the control of local government, which was lapsing into anarchy; it maintained the alliance with the Western Powers as popular support for the war against Germany was rapidly waning; the Provisional Government was forced to share power with the Petrograd Soviet.

6   The Bolsheviks: the acceptance of Lenin's 'April Theses'; the false start in the July Days; the Provisional Government under Kerensky and the Kornilov affair; the Soviet came to be dominated by Bolsheviks as workers became disillusioned and as local organisers came to see the Bolsheviks as the only sound base on which to build a new form of government.

7   The March Revolution occurred because of the crisis in Russia's economy and society, and because of the strains of the very rapid development to meet the demands of war; but the liberal bourgeois revolution did not work out in practice; there was no substantial liberal middle class and no true capitalist economic structure to form the base of a Western-style political order; the November Revolution occurred as a logical outcome, almost as a reaction, to Western theory and influence; the Bolsheviks alone seemed to offer a 'real' enough solution to the crisis of Russian society, more particularly the land question. Significantly, the Bolshevik takeover was consolidated by the decrees on land and peace.

3 'A great revolutionary, but not a great statesman'. How far would you accept this view of Lenin?

Tutorial note

This question appears to ask for a simple comparison of Lenin's achievement in gaining power in 1917 with his apparent lack of decisiveness subsequently and his failure to achieve the 'state' he described in *The State and Revolution*. However, this question asks whether you accept the view of Lenin propounded. It is legitimate to argue that it should be rejected because it gives a false perspective on Lenin's aims and understanding of events; the point is that Lenin became a 'statesman' by mistake.

You need to know about

Lenin's political beliefs and strategy. Russia's political and economic structure and its relation to Western Europe. Bolshevik ideas before the First World War. The events of 1917 and beyond, both in Russia and in Europe. Lenin's policies after 1917 and their consequences.

Suggested answer plan

1   Introduction: the view expressed might appear to be self-evident. The revolution-ary who wrote about the idyllic state in *The State and Revolution* became the founding father of one of the most repressive states in the world and failed to achieve his ideals. The end of Lenin's life was a story of failure and tragedy as he saw the growing dominance of a bureaucratic and oppressive state. However, this traditional view of Lenin as 'the revolutionary-who-fails-to-make-a-competent-statesman' is very misleading.

2   This is because: (a) the concept of 'statesmanship' used is a traditional one which he would not have accepted for himself; (b) he managed to retain power – on a simply pragmatic level he was a very good 'statesman' in that he preserved any government at all in the extremely chaotic circumstances after 1917; (c) he never expected to have to be a 'statesman' in the traditional sense at all. His policy after 1917 was a series of expedients, for he was anticipating the spread of revolution.

3   The Marxist concept of revolution and Lenin's expectation in 1917; the notion of 'permanent revolution' (Trotsky); Lenin was willing to make major conces-sions to Germany in the Treaty of Brest-Litovsk, not least because he believed that Germany would soon be engulfed in revolution.

4   Pure Marxist idealism lay at the heart of Lenin's rationale for 1917, but Lenin was a great revolutionary in practice as well as in theory; his organisation of the Bolshevik Party as a party of professional revolutionaries; his tactics between February and October 1917, especially the 'April Theses'; his disciplining of the Party; his capacity, once in power, for being very ruthless, viz. the dissolution of the Constituent Assembly and 'War Communism'; his pragmatism and flexibility in instigating the New Economic Policy.

5   Lenin was never a 'statesman' in the traditional sense; rather he was a pragmatic revolutionary in power; his legacy of strict party discipline and ruthlessness conflicted in its consequences with his idealistic wish for a 'stateless' world. These two strands were inherited respectively in the approaches of Trotsky (idealistic 'world revolution') and the 'Socialism in One Country' totalitarian dictatorship under Stalin.

6   It can be argued that Lenin remained a *revolutionary*. It was only with Stalin that the idea of 'statesman' returned to the Russian scene as the Bolsheviks turned towards 'building Socialism' within the bounds of the traditional state.

Question bank

1 Document question (The Russian Revolution and Lenin): study extracts I and II below and then answer questions (a) to (h) which follow:

Extract I

'The Provisional Government...should do nothing now which would break our ties with the Allies... . The worst thing that could happen to us would be a separate peace. It would be ruinous for the Russian revolution, ruinous for international democracy... . As to the land question – we regard it as our duty at the present time to prepare the ground for a just solution of that problem by the Constituent Assembly... .'

(Speech by Tseretelli, a minister in the Provisional Government, June, 1917)

Extract II

'Comrades!...Kerensky sends troops to suppress the peasants and to defend the landowners. Kerensky has again come to an agreement with the Kornilovist generals and officers who stand for the landowners.

'...If power is (put) in the hands of the Soviets...there will be in Russia a workers' and peasants' government; it will immediately, without losing a single day, offer a just peace to all the belligerent peoples... .

'...If power is in the hands of the Soviets...the landowners' lands will immediately be declared the property and heritage of the whole people... .

'...Are you willing to 'be patient' in order that the war may be dragged out longer, the offer of peace postponed, the tearing-up of the secret treaties of the former Tsar with the Russian and Anglo-French capitalists postponed?'

(Lenin, writing in October, 1917)

(a) Who first led 'the Provisional Government' and who succeeded him? (2)
(b) Explain Lenin's reference to 'Kornilovist generals'. (2)
(c) What do you understand by 'the Soviets'? (2)
(d) Identify 'the former Tsar' and explain briefly the circumstances in which he ceased to reign. (4)
(e) Summarise the main differences between the policy of the provisional government, as outlined by Tseretelli in Extract I, and that proposed by Lenin in Extract II. (4)
(f) What was the importance of the 'Constituent Assembly' in Russian political affairs in 1917–18? (5)
(g) Discuss how successful Lenin and his supporters were in obtaining 'a just peace'. (4)
(h) What problems arose concerning Lenin's intention to make the land 'the property and heritage of the whole people', and how far had these problems been overcome by the time of Lenin's death in 1924? (8)

2 'The real Russian Revolution occurred after 1917'. How far do you agree?
(NISEAC, June 1990)

3 How, and with what results to 1941, did Stalin succeed in asserting his personal authority over the USSR? (Cambridge, June 1991)

4 Consider the view that 'the purges and labour camps were inevitable consequences of Stalin's economic and political programme in the period 1929–53'. (AEB, June 1990)

5 How important was Lenin's influence in determining the outcome of the Russian Revolution of 1917? (Cambridge, June 1991)

READING LIST

Standard textbook reading

J. M. Roberts, *Europe 1880–1945* (Longman, 1967), chapter 13.

David Thomson, *Europe since Napoleon* (Penguin, 1977), chapters 22, 23, 25, 27.

Anthony Wood, *Europe 1815–1945* (Longman, 1975), chapters 26 and 29.

Further suggested reading

E. H. Carr, *The Russian Revolution from Lenin to Stalin* (Macmillan, 1980).

Robert Conquest, *The Great Terror: Stalin's Purge of the Thirties* (Penguin, 1968).

Isaac Deutscher, *Stalin* (Penguin, 1972).

S. Fitzpatrick, *The Russian Revolution 1917–32* (OUP, 1982).

G. Hosking, *A History of the Soviet Union* (Fontana, 1985).

L. Kochan, *The Making of Modern Russia* (Penguin, 1970); and *Russia in Revolution* (Paladin, 1978).

W. Laqueur, *The Fate of the Revolution: Interpretations of Russian History* (Weidenfeld and Nicolson, 1967).

M. McCauley, *Stalin and Stalinism* (Longman, 1983).

M. McCauley (ed.), *The Russian Revolution and the Soviet State 1917–1921* (documents) (Macmillan, 1975).

J. P. Nettl, *The Soviet Achievement* (Thames & Hudson, 1969).

Alex Nove, *An Economic History of the USSR* (Penguin, 1972).

D. W. Treadgold, *Twentieth-Century Russia* (Rand McNally, 1976).

A. B. Ulam, *Lenin and the Bolsheviks* (Fontana, 1969); and *Expansion and Coexistence: the History of Soviet Foreign Policy 1917–67*, (Secker and Warburg, 1968).

J. N. Westwood, *Endurance and Endeavour, Russian History 1812–1986* (OUP, 1987).

B. Williams, *The Russian Revolution 1917–21* (Blackwell, 1987).

A. Wood, *The Russian Revolution* (Longman, 1979).

CHAPTER 11

MUSSOLINI AND ITALIAN FASCISM

Units in this chapter

Chapter objectives

❶ The background of Fascist ideas; Fascism as a European phenomenon with origins in the prewar period; the emphasis on Nationalism; the rejection of parliamentary democracy, Liberalism and the ideas associated with the French Revolution of 1789; its appeal as a means of suppressing Socialism and Communism after the First World War.

❷ The Treaty of London and the grievances of Italy at the result of the Treaty of Versailles; the significance of the seizure of Fiume by Gabriele d'Annunzio.

❸ Mussolini's background and career before 1919; the formation of the Fascio di Combattimento; the events leading to and including the March on Rome; the 'Squadristi'; the role of the monarchy and the security forces.

❹ The political weaknesses in the Italian system which helped to make Mussolini successful in 1922 included:
* the Catholic Church's hostility to the Liberal Italian state:
* the effects of political management, especially the 'transformism' of Giolitti;
* the failure of the Italian Left to become a credible parliamentary alternative (the Left was divided between those who were willing to work within the parliamentary system and those who looked for a revolutionary alternative; the Socialists split in 1912 and 1921 on these issues);
* the domestic political significance of Italy's entry into the war in 1915 – the intervention crisis as a precedent for 1922.

❺ The demand for and appeal of strong leadership; the argument that the Italian parliamentary system had failed; the contribution towards Mussolini's success of the following groups:
* the Italian nationalists and patriots aggrieved by their country's failure to receive territories promised by the Treaty of London;
* the propertied classes frightened by the seizure of land and the occupation of the factories;

- all those who blamed the continuing inflation on the failure of government.
6. The consolidation of Mussolini's power and the means by which he established a one-party state; the new electoral law (1923); the Aventine Secession, following the murder of Matteotti; censorship; abolition of universal suffrage.
7. The economic policies of the Fascist State; the National Council of Corporations.
8. Mussolini's relations with the Roman Catholic Church and Papacy, particularly the significance of the Lateran Treaties (1929).
9. Mussolini's foreign policy: the Corfù incident; the origins, course and international impact of the Abyssinian War; the intervention in the Spanish Civil War; the invasion and conquest of Albania; Mussolini's relations with Germany: the Pact of Steel; the declaration of war on France and Britain.
10. The circumstances of Mussolini's fall from power; the dissolution of the Fascist Party.

Fascism marked a revolt against the liberal political ideas of the nineteenth century. It emphasised the power and unity of the state, as against individualism and the division of society into classes. It was militantly nationalistic and rejected pacifism and internationalism. It came to power in Italy against a background of acute economic difficulties, fear of revolution, disappointment at the territorial results of the Peace Settlement and the inability of Liberal governments to resolve these problems.

Mussolini became Prime Minister and *Duce* (leader) following the march on Rome in October, 1922. In subsequent years he proceeded to suppress political opposition and institute a dictatorship. Other major domestic developments included the setting up of the National Council of Corporations and the conclusion of the Lateran Treaties with the Catholic Church.

In 1935 he issued a major challenge to the international order and the League of Nations with his successful war against Abyssinia. This also drew him towards an alliance with Germany, with which he concluded the Pact of Steel. In 1940 he declared war on Britain and France.

In 1943 he was forced to resign after a coup by King Victor Emmanuel and Marshal Badoglio, and the Fascist Party was dissolved.

11.1 THE BACKGROUND

Fascism was a European phenomenon. It developed in the disturbed economic and social conditions which were common to most of Europe in the years after the First World War. Its origins, however, lie in the revolt against nineteenth-century liberal ideas and 'bourgeois' society in the prewar period.

In Italy the main target of this revolt was the dominant political figure, Giovanni Giolitti and his liberal, democratic, reform policies. The younger generation of post-war Italy rejected the cosy and comfortable middle-class values of Giolittian Italy. They demanded action and political excitement instead.

The leaders of the revolt were the Italian nationalists, who argued that Italy could only fulfil her imperial destiny and solve her persistent economic problems through successful war (there was already a strand of extreme nationalism in Italy dating from the struggle for unification). They also rejected Giolitti's compromises with the Socialist Party, which they regarded as the enemy of Italian patriotism. They advocated, in place of Socialist class struggle, the collaboration of all classes under an authoritarian, strong, nationalistic government.

Intervention and the First World War

The revolt against Giolitti most successfully asserted itself in the Intervention Crisis of 1915. The nationalists and their allies on the Right joined other forces violently hostile to Giolitti – the revolutionary Socialists (who included Mussolini at this time), the revolutionary syndicalists, radicals, republicans and democrats – to support Italian entry into the First World War. Giolitti and the majority of the Liberals opted for neutrality. So did the Socialists, thus reinforcing nationalist hostility to Socialism.

Eventually, the neutralist majority was overawed by the Interventionist press campaigns and street demonstrations. In May, 1915 the Italian parliament voted to go to war on the side of Britain, France and Russia, according to the terms of the Treaty of London.

11.2 THE BIRTH OF ITALIAN FASCISM

In March, 1919 some of the extreme Interventionist forces coalesced to form the first *Fascio* under the leadership of Benito Mussolini. The Left-wing origins of Fascism. were clearly visible in the political programme of the first Fascio, with its emphasis on anti-capitalism, anti-clericalism and republicanism. Indeed, Mussolini launched his movement as a patriotic alternative to the neutralist Socialist Party, but his appeal to the urban working class failed.

He did succeed, though, in attracting large numbers of ex-servicemen who were disillusioned with their return to civilian life and who were rebuffed by the Socialists. From the start, Fascism was characterised by extreme nationalism and violent anti-Socialism.

The crisis of the liberal state

At the same time as Italy, in common with other European countries in the postwar period, was facing serious economic, social and political problems, the system of government was paralysed by a difficult transition from a restricted franchise to full democracy. As a result of the introduction of universal male suffrage and proportional representation in the general elections of 1919, two strong mass parties, the Socialists and the Catholic Popular Party, emerged and the Liberals lost their parliamentary majority for the first time since the unification.

The Socialists obstinately refused to participate in parliamentary government, and the Popular Party would only do so on stringent conditions. To make matters worse, the Liberals were divided into several warring factions. Between the end of the war and October 1922; Italy was ruled by no fewer than six different coalitions. It was in any case a country with a tradition of anti-parliamentarism.

Not surprisingly, these weak, unstable governments proved incapable of resolving the grave problems facing Italy, and in their desire for strong, effective government many Italians turned to Fascism.

The three major problems facing the postwar governments were:

❶ The 'mutilated victory' Public opinion was dissatisfied with the gains made by Italy in the Peace Settlement of 1919. The nationalists and the Fascists claimed that Italy had been 'cheated' of her due reward for their war effort and they blamed the weak parliamentary governments for this. The aspect of the Peace which most outraged Italians was the allocation of the Italian-speaking town of Fiume to Yugoslavia, and in 1919 Gabriele D'Annunzio and his shock troops, the *arditi*, seized the town by force. The failure of the Italian Government to crush this rebellion further damaged its credibility, showing that it was powerless to prevent Right-wing violence and illegal acts.

➋ **Economic difficulties** Italian governments also failed to solve the economic problems of the postwar period, the run-down of industry, mass unemployment (swelled by demobilisation), high inflation and the land hunger of the peasantry. The immediate postwar period intensified deep-rooted problems in the economy, some of which could be clearly identified at the time of the Unification.

➌ **The fear of revolution** The years 1918–20 are known as the 'Red Two Years' by Italian historians, for they witnessed a violent upsurge of spontaneous working-class militancy – strikes, street demonstrations, riots and occupations of the factories and land. Though the leadership of the Socialist Party preached revolution, they were unwilling to bring it about. Nevertheless, the aggressive activities of the Socialists gave rise to a widespread belief that there was a real danger of a revolution. As one Socialist warned: 'We shall pay with tears of blood for this fright we have given the bourgeoisie'.

11.3 THE GROWTH OF FASCISM, 1920–22

Many who joined the Fascist squads did so because they seemed the only force willing and able to stop Socialism. The most widespread and violent reaction against the Left took place in the Po Valley. There, in the 1920 local elections, the traditional ruling class was unseated by a Socialist victory.

Control of the town halls gave them authority over the local labour exchanges, which the Socialist Peasant Leagues used to raise agricultural wages and force the farmers to accept more labourers then they needed. At the same time, they proclaimed that their ultimate aim was the **collectivisation** of the land, thus threatening not only the large landowners but the small peasant farmers as well. For these social groups it seemed that the revolution was already taking place and in their desperation they turned to the local Fascists for assistance.

Very quickly the Fascist squads were swelled by the unemployed, by students, peasants and all manner of unruly and anti-socialist elements eager for action and excitement. Between September 1920 and October 1922 the Fascist squads literally bullied, beat and burned their way to power in many areas of northern and central Italy. The police tended to turn a blind eye to these activities and in some cases they and the Army actually assisted the squads.

Even Mussolini was surprised by the speed with which 'agrarian fascism' grew. At this time he needed all his resources of energy, his national reputation as an Interventionist, his oratorical gifts and his ownership of the only Fascist daily newspaper, *Il Popolo d'Italia*, to preserve his leadership of the movement.

Power in three stages

In the general elections of May, 1921, Giolitti made a last attempt to restore the authority of the Liberal state by forming an electoral alliance of Liberals, Nationalists and Fascists, but he failed to win a majority. The only beneficiaries of his strategy were the Fascists, who won 35 seats and thus acquired a respectable parliamentary face which they used to win support and sympathy in conservative circles. Even the Vatican showed sympathy for Fascism, taking at face value Mussolini's brazenly opportunistic promise to settle the dispute between Church and State which had existed since the unification.

By October, 1922, the paralysis of parliamentary government was complete and the Fascists exploited the situation by threatening a March on Rome to give Italy a strong, effective government. On the 24th of that month Mussolini, speaking in Naples, laid down the challenge to the government: either solve Italy's problems or make way for the Fascists. Apprehensive that the alternative to capitulation, as the Fascists marched on Rome, would be civil war, the King, Victor Emmanuel III, gave in to this blackmail and appointed Mussolini as Prime Minister.

To consolidate his power, Mussolini persuaded Parliament to introduce a law controlling the press and set up a militia of Fascist 'squadristi' to defend Fascism against the Army should the Army move against him. Most important of all, he obtained approval for a reform of the electoral system, the Acerbo Law of 1923 which stipulated that the party which obtained the largest number of votes in excess of a quarter of the total would win two-thirds of the parliamentary seats. In the 1924 general elections the Fascists won their two-thirds majority, largely through violence and intimidation and because of the divisions of the opposition.

Within a few weeks, however, as a result of the abduction and murder by Fascist thugs of the Socialist leader, Giacomo Matteotti, Mussolini was fighting for his political life. Italian public opinion was outraged by the crime, not least because of Mussolini's alleged involvement.

The opposition parties abandoned parliament to form the Aventine Secession as a moral protest; however, they signally failed to exploit their last chance to overthrow Mussolini. Mussolini's allies – the industrialists, the Church and many liberal politicians – stood by him.

Prompted by the demands of the bosses of the Fascist Party, in January 1925 Mussolini declared that he accepted 'moral' responsibility for the Matteotti murder and for all other crimes committed during the 'Fascist Revolution'. During the next three years he suppressed the opposition, established a police state and the other institutions of the Fascist dictatorship.

Fascism in power: economic policy and corporatism

Despite the anti-capitalist demands of the early Fascist movement, Fascism in power showed considerable favour to the industrial and agrarian interests, beginning with the laissez-faire policies of the Finance Minister, De Stefani, appointed in 1922. On the other hand, in accordance with Mussolini's rule that 'economics is subordinate to politics', Fascist economic policy in the 1920s and 1930s was often dictated by prestige motives and the need to prepare for war.

The fixing of the exchange rate at the artificially high level of 90 Lire to the pound was typical of Mussolini's desire to raise Italian prestige abroad. Similarly the policies for autarky, or self-sufficiency in essential products, like the 'Battle for Grain' were pursued in the interests of defence and war. Under Mussolini substantial progress was made in this respect. By 1939 Italy was able to feed herself.

In the 1930s Fascism gained much respect from foreign statesmen because of its policy of corporatism: the establishment of corporations representing employers, employees and the state to regulate production and industrial relations. This policy was taken to its logical conclusion in 1939 with the abolition of the elected lower house of parliament and its replacement by a Chamber of Fasces and Corporations elected by the Corporations.

In fact the almost total absence of strikes in Fascist Italy was not the result of corporatism, but the effect of police repression, the outlawing of strikes, the dissolution of the free trade unions and their replacement by compulsory Fascist-controlled unions.

Mussolini and the Catholic Church

Mussolini's policy of wooing the Church paid handsome dividends in 1923–4 when the Vatican assisted his rise to power by abandoning the main parliamentary opposition force, the Catholic Popular Party. By 1926 the Vatican and the Fascist regime had developed cordial, even close relations, and over the next three yeas negotiated secretly to resolve the 60-year-old dispute between Church and State – the 'Roman Question'. On 11 February 1929, the Vatican and Italy signed the Lateran Pacts which established the State of the Vatican City and restored the Church's power and influence in Italy.

Mussolini's prestige was enormously strengthened both at home and abroad by the diplomatic triumph, and in the 1929 elections, or plebiscite, the Church ordered Italian Catholics to vote for the single Fascist list. But Fascism's relationship with the Church was not always harmonious: the 1931 crisis over Catholic Action showed the strength of anti-clerical, Fascist discontent with Mussolini's concessions to the Church. Further, though many Catholics approved of Mussolini's economic and corporatist policies and gave enthusiastic support to the Abyssinian War of 1935–6, they drew the line at the introduction of the Racial Laws in 1938. Pope Pius XI saw them as a highly unwelcome indication of the growing influence of Hitler over Mussolini. His successor, Pius XII, strongly disapproved of Italy's entry into the Second World War in 1940 and from this point on the Church sought to dissociate itself from Fascism.

11.4 FASCIST FOREIGN POLICY

Fascism was nothing if not violently nationalistic, and this nationalism manifested itself in the 1930s and 1940s in wars of aggression and colonial expansion. In the 1920s, however, Fascist Italy had little scope for aggression or expansion given the dominance of the international situation in the immediate postwar years by Britain and France. Only the 'gun-boat diplomacy' employed by Mussolini in the Corfù crisis of 1923 revealed the true nature of Fascist foreign policy.

Italy's opportunity for aggrandisement came with the Nazi assumption of power in 1933. By 1935 Britain and France were anxious for Italian support against a resurgent, rearming Germany. Mussolini, therefore, decided that they would condone his conquest of Abyssinia, on which he embarked in order to distract attention from the effects of the Great Depression in Italy. The Abyssinian War was both successful and popular with the Italian people, not least because the overwhelming majority resented the economic sanctions taken by the League of Nations.

Hitler was quick to exploit Mussolini's estrangement from Britain and France which resulted from the sanctions policy: he encouraged Italy to involve itself more and more deeply in the Spanish Civil War, thus preventing Mussolini from resisting the German invasion of Austria in 1938.

By 1939 relations between Italy and Germany had developed into a 'Rome-Berlin Axis', though Mussolini already showed signs of resenting Hitler's masterful methods. In March 1939, Mussolini invaded Albania to 'match' Hitler's occupation of Bohemia. Despite his doubts, Mussolini strengthened his ties with Germany, concluding the Pact of Steel in May 1939, and finally declaring war on Britain and France a year later.

11.5 THE FALL OF ITALIAN FASCISM

The War proved to be an unmitigated disaster for Mussolini and Fascism. By the summer of 1943 Italy had lost Greece and all her African colonies, in large part a result of her unpreparedness for war, for which Mussolini must take the blame. The civilian population was demoralised by the defeats, by the food shortages and the effects of the Allied bombing. The last straw was the Allied invasion of Sicily in July 1943, by which time demoralisation was almost as complete within the ranks of the Fascist Party as among the population at large.

On 24 July the Grand Council of Fascism passed a vote of no confidence in

Mussolini and he was dismissed. The Fascist Party was dissolved by order of the King. Fascism was in fact overthrown by a royal coup d'etat – the survival of the Monarchy had proved the Achilles heel of the regime. However, it should be noted that Fascism had never been able to obtain such a degree of obedience or totalitarian control as Nazism had in Germany. This can be seen, for instance, in the attitude of the Italian population towards the racial laws.

11.6 CHRONOLOGY

1915	April	THE TREATY OF LONDON: concluded with Britain, France and Russia. Clauses promised Italy the South Tyrol, Trentino and Trieste among other territories.
	May	Italian Government denounced the Triple Alliance and mobilised against Austria-Hungary.
1917	October–December	THE CAPORETTO CAMPAIGN: the defeat of the Italians by Austro-German advance.
1919	March	THE FORMATION OF THE FIRST FASCIO DI COMBATTIMENTO BY BENITO MUSSOLINI (1883–1945): Mussolini was a former socialist and editor of *Avanti*, who had turned interventionist and nationalist.
	April	President Wilson appealed against the Italian territorial claims on the Adriatic. The Italian delegation left the conference.
	September	THE SEIZURE OF FIUME BY NATIONALIST AND WAR HERO, GABRIELE D'ANNUNZIO, following President Wilson's rejection of the Italian claim to the town.
1920	August	A general lockout in the metallurgical factories leading to the occupation of the factories by workers.
	November	Treaty of Rapallo with Yugoslavia: Fiume to be an independent state.
	December	Declaration of war by d'Annunzio; Italian troops bombarded Fiume and forced him to evacuate it.
1921	January	Congress of the Socialist Party at Livorno: the Party split into radical and moderate wings.
	February	Communist and Fascist riots in Florence; the spread of clashes between the two factions.
	June	Fall of the GIOLITTI cabinet, replaced by Bonomi.
1922	February	New government headed by Facta.
	May	Fascists drove out Communist city government of Bologna. Conflict extended to all the larger cities.
	August	Fascists seized control of the Milan city government.
	October	Fascist Congress at Naples. Mussolini, having refused a seat in the Cabinet, demanded the resignation of Facta and the formation of a Fascist cabinet. THE MARCH ON ROME: the Fascists occupied Rome, the King having refused Facta's demand for the proclamation of martial law. Mussolini formed the Cabinet of Fascists and Nationalists.
	November	MUSSOLINI GRANTED DICTATORIAL POWERS BY THE KING AND PARLIAMENT: granted until the end of December 1923 to restore order and introduce reforms. Gradual consolidation of Fascist control. Constitution still technically in force.
1923	January	A voluntary Fascist Militia authorised by the King.
	August	THE CORFÙ INCIDENT: Greek appeal against Italy to the League of Nations.
	November	THE NEW ELECTORAL LAW: provision that any party securing the largest number of votes in an election (provided it had at least one-quarter of the total) should receive two-thirds of the seats.
1924	April	In the elections the Fascists received 375 as against the previous 35 seats.
	June	MURDER OF GIACOMO MATTEOTTI, Socialist deputy who had denounced the Fascists. THE AVENTINE SECESSION; majority of non-Fascist deputies left the Chamber.
	July	Rigid press censorship introduced.
	August	Meetings of opposition political groups forbidden.
1928	May	A NEW ELECTORAL LAW: universal suffrage abolished; the electorate reduced from 10 to 3 million. Candidates for election to be submitted to voters by the Fascist Grand Council.

1929	February	THE LATERAN TREATIES WITH THE PAPACY (ratified June) restored the temporal power of the Pope who was to rule over the Vatican City. A concordat with the Italian Government defined the position of the Church in the Fascist State; state indemnity for the Church.
	April	NATIONAL COUNCIL OF CORPORATIONS ESTABLISHED: to adjust disputes between various groups in the interests of national production. Composed of representatives from the syndicates, employers and government.
1933	July	THE FOUR POWER PACT: between Britain, France Italy and Germany.
1934	July	Attempted Nazi coup in Austria; Mussolini mobilised the army.
	November	Establishment of the Central Corporative Committee.
	December	Outbreak of conflict with Abyssinian troops at Wal Wal.
1935	January	FRANCO-ITALIAN AGREEMENT: in the hope of winning Italian support against Germany, Laval made large concessions to Italian claims in Abyssinia.
	April	THE STRESA CONFERENCE: called by France to consider action against German rearmament and to provide further guarantees for Austrian independence.
	October	ITALIAN INVASION OF ABYSSINIA, League Council declared Italy the aggressor.
	November	The League voted sanctions against Italy; failure of Powers to agree on oil sanction (1936).
1936	May	Italian army captured Addis Ababa. Annexation of all Abyssinia.
	July	League Council voted to discontinue sanctions. OUTBREAK OF THE SPANISH CIVIL WAR: from the start Mussolini supplied Francoist forces with men and equipment.
	October	Italian-German agreement over Austria: the basis for the Rome-Berlin Axis.
1937	December	THE WITHDRAWAL OF ITALY FROM THE LEAGUE.
1938	March	The German annexation of Austria. No objection offered by Italy.
	October	The Fascist Grand Council abolished the Chamber of Deputies, replacing it with a Chamber of Fasces and Corporations.
1939	April	ITALIAN INVASION AND CONQUEST OF ALBANIA.
	September	Italy declared neutrality at the outbreak of the Second World War.
1940	June	ITALY DECLARED WAR ON FRANCE AND BRITAIN.
	September	Italy, Germany and Japan concluded a three-power pact.
1943	July	MUSSOLINI RESIGNED and was placed under arrest. Replaced by MARSHAL BADOGLIO, who declared the Fascist Party dissolved.
	September	Badoglio accepted terms for Italian surrender. Mussolini rescued from captivity by German troops, proclaimed a Republican Fascist Party.
1945	April	Mussolini captured and executed by Italian anti-Fascist forces.

Illustrative questions and answers

1 To what extent is Mussolini's rise to power accounted for by the appeal of Fascism?

Tutorial note

This question invites a full discussion of the reasons why Mussolini came to power in 1922. The word 'appeal' in the question should be interpreted broadly, in terms of the promise of political stability, order and the revival of Italian national prestige as well as the narrower appeal of Fascist ideology.

You need to know about

The long-term causes of the abandonment of the parliamentary system in Italy and the forces and interests undermining it. The effect of the Versailles Treaty on Italian public opinion. The social instability in postwar Italy, e.g. the occupation of the factories. The forces demanding strong government and supporting Mussolini's Fascist bands. The political situation in 1922, particularly the attitude of the King and the Army.

Suggested answer plan

1   Introduction: postwar Europe saw a challenge to the parliamentary system – a particularly strong challenge to a democracy that had been recently established and was seen to be not working well; in Italy discontents with the political system were fuelled by a sense of grievance over the Versailles Treaty as it affected Italy, and by fears of general social disorder and the threat to property.

2   The weakness of the political structure: the Italian State was faced by a hostile Church; democracy was seen by the masses as a middle-class affair concerned with liberal freedoms rather than social betterment; democracy was undermined in 1915 by Italian intervention in the First World War; clear indication of the nature of a state dominated by interest groups.

3   The immediate postwar situation: the 1919 general elections, Liberals losing control of the Liberal state; difficulties in forming a stable and effective government – parliamentary paralysis; the effect on public opinion of the failure of the Versailles Treaty to fulfil earlier promises (e.g. the Treaty of London, 1915) to Italy.

4   The seizure of land; the occupation of factories; ex-servicemen form the nucleus of a new party and offer their services to the landed aristocracy and industrialists to suppress the Left; Fascism, which did so much to create disorder, appeared to many to promise the restoration of order; support for Fascism in the armed forces and Royal Family; the fear of Socialism leads the Catholic middle classes to rally to Mussolini.

5   The circumstances of Mussolini's appointment: this was not primarily due to the appeal of Fascism, which was vague and not widely known, but to the appeal of law and order and the fact that there appeared to be no credible alternative; the King who was fearful of being replaced by Aosta, agreed to the appointment of Mussolini in a coalition government; the significance of the March on Rome; official Italy favoured Fascism – a mainly Liberal parliament voted for Mussolini; the alternatives were seen to be military dictatorship or Bolshevism.

2   How did Mussolini consolidate his power in Italy after 1922?

Tutorial note

The question is asking for an examination of the means by which Mussolini transformed Italy from a parliamentary democracy into a Fascist state. It would be proper for you to look at, among other considerations, Church–State relations (as the Catholic Church had been hostile to the Italian State since the latter's creation). Though you may make reference to it, you should not dwell at length on his imperial policy.

You need to know about

Mussolini's use of emergency powers; the suppression of opposition newspapers and trade unions; and the creation of a special security force. New electoral laws. Control of education and the media. The corporate state, a National Assembly of Corporations replacing Parliament. Church–State relations and the Lateran Treaty.

Suggested answer plan

1 Introduction: Mussolini's assumption of power with the backing or connivance of the King, Army and industry; a *brief* assessment of the Fascist idea of the state.

2 The establishment of the new state on the basis of widespread national support; transformation of the political system: rule by decree replaced by a packed parliament based on the 1923 electoral law giving two-thirds of the seats to the Party getting one-quarter of the votes; the elections were managed by the police and the Blackshirts; there was support for Mussolini from numbers of Liberals and Catholics (the Clerico-fascists); Matteotti's published evidence of electoral malpractices led to his murder; the rigged Parliament further weakened in 1928 when the new electoral law enabled the Fascist Grand Council to decide who should be an MP; Mussolini was then President of the Grand Council and effectively Prime Minister for life; by 1934 this rump Parliament was in turn replaced by a National Assembly of Corporations.

3 The creation of a Fascist society: by 1927 there was the banning of non-Fascist parties, and the suppression of all opposition newspapers; strikes had been outlawed and trade unions of the traditional type had disappeared; there was the OVRA, the secret police; military tribunals had been empowered to deal with political offences; state employees were required to be Fascist Party members. To create a popular basis for a continuing support for Mussolini, the Ministry of Popular Culture was set up; Fascist textbooks had become compulsory and the youth were drafted into Fascist military-style organisations; propaganda in the press, on the radio and in the cinema; the Duce had become a symbol of the new Italy, virile, militaristic and united in purpose.

4 Mussolini's relationship with the traditional institutions; he was usurping more and more of the monarch's customary powers; the Church was won over by the Lateran Treaty, thus ending 60 years of Church–State rupture; the Church was protected by the regime; official Church support was given to the State – e.g. to the Fascist list of candidates in the plebiscite of 1929; Mussolini wooed the industrialists with new opportunities arising from the expansion in Africa and the development of the Italian air force.

3 Was Mussolini more than a 'sawdust Caesar'?

Tutorial note

You should concentrate on Mussolini's foreign policy and military achievements and failures and measure these against the grandiose imperial ambitions which he proclaimed for Italy.

You need to know about

Mussolini's declared imperial ambitions for Italy. Italian foreign policy under Fascism. The Italian campaign and conquest of Abyssinia and Italian intervention in the Spanish Civil War. Mussolini's contribution to the Second World War.

Suggested answer plan

1 Caesar had led his legions successfully against the barbarians; Mussolini's proclaimed ideal was to infuse Italians with martial ardour and to lead them against the contemporary barbarians (the Abyssinians), the effete races (the British and French) and such nations as Albania and Greece, which stood in the way of what he considered to be the natural path of Italian expansion, and the transformation of the Mediterranean into an Italian lake.

2 The Abyssinian campaign: even with relatively advanced military technology (aeroplanes, gas, etc) against half-armed tribesmen, Mussolini did not find it easy to defeat the Abyssinians. He was held up for two months and subsequently controlled the conquered territory by holding it in pockets and terroristic methods. However, the prestige victory over the Abyssinians (which

redressed the ignominious defeat of the Italians at the battle of Adowa in 1896) *seemed* gloriously successful to Italians at the time and Mussolini succeeded in rallying public opinion enthusiastically behind him. The defiance of the League had exposed British and French weakness – 52 nations had voted against Italy's action. It was a war which, in Denis Mack Smith's words, 'provided few casualties and many medals'. Mussolini now boasted that Fascist Italy, under strong leadership, had achieved what Liberal Italy had failed to do – to prove itself a major Power.

3 *However*, Mussolini's aping of Roman imperialism gave to Italians a wholly misleading impression of their country's potential strength, military preparedness and of his own capabilities as would-be Caesar. In fact, his megalomania and emphasis on 'Ducismo' proved more and more of a liability to Italy.

4 The Abyssinian War weakened the Italian economy and therefore restricted the likelihood of effective future military preparations; it depleted the war reserves and Italy ran into large budget deficits, in spite of recourse to compulsory loans and capital levies.

5 The impact on his foreign policy: initially he had been concerned to defend Austria against Germany but he abandoned Austria during the Abyssinian War and moved towards forging the 'brutal friendship' with Hitler. Mussolini convinced himself that he was the centre of European diplomatic activity (e.g. at Munich) but he was repeatedly upstaged and deceived by Hitler. He showed himself both fundamentally weak and unpredictable, – e.g. at one moment he vetoed the Anschluss and began to fortify the Brenner. At the next he announced that he was standing behind Germany. After the Anschluss his foreign policy showed a progressive subordination of Italian to German interests.

6 Mussolini declared that a major war was inevitable but he showed little aptitude for preparing for it. For instance (as contrasted with Germany) he did not use the Spanish Civil War to master new tactics or use new weapons. When Italy went to war, in June 1940, it was not merely militarily unprepared but in a state of marked political turmoil – the consensus which had supported the Abyssinian adventure was rapidly vanishing. 'Ducismo' was losing its hold and Mussolini had plainly not succeeded in militarising the spirit of the Italian people.

7 Mussolini admitted privately that Italy's unpreparedness for the First World War was as nothing in comparison with her unreadiness for the Second: equipment was antiquated and there was only enough ammunition for 60 days. Two weeks before his attack on Greece he had demobilised half his forces and then called up a fresh batch of 100,000 raw recruits. The attack proved a humiliating defeat and Italian troops were lucky to hang on to Albania. The subsequent German intervention in Greece and Yugoslavia put an end to Mussolini's ambitions in the Balkans. Note, too, the debacle in North Africa where 250,000 Italian troops were defeated by 30,000 British.

8 The case for describing Mussolini as a 'sawdust Caesar' can be fully substantiated. In his military and foreign policies it would be hard to argue that he was more than this. He *postured* as a great leader intent on grand imperialistic enterprises but he failed to plan effectively. He created large armies which he failed to equip. He proved himself very markedly inferior to Hitler as a dictator.

Question bank

1 Document question (Mussolini and the Rise of Fascism): study the extract below and then answer questions (a) to (g) which follow:

Extract

'When in the now distant March of 1919, speaking through the columns of the *Popolo d'Italia* I summoned to Milan the surviving interventionists who had intervened, and who had followed me ever since the foundation of the Fasci of revolutionary action in January 1915, I had in mind no specific doctrinal programme. The only doctrine of which I had practical experience was that of Socialism, from 1903–1904 until the winter of 1914 – nearly a decade. My experience was both that of a follower and a leader – but it was not doctrinal experience. My doctrine during that period had been the doctrine of action. A uniform, universally accepted doctrine of Socialism had not existed since 1905, when the revisionist movement, headed by Bernstein, arose in Germany, countered by the formation, in the see-saw of tendencies, of a Left-revolutionary movement which in Italy never quitted the field of phrases, whereas, in the case of Russian Socialism, it became the prelude to Bolshevism.

'The *Popolo d'Italia* described itself in its sub-title as "the daily organ of fighters and producers". The word "producers" was already the expression of a mental trend. Fascism was not the nurseling of a doctrine previously drafted at a desk; it was born of the need of action, and was action, it was not a party but, in the first two years, an anti-party and a movement. The name I gave the organisation fixed its character.

'The years preceding the March on Rome cover a period during which the need of action forbade delay and careful doctrinal elaborations. Fighting was going on in the towns and villages. There were discussions but…there was something more sacred and more important…death…. Fascists knew how to die. A doctrine – fully elaborated, divided up into chapters and paragraphs with annotations – may have been lacking, but it was replaced by something far more decisive – by a faith. All the same, if with the help of books, articles, resolutions passed at congresses, major and minor speeches, anyone should care to revive the memory of those days, he will find, provided he knows how to seek and select, that the doctrinal foundations were laid while the battle was still raging. Indeed, it was during those years that Fascist thought armed, refined itself, and proceeded ahead with its organisation. The problems of the individual and the state; the problems of authority and liberty; political, social, and more especially national problems were discussed; the conflict with liberal, democratic, socialistic, masonic doctrines and with those of the "Partito Popolare", was carried on at the same time as the punitive expeditions.'

(Mussolini, *Fascism, Doctrine and Institutions*, 1935)

(a) To whom is Mussolini referring as 'the surviving interventionists who had intervened'? (2)

(b) Why had Mussolini's experience of Socialism ended in 'the winter of 1914'? (2)

(c) Which sections of the Italian population were supposed to be included under the term 'producers'? (2)

(d) What were the 'political, social, and more especially national problems' of Italy in 1919–1922? (7)

(e) 'Fighting was going on in the towns and villages' of Italy in 1919–1922. Explain how this was important for the Fascists. (4)

(f) Compare the revolutionary activity of Italian Socialism in 1919–1922 with 'Russian Socialism' in 1917. (6)

(g) How far do Fascist slogans and Fascist doctrine support this explanation by Mussolini of the nature of Fascism in 'the years preceding the March on Rome'? (8)

2 What were the main features of Italian Fascism? (WJEC, June 1991)

3 'Little more than a show and a sham'. Discuss this view of Mussolini's domestic policies. (Oxford, June 1991)

4 How successful was Mussolini in implementing fascist policies in Italy between 1922 and 1939? (Oxford and Cambridge, June 1992)

5 Account for the collapse of democratic government EITHER in Italy in 1922 OR in Spain in 1936. (Oxford and Cambridge, 1991)

READING LIST

Standard textbook reading
J. M. Roberts, *Europe 1880–1945* (Longman, 1967), chapters 13, 15.
David Thomson, *Europe since Napoleon* (Penguin, 1977), chapters 23, 27, 28.
Anthony Wood, *Europe 1815–1945* (Longman, 1975), chapters 29, 31.

Further suggested reading
M. Blinkhorn, *Mussolini and Fascist Italy* (Methuen, 1984).
A. Cassels, *Fascist Italy* (Routledge, 1969).
F. Chabod, *A History of Italian Fascism* (Cedric Chivers, 1974).
M. Clark, *Modern Italy 1871–1982* (Longman, 1985).
H. Finer, *Mussolini's Italy* (F. Cass, 1964).

D. Mack Smith, *Italy – A Modern History* (Ann Arbor, 1969).
D. Mack Smith, *Mussolini* (Weidenfield and Nicolson, 1981).
G. Procacci, *A History of the Italian People* (Penguin, 1973).
E. M. Robertson, *Mussolini as Empire-builder: Europe and Africa 1932–36* (Macmillan, 1977).
Christopher Seton-Watson, *Italy from Liberalism to Fascism* (Methuen, 1967).
E. R. Tannenbaum, *Fascism in Italy: Society and Culture 1922–1945* (Allen Lane, 1973).
E. Wiskemann, *Fascism in Italy: its Development and Influence* (Macmillan, 1968).
S. Woolf, *European Fascism* (Weidenfeld and Nicolson, 1970).

CHAPTER 12

THE WEIMAR REPUBLIC AND NATIONAL SOCIALISM

Units in this chapter

Chapter objectives

❶ The end of the First World War; the origins and constitution of the Weimar Republic.

❷ The particular difficulties facing the new Republic; its association in the public mind with defeat and the unpopular Versailles Settlement; widespread social and political tensions and uprisings, e.g. the Kapp Putsch and the Spartacists; the weaknesses of the constitution; the dependence of Weimar on insecure coalitions; a sound understanding of the various parties and political alignments.

❸ The impact of the Ruhr invasion of 1923; the inflationary crisis.

❹ The importance of the relatively stable years 1924–9; the Dawes Plan; Gustav Stresemann and Locarno – Stresemann's objectives of understanding with the Western Powers and revision of the Eastern frontiers of Germany.

❺ The use made by the extremist parties of the unpopularity of the Versailles *Diktat* and the effect of the world depression which followed the crash of 1929; the origins of the Nazi Party and an explanation of its subsequent very rapid growth.

❻ Hitler's own background, personality and ideas; the appeal of his propaganda; the comprehensiveness of the Nazi movement with its appeal to an anti-Communist middle class, with its 'socialism' directed against Germany's traditional rulers and the promise of a restored German greatness; the importance to Nazism of the support from industrialists, bankers and Right-wing politicians.

❼ The 'Nazi seizure of power' in 1933; a detailed knowledge of the course of events leading to this and an explanation of how it came about; the Nazi emphasis on 'legality' and 'national revolution'; a consideration of the previous weakening of the Weimar democracy through government by presidential decree and the subsequent willingness of the parliamentary parties to vote their own end in the Enabling Law.

⑧ The process by which Nazi power was consolidated; the Reichstag Fire and the Enabling Act; the attitude to established institutions, e.g. the churches; the reign of terror; the racial laws.

⑨ Nazi economic and social policies.

⑩ Hitler's relationship with the Army, particularly the events leading to the Röhm purge (the Night of the Long Knives); the Army's attitude to the SA; the Army's oath of unconditional obedience to Hitler in his new role as Führer and Chancellor on the death of Hindenburg; the policies of conscription, rearmament and the reunification of the German people; the way in which these coincided with the Army's view of Germany's revival as a great Power.

The Weimar Republic was established as a presidential democracy following Germany's collapse in 1918. From the start it faced opposition from both the political Left and Right. It was widely associated in the German mind with the acceptance of the deeply resented Versailles *Diktat*, the implications of which were humiliatingly re-emphasised in the Ruhr invasion of 1923, by France and Belgium.

The period between 1924 and 1929 was one of relative stability in Germany. But after the economic collapse of 1929 political extremism gained the upper hand. The assumption of power in 1933 by Hitler, and the groups which supported him, exposed the widespread German opposition to Weimar democracy and the flaws in its constitution. Nazism, which had originated in postwar Bavaria, offered a mixture of violent nationalism, racialism and anti-Communism.

Once in power, and after the Reichstag fire, Hitler proceeded through legislation to set up a totalitarian order under the domination of the Nazi state and its *Führer* (leader). The process of the Nazi coordination of German society was accompanied by a reign of terror, of which a major element was anti-Semitic legislation and persecution. Socialistic social policies were combined with an attempt to secure maximum economic self-sufficiency and with preparations for war.

After the Night of the Long Knives, Hitler was granted an oath of unconditional loyalty from the Army and he merged the offices of Chancellor and President. The consolidation of Nazi power within Germany was the prelude to his expansionist foreign policy and military campaigns.

12.1 FOUNDATION OF THE REPUBLIC

The Weimar Republic was born out of Germany's defeat in the First World War. A combination of domestic upheaval and President Wilson's demands for the Kaiser's abdication led to its declaration by the new moderate Socialist Chancellor Ebert in November, 1918. The Republic constitution, drafted in the early months of 1919, established a democratically elected main chamber, the Reichstag; a second chamber, the Landrat, to represent the interests of the Länder (provinces); a popularly elected President and an electoral system with proportional representation.

Opposition to the Republic

From the start the new Republic was beset by difficulties. The Right-wing elements in German political life, which included the volunteer forces of ex-soldiers, the *Freikorps*, claimed that the new order had been brought about by revolutionaries. It was these, they argued, who had caused the internal collapse of Germany while the Army remained undefeated in the field. This was the legend of the 'stab in the back'.

The Republic also suffered from being forced by the Allies to accept the Diktat. In fact a large minority in the Reichstag voted against accepting the peace terms. In its early years, Weimar was assaulted by a series of attempted coups from both the extreme Left and the extreme Right such as the Spartacist revolt, the Kapp putsch and Hitler's abortive revolution in Munich.

In each instance, the Republic was dependent for its survival on the support or at least the neutrality of the Army, though the Kapp putsch was actually defeated by the actions of the German working class. But the Army was not the only institution left over from Imperial Germany on which the Republic was forced to rely.

Unable or unwilling to carry out a major change of personnel in the administration, the Republic's politicians continued to be served by a Civil Service and judiciary which had little sympathy for the new political system. As J. M. Roberts writes: 'The Right opposed Weimar parliamentarism as an affront to Nationalism; the Left regarded it as a cover for social conservatism.'

The weakness of the Weimar Constitution

The new political order was also flawed in its own constitutional structure. There were dangers in the system of proportional representation, which could lead to a multitude of small parties and instability. This was particularly so when they were faced with the violent nationalism of the Right and the militant emphasis on the unity of the German *Volk*.

There was potential danger in the popular election of the president, which created the possibility of his appealing to the German people over the head of the Reichstag; and in the presidential right to rule by emergency decree, a right designed and used originally to protect the Republic but one which could be used to undermine the democratic process. Further, in this system the Chancellor had a relative lack of control over his ministers, who were closely tied to the whims of the individual parties.

The main parties lending their support to the Weimar Republic were the Social Democratic Party, the Catholic Centre and the Liberal Democratic parties, though both of the latter drifted to the Right during the latter days of Weimar. The Communists and the National Socialists (Nazis), the extreme parties of the Left and Right, openly proclaimed their wish to overthrow the Weimar Republic. Stable coalitions of those parties willing to participate in a Republican government could only be achieved by either the exclusion of the Left or Right – both of which represented very powerful elements in Weimar society.

The Ruhr invasion and the Great Inflation

This vulnerable political structure and culture was further weakened by the French and Belgian invasion of the Ruhr in 1923, an action designed to secure reparations payments from Germany.

The German currency, already severely inflated by the government's need to pay for the war and its aftermath, spiralled into hyperinflation, due to a renewed crisis of confidence in the Mark and the government's resort to the printing press to finance its policy of passive resistance to the French. The result was the financial ruin of many middle-class Germans, many of whom already felt alienated from the Republic.

Inflation was finally halted with the introduction of a new stop-gap currency, the Rentenmark, and in 1924 an inter-Allied commission worked out the Dawes Plan for a revised arrangement for German reparations payments. This envisaged the economic recovery of Germany, a recovery which was financed largely on short-term loans borrowed from abroad, particularly from the US.

12.2 GUSTAV STRESEMANN

The German government accepted the Dawes Plan in spite of Right-wing opposition, and the German foreign minister, Stresemann, made further moves towards reconciliation with the West, reaching a high point with the Locarno Treaty of 1925. Stresemann's 'policy of fulfilment' was designed to make concessions which would return Germany to full sovereignty and independence as quickly as possible. But it did not abandon the aims of eventually removing reparations, achieving military equality and revising Germany's eastern frontiers. Though he did not exclude the possible use of force in the East, he was attacked by the Right wing as far too conciliatory and as a betrayer of German national interests.

The period 1924–29 was one of relative stability for Weimar, but the hostility of the Right towards Stresemann – arguably the Republic's most accomplished statesman, who was conspicuously patriotic and who was trying to restore Germany's status and strength within the framework of international relations – was ominous for the future. So, too, was the election in 1925 of the First World War hero Hindenburg to the Presidency. Although he was not the representative of the monarchist cause which some of the voters took him for, he was never a fervent supporter of Weimar and in his immediate circle there were many who were violently anti-Republican.

The move to the Right and the economic collapse

Following the accession of the press magnate Hugenburg to the leadership of the German Nationalists in 1928, the Party made a strong shift to the Right and was in the forefront of the 1929 campaign against the Young Plan, the new Allied scheme for reparations payments. The attack on the Young Plan was combined with a wholesale onslaught on the Republic, which brought into operation an alliance between the Nationalists and the National Socialists. Although, ultimately, the campaign failed to prevent the acceptance of the Young Plan, it was indicative of the scale of the Right-wing opposition to Weimar.

The year 1929 also saw the Wall Street crash, the prelude to the worldwide slump. This led to the recalling of those short-term loans on which Weimar's brief period of relative prosperity had been based. The subsequent depression led to a rapid rise in unemployment, reaching 6 million in 1932. It also resulted in the rapid spread of extremism in German life.

Because of the impossibility of maintaining a stable coalition, German chancellors were forced to rule from 1930 onwards by a combination of ad hoc majorities and presidential decrees. On the Left it was the Communists who gained most from the crisis; on the Right it was the Nazi Party which now – for the first time – became a really decisive force in German politics. In September, 1930, the Nazi Party won 107 seats in the Reichstag, and the Communists 77.

One should not overstate German hostility towards democracy. As Dr. Overy has reminded us, there were many in Germany who 'favoured the coming of democracy, Social Democrats, Liberals and the Catholic Centre Party among them.... The real problem was the stagnation of the German economy and the very unequal distribution of the economic cake, made it more difficult to produce a workable, effective, democratic political culture...'. The Nazi Party was 'a populist party feeding off social disillusionment on a grand scale.'

12.3 HITLER AND THE NAZI PARTY

The Nazi Party had its beginnings, in postwar Bavaria, as originally only one of a number of small radical Right-wing groups. Under the leadership of Adolf Hitler, with his extraordinary oratorical and propagandist talents, this rapidly became a significant force in Bavarian politics. The party suffered a major setback in 1923 with Hitler's abortive coup – an attempt in Munich to mount local forces and march on Berlin (in the year after Mussolini's March on Rome) led to his arrest, imprisonment and a temporary ban on the Party.

From this failure Hitler learnt one major lesson – power was not to be achieved by a coup, but through the democratic and constitutional processes of the Republic. Hitler chose the slower route of a legal accession to power, seeking to destroy Weimar from within rather than from without. This was the path he set out upon when the Party was reconstituted in 1925.

Hitler's ideology

Hitler, born an Austrian of lower-middle-class stock, had developed his basic ideas and prejudices as a layabout in Vienna in the early years of the century. These were a violent German nationalism, ideas of racial superiority, anti-semitism and anti-Marxism. These ideas were later combined with the fixed determination to overthrow the Versailles Settlement as well as the desire to acquire for Germany the massive addition of *Lebensraum* (living-space), in the East.

These themes are all contained in *Mein Kampf* ('My Struggle') which Hitler wrote in prison after the failed putsch of 1923. His experience as a soldier in the trenches during the First World War only served to strengthen these ideas as well as to develop in him an admiration for militaristic hierarchy. These ideas were presented to the German people with great political astuteness and had a widespread appeal, particularly among the demoralised lower middle classes with their deep fear of Communism, of the loss of social status and identity and their nostalgic hankering for the return of German greatness.

Nazism was presented as a movement that included the whole German Volk, not as a party in the traditional sense. In fact its objectives were the abolition of parties and factions, and the elevation of the power of the Nazi state and its leader over all – the creation of a totalitarian society. The Party had an anti-capitalist wing which promised to remove economic and social privilege. There were in the development of Nazism significant socialistic elements but Hitler tended to underplay them. He courted the support not only of the masses of the voters but also of the industrial, financial and politically conservative elites, setting out to persuade them that the Nazi Party was the only bastion against Communism. It should be noted that by no means all members of these groups supported National Socialism, for while they were inclined to endorse its anti-Communist and nationalistic appeal, they were apprehensive of its socially radical elements.

Hitler as chancellor

In the years 1930–32 the Nazi vote grew rapidly. Though he never gained an overall Nazi majority in the Reichstag, it was on the basis of that mass support that Hitler came to power. The Nazi use of the term 'seizure of power' is something of a misnomer. Hitler did not seize power. He was offered it. He had already demanded the Chancellorship in August, 1932 (the previous month the Nazis had become the largest party in the Reichstag with 230 seats) but had been refused by the current chancellor, Von Papen, and the president, Hindenburg.

However, neither Von Papen nor his successor, Schleicher, had been able to form a stable majority in the Reichstag. Von Papen continued negotiations with Hitler behind Schleicher's back and finally persuaded Hindenburg to give Hitler the Chancellorship in the National Socialist/Nationalist government.

As a representative of Germany's conservative elite, Von Papen believed that Hitler's party could be used to give mass popular backing to their attempt to create a conservative-dominated authoritarian state. This would, they hoped, return to Germany's privileged classes the political prominence they had enjoyed before Weimar. Hitler was to be their 'drummer'.

The conservative Right intended to use him to achieve *their* ends. In the event it was to be the other way round. Such a scheme could only operate in the context of the breakdown of parliamentary government and the consequently increased power of the President and the clique surrounding him.

The consolidation of Nazi power

The Nazis' legal takeover and their collaboration with the conservatives in the 'national revolution' was to prove an immense advantage to them when they began to consolidate their power. It provided them with full access to the administrative apparatus of the German state as well as with allies who were willing or eager to see the destruction of that state.

That consolidation or coordination (*Gleichschaltung*) proceeded along a number of lines. The legal basis for the Nazi takeover was established by two pieces of legislation.

First were the Reichstag Fire decrees which Hindenburg issued following the burning-down of the Reichstag by a Communist, possibly with the connivance of the Nazis. These suspended all civil liberties and provided the legal bases whereby the Land governments could be coordinated.

The second piece of legislation followed the March elections, when the Nazis and their nationalist allies gained an overall majority. This was the Enabling Act, which gave Hitler the right to rule by decree for four years and which was the prelude to the declaration of one-party rule. The Act allowed the government to pass laws without consulting the Reichstag.

The reign of terror A reign of terror was the background to the Nazi coordination, with beatings, murders and the establishment of concentration camps for political opponents. Some conservative institutions were fearful of Nazi radicalism. These Hitler bought off with promises which appealed to their self-interest: rearmament for the Army, a Concordat for the Roman Catholic Church, the suppression of the independent labour movement for big business (strikes were forbidden and the trades unions abolished, being supplanted by the Nazi Labour Front).

Hitler appeared to have something to offer for most groups in German society. The Jews, however, were to be ruthlessly excluded from the Aryan Reich. This was signalled by the official boycott of Jewish shops and the laws passed excluding them from public office. Anti-semitism was codified in particular in the Nuremberg Laws of 1935.

Economic policy Nazism wore the mask of benevolent Socialism for very many Germans. Not least, Hitler's job-creation schemes rapidly brought down the unemployment which had done so much to bring him to power. Here he expanded the work of previous governments in the provision of public-works programmes; by 1938 below half a million Germans were unemployed, this fall being also accounted for by the revival in world trade.

The policy involved state control over the German capital and credit system and the state direction of investment. By 1938 the State was investing five times as much money as in 1933. Strict controls were also imposed over prices and wages. The Nazi Goverment pursued a policy of economic nationalism which came close making Germany a siege economy.

The fear of indebtedness was lifted from thousands of German farmers by the hereditary farm law which guaranteed ownership in perpetuity; a new scheme was established to coordinate agricultural production. At the same time, new plans were developed to reduce Germany's expenditure of foreign currency, involving both complicated trading procedures and the encouragement of home production rather than imports. These programmes were designed not only to improve the performance of the German economy; they were also intended to make Germany self-sufficient in food and essential raw materials.

Totalitarian control Nazi rule penetrated every aspect of German life (its control and pervasiveness were markedly more comprehensive than that of Italian Fascism). Schools were purged of opposition elements amongst the staff and were instructed to teach in accordance with Nazi ideology. Membership of the Nazi Hitler Youth became obligatory in 1936 and gradually all other youth groups were dissolved. Marriage and population growth were promoted through propaganda and financial concessions.

Significantly, too, the historic subdivisions of Germany were done away with in

1933 and in fact the Nazi *Gleichschaltung* ended the dominance of Prussia in Germany which had been the legacy of the *Kleindeutschland* unification of Germany under Bismarck.

The Army Hitler still, however, required the support of powerful conservative institutions. His relationship with the Army, the institution which could have toppled him, was threatened by the SA, the Nazi stormtroops who, under Röhm, were seeking to usurp the Army's position. They also contained the most distinctively radical elements in the Nazi Party. Furthermore, the independent attitude of Röhm threatened Hitler's position within the Nazi movement itself. To deal with this threat, as well as to settle old scores with other figures, such as Schleicher, Hitler had the SA leaders and others removed in the Night of the Long Knives (30 June, 1934).

The Army, whose attitude had been equivocal towards Hitler, rewarded him for this action by granting him an oath of unconditional loyalty and by accepting his merger of the offices of chancellor and president, thus conferring on himself total dictatorial power.

But the elimination of the SA was not the only reason for the Army's allegiance to Hitler. In the following years he set about sweeping away the hated Treaty of Versailles, He introduced conscription, building up Germany's armaments and, on the basis of this strength, first through diplomacy and then by war, undid the territorial arrangements of the postwar settlement in order to restore Germany to the rank of a world power and to assert her hegemony over Europe.

12.4 CHRONOLOGY

1918	November	The ABDICATION OF KAISER WILLIAM ANNOUNCED IN BERLIN: a Republic proclaimed. The government entrusted to Friedrich Ebert and Philipp Scheidmann. A joint administration of Independent and Majority Socialists took control in Berlin. The struggle between the extreme Left SPARTACISTS and the Majority Socialists.
1919	January	THE SPARTACIST REVOLT IN BERLIN, crushed by the provisional government and the Army. Election of a national assembly to draw up a constitution.
	April	Soviet Republic established in Bavaria; overthrown by forces of the Federal Government.
	June	Proclamation of a Rhineland Republic. UNCONDITIONAL ACCEPTANCE OF THE PEACE TREATY. Germany signed the Treaty of VERSAILLES.
	July	ADOPTION OF THE WEIMAR CONSTITUTION: the President, elected for a seven-year term, was to appoint a Chancellor who in turn chose a cabinet which could command majority support in the Reichstag. By Articles 25 and 48 the President was empowered to suspend constitutional guarantees and dissolve the Reichstag in periods of national emergency. Federal rights were guaranteed. A system of proportional representation ensured that minority parties were represented. Also it meant government by coalition.
1920	February	HITLER PROCLAIMED THE 25 POINTS OF THE NATIONAL SOCIALIST PROGRAMME.
	March	THE KAPP PUTSCH: a monarchical coup involving the seizure of government buildings in Berlin. The Government fled to Stuttgart, but the movement collapsed as a result of the general strike of the trade unions.
	May	Germany received reparations bill of 132 billion marks.
	July	Spa Conference: the Germans signed a protocol of disarmament and arranged for reparations payments.
1921	March	Allied occupation of Düsseldorf, Duisburg and Ruhrort because of alleged German default in reparations payments.
1922	April	Treaty of Rapallo with Russia.
	June	Assassination of WALTHER RATHENAU.

1923	January	OCCUPATION OF THE RUHR by French and Belgian troops after Germany had been declared in default. The occupation was condemned by the British and Americans and led to passive resistance among the Ruhr workers. The Government supported this resistance.
	August	New government formed by GUSTAV STRESEMANN, leader of the People's Party.
	September	The government ended passive resistance. Astronomic monetary inflation in Germany.
	November	THE BEER HALL PUTSCH IN MUNICH: General Ludendorff and Adolf Hitler, leader of the growing National Socialist Party, attempted to overthrow the Bavarian Government. The rising was easily put down. Hitler was imprisoned, during which time he wrote *MEIN KAMPF*.
1924	April	THE DAWES PLAN: helped Germany to meet her treaty obligations in the period 1924–9. Gave stability to the German economy.
1925	April	FIELD MARSHAL VON HINDENBURG elected President of the Weimar Republic.
	October	The Reichstag ratified the Locarno treaties.
1926	September	Germany entered the League of Nations.
1929	September	French forced to evacuate demilitarised Rhineland.
	October	WALL ST CRASH, signalling the onset of the Great Depression.
1930	September	REICHSTAG ELECTIONS: emergence of Hitler's National Socialists as a major party (107 seats as against a previous 12).
1931	March	Project for a German-Austrian customs union; rejected by France and the World Court.
	May	The failure of the Austrian Credit-Anstalt, marking the start of the financial collapse in central Europe. By the beginning of 1932 the number of German unemployed was already more than 6 m.
	July	Hoover moratorium on reparations and war debts.
1932	May	BRÜNING resigned; VON PAPEN asked by President Hindenburg to form a Ministry responsible to the Executive alone.
	June	The government lifted the ban on the Nazi storm troops. Von Papen coup against the Socialist state government of Prussia.
	July	REICHSTAG ELECTIONS: the Nazis returned more candidates (230) than any other party.
	August	Hitler refused Hindenburg's request that he serve as Vice-Chancellor under Von Papen.
	September	The Reichstag dissolved: the impossibility of securing popular support for Von Papen.
	November	Resignation of Papen. Hitler rejected the conditional offer of the chancellorship. His demand for full powers was refused by Hindenburg.
	December	GENERAL VON SCHLEICHER formed a new cabinet.
1933	January	Schleicher was forced to resign after his efforts to conciliate the Left and Centre had failed. HITLER BECAME CHANCELLOR: the Ministry was regarded as a coalition of National Socialists and Nationalists.
	February	THE REICHSTAG fire: the Nazis claimed that it was the first move in a Communist conspiracy. Emergency decrees were issued, suspending the constitutional guarantees.
	March	The first Reichstag elections of the Weimar Republic: the Nazi terror. THE ENABLING ACT PASSED BY THE REICHSTAG AND REICHSRAT: the Nazi dictatorship firmly established. Suspension of the Weimar Constitution
	April	The Civil Service Law.
	July	THE NAZI PARTY DECLARED THE ONLY POLITICAL PARTY. CONCORDAT WITH THE VATICAN.
1934	January	THE REICHSRAT REPRESENTING THE STATES WAS ABOLISHED. Germany became a national rather than a federal state.
	May	Creation of the People's Court which was set up to try cases of treason. Proceedings to be secret. No appeal except to the Führer.
	October	Constitution of the NAZI LABOUR FRONT.
	June	THE RÖHM PURGE – THE NIGHT OF THE LONG KNIVES directed primarily against representatives of the more radical social revolutionary wing of the Nazi Party which aimed at far-reaching changes in society and the incorporation of the storm troops into the German Army.

	August	LAW CONCERNING THE HEAD OF STATE, COMBINING THE PRESIDENCY AND CHANCELLOR-SHIP. Death of Hindenburg. Plebiscite approved of Hitler's assumption of the presidency and of sole executive power.
1935	September	THE NUREMBURG LAWS: all Jews in Germany reduced to second-class citizens; professions closed to the Jews; the banning of intermarriage with them.
1936	October	THE FOUR-YEAR PLAN: policy of economic self-sufficiency which would make Germany independent, especially in raw materials, in the event of war.
1938	February	REORGANISATION OF THE MILITARY AND DIPLOMATIC COMMAND: VON BLOMBERG, War Minister and VON FRITSCH, Commander-in-Chief of the Army, were removed. Hitler assumed the Ministry of War

Illustrative questions and answers

1   How significant was the support of the German Army and its leaders in the establishment and consolidation of Hitler's power before the outbreak of the Second World War?

Tutorial note

The point is to assess just how much the Army had the power to stand in Hitler's way and whether or not it was the support of the Army which allowed Hitler to achieve his final mastery over Germany. You should give equal attention to both the establishment and consolidation of his power. Note that the question seems to assume that the Army supported Hitler from the start. This can be argued to be a mistaken assumption. One can, on the contrary, approach the question from the opposite angle, examining how Hitler managed to gain its support.

You need to know about

The relationship between Hitler and the German Army. The course of political events in Germany from 1918–39, with special regard to military involvement in civilian politics. The social basis of Nazi support.

Suggested answer plan

1   Nazism and German militarism are so synonymous in the popular imagination that the demise of the Weimar Republic and the emergence of the Nazi state *seemed* to follow inevitably, and the Röhm putsch (the Night of the Long Knives) of 1934 is seen as the culmination of the alliance between the Nazi Party and the Army which carried Hitler to absolute power. However, the relationship between the Army leadership and the Nazis was not so simple. The former were the old aristocratic Right of German society and antipathetic to the new 'radical Right'. It is not a simply story of the Army supporting Hitler from the start, but of Hitler *winning* army loyalty.

2   The initial Army attitude: there was some sympathy with the Nazis and SA (who were ex-Freikorps members) as a force against the Left, particularly the Communists and the trade unions; note that the Weimar Republic was supported by the 1918 Groening-Ebert pact against disorder; the Nazis were also seen, though, as a threat to order (e.g. Prussia, where the state was Socialist and the Nazis conflicted with authority).

3   The Army and Hitler's accession to power; the support for Brüning; note that the Army was working to try and block the Nazis from gaining power; in the end Hitler achieved prominence because of his popularity with the electorate, i.e. *despite* Army attempts to prevent him.

4   Once in power, Hitler worked to secure the trust of the Army leadership; they
     saw him, as many of the German industrialists did, as a bastion against the Left;
     they supported him against the radical wing of the Nazi Party, the SA. The Röhm
     putsch is a classic example of Hitler's capacity to divide and rule; standing by
     while the SS despatched the SA leadership and also killed off Schleicher and
     Bredow, the Army compromised themselves with the regime.

5   The personal oath of the Generals to Hitler; after the Hossbach Memorandum
     of 1937 Blomberg and Fritsch were dismissed; after this the Army was in Hitler's
     grip; the only resistance occurred in 1944 (the Stauffenberg plot), when the
     defeat of Germany loomed.

6   Ironically, then, it is not the Army's initial support but its failure to stop Nazism
     in 1932–3 which is all-important; the Army leadership's antipathy to Nazism
     was only overcome by the seeming irresistibility of Hitler's mass popularity with
     the electorate. Subsequently it is easy to see why the Army supported a leader
     who promised a re-emergence of the prestige of their institution in German life
     and who also shared their ambitions for national aggrandisement.

7   It could be argued that it was as much Hitler himself who caused the support
     of the Army; he used a natural sympathy for his nationalist and anti-Leftist aims
     (if not for his style) to subjugate an initially reluctant Army to offer unswerving
     loyalty. It was not so much the Army's support for Hitler that was important as
     his ability to produce that support in the first place and so to use the Army to
     enact his designs after 1939.

2   'Hitler's acquisition of power is more easily explained than his retention of it'.
     Do you agree?

Tutorial note

The question requires you to explain how Hitler first gained power. You must then
explain how he avoided becoming simply an instrument for the conservative wing
of German political life (a 'front man' for another coalition of the Right) and how he
went on to establish and consolidate the Nazi state.

You need to know about

The previous course of German politics, with particular attention to the years 1929–
33: the economic collapse, the rapid expansion of the Nazi Party and the
increasingly authoritarian nature of German government before Hitler. The reasons
for the appeal of Nazism and the basis of its support. Hitler's achievement of power
and the passing of the Enabling Act. The destruction of organised opposition; the
key role of the Army, particularly in the 1934 purge. The reason why Hitler's policies
were regarded as successful within Germany.

Suggested answer plan

1   Hitler's achievement of office was often thought of as a great tragic accident
     – due to a gamble, by the conservative upper classes through their representa-
     tives, which failed: it was seen as the gaining of power with their connivance
     in order to resist the Left; as outsmarting them and consolidating his political
     control through the 'Gleichschaltung'. On the other hand, one should not
     overstress the contribution of his personality and tactical astuteness at the
     expense of the underlying reasons why there was a wide basis of support for
     Nazism in German society.

2   An explanation of the collapse of the Weimar Republic: the economic slump
     sharply exposing a German lack of faith in democracy; constitutional weak-
     nesses; Brüning and government by decree; growing extremism at the expense
     of both liberal and conservative parties (e.g. the September 1930 elections);
     Right-wing radicalism in the face of a perceived threat to German society from
     Communism; this fear was skilfully used by Hitler, who won the support of
     bankers and industrialists, who in turn saw him as someone whom they could
     use to their own ends.

3   The immediate circumstances of Hitler's coming to power; the emphasis on the strength of popular support; note that subsequently the Enabling Act was passed with the support of all the parliamentary parties, except that of the Socialists and Communists. Note the skilful use of propaganda by the Nazis, particularly Goebbels' contribution.

4   Once in power by legal means, Hitler began to build the Nazi state and he banned, imprisoned and suppressed any opposition; within the Nazi movement the populist wing, the SA, was subordinated (with Army support) in the Röhm putsch, thus securing the loyalty of the Army to the regime.

5   In consolidating his control, Hitler depended partly upon the tradition of obedience to authority in German society and increasingly upon the image of a new, powerful and successful Germany. The ways in which he satisfied different groups in society: the working class with employment and social benefits; industrialists with rearmament and the pledge to defend society against Marxism; the Army with conscription and rearmament. He was helped by the economic recovery of the mid–late 1930s. Nazism appeared to offer national unity and purpose after the divisions of Weimar, and the great majority of Germans welcomed the success of Nazi foreign policy.

6   Both Hitler's acquisition and retention of power depended to a considerable extent on his political astuteness; he used the Weimar political system with great skill; once in power he used parliamentary means to suspend the constitution and then built his regime up by subordinating national institutions and organisations to Nazi purposes; his continuance in power rested on very widespread public support and also on his willingness to use methods which traditional German rulers would not normally have countenanced. Bearing these points in mind, it can, perhaps, be argued that his retention of power is more easily explained than his acquisition of it.

3   What grounds were there, by 1929, for believing that democracy had taken root in postwar Germany?

Tutorial note

This requires you to concentrate on the Weimar system of government and its relation to German public opinion. You should try and assess whether or not, before its collapse, it was working – and working *democratically*. You should then make some observations on the cause of the subsequent collapse.

You need to know about

Details of Weimar politics and a clear idea of the relations between the main interest groups, the industrialists, unions and the government. Economic developments and problems during Weimar, especially reparations, the Great Inflation and its social consequences. The constitution of the Weimar Republic and postwar attitudes towards it in Germany.

Suggested answer plan

1   Superficially things may have appeared stable in 1929; however, the prosperity and Liberalism of Weimar were largely a mirage and there were serious flaws in its democratic character.

2   The Western idea of democracy: the belief in government by the will of the majority of the people, with the rights of all protected by a constitution; also there was the connotation that the people would have the power to make its will effective through parliament.

3   Compare Weimar's constitution with this: show the extent to which it is 'democratic', viz. universal suffrage, the protection of rights, enactment by majority in the Reichstag; control of the executive through a democratically elected President with wide emergency powers over the state; Weimar was *formally* governed by 'vox populi'.

4   Note, however, that for democracy to work there must be a general consensus that the best way of settling differences is by each individual voting for a representative in a political party in an assembly which will then give the decision by vote; this approach of government is usually guaranteed by a protection of civil rights which 'all' accept as sacrosanct. Germany did *not* function in this way before or after 1929.

5   The inflation: the impact of this on the middle classes; those suffering from the economic crisis were alienated from the state, which was felt not to be acting in their interests; the pressure of the large-interest groups, not the ballot box, was felt to be deciding government policy; it was widely felt that Germany was operating on the cartel principle (of group interest) and not democratically (in the public interest); the middle classes felt ignored; see how, late in 1929, the question of social insurance created deadlock in the coalition.

6   Weimar politics was 'interest politics': the middle classes in particular were not reconciled to the social revolution and national defeat; all sides were only content so long as the economic prosperity of the Stresemann period continued; but this was a very fragile thing, dependent on loans.

7   Under the Weimar Republic, Germany in many respects remained backward-looking – to past glories of the Wilhelmine Reich rather than forward to a democratic future. By 1929 Germany had not truly taken to the democracy foisted on to her after defeat in 1918. Old forms of cartelisation and interest politics found new expression in the cobbled-together coalitions of Weimar. A large section of the population was in any case antipathetic to the new state.

Question bank

1   Document question (The Nazis in 1933): study the extracts below and then answer questions (a) to (h) which follow:

JANUARY 30th, 1933
'...Chief-of-Staff Röhm stands at the window the whole time, watching the door of the Chancellery from which the Leader must emerge... .

'The Leader is coming. A few moments later he is with us. He says nothing, and we all remain silent also. His eyes are full of tears. It has come! The Leader is appointed Chancellor. He has already been sworn in by the President of the Reich. The final decision has been made. Germany is at a turning-point in her history....'

FEBRUARY 3rd, 1933
'I talk over the beginning of the election campaign in detail with the Leader. The struggle is a light one now, since we are able to employ all means of the State. Radio and Press are at our disposal... . The Leader is to speak in all towns having their own broadcasting station. We transmit the broadcast to the entire people and give listeners-in a clear idea of all that occurs at our meetings.

'I am going to introduce the Leader's address, in which I shall try to convey to the hearers the magical atmosphere of our huge demonstrations.'

FEBRUARY 27th, 1933
'...Suddenly a phone call from Dr. Hanfstaengl: "The Reichstag is on fire!"....
There is no doubt but that Communism has made a last attempt to cause disorder....
Goering at once suppresses the entire Communist and Social Democrat Press. Officials of the Communist Party are arrested during the night. The S.A. is warned to stand by for every contingency.'

MARCH 24th, 1933
'The Leader delivers an address to the German Reichstag. He is in good form....
The Zentrum and even the Staatspartei affirm the law of authorisation...only the Socialists vote against it. Now we are also constitutionally masters of the Reich.

'...Now the discussions with the trade unions begin. We shall not have any peace before we have entirely captured these.'

MARCH 27th, 1933

'Dictate a sharp article against the Jewish horrors propaganda. The proclamation of <u>the boycott</u> already makes the whole clan tremble in their shoes.... The Jewish Press is whimpering with alarm and fear....'

MAY 1st, 1933

'The great Day of the German Nation has arrived.... An endless continuous stream of men, women and children flows to the Tempelhofer Feld…a million and a half people have assembled there…Then the Leader speaks…Germany is at stake, its future and the future of our children. A wild frenzy of enthusiasm has seized the crowd.

'…Tomorrow we shall seize the houses of the trade unions. There will hardly be any resistance anywhere. The struggle is going on!'

(Joseph Goebbels, *My Part in Germany's Fight*, 1935)

(a) Identify 'the President of the Reich'. (1)
(b) State briefly what happened to Röhm, and explain why it happened. (3)
(c) What was each of the following: 'the S.A.'; 'the Zentrum'; 'the boycott'? (3)
(d) Explain the importance of 'the law of authorisation'. (4)
(e) These extracts were written for publication. Comment on the style which Goebbels used. (3)
(f) Identify three groups of people whom, according to these extracts, the Nazis regarded as their enemies. (3)
(g) What do these extracts reveal of the methods by which the Nazis strengthened their position once they were in power? (6)
(h) On what grounds would you agree or disagree with the assertion that on 30 January 1933, Germany was 'at a turning-point in her history'? (8)

2 'We should not be surprised that it did not last, but astonished that it lasted so long'. Discuss this view of the Weimar Republic. (AEB, June 1988)

3 In what ways, and how successfully, did Nazi Germany attempt to deal with its economic problems between 1933 and 1945? (Cambridge, June 1991)

4 Why did Germans vote for Hitler and the Nazi Party up to 1933? (Cambridge, Summer 1986)

5 How important are economic factors in explaining the failure of the Weimar Republic? (Oxford and Cambridge, June 1992)

READING LIST

Standard textbook reading
J. M. Roberts, *Europe 1880–1945* (Longman, 1967), chapter 13.
David Thomson, *Europe since Napoleon* (Penguin, 1977), chapters 23, 25, 26, 27.
Anthony Wood, *Europe 1815–1945* (Longman, 1975), chapters 29–30.

Further suggested reading
K. D. Bracher, *The German Dictatorship* (Penguin, 1973).
M. Broszat, *The Hitler State* (Longman, 1981).
A. Bullock, *Hitler: a Study in Tyranny* (Penguin, 1968).
W. Carr, *Hitler: A Study in Personality and Politics* (Edward Arnold, 1986).
J. Fest, *Hitler* (Penguin, 1977).

J. W. Hiden, *The Weimar Republic* (Longman, 1974).
I. Kershaw, *Hitler* (Longman, 1991)
A. J. Nicholls, *Weimar and the Rise of Hitler* (Macmillan, 1979).
J. Noakes and G. Pridham (eds.), *Documents on Nazism 1919–1945* (Cape, 1974).
A. J. Ryder, *Twentieth-Century Germany from Bismarck to Brandt* (Macmillan, 1973).
W. L. Shirer, *The Rise and Fall of the Third Reich* (Pan, 1968).
J. P. Stern, *Hitler, the Führer and the People* (Fontana, 1984).
D. G. Williamson, *The Third Reich* (Longman, 1982).
E. Wiskemann, *Europe of the Dictators* (Fontana, 1973).

THE APPROACH OF WAR, 1933-9

Units in this chapter

Chapter objectives

❶ The significance of the following events in the breakdown of the international order during the 1930s: Japan's attack on Manchuria; the Abyssinian War; Hitler's reoccupation of the Rhineland; the Anschluss; the Czechoslovak crises.

❷ The significance of the intervention of Germany, Italy and the Soviet Union in the Spanish Civil War; the influence of the war on subsequent events and on the relations between the Powers; the role of Britain and France in the Spanish Civil War.

❸ A detailed grasp of the course of events from the Munich Conference to the outbreak of war in 1939: particularly the German occupation of Bohemia and Moravia; the Molotov-Ribbentrop Pact and the Polish crisis.

❹ The various arguments advanced in the West in favour of the appeasement of Germany and Italy; particularly the reasons why there was widespread acceptance that the Germans had good justification for violating the Treaty of Versailles; a clear understanding of the territorial, military and economic effects of the Treaty.

❺ How Britain helped to undermine the Versailles system by her failure to threaten action in the Rhineland crisis of 1936, by the Anglo-German Naval Treaty of 1935 (which represented a unilateral breaking of Versailles); Britain's willingness to accept the Anschluss and the sacrifice of Czechoslovakia; an explanation of official British policy during these events.

❻ The foreign policy of the Soviet Union in this period: the reasons why she was an unlikely ally for the Western democracies; the influence of the fear of Soviet Communism on Western policies; the belief in some quarters that the real enemy was not Germany but Communism and that a strong and rearmed Germany could be an effective bulwark against this danger; how this affected Anglo-French attitudes, for instance at the Munich Conference (where Russian interests were not considered); the negotiations between Britain, France and the Soviet Union in the weeks preceding the Russo-German pact.

⑦ The development of relations between Germany and Italy; an explanation of the Pact of Steel.

⑧ The reasons for the failure of the League of Nations to preserve peace; a consideration both of its weakness as a peace-keeping organisation and of its handling of the crises which confronted it, with particular reference to the Abyssinian War; the League and public opinion.

⑨ Hitler's foreign policy: his aims and ideas of German aggrandisement and racist domination; his tactics for their achievement; the extent to which his actions were determined by long-term calculations and ambitions or by opportunism; the extent to which a widespread acceptance of the German case for revision of the Versailles Treaty worked for him up to and after the Munich Conference.

⑩ The British and French responses to German policy after the Munich Conference, e.g., the guarantee to Poland; the revolt of public opinion against appeasement and its influence in the immediate prewar period.

During the 1930s the hopes of the peacemakers of 1919 were destroyed and the League of Nations proved unable to prevent the aggression of Germany, Italy and Japan. The Manchurian crisis revealed the weakness of the League as an institution capable of preserving peace. Its credibility was at an end when it failed to impede Mussolini's conquest of Abyssinia. From 1933 onwards Hitler and Mussolini challenged the existing order.

The origins of the Second World War lie both in their actions and in the other Powers' reaction – or lack of effective reaction – to them. Soon after coming to power in 1933 Hitler withdrew Germany from the disarmament negotiations at Geneva and pulled out of the League of Nations. He announced his determination to reverse the 'humiliation' of the Versailles Treaty and also demanded the conquest of 'Lebensraum' (living space) for the German people in the East and the subjugation of the Slavs.

The major events leading towards war were the German reoccupation of the Rhineland, the Spanish civil war, the Anschluss, the ceding of the Sudentenland to Germany after the Munich Conference, the subsequent dismemberment of Czecho-slovakia and the German-Polish dispute.

There was a very strong public sentiment in favour of peace in these years and a marked willingness of the Western governments – for a range of reasons – to appease the aggressor Powers. British and French policy did much to convince Hitler that they would not resist his demands by military means. The mutual distrust between the Soviet Union and the Western Powers further weakened the prospect of peace.

The Molotov-Ribbentrop Pact, in which Russia and Germany agreed on the partition of Poland, together with the Western guarantee to Poland set the scene for the invasion of September 1939, and the subsequent wider conflict.

13.1 THE ECONOMIC CRISIS

The world economic crisis of 1929–33 was a major cause of the collapse of the Versailles settlement. The economic breakdown, with a shrinking export trade and mass unemployment, led to political upheaval, hostility between states and the end of peace.

Particularly it encouraged political extremism, both of the Left and the Right. Germany was the most striking example of this. There, massive unemployment reinforced the existing deep resentment against the Diktat, reparations and the Weimar Republic. It dramatically boosted the fortunes of Hitler's Nazis.

The collapse of the national economies led countries to be more than ever preoccupied with their domestic social and economic problems. The prospect of costly rearmament, funded by heavy taxation or loans, was more than ever unwelcome to those democratic countries whose most pressing concern was to achieve economic recovery. This strengthened the argument for appeasement and encouraged the Western Powers (Britain and France) to conciliate Italy and Germany.

13.2 THE BREAKDOWN OF INTERNATIONAL ORDER

Manchuria

The Manchurian affair of 1931–3, which began when Japanese forces seized key points in Manchuria from Chinese garrisons, damaged the authority of the League of Nations and the credibility of the idea of collective security or international peace-keeping. It weakened the confidence particularly of those in the democratic states who believed that peace could be preserved by such an organisation.

Following the Lytton Commission, which went to investigate the situation in the Far East and censured Japan for resorting to force, Japan left the League. This example of a successful aggressor power defying the League was not lost on the leaders of Germany and Italy.

German demands for equality and rearmament

Hitler's impact on international affairs was felt soon after his accession to power in January 1933. Germany had insisted on equality of rights in the Geneva disarmament talks. Such demands were regarded by France – which sensed herself to be very vulnerable in the event of any expansion of German power – as quite unacceptable. In October 1933, Hitler ended German participation in the conference and openly rejected disarmament clauses of the Treaty of Versailles.

In the spring of 1934 France rejected further disarmament discussions. She attempted, without success, to establish the same sort of guarantee for Eastern Europe (an 'Eastern Locarno') as had been achieved in 1925 for the West (see Chapter 9). France signed a pact with Soviet Russia in 1935 but this did not strengthen her position; in some respects it weakened it. It was highly controversial, being violently opposed by Right-wing political circles, and there were no subsequent staff talks between the French and Russian military. In 1936 France began to rearm.

The Abyssinian crisis

The consequences of Mussolini's invasion of Abyssinia were no less grave: the League imposed sanctions on Mussolini but not the oil embargo, which could have stopped him. Britain and France tried to put off Mussolini with the Hoare-Laval Pact of December, 1935, by which two-thirds of Abyssinia would have been ceded to Italy.

This brought speedy condemnation in the British Parliament and from supporters of the League. The Government were seen on the one hand to be openly supporting the League and on the other to be doing a deal with the aggressor. Within six months the Italians had conquered Abyssinia. The results for international relations of the Abyssinian crisis included the following:

❶ The recently constructed Stresa 'front' of Britain, France and Italy, whose purpose was to defend the international order and more specifically to guard against German aggrandisement, was destroyed.

❷ The League of Nations could no longer be considered an effective peace-maker and it exercised no significant influence on subsequent events.

❸ Italy was isolated. This led to the Rome-Berlin Axis of October 1936, the prelude to the wartime alliance of the Fascist Powers.

❹ Italy abandoned her resistance to the German domination of Austria. This was shown during the Anschluss (the takeover of Austria) and contrasts with Mussolini's reaction at the time of the murder of Dollfuss and the abortive Nazi putsch in July 1934.

❺ Hitler was given further evidence of British and French unwillingness to resist aggression.

The German reoccupation of the Rhineland

While Britain and France were distracted by the Abyssinian war, Hitler struck his first blow against the territorial order. In March 1936, he reoccupied the Rhineland. In order to justify this he argued that the Franco-Soviet Pact of 1935 contradicted the Treaty of Locarno and threatened Germany. In fact, his invasion and remilitarisation violated both the Treaty of Versailles and the Treaty of Locarno.

This action was of very great strategic, as well as political, significance and was the essential prelude to any revision of the eastern boundaries of Germany. By closing the gap in Germany's western frontier, Hitler could block a French offensive in aid of Poland or Czechoslovakia.

It was a major gamble, but the failure of Britain and France to stop Hitler confirmed further his diagnosis of the weakness of the Western democracies while at the same time enhancing his own reputation within Germany.

The Spanish Civil War

Immediately after the outbreak of the civil war in July 1936, the Spanish Popular Front government asked France for arms. At the same time, General Franco, leader of the military revolt, requested help from Germany and Italy. Within weeks Italy, Germany and the Soviet Union were supplying men and arms. The French Popular Front government proposed a non-intervention agreement. Of the Powers, only Britain fully respected this while France allowed a small quantity of supplies to reach Spain.

The Spanish Civil War deeply divided public opinion and nowhere more so than in France, which was already at odds over the Franco-Soviet Pact. The decisive consideration for Britain and France, though, was the danger of a general European war if they became involved in Spain. Such a war neither of them were willing to contemplate. On the contrary, Chamberlain was working to restore relations with Italy and regarded the Spanish conflict as an obstruction to his strategy for European security.

13.3 THE NAZI EXPANSION

Within a few weeks of coming to power Hitler was addressing his High Command on the need for 'the conquest of new Lebensraum (living space) in the East and ruthless Germanisation'. Following his reoccupation of the Rhineland his aggressive intentions became increasingly apparent.

Though he did not have a clearly predetermined timetable, his objectives were constant:

❶ the full revision of the Versailles Treaty in Germany's interest in Europe;

❷ the inclusion of all people of German race within an enlarged Reich;

❸ the establishment of a massive German preponderance in the East through the conquest of Lebensraum.

The pace of German rearmament indicates that Hitler was not preparing for a general war. For instance, when war broke out in 1939 he had only six weeks' supply of munitions. He adopted a *Blitzkreig* strategy in the event – a series of short wars. The war which the Western democracies expected and prepared for – a war of attrition similar to that of 1914–18 – was the war Hitler wanted to avoid.

The Anschluss

As Hitler accelerated his programme of expansion, the British Prime Minister, Chamberlain, set out to achieve a reconciliation with Italy. Hitler, exploiting the opportunity provided by the decision of Austria's Chancellor Schuschnigg to hold a plebiscite on the future of Austria, improvised invasion plans and German troops occupied Austria in March, 1938.

He proclaimed the annexation of Austria as a province of the German Reich. As an Austrian by birth, the incorporation of his homeland in a greater Germany had been a primary and unchanging aim, stated on the first page of *Mein Kampf.*

Czechoslovakia

After the invasion of Austria, Czechoslovakia was the obvious next target for Nazi expansion. She had a strong army, and alliances with France and the Soviet Union. She was a barrier to German control of Central Europe. The Anschluss now made her very vulnerable to economic pressure. She did not have the undivided loyalty as a state of her inhabitants. There were Hungarian, Slovak, Ruthenian and German minorities. Hitler's justification for now turning his attention to Czechoslovakia was the 3.5 million minority of Germans living in the Sudetenland in Western Czechoslovakia. By her treaty of 1925 France was pledged to aid Czechoslovakia if the latter were attacked. Her own safety was bound up with the fate of Czech fortifications on Germany's opposite frontier.

Faced with German pressure on Czechoslovakia in 1938, she decided that she could not help her ally directly. Britain had made up her mind that Czechoslovakia could not be defended and that no guarantee should be given to France on that account.

Both Powers agreed that the Czechs should be encouraged to make large concessions to the Sudeten German minority.

The arguments for appeasement

The arguments for yielding to Germany's pressure were various:
* There was the widespread horror of war.
* There was fairly wide acceptance that the Germans had a good case for violating the Treaty of Versailles. There was the practical criticism of the settlement and the view, advanced by J. M. Keynes and others, that it had been morally unacceptable.
* There was the belief that a strong Germany could act as a bulwark for the West against the spread of Soviet Communism.
* Economic considerations – the cost of war preparations and of war. There was no guarantee, for instance, that Britain would receive economic assistance in the event of war from the US.
* British and French policies were also swayed by imperial and strategic considerations. Could the British Empire survive a major war? Italy and Japan, as well as Germany, were now counted as potential enemies. Britain could not, without substantial assistance, confront all three and hope to win.

Munich

On 30 May, 1938, Hitler secretly decided to invade Czechoslovakia in the near future. Military preparations were to be completed by October, 1938. During the last week of September, German troops were massed on Czechoslovakia's borders.

Following appeals from Chamberlain (who had already discussed the issue of the Sudetenland with Hitler at Berchtesgaden and at Godesberg), and from Mussolini and President Roosevelt, invitations were issued by Hitler to a conference at Munich on 29 September.

The agreement signed there provided for the German occupation of the Sudetenland in ten days from October 1. The operation was to be supervised by an

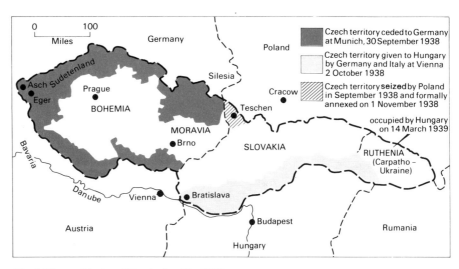

Fig. 6 The partitioning of Czechoslovakia, 1938

international commission. A Four-Power guarantee of the dismembered State would replace the Franco-Czechoslovak treaty once Polish and Hungarian claims in Czechoslovakia had been settled.

Arguments justifying the Munich agreement include:

❶ that public opinion supported it;
❷ that Britain was unprepared for war and was given an extra year for rearmament;
❸ that it offered a last chance for Hitler – if he went further he would condemn himself in the eyes of world opinion, not least in the US.

To set against this, the arguments of the anti-appeasers were:

❶ that the nature of Nazism and Hitler were such that he would go on to further conquests unless a firm stand were taken;
❷ that Munich would only encourage him to take further risks;
❸ that a major betrayal of Czechoslovakia was involved;
❹ militarily he could have been resisted in September, 1938.

13.4 THE PRELUDE TO WAR

Hitler's immediate objectives after the Munich agreement were:

❶ an understanding with Poland on Danzig and the Polish Corridor;
❷ a military alliance with Italy and Japan;
❸ the capitulation of what remained of Czechoslovakia.

On 15 March, 1939, Germany occupied Prague and announced the annexation of Moravia and Bohemia. The same day Hungary occupied the Carpatho-Ukraine. Slovakia survived as a vassal state.

The immediate results of this coup were:

❶ a decisive hardening of public opinion against Hitler in Britain and France – though the appeasers did not give up hope, they now faced mounting criticism;
❷ Anglo-French guarantees were given to Poland, Greece and Rumania.

Hitler occupied Memel and Mussolini invaded Albania.

Poland

Hitler hoped to win Danzig by peaceful means, but the seizure of Memel convinced Poland that a German attack was imminent and strengthened their resistance. On

3 April he ordered plans to be prepared for the invasion of Poland by 1 September. It would be attacked, he informed his generals, 'at the first suitable opportunity…but it must not come to a simultaneous showdown with the West'.

On 23 August, following the failure of Stalin and the Western Powers to reach an understanding, Germany and the Soviet Union signed the Molotov-Ribbentrop Pact. This contained a secret protocol providing for the partition of Poland and designating Nazi and Soviet spheres of influence in Eastern Europe.

With this crucial promise of benevolent neutrality, Hitler was freed – for the moment – from the threat of war on two fronts.

In recent years, some historians have paid particular attention to the domestic economic difficulties within Germany, shortages of raw materials and skilled labour and an 'overheated' economy which they consider exercised a major influence on Hitler's decision to go to war in 1939. This was undoubtedly a consideration, but one should remember that Hitler had reasonable grounds for reassurance. Germany was well prepared to defeat the Poles. She had a non-aggression pact with the Soviet Union, a treaty with Italy and the track-record of Britain and France in previous crises suggested they might protest, but would hardly go to war over Danzig. Hitler had plans for the further massive rearmament of Germany by the mid-40s. He was certainly not ready for a 'world war' in 1939. But in 1939 he was not engaged in a world war.

It only became a truly global conflict in 1941 with the attack on the Soviet Union and the failure to defeat her in the first six months, and when Japan bombed Pearl Harbour in December of that year. Then two very separate conflicts, caused by German expansionism in the West and Japanese aggrandisement in the Far East, were joined.

13.5 CHRONOLOGY

1933	January	HITLER BECAME GERMAN CHANCELLOR.
	February	Japan left the League of Nations following the reception of the Lytton Report by the League on Manchuria.
	October	GERMANY LEFT THE DISARMAMENT CONFERENCE AT GENEVA AND THE LEAGUE OF NATIONS.
1934	January	NON-AGGRESSION PACT BETWEEN GERMANY AND POLAND – the first break in the French alliance system.
	July	THE MURDER OF DOLLFUSS: attempted Nazi takeover in Austria.
	September	The Soviet Union joined the League of Nations reflecting her fear of German aggrandisement.
1935	March	HITLER ANNOUNCED CONSCRIPTION AND THE CREATION OF A MILITARY AIR FORCE.
	April	THE STRESA AGREEMENTS between Britain, France and Italy in the face of growing German power.
	May	THE FRANCO-SOVIET PACT: concluded for five years. Each party promised the other aid in the event of unprovoked aggression.
	June	THE ANGLO-GERMAN naval agreement. Franco-Italian military convention.
	October	THE ITALIAN INVASION OF ABYSSINIA: the League declared that Italy had resorted to war in disregard of her obligations under Article XII; voted to impose sanctions.
	December	THE HOARE-LAVAL PLAN.
1936	March	THE GERMAN REOCCUPATION OF THE RHINELAND: Hitler denounced the Locarno agreements, taking advantage of the Abyssinian crisis and pleading danger to Germany from the Franco-Soviet Pact.
	July	THE SPANISH CIVIL WAR BEGAN: became the focus of Fascist and anti-Fascist intervention.
	August	The French proposed a non-intervention agreement for the Spanish civil war.

	November	ROME-BERLIN AXIS announced. Germany and Japan signed the Anti-Comintern Pact.
1937	May	NEVILLE CHAMBERLAIN became British Prime Minister.
	July	Japanese invasion of China.
	November	THE HOSSBACH CONFERENCE. Italy joined the Anti-Comintern Pact.
	December	Italy left the League.
1938	March	GERMAN OCCUPATION OF AUSTRIA AND THE ANNEXATION (ANSCHLUSS).
	April	Anglo-Italian agreement signed (implemented in November 1938).
	September	HITLER AND CHAMBERLAIN MET AT BERCHTESGADEN: Hitler stated his demand for the German annexation of the German areas of Czechoslovakia. Anglo-French plan for the Czech cession of the Sudetenland to Germany. HITLER AND CHAMBERLAIN MET AT GODESBERG: further demands by Hitler for the immediate surrender of the Sudetenland without the dismantling of military or industrial establishments. MUNICH CONFERENCE AND AGREEMENT: Chamberlain and Hitler signed the Anglo-German Declaration. The transfer of the frontier region and provision for Polish and Hungarian claims on Czechoslovakia. The Polish ultimatum to Czechoslovakia over Teschen (occupied by Polish forces in October).
	November	Southern Slovakia and part of Ruthenia given to Hungary.
	December	Italy denounced the Rome agreements of 1935.
1939	March	GERMANY OCCUPIED BOHEMIA AND MORAVIA. Hungary occupied Carpatho-Ukraine. Lithuania ceded Memel to Germany. Madrid surrendered to General Franco. Anglo-French staff talks began. PROVISIONAL ANGLO-FRENCH GUARANTEE TO POLAND.
	April	ITALY INVADED ALBANIA. ANGLO-FRENCH GUARANTEES TO GREECE AND RUMANIA. Hitler denounced both the Anglo-German naval agreement and the German-Polish Pact.
	May	Provisional Anglo-Turkish pact announced. GERMAN-ITALIAN PACT OF STEEL SIGNED. Hitler addressed his generals on Danzig and Poland.
	July	Scare over Danzig.
	4 August	Danzig-Polish customs crisis.
	12	Anglo-French-Soviet military talks began in Moscow.
	23	MOLOTOV-RIBBENTROP NON-AGGRESSION PACT SIGNED IN MOSCOW: the Nazi-Soviet Pact included pledges to maintain neutrality if either country was at war. Secret clauses gave Lithuania and western Poland to Germany and eastern Poland, Estonia, Latvia, Finland and Bessarabia to the Soviet Union. Mussolini suggested that Britain should persuade Poland to surrender Danzig to Germany.
	24	Danish-Polish customs talks broken off.
	25	ANGLO-POLISH AGREEMENT SIGNED.
	28	Hitler demanded Danzig; the Polish Corridor and parts of Silesia.
	29	Poland persuaded by Britain and France to postpone full mobilisation. Mussolini urged Hitler to accept the British proposals as a basis for settlement.
	30	Polish mobilisation announced.
	31	Poland informed Germany that she was considering the British proposals of direct negotiation. Mussolini proposed conference to discuss Versailles grievances.
	1 September	GERMANY INVADED POLAND. Britain and France warned Germany.
	2	French moves in support of an Italian idea for a conference. Protests in the House of Commons over the government's appeasement of Germany.
	3	BRITISH AND FRENCH ISSUED ULTIMATA TO GERMANY – DECLARATION OF WAR.

Illustrative questions and answers

1 How far is it true that World War II was essentially the result of Hitler's aggressive policies?

Tutorial note

As with any 'how far' question, this one invites you to show precisely *in what ways* Hitler's policies contributed to the coming of war. You should consider how these policies were 'aggressive'. You should refer to the outbreak of the *world* war in 1941, as well as of the *European* war in 1939.

You need to know about

Hitler's underlying ideas and objectives. The relations between Germany and the Western Powers, 1933–39. The relations between Germany, the USSR and the US, 1939–41.

Suggested answer plan

1 A war is possible only if *two* sides are willing to use force. Both Hitler and the Western Powers must be examined.

2 Hitler's objectives, as set out in *Mein Kampf* and elsewhere, fall into two main groups:

   (a) The regaining of Germany's freedom of manoeuvre as a great Power by breaking out of the constraints imposed by the Treaty of Versailles. By 1937 this had largely been achieved through: (i) (above all) successful rearmament; (ii) the remilitarisation of the Rhineland in March, 1936, allowing the construction of defences for Germany's western industrial areas; and (iii) the breach in the unity of World War I victors caused by the Abyssinian crisis and the formation of the Rome-Berlin Axis. By 1937 war was, therefore, *possible* because Germany was again in a position to fight one. In allowing this to happen, the Western Powers perhaps had a 'passive' responsibility for the war but this must be carefully distinguished from Hitler's 'active' one.

   (b) Hitler's first set of objectives was not 'aggressive', in the sense of entailing threats against and attacks on Germany's neighbours. But he also desired Lebensraum (living space) – i.e. the conquest of an empire in the USSR and Eastern Europe. This was aggressive by any definition. Yet, when Hitler began to expand outside Germany's frontiers in 1938–9, his intentions appeared at first to be confined to bringing all the Germans of Eastern Europe within the Third Reich. Hence the absorption of Austria and the Sudetenland in 1938; and the crisis over Danzig and Poland in 1939.

3 Britain and France. The second precondition for war was the shift on the Western side from 'appeasement' (notably the Munich Settlement of September, 1938) to a policy of resistance to Hitler (the British guarantee to Poland in March, 1939). The British government was *not* prepared to fight over the issue of incorporating the Eastern European Germans in the Third Reich. But by March, 1939, it was convinced that Hitler also threatened the *non-Germans* of Eastern Europe (evidenced by the occupation of Prague, and of reported German threats to Rumania and Poland). Rather than permit German domination of Eastern Europe, the British were willing to risk war by issuing guarantees to Poland and (later) Rumania. When Hitler invaded Poland in defiance of the guarantee, in September, 1939, Britain and France declared war on Germany. The West, therefore, took the final step – but note paragraph 4 below.

4 Unlike his position on Czechoslovakia in 1938, Hitler was determined to settle the Polish crisis by force rather than compromise. He gambled (because of the Nazi-Soviet Pact) that Britain and France would back down rather than honour

the guarantee. The issue in 1939 was not just Danzig and the German minority in Poland but whether Germany should dominate Eastern Europe.

5   The events of 1939 were not the end of the story. In 1941 Hitler invaded Russia, as he had always intended to do. This was then more clearly aggressive than his actions in 1938-9. In December, 1941, he declared war on the US. It is true that the US had been greatly assisting both Britain and the USSR in their war against Germany (e.g. Lend-Lease; destroyers for convoy duty, etc.) but these American actions in turn were in response to Hitler's policies in the preceding years.

2   How far was the destruction of the peace treaties the mainspring of German foreign policy after 1933?

Tutorial note

You are being asked for an evaluation of Hitler's foreign policy.

The German leader was insistent on the need to revise the treaties in Germany's interest and the achievement of equal status among the Powers; but he was also driven by an ambition for a greatly expanded Reich and for racial domination in the East. Assess the relative significance of these as driving forces in his foreign policy.

You need to know about

The clauses of the peace treaties, particularly Versailles, and the reasons for their unpopularity in Germany. Hitler's foreign policy objectives. The course of this policy after 1933 and the relation of the major developments (e.g. the reoccupation of the Rhineland) to the revision of the treaties and to Hitler's wider aims.

Suggested answer plan

1   German foreign policy in the 1930s demanded equality of status, a revision of the treaties and the incorporation of previously German territories and populations and the unification with Austria; but Hitler's ultimate objectives were far more ambitious, embracing the domination of Central and Eastern Europe and the achievement of Lebensraum (living space) for the Third Reich.

2   The challenge to the peace treaties included: rearmament, the reoccupation and remilitarisation of the Rhineland, following the Anglo-German naval treaty which broke the Versailles Treaty; the Anschluss (forbidden by the Austrian Peace Treaty); the Sudetenland (incorporated in Czechoslovakia by the Peace Treaty for strategic and economic reasons); the Munich Conference, being the apogee of Hitler's foreign policy success without war; after this the wider nature of his objectives became more apparent to the Powers and to public opinion.

3   The moves to achieve German security: Hitler's intervention in Spain was partly directed towards establishing a state well disposed to Germany on France's frontiers to reduce the threat of France; the Rome-Berlin Axis and Anti-Comintern Pact; the Nazi-Soviet Pact ensuring that Germany would not be faced with the possibility of a two-front war when she attacked Poland.

4   The expansion of the Reich: in his speech of 5 November, 1937, Hitler expounded his overall purpose of expanding Germany into European Russia. His foreign policy followed this aim: the occupation of the rump of Czechoslovakia in March, 1939; the partition of Poland after the Polish campaign; Operation Barbarossa in 1941; plans for the establishment of German colonists in Russia and the driving back of Russian peoples into Asia.

5   If the destruction of the peace treaties had been *the* mainspring of German foreign policy in the Nazi period, it is arguable that this process could have been completed without war. But this objective was only part of, and means towards achieving, a far larger design; though the justification offered by Hitler was, in terms of righting 'wrongs' done to Germany in the peace treaties, the essential driving force was to complete a far more comprehensive design.

3 Examine the extent to which the policies of Nazi Germany, Fascist Italy and Soviet Russia were responsible for the outbreak of war in 1939.

Tutorial note

This requires you to analyse the contribution of the policies of the three Powers to the outbreak of the war and to weigh their respective responsibility. Your answer must obviously also indicate an awareness of the role of the other Powers. The question should not be taken as an invitation to give a narrative account of the origins of the war.

You need to know about

A comprehensive understanding of the course of events leading to war, and the relations between the Powers. German foreign policy, particularly from 1936 onwards. Italian foreign policy. Soviet policies, particularly the Nazi-Soviet Pact.

Suggested answer plan

1   Introduction: the impact of the rise of the dictators; the revisionist Powers; Germany and Italy, eager to reverse the consequences of the First World War; and willing to resort to aggression and intervene in the affairs of other states; contrast this with the policies of the Western Powers; responsibility means not simply the immediate responsibility, but also the contribution of these policies to a warlike climate in international relations.

2   Fascist Italy: Mussolini's advocacy of violence and war as a means of reviving Italian greatness; his invasion of Abyssinia gave evidence of the willingness of Italy to use force to achieve her foreign policy objectives and destroyed the credibility of the League of Nations as a preserver of peace; Italy's new relationship with Germany and her breach with France and Britain; intervention in Spain; in 1938 Mussolini acted as an 'honest broker' at the Munich Conference; in 1939 his role might be seen as one of trying to restrain Hitler; Mussolini's overall responsibility is to be seen more in his role as a pioneer to Hitler's defiance of the Western Powers and as distracting them from the greater threat of German aggrandisement.

3   Nazi Germany: initially Hitler's policy was regarded with some international sympathy as redressing the wrongs of Versailles; but one should emphasise the aggressiveness of the Nazi creed and the far more extensive aims of Hitler's foreign policy; Germany's intervention in the Spanish civil war, such actions as the bombing of Guernica and Madrid intensifying the apprehensions of the Western Powers; German intentions more clearly revealed in the Czech crises, more particularly after the Nazi occupation of Bohemia and Moravia, which led public opinion in Britain to turn against appeasement.

4   Hitler's policy towards Poland led inevitably, after Britain's guarantee to her, towards war; consider the argument that, even without the Nazi-Soviet Pact, his determination and vision of a new Reich would have forced him inexorably on.

5   Soviet Russia: Soviet involvement in Spain intensified British and French suspicions and was seen as part of that worldwide drive to establish Communism, which those distrustful of Stalin's Russia saw as her ultimate foreign policy aim; this weakened the prospect of collective security; Russian policy was essentially defensive; the Nazi-Soviet Pact, which seemed to buy security by extending Russian frontiers westwards into Poland; responsibility lay too with Britain and France in failing to secure a pact with Russia which would make the guarantee to Poland a military reality; the Pact, however, was of crucial assistance to Hitler in pursuing his objective of further German aggrandisement.

6   What made war certain was the Polish guarantee, but only to the extent that Britain and France were forced into war; the overwhelming responsibility was Germany's, given the scale of Hitler's ambitions and his unwillingness to limit them; wars between Germany and Poland and Germany and the Soviet Union

were inevitable in these circumstances; so was war with the Western Powers, unless they were willing to tolerate the creation of a German Europe; while Italian and Soviet policies, as well as the actions of Britain and France, helped to *contribute* towards the outbreak of war, they were not ultimately the decisive factor.

Question bank

1 Document question (Diplomacy – 1939): study the extract below and then answer questions (a) to (f) which follow:

'Duce,
'For some time Germany and Russia have been meditating upon the possibility of placing their mutual political relations upon a new basis. The need to arrive at concrete results in this sense has been strengthened by:
'1 The conditions of the world political situation in general.
'2 The continued procrastination of the Japanese Cabinet in taking up a clear stand. <u>Japan was ready for an alliance against Russia</u> in which Germany – and in my view Italy – could only be interested in the present circumstances as a secondary consideration. She was not agreeable however to assuming any clear obligations regarding England – a decisive question from the German side, and I think also from Italy's... .
'3 <u>The relations between Germany and Poland have been unsatisfactory since the spring</u>, and in recent weeks have become simply intolerable, not through the fault of the Reich, but principally because of British action.... These reasons have induced me to hasten on a conclusion of the Russian-German talks. I have not yet informed you, Duce, in detail on this question. But now in recent weeks the disposition of the Kremlin to engage in an exchange of relations with Germany – a disposition produced from the moment of the <u>dismissal of Litvinov</u> – has been increasingly marked, and has now made it possible for me, after having reached a preliminary clarification, to send my Foreign Minister to Moscow to draw up a treaty which is far and away the most extensive non-aggression pact in existence today, and the text of which will be made public. The pact is unconditional, and establishes in addition the commitment to consult on all questions which interest Germany and Russia. I can also inform you, Duce, that, given these undertakings, the benevolent attitude of Russia is assured.'

(Letter from Hitler to Mussolini, August, 1939)

(a). Explain why 'relations between Germany and Poland have been unsatisfactory.' (6)
(b) (i) Who was Litvinov and who replaced him? (2)
(ii) Why did Hitler regard this as an important change? (2)
(c) Explain why Japan 'was ready for an alliance against Russia'. (5)
(d) What was Hitler's purpose in informing Mussolini of the imminent agreement between Germany and Russia? (4)
(e) Mussolini replied to this letter: 'As far as Russia is concerned, I completely approve.' Why could the publication of such sentiments in Italy have constituted a political embarrassment to him? (4)
(f) Discuss the view that the information revealed in this letter meant that the outbreak of a European war in the near future was inevitable. (8)

2 At what stage, and for what reasons, did it become apparent in the interwar years that the League of Nations was doomed to ineffectiveness in trying to keep the European peace? (London, June 1990)

3   'Hitler's foreign successes between 1933 and 1941 rested on his remarkable tactical skills and ability to exploit his opponent's weaknesses'. Discuss.
(Oxford, June 1989)

4   Was general war the intended result of the aims and conduct of Hitler's foreign policy, 1933–39?
(WJEC, June 1991)

5   Why, and with what consequences, did Stalin enter into a pact with Hitler in 1939?
(AEB, June 1988)

READING LIST

Standard textbook reading
J. M. Roberts, *Europe 1880–1945* (Longman, 1967), chapter 15.
David Thomson, *Europe since Napoleon* (Penguin, 1977), chapters 26–28.
Anthony Wood, *Europe 1815–1945* (Longman, 1975), chapters 29–30.

Further suggested reading
A. Adamthwaite, *The Making of the Second World War* (Allen and Unwin, 1977).
C. J. Bartlett, *The Global Conflict 1880–1970* (Longman, 1984).
P. M. H. Bell, *The Origins of the Second World War in Europe* (Longman, 1986).
A. Bullock, *Hitler: a Study in Tyranny* (Penguin, 1968).
E. H. Carr, *International Relations between the Two World Wars* (Macmillan, 1947).
W. Carr, *Arms, Autarchy and Aggression* (E. Arnold, 1972).

F. H. Hinsley, *Power and the Pursuit of Peace* (CUP, 1963).
G. Martel (ed.) *The Origins of the Second World War Reconsidered: The A. J. P. Taylor Debate after Twenty-five Years* (Allen and Unwin, 1986).
C. L. Mowat (ed.), *The New Cambridge Modern History 1898–1945*, volume XII (CUP, 1968), chapter 23.
R. J. Overy, *The Origins of the Second World War* (Longman, 1987).
R. Sontag, *A Broken World 1919–39* (Harper and Row, 1971).
A. J. P. Taylor, *The Origins of the Second World War* (Penguin, 1963).
C. Thorne, *The Approach of War 1938–39* (Macmillan, 1976).
D. C. Watt, *How War Came: the Immediate Origins of the Second World War* (Heinemann, 1989).
E. Wiskemann, *Europe of the Dictators* (Fontana, 1973).

THE COLD WAR AND EUROPE

Units in this chapter

Chapter objectives

❶ As background: an understanding of relations between the Soviet Union and the Western Powers during the pre-Second World War period; Western attitudes to the Russian Revolution; the involvement of the Powers in the Russian Civil War; the Soviet view of the West, and Stalin's policies.

❷ The significance of the Atlantic Charter; the Tehran, Yalta, San Francisco and Potsdam conferences; the significance in particular of the decisions over the future of Poland and Germany; a clear grasp of the territorial changes involved and the conflicting views of the Allied Powers.

❸ The division of Germany and Berlin; the key role of Germany in the postwar period, noting particularly the intensification of conflict between East and West over the Berlin blockade and airlift; the question of German rearmament; the emergence of the Federal Republic of West Germany, and the Berlin Wall; the policies of Chancellor Adenauer; how the concept of a united Germany was abandoned by both East and West as a result of the considerations of military security.

❹ The extent to which President Roosevelt's death and his replacement by President Truman affected US policy towards the Soviet Union; the contrasting views of President Roosevelt and Stalin on the postwar world order; Russian considerations of national security; the doctrine of containment; the role of the atom bomb in East-West relations; the impact of the Korean War.

❺ The Marshall Plan (offered initially to Eastern Europe as well as to the nations of Western Europe); the Brussels Treaty; NATO; the purpose and significance of each of these and its influence on the growing divergence of East and West.

❻ The ideological conflict; the development of the notion of a world divided into two blocs, Communist and anti-Communist; the extent to

which the Cold War was a conflict of ideas; the growth of anti-
Communism in the West; the significance of the Communist parties of
France and Italy in Western calculations.

⑦ The Sovietisation of Eastern Europe and the consolidation of Russian
power; the process of transformation from 'Peoples' Democracies' to
satellite states; Comecon; Cominform and the Warsaw Pact; the
significance of the rift between Yugoslavia and the Soviet Union;
developments in Eastern Europe after the death of Stalin, particularly
the Hungarian Revolution.

⑧ The crises over Berlin and Cuba, 1958–62; the construction of the Berlin
Wall. The respective roles of the German Chancellor Konrad Adenauer
and the French President Charles de Gaulle in the East-West conflict.

⑨ Détente in Europe during the 1960s and 1970s, in particular the West
German 'Ostpolitik'; the significance of the 'Prague Spring' and Warsaw
Pact invasion of Czechoslovakia in 1968; the 'Brezhnev Doctrine'.

⑩ The reasons for the 'New Cold War'; Afghanistan; Polish Solidarity and
its suppression; nuclear modernisation, in particular the significance of
the dual-track decision and research on SDI. The revival of détente in
the mid-1980s; Mikhail Gorbachev; the INF Treaty. The crisis of
Communism, transformation of Eastern Europe after 1989 and the
reunification of Germany.

The term 'Cold War' describes the mounting tension between East and West which
dominated the international scene during the years after the Second World War.
There had already been considerable disagreements between the Soviet Union and
the Western Powers during the war and there was a legacy of acute distrust which
went back to the Russian revolution of November 1917, and the subsequent civil war.

In August 1941, Roosevelt and Churchill had drawn up the Atlantic Charter to lay
the basis for an enduring peace. In this they declared that boundaries would be drawn
up in accordance with the principles of national self-determination. However, the
Soviet Union informed the West that they expected to keep those territories which
they had won during their pact with the Nazis. At the same time, American troops
remained in Europe, particularly as occupation forces in Germany and Austria, and
American economic dominance was overwhelming.

The new juxtaposition of the superpowers brought them into direct confrontation.
This was ideological as well as being territorial and was concerned with considerations
of security. The conflict of interest was first sharply apparent over Poland and then
Germany. Berlin was a particular focus of East-West hostility and Germany was
divided between the Western and Soviet blocs.

President Truman announced a policy of 'containment' of Communism and offered
extensive military and economic aid to Turkey and Greece. This was followed by the
setting up of the North Atlantic Treaty Organisation. The conflict intensified with
the Sovietisation of Eastern Europe and the Russian acquisition of the atom bomb.
The Cold War widened into a global conflict with the outbreak of the Korean War.

14.1 THE BACKGROUND TO THE COLD WAR

The postwar division of Europe into Eastern and Western Blocs dates from the
wartime agreements of the Allies. As early as January 1943, they agreed to demand
the unconditional surrender of Germany. This ensured the creation of a 'power
vacuum' in Central Europe which would inevitably be filled by Germany's
conquerors. An agreement was reached between Stalin and Churchill in October 1944,

in which the two leaders divided the Balkans into spheres of influence. As a result of the 1943 armistice, Britain and the US had already brought Italy firmly into their sphere of influence.

The confrontation between the Soviet Union and the Western Powers which developed into the Cold War can be traced through an almost continuous series of wartime diplomatic meetings, during which major differences emerged between the Powers. At the same time it should be understood in the context of the original deep ideological hostility and mutual suspicion between Russia and the West which followed the revolution of 1917 and Allied intervention in the Russian Civil War.

There was the conference of foreign ministers in Moscow in October–November 1943, followed by the summit meeting at Tehran, which brought the three great wartime leaders, Churchill, Stalin and Roosevelt together for the first time. Particularly crucial for subsequent developments were the conferences of Yalta and Potsdam. Unlike in 1919, the victors could not agree on the terms of the treaty to be signed with their main enemy, Germany.

The Soviet Union and Europe

The Soviet Union wanted certain clearly defined benefits from the peace: reparations for the damage done to her by the German invasion, security against any possible repetition of it, the recognition of her status as a Great Power and security for the future of the Communist system.

Between 1941 and 1945, in addition to about 20 million lives, one-third of the production resources of the Soviet Union had been destroyed; reparations or aid were very seriously needed. She set out to safeguard herself from any recurrence of German invasion by military alliances, territorial annexations and control over the satellite buffer states of Eastern Europe. Above all, Stalin was determined to incorporate into the Soviet Union those territories which had been taken away from Russia after the First World War. Russia took advantage of victory to recover territories – extending from the Baltic to the Black Sea – which had been part of Tsarist Russia before 1917.

These included the areas through which Germany had attacked her in both wars. This was particularly true of the large area of Poland which she now recovered, encouraging the Poles to make up for the loss by moving westwards at the expense of Germany. The dominant motive for this annexation was security.

The Sovietisation of Eastern Europe

It was soon clear that Stalin thought of the 'Peoples' Democracies', which were set up in Eastern Europe in the wake of the Red Army at the end of the war, as interim regimes at best. Originally he had hoped to obtain American aid and at the same time to control and exploit Eastern Europe to the Soviet Union's own economic and political advantage. Failing in the former, he concentrated on the latter. One after another, the Eastern European countries succumbed to Communist plots and manipulation which brought them more and more under Russian control: in Poland, Rumania, Bulgaria and Hungary, non-Communist politicians were eliminated and the peasant parties outmanoeuvred or taken over. By 1947 all four countries had virtually become Russian satellites, and in February 1948, Czechoslovakia fell victim to a Communist coup. Yugoslavia and Finland were left out. Tito's independence and defiance of Stalin led to the expulsion of the Yugoslav state from the Communist Bloc and also to purges in other Eastern European countries.

During the interwar years Russia had resented the role of Eastern Europe (as envisaged by Churchill and others) as a buffer against the spread of Bolshevik ideas. Now this area became a 'cordon sanitaire' against the penetration of Western and 'cosmopolitan' ideas and influence in Russia. Whether a state had been an ally of Nazi Germany or a victim, the process was the same. After a period of coalition government in which the Soviet occupying forces saw to it that Communists gained leading positions, all the satellites were sooner or later transformed into one-party states with governments dependent on and subservient to the Soviet Union.

Fig. 7 The division of Europe

The US and Europe

At the end of the Second World War the US had more than doubled its industrial production and was determined to reorganise the world to make it free for trade. In August, 1941, Churchill and Roosevelt had met to draft the Atlantic Charter, a general statement of principles on which a postwar settlement might be based.

Both powers disavowed any national gain or the implementation of any territorial changes contrary to the wishes of the inhabitants. All peoples should have the right to choose their own forms of government in a new world of economic cooperation. In January, 1942, these were embodied in the Declaration of the United Nations, which all governments at war with Germany signed.

In contrast to the very specific Russian objectives, the postwar aims of the US in world affairs appear more theoretical and less tangible. It is clear that President Roosevelt expected the Soviet Union to try to establish its control over the states of Eastern Europe and that this could well have unpleasant consequences for the people of Poland and the other states involved. He seems to have believed that the fundamental interests of the US and the USSR could be reconciled without too much conflict or confrontation. He expected, or at least hoped, that the United Nations Organisation would develop into a functioning world peace system.

If he had taken a different line in 1945, leaving considerable American forces in Europe in an attempt to stand up actively to Soviet pressure, he would have run into powerful opposition at home. During the Yalta Conference, Roosevelt told Stalin that within two years of the war's end there would be no American troops left in Europe. The US army was reduced from about 5 millions in May 1945, to less than half a million in March 1946. While the US possessed the atom bomb, the Soviet Union had a very marked superiority of conventional forces in Europe.

The question of Poland

After Roosevelt's death on 12 April, 1945, tension between Russia and her allies very noticeably increased. His successor, Harry Truman, right from the start of his presidency took a much firmer line with the Russians.

In January, 1945, the 'puppet' Provisional Government of Poland at Lublin had been recognised, in spite of the existence of the Polish government-in-exile in London. At Potsdam, in July, Churchill complained bitterly to Stalin that the Russians were surrounding parts of Eastern Europe with an 'iron fence'.

During the summer of 1945 American Lend-Lease aid to her allies, including Russia, was abruptly terminated. Stalin's request for an American loan, originally made early in 1945, was finally turned down in March 1946. It was the Soviet defiance of the American wish for liberal democratic regimes and particularly their attitude towards Poland that provoked the tougher attitude on the part of Roosevelt's successors. As early as the summer of 1945, when the Soviet Union was plainly unwilling to allow a Western-type democratic regime to be established in Poland, Britain and America were protesting at the breach of the Yalta agreement.

The question of Germany

At the end of the war the US, Britain and the USSR were agreed that Germany should be kept under strict control and that she should remain a single unit. In fact, by 1949, two new German states had come into existence. Germany, as well as Europe, was partitioned as a result of the Cold War.

The reasons for this included the inability of the victors to agree on other aspects of the German problem, the very great political, economic and strategic importance of Germany itself (neither East nor West could allow the other side to monopolise it), and the external circumstances of the Cold War, of which the Korean War was the most important.

Reparations The major victors in 1945 were agreed that Germany should be disarmed and de-Nazified, divided *administratively* into zones of occupation but treated *economically* as a single unit. It was intended that she should pay for imported necessities out of current production.

The idea of dismembering Germany, which had been put forward during the war, was quietly forgotten. But she lost East Prussia to the USSR and all other territories beyond the Oder and the Western Neisse rivers, which were left under Polish administration. The Potsdam decision meant that Germany lost nearly a quarter of her pre-1938 territory. The policy of economic unity was contradicted by the problem of reparations.

At the Potsdam Conference the Russians, whose need for reparations was very great, secured agreement for the removal of goods from their zone of occupation, but nothing was settled with the Western Allies about the *extent* of these claims. The Allies were similarly to be entitled to dismantle and remove property. They soon found, however, that this process left them with an obligation to provide their own zones with imported food which had to be paid for by their own taxpayers since German production was unable to foot the bill. Soon, therefore, the West called for the restoration of German industrial capacity and production.

Berlin Berlin had been excluded from the zonal system. It lay deep inside the Soviet zone of occupation but it was placed, in joint occupation, under a separate joint allied authority, the Kommandatura. From the start Berlin was a crucial point of confrontation in the Cold War. During 1947–8, steps were being taken by the Western Powers to establish a West German state. which contradicted the idea of a unitary Germany. In order to bring pressure to bear on the West, Stalin ordered the blockading of Berlin and the Allies – having considered sending an armed convoy to force its way along the road from the British zone – decided instead to keep the city going by the airlift of essential supplies. The Soviet blockade was lifted after 318 days, but the problem of Berlin remained as one of the most vexed issues in East-West relations.

The German Federal Republic After elections in August, 1949, the German Federal Republic came into existence with its capital in Bonn and with Konrad Adenauer as Chancellor. Adenauer postponed any serious pursuit of German reunification and concentrated on integrating the new state within Western Europe. A year later the question of German rearmament became a live issue, following the outbreak of the war in Korea in June 1950, and the US announcement that a substantial West German contribution was essential to the defence of Western Europe. (See Chapter 15).

14.2 THE COLD WAR AND 'CONTAINMENT'

The principal features of the Cold War were clearly apparent in 1946 in the 'Iron Curtain' speech of Sir Winston Churchill at Fulton, Missouri, and in that of President Truman's Secretary of State, J F Byrnes, at Stuttgart in the same year in which he announced the merging of the British and American zones (Bizonia). These clearly indicated that the wartime alliance had been superseded by East-West confrontation and that the US now regarded Western Europe as an essential sphere of influence.

Though President Truman had to accept the exclusion of western influence from Central and Eastern Europe, he warned the Soviet Union – the Truman Doctrine of March, 1947 – that further pressure would meet with American resistance. This may be taken as the first fully comprehensive statement from either side of the existence of the Cold War. This announcement was precipitated by the economic weakness of Britain in 1946–7, which forced her to give up her military and economic support to Turkey and Greece.

The Truman Doctrine spelled out the policy of 'containment', which was designed to curb Russian-expansionism and to resist the spread of Communism. This was further underlined by the strengthening of the West European economies by Marshall Aid and the creation of NATO.

NATO was an association of 11 states which declared that an armed attack on any one of them in Europe or in North America would be regarded as an attack on them all. In such an event each would go to the help of the ally attacked. Its creation meant the formal collapse of the World II alliance. The European policy of resisting Communist expansion was transformed into a worldwide confrontation by the outbreak of the Korean War.

The Cold War embodied both a conflict of interests between the superpowers and their allies (some historians see Stalin's policies essentially in terms of Russian nationalism) and a confrontation of ideas, Western democratic and Communist.

Both sides exaggerated the other's intentions. On the one hand, the Soviet Union accused the United States of trying to establish anti-Soviet regimes in countries on the borders of the USSR; on the other, the US appeared to take with very great seriousness the theoretical Communist aim of spreading revolution to the whole world and regarded every increase in Soviet influence and strength as a step towards that end. The American fear of the Soviet Union was matched by an often hysterical fear of Communist subversion at home. This was intensified by the ending of the Western monopoly of nuclear weapons in 1949 and the atomic arms race.

14.3 AFTER 1955

The issue of Germany remained a central preoccupation after West Germany was rearmed in 1955. The Federal Republic claimed to be the custodian of the sovereignty of the whole of Germany. At the same time it experienced dramatic economic growth, the 'economic miracle', which made it the leading industrial power in Western Europe. But it was vulnerable and was very much made to feel its insecurity in the Cold War years. The Western Allies insisted for many years that they did not accept its division and that their objective was reunification 'in security and freedom'. The German Chancellor Adenauer argued that the West would from 'a position of strength' be able to force the Soviet Union to accept a solution of the Germany question on Western terms.

In practice, after the rearmament of Western Germany, the West tacitly accepted until 1989 that Germany would not be reunited in the foreseeable future. In the Cold War years, Adenauer's hope seemed unrealistic. How could one force the Soviet Union in the nuclear age? At the same time the Soviet Union also reconciled itself to this division, though it attempted to make the West recognise the legitimacy of the German Democratic Republic. This led to serious renewed tension over Berlin between 1959 and 1961 and the construction of the Berlin Wall in August 1961. The West refused to accept Soviet terms for peaceful coexistence, because this meant acceptance of the finality of separate spheres of influence. Soviet frustration over Berlin also encouraged the Soviet leader Krushchev to gamble on introducing nuclear missiles into Cuba in 1962. The Cuban Missile Crisis and Berlin represented, arguably, the two most dangerous crises of the Cold War.

14.4 DE GAULLE

The leading political figure in Western Europe during the 1960s was the French President Charles de Gaulle. As he saw it, the Cold War impasse offered either the threat of nuclear catastrophe or condominium of the superpowers. He campaigned against US influence and 'Anglo-Saxon' dominance and called for a 'European Europe', while France at the same time remained under the umbrella of NATO nuclear protection. He vetoed Britain's application to join the Common Market, was unenthusiastic about President Kennedy's attempts to improve US-Western European relations, opposing the US proposal for a multilateral nuclear force within NATO. (Under de Gaulle France became an independent nuclear power.) In 1966 he withdrew France from the command structure of NATO. Instead he opened up relations with Communist China and Eastern European states and talked of the recreation of a common European identity – a Europe 'from the Atlantic to the Urals'. At the same time he was widely critical of US policy outside Europe, for instance in Vietnam and the Middle East. Just as Adenauer's reunification of Germany through strength seemed unrealistic at the time, so too, de Gaulle's Europe 'from the Atlantic to the Urals' seemed an incredible aspiration as Warsaw Pact forces invaded Czechoslovakia in 1968 to suppress the Czechoslovakian liberalisation process of the 'Prague Spring'.

Ostpolitik

After de Gaulle's departure, the initiative for détente with the Eastern Bloc passed to Germany. The rigidity of Adenauer's approach to the Soviet Union and her allies now made way for the so-called Ostpolitik. (Already, as early as 1963, his successor Ludwig Erhard had established trade links between the Federal Republic and Eastern Europe.) Ostpolitik was particularly associated with the Chancellorship of the Social Democrat Willi Brandt. It led to the recognition of two German states, though only as parts of a single German nation. It also achieved greater normalisation of relations with the Soviet Union and other Eastern European states. Fundamentally, it accepted the implications of the postwar distribution of power in Europe. At the same time it reorientated the Federal Republic towards Eastern Europe, contributing significantly to the East-West détente of the late 1960s and early 1970s, illustrated by the Strategic Arms Limitation Treaty of 1972 between the Superpowers. One of the key elements in this rapprochement was the 1971 Quadripartite Agreement on Berlin. This was between the occupying powers, and the FRG was not directly involved, but a proper settlement over Berlin was an obvious precondition for treaties with the East.

14.5 THE 'NEW' COLD WAR

By the mid–1970s it seemed, then, that East and West had basically accepted the continental division in Europe. By the end of the decade, though, détente, never popular with some leading elements in the US, came under strain. The Helsinki Accords, for instance, were accused by some of legitimising the Soviet system in Eastern Europe without producing anything meaningful in return. In 1979 the Soviet Union invaded Afghanistan; in 1981 the Solidarity movement in Poland was suppressed by General Jaruselki's imposition of martial law. Rapid rearmament ensued, including the deployment of Cruise and Pershing missiles (the SALT II agreements were significantly not ratified). The rhetoric between the Superpowers was reminiscent of the 1950s, and the early 1980s came to be characterised as the 'New Cold War'. Sharply deteriorating US-USSR relations were also accompanied by considerable strains between the US and continental Western Europe, reflected not least in the rapid revival of the peace movement and campaigning against nuclear deployment.

14.6 THE 'END' OF THE COLD WAR

In 1985 this tension started to abate. In this year Moscow reopened the talks over intermediate nuclear forces and Mikhail Gorbachev succeeded to the Soviet leadership. After various setbacks the INF Treaty was signed in 1987. It removed all missiles from Europe with ranges between 300 and 3000 miles. At the same time the Communist system imposed by Stalin after the war started to unravel. With the introduction of democratic elections, market economics and the resurgence of nationalism, the Cold War framework of Europe disintegrated. The most evocative symbol of the end of the old order was the removal of the Berlin Wall in 1989. The Cold War had resulted in the division of Germany and Europe and the imposition of single-party rule in Eastern Europe. After 1989 the way was open for the reunification of Germany, though not with her prewar borders in the East. At the same time the crisis of Communism, leading to free elections and dramatic transformation in Eastern Europe and the Soviet Union also opened the way for nationalist upheavals, as seen most dramatically in what was Yugoslavia. The tension and uncertainty of the Cold War confrontation (which had, curiously, provided a stability of a sort) was now succeeded by other tensions and uncertainties, more reminiscent of Europe at the end of the First World War than of any time since 1945.

14.7 CHRONOLOGY

1941	August	THE ATLANTIC CHARTER: PRESIDENT ROOSEVELT and WINSTON CHURCHILL issued a statement of fundamental principles for the postwar world, emphasising opposition to any territorial changes contrary to the wishes of those immediately concerned. Sovereign rights and self-government should be restored to those who had been deprived of them.
1943	October	Moscow Conference of British, US and Soviet Foreign Ministers: agreement to set up an international organisation for peace and security.
	November	THE TEHRAN CONFERENCE: the first inter-allied summit attended by Stalin as well as Roosevelt and Churchill. Discussion of a landing in France and of cooperation in the peace settlement.
1945	February	THE YALTA CONFERENCE: Stalin agreed to enter the war against Japan – accepted the Curzon Line as the Soviet-Polish frontier; conceded that Poland would have the Oder-Neisse Line as a western boundary and agreed to Poland having free elections as soon as possible.
	May	TERMS OF UNCONDITIONAL GERMAN SURRENDER SIGNED: supreme authority vested in the Allied Control Council of Great Britain, France, the US and the Soviet Union. Each of these powers administered its own occupation zone. Berlin was divided into four sectors.
	June	THE SAN FRANCISCO CONFERENCE: completion of the Charter for the United Nations Organisation.
	August	THE POTSDAM CONFERENCE: discussion of allied control in Germany, reparations, disarmament and of the dissolution of Nazi institutions; the Oder-Neisse Line and Russian intervention against Japan also discussed.
1946		Economic fusion of the US and British Zones of Germany, (Bizonia).
1947	March–April	MOSCOW CONFERENCE OF FOREIGN MINISTERS: showed considerable disagreement on the German question. Conflict between Russian demands for reparations and the Western policy of making Germany economically self-supporting.
	July	THE MARSHALL PLAN: a programme of European recovery proposed by George Marshall, US Secretary of State. A committee was set up to draft a EUROPEAN RECOVERY PROGRAMME. The Soviet Union and its satellites refused to participate in this programme.
	October	THE COMMUNIST INFORMATION BUREAU (Cominform) established by the Communist parties of the Soviet Union, Yugoslavia, Bulgaria, Hungary, Poland, France, Italy and Czechoslovakia to coordinate the activities of the European Communist parties.
1948	February	COMMUNIST COUP AND PURGE IN CZECHOSLOVAKIA.
	March	Soviet delegates walked out of the Allied Control Council after charging the Western Powers with undermining the quadripartite administration of Germany. THE BRUSSELS TREATY: signed by Great Britain, France, Belgium, the Netherlands and Luxembourg. It constituted a 50 year alliance against attack in Europe and provided for economic, social and military cooperation.
	June	YUGOSLAVIA EXPELLED FROM THE COMINFORM: for alleged doctrinal reasons and hostility to the Soviet Union.
	July	Disagreement between the Soviet Union and the West over the latter's programme of economic and currency reforms brought complete Soviet stoppage of rail and road traffic between Berlin and the West – THE BERLIN AIRLIFT.
1949	January	THE COUNCIL FOR MUTUAL ECONOMIC ASSISTANCE (COMECON): originally intended by Stalin to enforce an economic boycott against Yugoslavia.
	April	THE NORTH ATLANTIC TREATY ORGANISATION (NATO): between Great Britain, Belgium, Canada, Denmark, France, Iceland, Italy, the Netherlands, Norway, Portugal and the US – for mutual assistance in the event of attack.

	May	The three Western Powers agreed on an OCCUPATION STATUTE for Western Germany, which assured the Germans of considerable self-government, while reserving far-reaching powers to the occupation authorities.
		The Western Parliamentary Council adopted the BASIC LAW for the Federal Republic of Germany.
	September	KONRAD ADENAUER elected Chancellor of the Federal Republic.
		Soviet Union renounced its treaty of friendship with Yugoslavia.
1950	June	OUTBREAK OF THE KOREAN WAR.
1952	February	GREECE AND TURKEY JOIN NATO.
	May	THE EUROPEAN DEFENCE COMMUNITY: an attempt to create a supranational European army with common institutions. Rejected by the French Assembly, 1954.
1953	May–August	The death of Stalin. The USSR proposed that a Big Four Conference be held within six months on a German peace treaty. Moscow suggested that East and West Germany met first to set up a provisional all-German regime.
1955	May	The Federal Republic of (Western) Germany gained sovereign status; joined NATO.
		THE WARSAW PACT: set up to provide for the establishment of a unified military command with headquarters in Moscow – 'The Eastern European Mutual Assistance Treaty'.
1956	October–November	THE HUNGARIAN UPRISING.
1957	October	The Soviet Union launched first earth satellite, 'Sputnik I'.
1960	February	France exploded its first atomic bomb.
	May	The Soviet Union shot down a US U-2 spy plane.
		PARIS SUMMIT CONFERENCE.
	November	J. F. Kennedy elected President of the United States.
1961	June	Kennedy and Krushchev met in Vienna as crisis over Berlin escalated.
	August	GERMAN DEMOCRATIC REPUBLIC ERECTED THE BERLIN WALL.
1962	October	THE CUBAN MISSILE CRISIS.
1963	June	Establishment of the 'hot line' between Washington and Moscow.
	August	The Soviet Union, the United States and Britain signed the first nuclear test-ban treaty.
	November	Kennedy assassinated.
1964	October	Krushchev deposed. Leonid Brezhnev succeeded as First Secretary of the Communist Party.
1968	January	Alexander Dubcek elected First Secretary of the Communist Party in Czechoslovakia.
	July	The United States, Britain, the Soviet Union and 58 non-nuclear states signed a nuclear non-proliferation Treaty. This came into effect in 1970.
	August	WARSAW PACT FORCES ENTERED CZECHOSLOVAKIA TO HALT THE LIBERALISATION PROGRAMME.
1970	August	The Federal Republic and the Soviet Union signed the Moscow Treaty of Reconciliation and Peaceful Cooperation.
1972	May	THE UNITED STATES AND THE SOVIET UNION SIGNED THE SALT I TREATY.
	June	FOUR-POWER AGREEMENT ON BERLIN SIGNED.
1979	June	THE SALT II AGREEMENT BETWEEN THE SUPERPOWERS.
	December	The Soviet Union occupied Afghanistan.
1981	August	The Polish Government and Lech Walesa, leader of the Solidarity Movement, signed the Gdansk agreement granting extensive rights to trade unionists.
1981	December	MARTIAL LAW WAS DECLARED IN POLAND UNDER GENERAL JARUSELKI, LEADING TO THE BANNING OF SOLIDARITY.

1987	December	THE UNITED STATES AND THE SOVIET UNION SIGNED THE INTERMEDIATE-RANGE NUCLEAR FORCES (INF) TREATY.
1989	November	THE BERLIN WALL WAS DEMOLISHED.
1990	September	THE FEDERAL REPUBLIC, THE DEMOCRATIC REPUBLIC, BRITAIN, FRANCE, THE UNITED STATES AND THE SOVIET UNION SIGNED THE TREATY ON FINAL SETTLEMENT WITH RESPECT TO GERMANY.
	October	THE REUNIFICATION OF GERMANY.
1991	July	The Warsaw Pact was officially ended.
	August	The Supreme Soviet voted to suspend all activities of the Communist Party in the Soviet Union.
	December	Presidents of eleven former Soviet republics met at Alma Ata and declared the end of the Soviet Union and the creation of a Commonwealth of Independent States. They agreed that the United Nations Security Council seat previously occupied by the Soviet Union should go to the Russian Republic.

Illustrative questions and answers

1   Why, after the Second World War, did Germany, occupy so important a place in the quarrels between West and East?

Tutorial note
A straightforward question which needs to be answered, however, at both a general and a specific level.

You need to know about
Developments in Germany, c. 1945–54, and their effect on East-West relations.

Suggested answer plan
1   Start by presenting a paradox: during 1941–5 the Allies were all agreed that Germany must be completely defeated. There was also substantial Soviet-US agreement about how Germany should be treated after the war: it should lose territory, be disarmed, economically weakened, and possibly split up (viz. the 1944 Morgenthau Plan). Yet, by 1948–9, the future of Germany caused the most serious US-Soviet crisis of the early Cold War. Why?
2   The general reasons for Germany's importance were (a) its geographical position – Western and Soviet troops and along the Elbe, and West Berlin remained as a Western enclave that was highly vulnerable; and (b) Germany's potential, shown in both World Wars, as an extremely formidable military and industrial Power, and the evidence of the interwar years that it could rapidly recover from defeat. Neither the Western Powers, especially France, nor the USSR, which had just lost 20 million dead, wanted Germany to recover as an *independent* Power. But if it were to recover as a *dependent* Power it might give a decisive advantage to whichever of the postwar blocs it was attached to. The wartime solution to this dilemma was to prevent Germany from recovering economically and militarily at all. This, however, proved very difficult to implement in the postwar years. Because of all these difficulties, there was no precise agreement over a peace treaty with Germany even when East-West relations were good. Once the Cold War had begun, all chance of a peace treaty with Germany was ended.
3   The *specific* course of events: Germany was not the issue which started the Cold War. American–Soviet tension began over Poland and Eastern Europe in 1944–5. It intensified over the crises in the Near East in 1946–7 (i.e., Iran, Turkey and Greece). In 1945–6 the main dispute in Germany was over the

USSR's desire for reparations (and especially its desire to take these from the Western occupation zones). This, however, was relatively minor. Once tension had begun elsewhere it became important to prevent Left- or Right-wing extremism winning support in Western Germany. By 1947 industrial recovery in Germany had become essential to prevent an economic crisis and possible social revolution in Western Europe as a whole. Hence the development of a Western commitment to a unified and prosperous West Germany (e.g., J. F. Byrnes's Stuttgart speech, September 1946; the economic fusion of the British and US occupation zones, January 1947; the Marshall Plan, announced in June 1947; the London Conference (February–June, 1948) agreed on a West German currency and state; the June 1948, currency reform; the West German constitution adopted, May 1949).

This re-emergence of a German state (with two-thirds of the German population and the main industrial areas) was what the USSR had wished all along to prevent. Hence Stalin responded by: (a) tightening his control of Eastern Europe, and (b) the Berlin blockade, a direct response to the currency reform but frustrated by the Berlin airlift. The final phase came as a result of the USSR acquiring an atomic bomb and the invasion of South Korea. The US now pressed for Western Europe's non-nuclear defences to be strengthened by the creation of a West German Army and West Germany's admission into NATO (provided by the Paris agreements of October, 1954). In May 1955 the USSR responded with the creation of the Warsaw Pact.

4   The Cold War did not start over Germany but, once it had begun, there was an irreconcilable conflict between the Western desire to see a united, prosperous (and eventually rearmed) West Germany and the Soviet desire to prevent this.

2   Show how and why a 'cold war' developed after 1945. What were its consequences?

Tutorial note

The question asks you to explain (and not just to narrate) the transformation of the relationship between the United States and the Soviet Union from an alliance against Germany (and Japan) during 1941–5 into open hostility, with the formation of opposed alliances and the beginning of an arms race.

You need to know about

Soviet and US foreign policy, 1944–50. The outlines of European political history over the same period.

Suggested answer plan

1   At the most general level, the Cold War was made probable by the emergence in 1945 of the US and the USSR as by far the two most powerful nations in the world. The war had caused the defeat or enfeeblement of all the other Powers. It also made the US and the USSR more anxious to eliminate threats to their 'security' than they had been before. But they had little in common once Germany was defeated (the US, unlike the USSR, was a private enterprise democracy without vulnerable land frontiers or a history of foreign invasion), and they disagreed radically in their desires for a postwar settlement.

2   In addition to these general points, it is necessary to explain the circumstances and timing of the 'outbreak' of the Cold War, and to study the motives of both sides.

(a)   *The USSR*: Stalin's maximum aims are not known. His minimum aims certainly included (i) preventing Germany from ever recovering as a military threat to the USSR; (ii) establishing a security screen in Eastern Europe, which would probably require reliable Communist dictatorships in the countries occupied by the Red Army in 1944–5; and (iii) similar buffer zones in the Far East (e.g. Manchuria) and possibly the Middle East (e.g. northern Iran).

(b) *The USA*: The US leaders were initially close to Stalin's view about Germany (eg. the Morgenthau Plan, September, 1944). For reasons of idealism (e.g. the Atlantic Charter, 1941) and domestic circumstances (e.g. the sizeable Polish vote), however, they criticised and tried to limit the establishment of Communist dictatorships in Eastern Europe (notably in the Yalta agreement over Poland). But they could do little more than slow this process down. More important was the evidence in 1946–7 that appeared to show a desire by the USSR for unlimited expansion *outside* Eastern Europe (e.g. the Iran crisis, March 1946; Turkey, August 1946; and the Greek civil war). To this the US leaders responded by announcing the policy of 'containing' Communist expansion (e.g. the Truman Doctrine, March 1947, and aid to Greece and Turkey); and giving aid to prevent economic crisis and social disorder in Western Europe (i.e. the Marshall Plan, announced June 1947). The US leaders were encouraged by (i) historical analogy – e.g. the failure of appeasement in the 1930s; and (ii) geopolitics – the belief that the US would be threatened if Western Europe's industrial resources fell under Soviet control.

3 But the Marshall Plan required the economic recovery of West Germany (accompanied by the formation of the West German state). This appeared to threaten the Soviet Union and started a process of 'escalation' (e.g. the Berlin blockade of 1948–9) causing the US to enter a defensive alliance with the Western Europeans (the North Atlantic Treaty, April 1949). After the USSR acquired an atomic bomb (1949) and the invasion of South Korea (1950), the US pressed for the rearmament of West Germany (agreed in 1954). By then Europe was more stable, and Asia had become the main theatre of East-West conflict.

4 *Consequences*:

(a) The ceasefire lines of 1945 became the boundary between two Germanies and two Europes with very different political and economic systems.

(b) Suspicion and rivalry between the US and USSR both within and outside Europe.

(c) The Cold War and the division of Germany made it possible to heal the old France/Germany conflict. But while East-West tension continues both East and Western European states remain dependent on the US and the USSR, and have little diplomatic manoeuvre.

(d) Note, finally, that outside Greece the Cold War in Europe did not become 'hot'.

3 To what extent was the Cold War 'a conflict between two irreconcilable ideologies'?

Tutorial note

This is a difficult question which requires you to identify the ideological elements of the Soviet-American conflict and to balance them against other possible explanations of that conflict.

You need to know about

Soviet-American relations, c. 1943–50. The domestic political and economic systems of the US and the USSR, and the fundamental assumptions of their leaderships.

Suggested answer plan

1 Officially Marxist-Leninist, the USSR after World War II was a command economy under a single-party dictatorship; the US was a liberal democracy

with a predominantly market economy. The ideological element in the Cold War was the belief of each side in the superiority of its domestic system, and its willingness, if necessary by force, to preserve and/or expand the geographical area covered by that system. This has to be set against the alternative explanations of the Cold War as a conflict of economic interests or (more convincingly) as a conflict between rival states which would have taken place whatever the domestic political system.

2   The US and the USSR had had different domestic systems for many years. But during the interwar years they did not fear attack from each other – unlike the period after 1945; and in the years 1941–5 they were preoccupied with the danger from Germany and Japan. By 1945 Germany and Japan were defeated, and other Powers (Britain, France, China) were so weakened that the US and the USSR were far stronger than any other states except each other. If *both* states had been democratic, or *both* Communist, conflict might still well have occurred. But the conflict was much harder to control because of the ideological suspicion each side felt for the other, which encouraged each to interpret the other's actions in the worst possible light. To explain the *timing* and *circumstances* of the conflict, however, it is necessary to be far more precise.

3   *The USSR*: There was the widespread belief in the US by 1950 that the USSR wished to impose Communist dictatorships throughout the world. But (a) many Communist movements – e.g. in China, Yugoslavia, and Greece – were not under Soviet control; and (b) the USSR was responsible for the communisation of the areas of Eastern Europe occupied by the Red Army. But this can be explained as the result of a devastating war with Germany. Stalin wanted a security screen of reliable governments on his border, and Communist control of the governments was the best way to make them reliable. Ideology was, therefore, at the service of security. It *may* be, however, that the USSR felt its security also required the Communist control of Western Europe. This is still unknown.

    The USA: The American government pressed in 1945 for non-communists to be included in the East European governments. But what persuaded the Americans of a need for 'containment' was the evidence that the Soviet Union wished to expand *outside* Eastern Europe (e.g. Iran and Turkey, 1946; Greece, 1947). If Communist governments came to power in Western Europe, democracy and private enterprise would be endangered. But the US would itself feel under threat if the USSR controlled Western Europe's industrial resources. To prevent this, the US supported the economic and military recovery of Western Germany after 1947: this was precisely the threat which the Soviet Union had wished to guard against. From this point on, suspicion on the two sides was self-reinforcing.

4   The motives of security and ideology on the two sides were inextricably interlinked but, during the years 1946–8, ideological differences came to seem more threatening than before because of the elimination of the other Powers. Soviet behaviour in Iran, Greece and Turkey in 1946–7, and US policy towards West Germany in 1947–8, seem to have persuaded each side that the other endangered its existence.

Question bank

1   Document question (the Cold War): study extracts I, II and III below and then answer questions (a) to (g) which follow:

Extract I

'From Stettin in the Baltic to Trieste in the Adriatic <u>an iron curtain</u> has descended across the continent. Behind that line lie all the capitals of the ancient states of Central and Eastern Europe.

'...Athens alone...is free to decide its future at an election under British, American and French observation. The <u>Russian-dominated</u> Polish government has been encouraged to make enormous and wrongful inroads upon Germany.... <u>The Communist parties....in all these Eastern States of Europe, have been raised to pre-eminence and power far beyond their numbers and are seeking everywhere to obtain totalitarian control...and, so far, except in Czechoslovakia, there is no true democracy.</u>'

(Winston Churchill, Speech at Fulton, Missouri, 5 March, 1946)

Extract II

'Since the war Turkey has sought additional financial assistance from Great Britain and the United States for the purpose of effecting that modernisation necessary for the maintenance of its national integrity. That integrity is essential to the preservation of order in the Middle East... .

'To ensure the peaceful development of nations, free from coercion, the United States has taken a leading part in establishing the United Nations. The United Nations is designed to make possible lasting freedom and independence for all its members. We shall not realise our objectives, however, unless we are willing to help free peoples to maintain their free institutions and their national integrity against aggressive movements that seek to impose upon them totalitarian regimes. This is no more than a frank recognition that totalitarian regimes imposed upon the peoples, by direct or indirect aggression, undermine the foundations of international peace and hence the security of the United States.'

(President Truman to Congress, 12 March, 1947)

Extract III

'The American arguments for assisting Turkey base themselves on the existence of a threat to the integrity of Turkish territory – though no one and nothing actually threatens Turkish integrity. This 'assistance' is evidently aimed at putting this country also under US control. Some American commentators admit this quite openly...that an American alliance with Turkey would give the USA a strategic position incomparably more advantageous than any other, from which power could be wielded over the Middle East... .

'We are now witnessing a fresh intrusion of the USA into the affairs of other states... . But the American leaders...fail to reckon with the fact that the <u>old methods of the colonisers and die-hard politicians</u> have out-lived their time and are doomed to failure.'

(Article in *Soviet News*, 15 March, 1947)

(a) What did Churchill mean by 'an iron curtain'? (2)
(b) Explain why Churchill considered the Polish government to be 'Russian-dominated' and how this situation had come about. (4)
(c) Explain what Churchill meant by 'The Communist parties...in all these Eastern States of Europe, have been raised to pre-eminence and power far beyond their numbers and are seeking everywhere to obtain totalitarian control'. (4)
(d) Explain the particular circumstances which led Truman to enunciate his 'doctrine' (Extract II). (4)
(e) Why did the writer of Extract III refer to 'the old methods of the colonisers and die-hard politicians'? (4)
(f) Compare the reasons advanced in Extract II with those advanced in Extract III for United States policy towards Turkey. (5)
(g) What developments in Europe in 1947 and 1948 led to an even greater rift between the Communists and the Western democracies? Which of these developments would have made Churchill revise the last assertion in Extract I, 'except in Czechoslovakia, there is no true democracy'? (7)

2 Why was no peace treaty signed with Germany after 1945?

(Oxford, June 1988)

3 Discuss the nature and extent of American influence in Europe after the Second World War.   (NISEAC, June 1991)

4 Why was Berlin the focus of so much international attention from 1948 to 1970?   (AEB, June 1989)

5 To what extent, and for what reasons, did the people of Eastern Europe welcome the establishment of Communist rule, 1945–49?
                                                                      (WJEC, June 1991)

READING LIST

Standard textbook reading

H. Stuart Hughes, *Contemporary Europe: A History* (Prentice-Hall, 1976), chapters 13, 14, 15, 17, 19.

David Thomson, *Europe since Napoleon* (Penguin, 1977), chapters 29–30.

Further suggested reading

C. J. Bartlett, *The Global Conflict 1880–1970* (Longman, 1984).

M. Crouzet, *The European Renaissance since 1945* (Thames and Hudson, 1970).

A. W. DePorte, *Europe between the Superpowers* (Yale Universal Press, 1979).

Isaac Deutscher, *Stalin* (Penguin, 1972).

André Fontaine, *History of the Cold War, volumes 1 and 2* (Vintage Books, 1970).

Alfred Grosser, *Germany in our Time* (Pall Mall, 1971).

L. J. Halle, *The Cold War as History* (Harper and Row, 1975).

J. Joll, *Europe since 1870* (Weidenfeld and Nicolson, 1973).

W. LaFeber, *America, Russia and the Cold War 1945–1984* (5th ed) (Knopf, 1985).

W. Laqueur, *Europe since Hitler* (Weidenfeld and Nicolson/ Penguin, 1970).

M. McCauley, *The Origins of the Cold War* (Longman, 1983).

R. C. Mowat, *Ruin and Resurgence 1939–65* (Blandford, 1966).

R. Okey, *Eastern Europe 1740–1980: Feudalism to Communism* (Hutchinson, 1982).

J. W. Young, *Cold War Europe 1945–89*, (Edward Arnold, 1991).

CHAPTER 15

WESTERN EUROPEAN INTEGRATION

Units in this chapter

Chapter objectives

❶ Western Europe in 1945: the political, economic and social consequences of the Second World War – particular attention to be paid to Germany, France and Italy; the scale of destruction and the factors favouring economic reconstruction; the significance of the movement of populations from Eastern Europe; the restoration of democracy.

❷ The historical antecedents of the postwar ideas for European unity, e.g. the influence of the resistance movement against Hitler.

❸ The economic arguments in favour of integration, such as the need for large markets, competitiveness and technological advance.

❹ The political arguments in favour of integration: the influence of the loss of faith in Nationalism as a result of the Second World War; the decline of European power in the world; the fear of the Soviet Union and the spread of Communism; the desire to contain Germany and to prevent any future European war; American encouragement for moves towards German unification.

❺ The difference between the federalist and functionalist approaches to European integration; the contribution of leading European statesmen to the European movement, particularly Konrad Adenauer and Alcide de Gasperi; the particular role of Jean Monnet.

❻ The Marshall Plan or European Recovery Programme; its aims, scope and results; the OEEC; Benelux; the Council of Europe.

❼ The revival of Germany: the transition from occupation to Federal Republic; the 'Economic Miracle'.

❽ The Schuman Plan and the European Coal and Steel Community; the various reasons for the Plan and the institutions and organisation and institutions of the ECSC.

❾ The question of European defence: the Brussels Treaty and Nato; the Pleven Plan and the debate over the European Defence Community; the reasons for the defeat of the EDC and the role of public opinion in this debate.

⑩ The Messina Conference and the Rome Treaties; the institutions and working of the EEC; the role in particular of the Commission, the Council of Ministers and the European Parliament.

⑪ The effects of the EEC on the development of Western European industry and agriculture.

⑫ General de Gaulle and the EEC: the Fouchet Plan, the veto of British entry in 1963 and 1967 and the reasons for this; the Gaullist view of Europe in the world and of France in Europe; the Franco–German Treaty (1963); the boycott of Community institutions (1965).

⑬ The enlargement of the Community (1973).

⑭ The introduction of the European Monetary System (EMS) and direct elections to the European Parliament.

⑮ The further enlargement of the Community to the Twelve with the inclusion of Greece, Spain and Portugal.

⑯ The issues of budgetary contributions to the Community and of Common Agricultural Policy, in particular the relations between Mrs. Thatcher, her Community partners, and the Institutions.

⑰ The Single European Act, '1992' and the Maastricht Treaty; the debate over the 'widening' and 'deepening' of the Community and over 'subsidiarity'.

Most of the countries of Western Europe faced a painful task of reconstruction after 1945; economic revival was the primary requisite after the devastation of the Second World War. Following the war, American aid provided statesmen in most of the non-Communist states with vital experience in economic cooperation. The Marshall Plan required recipients to coordinate their economic policies in order to use the aid to the best advantage.

During the war leaders of the Resistance movement in many countries had voiced the desire for a postwar reorganisation of the European states system, for the reduction of national autonomy and even for a federal Europe. The Cold War threat to Europe and the problem of how to contain the revival of German power offered further encouragement to ideas of greater European integration.

The first really major step in this direction was the Schuman Plan, which led to the setting up of the Coal and Steel Community. This was followed by the abortive attempt to create a European army, the European Defence Community. In 1957 the nations of the Six pooled their nuclear energy resources in Euratom and established the European Economic Community, which became the Nine in 1973, the Twelve by 1986, with further extension under negotiation.

15.1 EUROPEAN INTEGRATION

By 'integration' we mean the process of political and economic unification of the nation-states of Western Europe since the end of the Second World War in 1945. 'Integration' is to be distinguished from 'cooperation' by the fact that the participants in integration must delegate part of their national sovereignty to a body with supranational powers.

The idea of the unification of Europe was not new. Thinkers from the sixteenth century onwards had put forward schemes for a more or less federal European government. There had been Pan-European movements between the two world wars and the demand for European union was very strongly advanced by the resistance movement against the Nazis.

Common opposition to the Hitler regime had brought resistance fighters and exiled governments of different nationalities closer together. This movement condemned the system of nation-states and nationalism as the cause of Europe's war. As resistance activists expressed it in July 1944: 'Federal union alone can ensure the preservation of liberty and civilisation on the Continent of Europe, bring about economic recovery and enable the German people to play a peaceful role in European affairs.'

Factors favouring integration

There were a number of reasons why European statesmen were persuaded to move in the direction of European integration after 1945. The major ones were:

❶ The discrediting of Nationalism and the fact that, during the war, the nation-states of Europe had not been able to offer a minimum of security to their inhabitants against the aggressor.

❷ The impact of the Cold War and the need for European defence.

❸ Europe had ceased to be the dominant force in world affairs and was now replaced by the two superpowers, the US and the USSR. The idea grew of giving to Europe the necessary strength to preserve its independence and identity in the world.

❹ The need for large markets and the coordination of economic efforts in a modern technological economy if European countries were going to be able to compete, for instance with the US.

❺ American support for a strong Europe capable of resisting Soviet aggression – the US consistently exerted pressure in favour of integration.

❻ A means of solving 'the German question', by incorporating her in a larger unit on the basis of reconciliation with France.

❼ A general disposition towards European union on the part of the Catholic parties.

15.2 FEDERALISM AND FUNCTIONALISM

The federalist movement, which derived such encouragement from Resistance circles, called for European unity through the transfer of political sovereignty to a new central authority. In practice, though, at the end of the war the occupying armies handed over political control to restored national governments.

There was also the functionalist approach, represented most notably in the plans of M. Jean Monnet. He had had long experience of international affairs, having been Deputy Secretary General of the League of Nations. At the end of the war he became the first head of the French Economic Planning Commission. He was to be one of the most influential figures in the movement towards European integration.

He argued that a new international order could be built not, as the federalists hoped, by an out-and-out attack on the principle of state sovereignty and independence, but by the establishment of specialised agencies with real power to carry out certain functions, which would attract authority away from national governments. In the first instance the integration was to be economic, though the longer-term objective was political. The hope was that, just as the *Zollverein*, had helped to pave the way for German unification during the nineteenth century, so too the economic integration of Europe would prepare the way for political cohesion. There was in any case a widespread recognition, going far beyond those who were enthusiastic for European unification, that the economic and political problems of the Western European governments could not be solved within a purely national framework.

15.3 THE MARSHALL PLAN

A particularly strong impetus towards European unity came from the United States, as a result of the growing Cold War conflict between East and West, with the Truman Doctrine and the Marshall Plan.

The background to this was the collapse of British power and a desperate economic situation in Europe. The Cold War was the context within which the European integration movement was really reborn. The American Secretary of State, George Marshall, put forward a programme of massive economic aid to Europe. This was prompted, not least, by the political risks as the Americans saw them; an extremely weakened Europe would be vulnerable to Soviet pressure both from without and from within. They viewed with apprehension the existence of very large Communist parties in both France and Italy.

By April, 1948, the Organisation for European Economic Cooperation had been established to administer the aid programme. Through the plan more than 11 billion dollars of aid were made available by 1951 to the principal Western European countries. With this assistance their economies were able to recover, by that time, their prewar level. Once this process of substantial economic reconstruction had been set in motion it also became possible for statesmen to think purposefully in terms of Western European economic integration. This represented a change from the immediate postwar period, when the various governments had been hard-pressed simply to rebuild their devastated economies.

The offer of economic aid was made to the whole of Europe, including the Soviet Union. Before Moscow forced them to withdraw, Poland and Czechoslovakia had accepted the Marshall Plan with enthusiasm.

The OEEC succeeded in three principal tasks:
❶ cooperating in the distribution of Marshall Aid;
❷ freeing trade between its members from tariffs and other barriers;
❸ creating the European Payments Union for monetary transfers.

It was, however, an inter-governmental organisation with no supranational powers of decision. Awareness of its limitations and the success of the integration of Belgium, the Netherlands and Luxemburg (Benelux) helped to encourage the movement towards more effective integration.

15.4 NATO AND THE COUNCIL OF EUROPE

The two most significant Western organisations to be set up in 1949 were NATO (The North Atlantic Treaty Organisation) and the Council of Europe. NATO committed its members to consult together on the means of planning their common defence and to 'take such action as it deems necessary' in case of attack.

In fact the Western European countries had begun to establish a system of defensive military alliances before the escalation of the Cold War conflict in 1947. Both the Franco-British Treaty of Dunkirk and the Treaty of Brussels, signed by Britain, France and the Benelux countries were, however, signed partly with fears of a revived Germany in mind.

The crisis that led the West to expand the Brussels Treaty into NATO was the Berlin blockade of June, 1948–May, 1949.

The European Coal and Steel Community

In May 1950, the French Foreign Minister, Robert Schuman, following the suggestion of Jean Monnet, proposed a European Coal and Steel Community.

One motive behind this initiative was that French political leaders wished to ensure that German strength would never dominate Europe again. In particular, France wanted to maintain some control over the Ruhr industrial area. The pooling of coal and steel production would help to solve this problem.

There were other major considerations. In his announcement of the plan, M. Schuman declared: 'The pooling of coal and steel production will immediately provide for the establishment of common bases for economic development as a first step in the federation of Europe and will change the destinies of those regions which have long been devoted to the manufacture of munitions of war, of which they have been the most constant victims'.

The Coal and Steel Community (ECSC) was formally set up in April, 1951 and was a supranational organisation. The High Authority of the Community had real power to enforce its decisions on member states, even though its functions were limited to the control of the coal and steel industries.

The essential feature of the Schuman Plan was that six European governments were prepared to accept voluntary limitations on their national sovereignty in a vital part of their economic life with the political aim of progressing towards a united Europe. One of the main purposes of the ECSC was to serve as a pioneer for other movements towards integration.

The West German Chancellor, Konrad Adenauer, welcomed the Plan, of rehabilitating Germany and giving her greater status. He was intent on integrating West Germany into the West as a priority over German reunification. In Italy, Alcide de Gasperi was equally anxious to find a European framework which would offer his country a stable economic background against which to resolve its internal problems. The Benelux countries were already committed to a customs union and were looking beyond this to a closer economic union.

The European Defence Community and the European Political Community 1950–54

The outbreak of the Korean War led to American fears that the Soviet Union might move against Western Europe. The next area in which integration was proposed was that of defence. The Pleven Plan was a French proposal for solving the problem of fitting Germany into the Western Alliance in response to the American pressure for German rearmament.

The idea of a strong, independent German national army was unacceptable to very many Europeans, not least to large numbers of Germans. If German rearmament was essential – as the US argued it was – then it was logical for the armed forces to be controlled by a similar system. The federalists went further, to argue that a European army could only be directed by a European government. On the proposal of de Gasperi and Robert Schuman, an ad hoc assembly, formed by an enlargement of the Common Assembly of the ECSC, was directed to draw up a political statute for a European Political Community.

From 1950–54, the arguments for and against the European Defence Community (EDC) dominated the political life of France and Germany. In the first place it raised the fundamental question as to whether Germany should be rearmed at all. It was only five years since the Allies had resolved to abolish German militarism for ever and the German people had to a large extent supported the decision that the new Federal Republic would have no armed forces. There was also a marked resistance in France to the idea of the French Army merging its identity in a common European army.

The refusal of the French Assembly to ratify the EDC led to a serious setback for the European integration movement, but arrangements were speedily made for the rearmament of West Germany in a new and acceptable form. The outcome was the agreement of October 1954, to enlarge the Brussels Treaty organisation into a Western European Union into which Germany and Italy would both be admitted. They were also to become members of NATO and the function of the WEU was essentially to ensure that Germany did not create armed forces larger than 12 divisions and that she respected her pledge not to manufacture atomic, biological or chemical weapons. Britain also undertook to keep four army divisions and her tactical air force on the Continent.

15.5 THE TREATY OF ROME

The movement towards further European integration was revived with the Messina Conference of June, 1955. In October of that year, M. Monnet announced the formation of the Action Committee for the United States of Europe. These laid the basis for the Treaty of Rome by which the six members of the ECSC agreed to go ahead with the integration of their economies on a much broader scale, which was to include agriculture. This was signed in March, 1957, and at the same time the Six authorised the establishment of Euratom.

The provisions of the Treaty of Rome contained articles of two categories, those designed to achieve:
❶ 'positive' and
❷ 'negative' integration.

The first included such aims as the development of common European policies for industry and technology and the second involved all measures aimed at removing tariff barriers and obstacles to the free movement of labour and capital.

The major Community institutions which came into existence were:
❶ the executive Commission;
❷ the Council of Ministers;
❸ the European Parliament, with largely consultative powers;
❹ the Court of Justice.

The EEC emerged as more than a traditional inter-governmental organisation but less than a full federal structure. The Commission represented the unity of the Community, but final decisions were taken by the representatives of the individual member states in the Council of Ministers.

The enlargement of the Community

The EEC was helped by various factors to establish itself. One of these was the continuing rapid pace of economic growth and prosperity, to which it contributed. Another was the continued support of the US.

To start with, the British – who had seen themselves primarily as a World Power with overriding overseas commitments – reacted to the EEC by proposing a wider free-trade area of which Britain, the Community and the other OEEC countries could be a part. Negotiations for this broke down and Britain, under pressure from the Scandinavian countries, decided to go ahead with the construction of a smaller free-trade area. This led in 1960 to the setting up of EFTA with seven members – Britain, Denmark, Norway, Sweden, Switzerland, Portugal and Eire.

A year later the British Prime Minister, Mr. Macmillan, announced his government's decision to apply for membership of the Community. This application was vetoed by General de Gaulle in January, 1963. De Gaulle had moved from his previous hostility to the Community to the view that the Six was not only a useful economic group but one which could serve French political interests. This lay behind his initiative, the Fouchet proposals. There is little doubt that his veto was motivated primarily by political considerations: he wished to exclude a potential rival from the Community, and to resist Anglo-Saxon dominance in Europe.

De Gaulle also in 1965–6 effectively boycotted the instutions of the Community over agriculture and the financing of the Community, until won back with the Luxembourg Agreement which specified that an important national interest could be used as a reason for vetoing a decision in the Council of Ministers. The attitudes of

De Gaulle and, subsequently, Margaret Thatcher, with her well-advertised opposition to supranationalism or 'federalism', emphasise the tenacity of the national idea in conditions of increasing economic interdependence.

The final and successful negotiations for the enlargement of the Community were opened in June, 1970, during the presidency of de Gaulle's successor, M. Pompidou. All the major issues of the British case were settled within a year. In January 1973, the Six became the Nine with the accession of the UK, Denmark and Eire.

Membership did not, however, end debate in the UK. In particular, there was strong hostility within the British Labour Party and Trade Union movement. This forced Harold Wilson, returned to power in 1974, to call a referendum on membership in 1975. Two-thirds of those voting opted to remain in the Community, but major unresolved issues persisted, notably the unpopular Common Agricultural Policy and the size of the British contribution to the Community budget. These became headline news in the 1980s with Mrs. Thatcher's celebrated exchanges with her Community partners and the Commission.

In 1979 Direct Elections were held for the first time to the European Parliament (up till then it had consisted of nominees from the national parliaments). The other major innovation at this time was the creation of the European Monetary System (EMS) with its Exchange Rate Mechanism (ERM). Its purpose was to produce a 'zone of monetary stability' after the chronic instability in world financial markets of the 1970s, following the end of Bretton Woods and the fourfold increase in world oil prices after the Arab–Israel War of 1973. From the 1960s onwards, though, the Community signed a significant series of agreements with Third World Countries, especially African States, which emphasise her importance as a burgeoning world economic power.

Further enlargement and institutional reform

By the mid-1980s there was widespread fear that the Community was stagnating economically and in the grip of institutional paralysis. Renewed interest was shown in 'European political union' and it was decided to create a genuinely free market by abolishing the non-tariff barriers within the Community.

This led to the major innovation of the Single European Act (SEA) which came into effect in 1987. It called for the completion of the single market by the end of 1992 and brought in qualified majority voting (as against unanimity) for a number of measures. The 1980s also saw the enlargement of the Community to include Greece, Spain and Portugal. The original Six became the Twelve. With the collapse of Communism in Eastern Europe and the reunification of Germany, the Community now faces application for membership from both Western European states, such as Austria, and erstwhile Communist states, such as Poland and Czechoslovakia. The need to adapt to very changed circumstances is one of the principal motives behind the much-debated Maastricht treaty of December 1991. The original debate over membership has now given way to discussions over whether the Community should be 'widened' or 'deepened', or both, over its territorial extent and the extent of centralised decision-making. These discussions include such questions as to whether the Community should have an integrated defence policy, or a European Central Bank.

15.6 CHRONOLOGY

| 1946 | September | WINSTON CHURCHILL'S ZÜRICH SPEECH, calling for Franco-German reconciliation within a 'United States of Europe'. |
| 1947 | July | ANNOUNCEMENT OF MARSHALL AID: to stimulate European recovery. A committee set up to draft a European Recovery Programme; European Payments Union set up to distribute this. |

	October	Economic union of Belgium, the Netherlands and Luxembourg – BENELUX.
1948	March	The Brussels Treaty: Benelux; France and England.
	April	The OEEC (Organisation for European Economic Cooperation) formed.
1949	April	NATO (North Atlantic Treaty Organisation) formed.
	May	The Statute of the Council of Europe signed, consisting of the Brussels Treaty powers plus Sweden, Denmark, Eire, Norway, Italy, Iceland, Greece, Turkey, West Germany and Austria.
1950	May	THE SCHUMAN PLAN: to place French and German coal and steel under a common authority.
	October	THE EUROPEAN DEFENCE COMMUNITY: devised and presented by M. Pleven. Recommendation of a European Ministry of Defence and the integration of Germany into the defence of Western Europe rather than the rearmament of West Germany as an independent unit. After four years of debate it was rejected by the French National Assembly.
1951	April	THE EUROPEAN COAL AND STEEL COMMUNITY (ECSC) TREATY signed by the Six – Benelux, France, Germany and Italy – to become operational in 1953. This Treaty set up the first common European authority, the ECSC High Authority, subject to democratic control through an assembly and to the rule of law through the Court of Justice.
1954	October	Western European Union formed: the Six plus Britain.
1955	June	MESSINA CONFERENCE of the foreign ministers of the Six. Set up a committee under M. Spaak to study ways in which 'a fresh advance towards the building of Europe could be achieved'.
1957	March	ROME TREATIES SIGNED, setting up the European Economic Community and Euratom.
1958	January	THE ROME TREATIES CAME INTO EFFECT.
1959	May	EUROPEAN FREE TRADE ASSOCIATION (EFTA) formed by Austria, Denmark, Norway, Sweden, Switzerland, Portugal and the UK.
1962	March	The UK applied for membership of EEC.
1963	January	Signing of Franco-German Friendship Treaty. DE GAULLE VETOED BRITISH ENTRY INTO EEC.
1965	July	French boycott of Community institutions for seven months in opposition to the Commission's proposal that all import duties and levies be paid to the Community budget, and that the powers of the European Parliament be increased.
1966	January	The 1965 crisis was ended by the Luxembourg compromise which stated that the other community member states would not overrule a country that opposed a piece of draft EC legislation on the ground that a vital national interest was at stake.
1967	May	The UK, Eire and Denmark submitted applications for membership.
	July	COMMUNITY EXECUTIVES MERGED INTO A SINGLE COMMISSION.
	December	Council reached deadlock after de Gaulle's refusal to accept UK entry.
1969	April	The resignation of General de Gaulle.
	December	The Hague Summit – the Six agreed to enlarge the Community.
1971	June	Agreement reached on Britain's entry to the EEC.
1973	January	DENMARK, EIRE AND THE UK JOINED THE COMMUNITY. The Six became the Nine.
1973	December	Copenhagen Summit meeting.
1974	January	Oil crisis. Price of oil quadrupled in three months.
	December	Paris Summit. Agreement to set up Regional Development Fund.
1975	March	Regional Development Fund in operation.
	May	LOMÉ CONVENTION SIGNED BY THE COMMUNITY WITH 47 DEVELOPING COUNTRIES.

	June	Referendum in the UK showed a two-thirds majority in favour of remaining in the Community
1976	January	Tindemans Report on Economic and Political Union.
1977	July	Spain applied to join the Community.
1978	July	THE HEADS OF GOVERNMENT AT THE EUROPEAN COUNCIL IN BREMEN AGREED TO SET UP THE EUROPEAN MONETARY SYSTEM (EMS).
	October	Negotiations opened for the accession of Portugal.
1979	February	Negotiations opened for the accession of Spain.
	March	EMS CAME INTO OPERATION WITH FOUR MAIN COMPONENTS, A CURRENCY UNIT (ECU), EXCHANGE RATE MECHANISM, CREDIT FACILITIES AND TRANSFER ARRANGEMENTS.
	June	First direct elections to the European Parliament held.
	October	SECOND LOMÉ CONVENTION.
1981	January	Greece became the tenth member of the Community.
1982	July	The European Parliament passed a resolution in support of reform of the Treaties and the achievement of European Union.
1983	June	Second elections to the European Parliament.
1985	June	The Commission issued White Paper on the Single European Market.
	December	THE DRAWING UP OF THE SINGLE EUROPEAN ACT AT THE LUXEMBOURG EUROPEAN COUNCIL – THE CREATION OF A SINGLE EUROPEAN MARKET BY THE END OF 1992.
1986	January	Spain and Portugal joined the Community.
1987	July	THE SINGLE EUROPEAN ACT (SEA) CAME INTO EFFECT. This amended the treaties of Rome to improve EC functioning both by allowing for the adoption of legislation by less than unanimous vote of the member states, and by expanding Community powers.
1988	February	Summit Agreement where reform of the Common Agricultural Policy (CAP), budget reform and the doubling of regional aid were agreed.
1989	June	Third elections to the European Parliament.
1991	December	THE MAASTRICHT TREATY PROVIDING FOR THE CREATION OF A COMMON EC CURRENCY AND CENTRAL BANK BY 1999 AND EXTENDING THE ROLE OF THE COMMUNITY.
1993	January	THE SINGLE EUROPEAN MARKET TO COME INTO FORCE.

Illustrative questions and answers

1 Would you agree that the Marshall Plan saved Europe from certain economic collapse?

Tutorial note

A precise answer to this question cannot be given but you can explain the economic crisis which the Marshall Plan was intended to solve, and speculate on what might have happened without it.

You need to know about

The European economic crisis of 1947, and its political background. The Marshall Plan and its effects.

Suggested answer plan

1   The nature of the Western European economic crisis of 1947: (a) shortages of food and raw materials (especially coal), due to a delayed recovery of production, was worsened by a bad harvest and a harsh winter; this led to inflation, and labour unrest; (b) the financial crisis (the 'dollar gap') – Europe's export industries had been dislocated, and it had difficulty in earning foreign currency, especially as its prewar foreign investments had mostly been lost; in particular, most European countries ran very large balance-of-payments deficits with the USA, because of their imports from it of the capital goods and machinery needed for reconstruction (Germany had been the other big prewar exporter of machinery but industrial production in West Germany was one-third of the prewar level); the danger was that the European countries would halt their economic expansion programmes due to a shortage of dollars, thus leading to further social unrest and to political crises which would benefit the Left in Germany and elsewhere, in turn further damaging business confidence.

2   The Marshall Plan and its effects: the Plan was announced in principle in Secretary of State Marshall's Harvard speech, in June, 1947. The distribution of the US aid was worked out by the European nations (including West Germany but *not* members of the Soviet bloc) in the Organisation for European Economic Recovery (OEEC). The aid was used for: (a) the finance of European imports from the US, especially capital goods; (b) investment in basic industries in Europe. In its first year the Plan accounted for 4% of the national income of the 14 European recipients. It allowed: (a) a continuing, very fast industrial growth (especially in West Germany); (b) the restoration of the trade balance between Western Europe and the US by 1950–1.

3   The contribution of the Plan was: (a) economic – the removal of the bottleneck of the dollar gap, and the revival of German machinery production for supply to the rest of Europe (other measures, such as the German currency reform of 1948, helped here); and (b) political – the solution to the problem of German recovery. Germany's neighbours (especially France) needed what it could produce but feared that Germany's economic revival would enable it again to become a military threat. The Plan overcame this obstacle because: (a) Germany's recovery would take place only as part of a recovery of Western Europe as a whole and hence would, in relative terms, be less threatening; (b) Germany's neighbours would not get reparations but would be compensated for this by US aid; and (c) German recovery would be less dangerous if it was within the political framework of a continuing presence of US troops in Europe and of French alliances with Britain (e.g. the Dunkirk and Brussels treaties, 1947 and 1948) and with the USA (the North Atlantic Treaty, 1949).

4   The Marshall Plan therefore not only solved the problem of the 'dollar gap' but also permitted German economic recovery to take place without the controversies over reparations and French security that followed the First World War (though, while reassuring France, it gravely alarmed the USSR).

2   Examine why it was possible to establish a European Economic Community but not a European Defence Community.

Tutorial note

A straightforward question requiring you to compare the failure of the proposed EDC (1950–4) with the successful establishment of the EEC in 1955–8.

You need to know about

The history of the European integration movement, c. 1950–8. Attitudes towards it of the various national governments, notably Britain, France, West Germany and the US.

1   Set the context: the early 1950s were the most favourable historical moment for moves to pool sovereignty in Western Europe. Before that point there was no West German state, and wartime memories were still too bitter; also, by the late 1950s, traditional national consciousness was reasserting itself (especially in France after 1958 and De Gaulle's assumption of power). In 1950 two initiatives were launched by the French government: (a) the Schuman Plan, which was to lead on to the European Coal and Steel Community, and later to the EEC; and (b) the Pleven Plan, for the European Defence Community, which did not succeed. Agreement, therefore, was reached over economic questions but not defence, which was much closer to the essence of national sovereignty.

2   Both the Schuman and the Pleven plans were French attempts to reduce the risks of German recovery: French reasons were (a) economic, in the case of the ECSC – e.g. the need to assure France supplies of German coking coal and to keep some international control over the Ruhr; and (b) military, in the case of the EDC – e.g., the US government, as a result of the Korean War, had pressed for the creation of West German armed forces, and the Pleven Plan, intended as an *alternative* to this, proposed a European force which would include German units but with a multinational command. In the emergency caused by the Korean War, the Plan was approved by the French parliament; the EDC treaty was signed in 1952 and approved by most of the parliaments of the ECSC 'Six' but defeated by the French parliament in August, 1954 by a combination of Communist votes with those of nationalists hostile to German rearmament.

3   Why did the French reject the EDC treaty? Reasons include (a) the lukewarm attitude of the French Premier, Mendès-France; (b) after the death of Stalin in 1953 and the resulting slackening of East-West tension, any strengthening of West European defences seemed less urgent; and (c) the reluctance of Britain to participate in the EDC as a possible counterweight to Germany. Note, however, that the October 1954 Paris accords (which the French parliament approved) *did* provide for a West German army but this was to be balanced by a British commitment to keep troops indefinitely on the Continent. This settlement of the defence question made further integration easier.

4   The EEC: this was accepted in principle by the ECSC 'Six' at Messina in June, 1955 and confirmed by the Treaty of Rome, March 1957, which all six parliaments ratified. There were four main reasons for this success:

    (a)   the project was deliberately *not* presented as leading on to political unification but rather took the form of a broadening out of the successful ECSC, which had benefited the European coal and steel industries while not infringing intolerably on national sovereignty, and whose institutions were copied by the EEC;

    (b)   agreement was probably assisted by the revival of the Cold War (Hungary, October–November, 1956);

    (c)   Britain's absence was less serious than for the EDC, and made negotiations simpler;

    (d)   a successful balance was struck between Germany's desire for larger export markets and the interests of France: France obtained (i) European assistance for the French civil nuclear programme, through Euratom, (ii) European aid for France's colonies, and (iii) special transitional arrangements to protect French industry.

5   *Conclusion.* The EDC was a much more ambitious project than the EEC, which was built on the earlier success of the ECSC. The French attitude was the key: France was given adequate reassurances over the EEC but not over the EDC.

3   Examine the historical origins of the European Economic Community.

An open-ended question, which requires you to balance long- against short-term explanations.

You need to know about

The historical antecedents of European unification. The stages of European integration, c. 1950–8.

Suggested answer plan

1   (a) The origins of 'European' consciousness are very old; there were the precedents of the Roman Empire, Charlemagne, medieval Christendom at war with the Saracens and later with the Turks, and the nineteenth-century cooperation of the Powers in the 'Concert of Europe'. Since the sixteenth century, however, there had been the rise of rival allegiances – the Reformation, the spread of national consciousness in Europe, and ideological divisions caused by the French and Russian revolutions and by the spread of Fascism. (b) On the economic side, there had been the spectacular increase in intra-European trade due to the industrial revolution and the railways before 1914; there was evidence also (e.g. from the German Zollverein) that a customs union could promote economic growth and political unity (cf. also the US). The growth, however, of intra-European trade was much weaker between the wars. (c) The 'European' movement: advocates of surrendering some or all national sovereignty to pan-European institutions. This grew stronger between the wars and won over some statesmen (e.g. Briand and Herriot in France).

2   These long-term trends are less important than the following specific circumstances after 1945:
    (a)   The strengthening of the European movement by the Second World War; many of the postwar statesmen most concerned were in opposition or exile during the war (e.g. Monnet, Schuman, Adenauer), and there was also the wartime Resistance. Favourable circumstances for the spread of the pan-European movement included: (i) the rival economic power of the US seemed more formidable than ever; (ii) East European Communist parties were now backed by the Red Army; and (iii) there was increasing hostility to the colonial Powers outside Europe. All of these, among other reasons, made continuance of European internal political and economic conflicts appear suicidal.
    (b)   In spite of this, there was deep resentment against Germany in the former German-occupied states of Western Europe. The timing of the unification movement is explained by the British/US rehabilitation of West Germany due to the Cold War – i.e. the economic recovery under the Marshall Plan; the West German constitution (1949) and West German rearmament (agreed by 1954). The biggest obstacle to European integration was Franco-German hostility. This was overcome by: (i) the European movement; (ii) the need to strengthen Western defences against the USSR; (iii) the presence in Germany of British and US forces, which was a reassurance to France against possible renewed German aggression. But it was the acceptance of the Schuman Plan (1950) – the French proposal for a European Coal and Steel Community designed to assure France's coking coal supplies and to keep German heavy industry under some international control – which proved to be the crucial breakthrough; the Plan's function was to reassure France about the consequences of German economic recovery.

3   The foundation of the EEC was a smaller step than that of the ECSC, and needs less explanation. 'European' enthusiasts in the governments of the Six were seeking a new line of advance after the 1954 failure of the European Defence Community, and chose to broaden the methods of cooperation of the ECSC to other branches of industry. Purely economic motives were by now increasingly important rather than political ones, though agreement helped by the revival of the Cold War (e.g. Hungary, October–November 1956; the launch of the Sputnik, October 1957). There was wide acceptance of the view that the

removal of international barriers would encourage economic stability and growth, and there was the German desire for larger markets.

4   *Conclusion*. The EEC was made possible by the ECSC, which was a solution to the problems of German recovery. The EEC was made possible also by economic growth, which it accelerated, and by the European movement, which paradoxically declined after 1958.

Question bank

1   Document question: Study extracts I and II below and answer questions (a) to (g) which follow:

Extract I

'...Since 1947, we have confounded both the Communists and the other cynics by proving, first, that together we could successfully start economic recovery in Western Europe;and, second, that we could join in <u>laying the foundations for security against attack upon our Atlantic Community</u>... .

'The European Recovery Programme is now approaching the halfway mark. The time has come to consider carefully what more must be done to hold the ground already gained and to assure the further progress that is vitally needed. We must now devote our fullest energies to the major tasks.

'These tasks are: First to balance Europe's dollar accounts so that Europe can buy the raw materials and other items which mean employment and better living. The second...is to move ahead on a far-reaching programme to build in Western Europe a more dynamic, expanding economy which will promise steady improvement in the conditions of life for all its people. This, I believe means nothing less than an integration of the Western European economy... .

'The substance of such integration would be the formation of a single large market within which quantitative restrictions on the movement of goods, monetary barriers to the flow of payments and, eventually, all tariffs are permanently swept away... . <u>The creation of a permanent, freely trading area</u>, comprising 270,000,000 consumers in Western Europe would have a multitude of helpful consequences.... This would make it possible for Europe to improve its competitive position in the world and thus more nearly satisfy the expectations and needs of its people.

'This is a vital objective. It was to this that Secretary Marshall pointed in the speech which sparked Europe to new hope and new endeavour. It was on this promise that the Congress of the United States enacted the ECA act. This goal is embedded in the Convention of the OEEC.'

(Speech of Paul Hoffman to the OEEC Council in Paris, 31 October 1949)

Extract II

'It is becoming more and more evident to everyone that the implementation of the Marshall Plan will mean placing European countries under the economic and political control of the United States and direct interference by the latter in the internal affairs of those countries. Moreover, this plan is an attempt to split Europe into two camps and, with the help of the United Kingdom and France, to complete the formation of a bloc of several European countries hostile to the interests of the democratic countries of Eastern Europe and most particularly to the interests of the Soviet Union. An important feature of this Plan is the attempt to confront the countries of Eastern Europe with a bloc of Western European States, including Western Germany. The intention is to make use of Western Germany and German heavy industry (the Ruhr)as one of the most important economic bases for American expansion in Europe in disregard of the national interests of the countries which suffered from German aggression... .'

(Andrei Vyshinsky: *A Criticism of the Truman Doctrine and the Marshall Plan*, 18 September 1947)

(a) Explain the reference to 'laying the foundations for security against attack upon our Atlantic Community'. (2)

(b) Describe the purposes and limitations of the OEEC as perceived at this time. (4)

(c) Explain the circumstances which led to the foundation of the European Recovery Programme. (5)

(d) Account for the contrasting views in Extracts I and II towards Western European integration. (7)

(e) How does Extract I reflect a changed attitude on the part of the US towards European integration? To what extent does Extract II explain the reasons for that change? (7)

(f) What other 'helpful consequences' might the creation of a 'permanent, freely trading area' have been expected to have? (5)

2 What conditions encouraged the growth of cooperation between the western democracies after the Second World War?   (Cambridge, June 1991)

3 Why did France and West Germany lead the movement towards Western European cooperation and unity after 1945?   (London, June 1986)

4 Compare the approaches taken to post-1945 economic reconstruction in 'western Europe' with those taken in 'eastern Europe.' (NISEAC, June 1990)

5 Evaluate the political and economic consequences, to 1973, of the formation of the European Economic Community.   (AS Level, AEB, June 1989)

READING LIST

Standard textbook reading
H. Stuart Hughes, *Contemporary Europe: A History* (Prentice Hall, 1976), chapters 15, 17, 19, 20.
David Thomson, *Europe since Napoleon* (Penguin, 1975), chapter 30.

Further suggested reading
C. Black et al., *Rebirth: A History of Europe since World War Two* (Westview, 1992).
M. Blacksell, *Post-War Europe: A Political Geography* (Hutchinson, 1981).
Brian Crozier, *De Gaulle: the Statesman* (Methuen, 1974).
A. Grosser, *Germany in our Time* (Pall Mall, 1971).

J. Joll, *Europe since 1870* (Weidenfeld and Nicolson, 1973).
P. Lane, *Europe Since 1945* (Batsford, 1985).
A. Milward, *The Reconstruction of Western Europe 1945–51* (Methuen, 1984).
J. Monnet, *Memoirs* (Collins, 1978).
R. C. Mowat. *Ruin and Resurgence 1939–45* (Blandford, 1966).
A. J. Ryder, *Twentieth-Century Germany from Bismarck to Brandt* (Macmillan, 1973).
D. W. Urwin, *The Community of Europe* (Longman, 1991).
D. Weigall and P. Stirk (ed.) *The Origins and Development of the European Community* (Leicester University Press, 1992).
R. Vaughan, *Twentieth-Century Europe: Paths to Unity* (Croom Helm, 1979).

TEST RUN

In this section:

Test Your Knowledge Quiz

Test Your Knowledge Quiz Answers

Mock Exam

Mock Exam Suggested Answer Plans

This section should be tackled towards the end of your revision programme, when you have covered all your syllabus topics, and attempted
the practice questions at the end of the relevant chapters.

The Test Your Knowledge Quiz contains short-answer questions on a wide
range of syllabus topics. You should attempt it without reference to the
text.

Check your answers against the Test Your Knowledge Quiz Answers. If
you are not sure why you got an answer wrong, go back to the relevant
unit in the text: you will find the reference next to our answer.

The Mock Exam is set out like a real exam paper. It contains a wide spread
of question styles and topics, drawn from various examination boards. You
should attempt this paper under examination conditions. Read the instructions on the front sheet carefully. Attempt the paper in the time allowed,
and without reference to the text.

Compare your answers to our Mock Exam Suggested Answer Plans. We
have provided tutorial notes to each, showing why we answered the
question as we did and indicating where your answer may have differed
from ours.

TEST YOUR KNOWLEDGE QUIZ

1   What is meant by Absolutism?

2   What were the main points in the French Charter of 1814?

3   Which key statement of this period contained the following words:

> States which have undergone a change of government, due to revolution, the results of which threaten other states *ipso facto* cease to be members of the European Alliance, and remain excluded from it until their situation gives guarantees for legal order and stability. If, owing to such alterations, immediate danger threatens other States, the powers bind themselves, by peaceful means, or if need be, by arms, to bring back the guilty State into the bosom of the Great Alliance.

4   What was the significance of the Belgian revolution of 1830?

5   What were the National Workshops?

6   What was the role of Daniele Manin in 1848–9?

7   What did the supporters of a 'grossdeutsch' solution to the question of German unification want in 1848?

8   What was the significance of the Convention of Olmütz?

9   What was the Philiké Hetairia?

10 In what circumstances was the Treaty of Unkiar Skelessi concluded?

11 What were the Vienna Four Points?

12 What was the significance of 'Young Italy'?

13 What was the Statuto?

14 Explain, briefly, what is meant by the 'Roman Question'.

15 What was the Cobden-Chevalier Treaty?

16 Explain what is meant by the right of interpellation.

17 What was the Luxembourg Crisis of 1866–67?

18 What were the major points in the Treaty of Frankfurt of 10 May 1871?

19 What was the Zollverein?

20 What were the terms of the Gastein Convention of 14 August 1865?

21 What was the purpose of the Indemnity Bill of 3 September 1866?

22 Explain the term 'Realpolitik'.

23 Who were the Populists?

24 In what ways was Sergei Witte a significant political figure?

25 What was the purpose of the Stolypin agrarian reforms?

26 What was 'La Revanche'?

27 Explain what is meant by Pan-Germanism in this period.

28 What did the idea of a Continental League involve?

29 What was the significance of the Algeçiras Conference of 1906?

30 What is meant by self-determination?

31 What reparation payments were demanded from Germany after the First World War and to what extent were these demands met?

32 What was the Chanak Crisis?

33 What were the 'April Theses'?

34 What demands were issued by the Kronstadt mutineers in 1921?

35 Who was Nikolai Bukharin?

36 What were the major points of the Stalin Constitution of 1936?

37 Who were the Squadristi?

38 What was the Corfù Crisis of 1923?

39 What did the Roman Catholic Church gain from the Lateran Pacts of 1929?

40 Who were
i) the Freikorps?
ii) the 'November Criminals'?

41 What was the significance of the Enabling Act of 23 March 1933?

42 What was the Fritsch Plot?

43 What was the significance of the London Naval Agreement of 18 July 1935?

44 What was the Hossbach Protocol?

45 What were the terms and what was the significance of the Anti-Comintern Pact of 25 November 1936?

46 What was the Katyn Forest Massacre?

47 What is the 'force de frappe'?

48 Explain what was meant by the 'Brezhnev Doctrine'.

49 What was the significance of the Messina Conference of 1955?

50 What was the Luxembourg Compromise of 1966?

51 What is the EMS?

TEST YOUR KNOWLEDGE QUIZ ANSWERS

1 A system of government in which the governed possess no representation, right to vote or part in the administration and in which there are no legal or constitutional restraints on the ruler (contrast constitutional government). Absolutist, hereditary monarchies could not be challenged or opposed in the name of government, but their exercise of power was constrained by natural law, traditions and a sense of responsibility to God.

2 Its declared principles were:
   ❶ representative government
   ❷ ministerial responsibility
   freedom of religion, of the press and 'of persons'. The first point declared: 'Frenchmen are equal before the Law, whatever may be their titles and their ranks'. Three powers were specified:
   i   the hereditary Crown
   ii the Chamber of Peers
   iii the Chamber of Deputies.

   The Charter retained most of the liberties won by the Revolution. Lands confiscated from the Church and nobility remained in the hands of the new owners. It also abolished conscription.

3 The Troppau Protocol, 1820.

4 The Belgian revolution was the first major territorial departure from the Vienna Settlement and led to the establishment of a new state with a liberal constitution.

   In 1815 Belgium had been united to Holland as a buffer against resumed French expansion. Friction over the position of Belgian Catholics, Belgian under-representation in the States-General and economic difficulties had led to the revolution.

   The London Conference of November 1830 proposed that Belgium should be established under perpetual guarantees of neutrality and inviolability. The Dutch were ejected in 1831 and a Five-Power Treaty guaranteeing neutrality was signed in 1839.

5   An attempt by the Provisional Government of the Second Republic in 1848 to alleviate the problem of mass unemployment. Not only Parisians, thousands of provincial unemployed too. The workshops proved ruinously expensive and offered limited relief work. The cost could only be met by an unpopular increase in taxation, felt most onerously by the peasantry. The newly elected Assembly decided to close them, provoking the insurrection of the June Days in Paris.

6   Leader of the Venetian revolution and inspiration behind its long defence in 1849. He organised a popular movement which ousted the Venetian Provisional Government and proclaimed the Republic of St. Mark in March 1848. He was elected President and established ties with other revolutionary governments in Italy. He supported the annexation of Lombardy to Piedmont-Sardinia and the attempt of Charles Albert to occupy Venetia. After the Piedmontese monarch's second defeat, Manin held out against the Austrians until August 1849.

7   The extent of a united Germany was complicated by other nationalities, such as the Danes of Schleswig and the Poles of Posen. The 'grossdeutsch' solution meant the inclusion of Austria in a reformed Bund. Austria was excluded from Germany after her defeat by Prussia in 1866 ('Kleindeutsch').

8   This was the result of the meeting in November 1850 between Schwarzenberg and Manteuffel. Prussia accepted the Federal solution to the crisis over Hesse and acknowledged Austria's superiority within the Bund. After the failure of the Frankfurt Parliament, Radowitz had tried to build up a Prussian union of Princes which would unify Germany and exclude Austria. At this time, though, Austria still had Russia's support.

9   The 'Friendly Society' – the secret Greek nationalist movement founded by three Greeks in the Russian city of Odessa in 1814. By the time of the outbreak of the Greek War of Independence in 1821 it had managed to recruit members from nearly every major regional and social group in the Hellenic world. It played a role in the events which led to the Greek revolt and encouraged the belief that the Tsar would come to the aid of the Greeks against Ottoman rule.

10 This Russo-Turkish defensive alliance (1833) followed the first Mehemet Ali Crisis. The Russians had intervened with 30 000 troops, saving Asia Minor and Constantinople at the Straits, from the Pasha of Egypt. The Treaty was the price for that support and regretted by Britain, whose Navy had been engaged off Holland and Portugal at this time.

11 The suggested conditions for peace between Russia and Turkey during the Crimean War (1854). They specified:
    ❶ collective guarantee of the position of the Principalities and Serbia
    ❷ free passage of the mouth of the Danube
    ❸ a revision of the Straits Convention in the interests of the balance of power
    ❹ Russian abandonment of claims to a protectorate over the Sultan's Christian subjects.

12 Founded by Giuseppe Mazzini in Marseilles in July 1831, the 'Young Italy' movement set out to propagate republican nationalism throughout the peninsula. It concentrated on the political education of the Italian people. After a failed insurrection in Savoy in 1833, Mazzini was condemned to death 'in absentia'. In 1834 he went on to set up the 'Young Europe' movement. He was the leading prophet of Italian unification and led the Roman Republic in the revolutions of 1848–9.

13 The Sardininan Constitution of 1848 which became the Constitution of the Kingdom of Italy in 1861. Proclaimed by King Charles Albert, it sanctioned a sharing of power between the monarch and a parliament chosen on the basis of a highly restricted electorate. The Statuto proclaimed Roman Catholicism to be the state religion, but also safeguarded the rights of religious minorities.

14 This term covers several problems in Italian Church–State relations between the decade of Italian unification and the Lateran Accords of 1929. Between

1859 and 1861 it centred on the protest of Pope Pius IX against the seizure of the Papal States by the new Italian State. From 1861–1870 it turned on the question of the acquisition of Rome as capital of the new State. This was attempted both by negotiation, by Cavour among others, and by force, by Garibaldi. The Pope secluded himself in the Vatican, rejecting the privileges and assurances of the Law of Papal Guarantees and refusing to recognise the new Kingdom of Italy.

15 The Treaty was an Anglo-French tariff agreement signed in January 1860. Britain and France lowered or eliminated duties on each other's goods and France abolished prohibition. It was the first of a series of similar commercial agreements between European States which introduced low tariffs. It was intended to facilitate economic expansion, stimulate an economy that had suffered commercial crisis in 1857 and, Napoleon III hoped, encourage improved relations between France and Britain, which had deteriorated during the French intervention in Italy in 1859.

16 A procedure by which a minister could be called before Chamber to explain his actions. If the Chamber was not satisfied, it could register a vote of no-confidence against the Government. This practice had begun during the French Revolution (1791); Napoleon III suspended it (1852–69) and the Third Republic reconfirmed it in the Law of 13 March 1873.

17 An episode in the Franco-Prussian territorial compensation negotiations after Prussia's defeat of Austria in 1866. The French proposed to acquire Luxembourg with suitable compensation for the King of Holland. Bismarck voiced opposition to conceding Luxembourg, which many thought to be German. A conference in London, attended by representatives of Britain, Russia, Austria, Prussia, France and Luxembourg agreed in 1867 to respect the neutrality of the Duchy. The Prussian garrison was withdrawn and the Duchy put under collective European guarantee. This agreement ended French hopes of compensation, which Bismarck had led Napoleon III to believe he would receive. The crisis contributed to that deterioration of relations which led in 1870 to the Franco-Prussian War.

18 The Treaty of Frankfurt ended the Franco-Prussian War.
    ❶ An indemnity of five thousand million francs was imposed on France.
    ❷ The province of Alsace and a third of Lorraine were separated from France in spite of Bismarck's objection.
    ❸ German troops were to be stationed on French soil until the indemnity was settled.

19 The customs union founded mainly within the German Confederation (Bund) in 1834, but excluding Austria. The Zollverein removed anachronistic tariff barriers but soon erected new ones to protect the rising industry of Prussia. It confirmed Prussian economic leadership in Germany and prepared the way for the 'kleindeutsch' solution of German unification. Efforts made by Austria to join after 1850 were frustrated.

20 This agreement, reached between Bismarck and the Austrian envoy Count Blome in August 1865, regulated the occupation rights of Prussia and Austria in Schleswig-Holstein after the war against Denmark. Schleswig was to be administered by Prussia, and Holstein by Austria. Lauenburg was ceded to Prussia as an indemnity and Prussia was granted the right to establish naval dockyards in Kiel. None of the other members of the German Confederation was consulted. Gastein, described by Bismarck as a 'papering-over of the cracks', did not avert the Austro-Prussian War which broke out in 1866.

21 This Bill called for a retrospective endorsement of the expenses incurred by the Government during the constitutional crisis over the Roon Army Reforms. The dispute over the Army had developed into a full constitutional crisis, with Bismarck arguing the 'gap theory': since the constitution did not provide for the eventuality of both Houses failing to agree on a budget, it was possible to govern without one. After the Prussian victory over Austria, Bismarck hoped to appease the opposition in Prussia and gain the support of

the non-Prussian Liberals in the North German Confederation. The Conservatives voted en bloc for the indemnity. The Liberals split, the majority supporting it too. This also meant that the unification of northern Germany was achieved on Prussian conservative rather than liberal parliamentary terms.

22 This term was coined by Ludwig von Rochau in 1853. It means the pursuit of objectives which have a realistic chance of success. Originally used to criticise the impractical idealism of the Frankfurt Assembly Liberals (1848), it has often been used to describe Bismarck's approach to foreign policy in which he adjusted his aims realistically to circumstance.

23 Members of the widespread movement opposed to Tsarist authority and the centralised Russian state apparatus, who wished to replace it by a loose federation of socialist self-governing units based on the commune. Populism developed against the background of disappointment with the consequences of the 1861 emancipation of the serfs and it tended to idealise peasant life and to encourage the belief that capitalist development could be bypassed.

24 As Tsarist Minister of Finance and Chairman of the Council of Ministers, he was largely responsible for the government-sponsored programme of industrialisation at the end of the century and for the implementation of Reform during the 1905 Revolution. His policies included:
- reorganisation of the protective tariff system,
- encouragement of foreign investment,
- introduction of the Gold Standard.

His period of office also saw:
- construction of the Trans-Siberian Railway,
- establishment of the Russo-Chinese Bank,
- encouragement of settlement in Siberia.

25 Introduced by the ukase of November 1906 and the laws of June 1910 and June 1911, the Stolypin reforms were meant to counter revolutionary influences among the peasantry by:
- introducing them to private property,
- granting them the right to leave the village commune,
- allowing them to acquire their own plots of land.

The aim was to transform the mass of the peasantry into a class of small and medium farmers which would have a stabilising influence in the countryside.

26 This was used to refer to the French wish to be revenged on Germany for the humiliation of the Franco-Prussian War, and to specifically, their desire to win back Alsace-Lorraine.

27 The idea of an expanded Germany to include all German-speaking peoples in Europe and some of their neighbours (e.g. Dutch, Flemish and Swiss-German). In the 1890s its supporters became organised in the Alldeutscher Verband (the Pan-German League).

28 The idea of a Continental League against Great Britain was floated by the German government between 1895 and 1905 and reflected deteriorating relations between the two countries. The purpose was either to draw Britain out of her reserve towards Germany, or to avoid the danger of a war on two fronts.

29 A three-month international meeting to settle the dispute between France and Germany over control of Morocco. It reaffirmed French rights there, though France was not allowed to annex the country. It aroused suspicions about German imperialist objectives and drew France and Britain closer together. Ostensibly championing Moroccan independence, the Kaiser wished to extend German influence and weaken the Anglo-French Entente.

30 The aspiration of a group of people, grounded in some existing sentiment of national or racial identity associated with common territory, language and religion, to govern itself. This aspiration was encouraged by President Woodrow Wilson's Fourteen Points and the effects of self-determination are particularly in evidence in the disintegration of the Habsburg Empire.

31 In 1921 the Allies fixed the reparations dues at 226 000 million gold marks, to be paid in 42 annual instalments. After Germany's inflationary collapse in 1923 the Dawes Plan (1924) and subsequently the Young Plan (1929) reduced them. In 1931, in the wake of the collapse on Wall Street, a year's moratorium was granted. The Lausanne Agreement of 1932 envisaged a final payment of 3000 million, which was never made. By then, Germany had paid one-eighth of the sum originally demanded and received loans equivalent to one-fifth.

32 The Treaty of Sèvres had given European Turkey as well as Smyrna to Greece. In 1922, Mustapha Kemal defeated the Greeks, occupied Smyrna and threatened to cross to Constantinople. British troops at Chanak on the Dardanelles were reinforced on the orders of the British Prime Minister Lloyd George who was strongly pro-Greek. There was a tense military situation before Kemal accepted a compromise. This crisis led to the fall of Lloyd George and the Treaty of Lausanne (1923) granted Turkey Eastern Thrace and Constantinople.

33 Printed in *Pravda* on 7 April 1917, Lenin's statement after he returned to Petrograd after an absence of ten years from Russia. Titled 'Tasks of the Proletariat in the Present Revolution', the theses argued that neither the war nor the Provisional Government merited support. Lenin called for the creation of a republic of Soviets at home. He claimed that the Russian Revolution was an ongoing process. It would not end with the overthrow of the Tsarist order, nor would it be confined to Russia. A second stage 'must place power in the hands of the proletariat and poorest peasantry'. Estates should be confiscated. Lenin also advocated fraternisation with enemy troops at the front.

34 This was the first organised revolt against the authority of the Bolshevik Party from the Left. Their demands included the following:
- freedom of speech and press for all Left wing parties;
- fresh elections to the Soviet by secret ballot;
- freedom of assembly for trade unions and peasant organisations;
- withdrawal of all grain-requisitioning squads;
- re-establishment of a free market for the peasants;
- release of all Socialist political prisoners;
- abolition of the Communist-appointed political departments;
- equal rations for all working people;
- abolition of Communist fighting detachments in the Army;
- removal of Communist guards from factories.

35 Nikolai Bukharin (1888–1938), leading theoretician of Soviet Communism and Old Bolshevik, played a prominent role in the early stages of the new state. Author of the *ABC of Communism*, he initially supported Stalin against Trotsky. From 1926–9 he was in charge of the Comintern. He later opposed Stalin over the collectivisation of agriculture and was expelled from the Party. Branded as a 'Right-wing deviationist', he was executed on trumped-up charges of treason in 1938, one of the most prominent victims of the purges.

36 The Soviet Union was defined as 'a Socialist State of workers and peasants' and the Communist Party was described as its vanguard. Reaffirmed socialist ownership of the means of production and enacted a federal bill of rights and duties.

There was to be a two-chamber Supreme Soviet with power to amend the Constitution by a two-thirds majority vote (supplanting the earlier Congress of Soviets).

In practice, federal authority was all-embracing. There was also no provision for judicial review of the constitutionality of the laws.

37 The armed bands of Italian Fascists who played a decisive role in the emergence of Fascism as a major political force between 1920 and 1922. From the start Fascists had stressed military organisation. Their violence and unwillingness to accept compromise with non-Fascists later became a liability for Mussolini, anxious to win over respectable elites and foreign public

opinion. In October 1925 he had the squads officially disbanded and disarmed.

38 The crisis arising from the Italian naval seizure of the Greek island. The justification offered was that this was a guarantee for reparations after the murder of an Italian general and several of the staff of the Conference of Ambassadors who were delimiting the Greco-Albanian frontier. Corfù also served Italy's strategic interest and national ambition. Greece appealed to the League of Nations and Mussolini indicated that he would occupy the island permanently if the League intervened. In the event, the Conference of Ambassadors arbitrated. They imposed heavy reparations on Greece and Mussolini withdrew his forces from the island.

39 It won a privileged place in Italian society and protection for its lay movement, Catholic Action. The financial convention indemnified the Holy See and also granted it the sovereign independence which it had always insisted was essential to its spiritual mission. Outside Italy the Lateran Pacts helped to rally Catholic support for Mussolini. After the long estrangement of Church and State in Italy, they appeared to be a signal political achievement. In practice, though, tensions surfaced soon after and in the end Mussolini reverted to his original anticlericalism.

40 i) The Rightist volunteer paramilitary units which sprang up across Germany from 1918. Composed of officers and soldiers from the Imperial Army and the unemployed, these fanatically nationalistic groups called for the elimination of 'traitors to the Fatherland' and were involved in numerous acts of murder and violence against political opponents and representatives of the Weimar Republic.

ii) The term used by the Nazis to describe those responsible for concluding the armistice at the end of the First World War. German leaders had agreed to suspension of hostilities pending a definitive peace settlement.

41 This empowered the Government to proclaim and enforce laws without the approval of Parliament. It required a two-thirds majority which was achieved because the KPD (German Communist Party) had forfeited their seats and several Social Democrats had been elected. The Centre Party and the small Liberal parties consented after Hitler gave them the guarantee that the Constitution would be respected. This did not prove to be the case. In passing this Act, the Reichstag surrendered its powers and laid the legal basis for Nazi dictatorship.

42 The Nazi ploy to bring about the removal of the commander of the Wermacht. Von Fritsch had doubted the capacity of the Army to achieve Hitler's military aims. He was unjustly accused of homosexuality in order to force his resignation. He was replaced by Brauchitsch. Later, Hitler assumed supreme command. The removal of Fritsch therefore greatly assisted the Nazis in gaining control over the Army.

43 This was concluded by an exchange of notes between the British and German governments. The proportion of war-shipping tonnage was fixed at a ratio of 100:35 of British to German, though in emergency Germany was allowed full equality in the submarine tonnage. This agreement was very badly received by the French. It meant disregarding the naval clauses of the Versailles Treaty and appeared to endorse German rearmament. British intention was to avoid a navy race such as that before 1914.

44 The Hossbach Conference was a meeting at the Reich Chancellery on 5 November 1937, in which Hitler informed his closest advisers that he planned to go to war and outlined the options. Colonel Hossbach, who was Hitler's adjutant, wrote the record of this meeting. In the memorandum Hitler envisages the outbreak of war not later than 1943–5. The first blow was to be struck against Austria and Czechoslovakia.

45 This agreement called for consultation and collaboration between Germany and Japan to counter the actions of the Third Communist International. Italy joined in November 1936. Though not a military alliance, the Japanese felt

the pact would serve as a deterrent to the Soviet Union. Hitler recognised Japan's puppet government of Manchukuo. Germany and Japan never fully agreed on the meaning of the pact. Germany refused to recognise Japan's war against China as one against Communism, interpreting the pact as applying only to the spread of Communism within the territories of the nations that had signed the pact.

46 The execution of more than 4000 Polish prisoners of war, with 11 000 unaccounted for, in 1940 near Smolensk. The area at this time was under the control of the NKVD. Three commissions identified the time of the massacre as predating Hitler's invasion of the Soviet Union and therefore disproving Stalin's claim that it was a Nazi atrocity. Britain and the US at the time were unwilling to admit the compelling evidence of Soviet guilt.

47 The French independent nuclear deterrent. The decision to become a nuclear power was taken at the end of the Fourth Republic and the programme of development was completed under General de Gaulle, who laid considerable emphasis on France's status as a nuclear power.

48 The idea of 'limited sovereignty'. After the Warsaw Pact invasion of Czechoslovakia in 1968, the Soviet leader asserted that the 'Socialist Community as a whole' had the right to intervene in the territory of any one of its members whenever forces hostile to Socialism threatened its ideological alignment. The ideological unity of the Communist bloc, he argued, must take precedence over the liberty of individual states.

49 The meeting of the Foreign Ministers of the Six members of the European Coal and Steel Community (France, Germany, Italy, Belgium, Holland and Luxembourg), at which it was decided to launch 'a fresh advance towards the building of Europe' and to create a market 'free from all customs duties and all quantitative restrictions'. An intergovernmental committee set to work after this meeting under the chairmanship of the Belgian Minister Paul-Henri Spaak to work out detailed proposals. These were to result in the Treaty of Rome (1957).

50 This resolved the 'empty chair crisis' in which President de Gaulle had effectively boycotted the European Community in 1965 in protest against its timetable for the increasing use of qualified majority voting. At Luxembourg, the Six agreed to disagree, and to accept the right of any member state to veto proposals before the Council of Ministers whenever it believed its own national interests might be affected. The compromise acted as a brake on the process of political integration.

51 The European Monetary System, established in 1979. Its main elements are:
   ❶ the European Currency Unit (ECU) (its value is a weighted average 'basket' of EC currencies);
   ❷ the Exchange Rate Mechanism, in which member states keep the value of their currencies within an agreed band.

LETTS SCHOOL EXAMINATIONS BOARD
General Certificate of Education Examination

ADVANCED LEVEL
EUROPEAN HISTORY

Time allowed: 3 hours

Attempt question 1 and any 3 others

1 The Unification of Italy 1815–71

Read the extracts below and then answer all the questions which follow.

Document A: From Charles Albert's proclamation to Lombardy and Venice, Turin, 23 March 1848.

> We, out of love for our common race, understanding, as we do what is now happening, and supported by public opinion, hasten to associate ourselves with the unanimous admiration which Italy bestows on you.
>
> Peoples of Lombardy and Venetia, our arms, which were concentrating on your frontier when you forestalled events by liberating your glorious Milan, are now coming to offer you in the latter phase of your fight the help which a brother expects from a brother, and a friend from a friend.
>
> We will support your just desires, confident as we are in the help of that God who is manifestly on our side: of the God who had given Pius IX to Italy; of the God whose helpful hand has wonderfully enabled Italy to rely on her own strength (*Italia farà da sé*).
>
> In order to show more openly our feelings of Italian brotherhood, we have ordered our troops as they move into Lombardy and Venice to carry the Cross of Savoy imposed on the tricolour of Italy.

Document B: From the Allocution of Pius IX of 29 April 1848.

> Seeing that some at present desire that We too, along with the other princes of Italy and their subjects, should engage in war against the Austrians. We have thought it convenient to proclaim clearly and openly, in this our solemn assembly, that such a measure is altogether alien from our counsels.
>
> And in this place We cannot refrain from repudiating before the face of all nations, the treacherous advice, published moreover in journals, and in various works, of those who would have the Roman Pontiff to be the head and to preside over the formation of some sort of novel republic of the whole Italian people. Rather on this occasion, moved hereto by the love We bear them. We do urgently warn and exhort the said Italian people to abstain with all diligence from the like counsels, deceitful and ruinous to Italy herself and to abide in close attachments to their respective sovereigns.

Document C: From Count Casati. *New Revelations* on the facts in regard to Milan during 1847–48 published in 1885. Casati was Mayor of Milan in 1848.

> The subsequent story that Charles Albert had been counting the days until he could attack Austria does not square with the fact that his army was entirely unprepared for such a war. It evidently had no plans nor even any maps of Lombardy, and almost all its strength was rather posted on the French frontier as a defence against the menace of republicanism.
>
> Four days were wasted at Turin in deciding whether or not to fight. Then with greatly superior forces, a slow, timid advance took place which did nothing at all to harry Radetzky or to seize the mountain passes and cut off his supplies. Instead of marching at once on Brescia or Verona, not until the second week in April did any serious fighting commence, and by that time the Austrians were well protected inside the Quadrilateral. Garibaldi's offer of help was turned down by the king on the grounds that to accept support from mere volunteers and ex-outlaws would be dishonourable for the army.
>
> This fundamental military weakness was made worse by political differences. Instead of playing for support from the popular elements who had chiefly manned the barricades at Milan and other towns, Charles Albert preferred the small aristocratic element in Lombardy. Instead of concentrating on the war, he insisted on holding a plebiscite to make sure of the political fusion of Lombardy and Venice with Piedmont, even though this was bound to arouse suspicions of Piedmontese aggrandisement and discourage other elements in Naples, Tuscany and Rome who wanted a new union of Italy. Politics at once

became bitter, and the republicans and federalists gradually broke away from what looked to them like an essentially royalist anti-revolutionary war.

(a) What reasons does Casati give in Document C for the ineffectiveness of Charles Albert's invasion of Lombardy? (4)

(b) What was meant by 'Italia farà da sé', in Document A line 9 and who advocated this solution to Italy's problems? (6)

(c) Compare Documents A and C as sources for Charles Albert's motives for invading Lombardy. (7)

(d) How fully do Documents A, B, and C explain the failure of the 1848 revolutions in Italy? (8)

2 Why, in spite of praiseworthy intentions, were the results of the Congress System of 1815–25 disappointing and limited?

3 Explain both the initial successes and the ultimate failure of the 1848 revolutions in the Habsburg Empire.

4 Do you agree that while its causes were insignificant, the consequences of the Crimean War were of enormous significance?

5 How far was Napoleon III's foreign policy shaped by the Napoleonic legend?

6 Is it fair to say that Tsar Alexander II achieved nothing of real substance for Russia?

7 'Austria-Hungary's reckless and provocative behaviour in the period 1908–14 contributed significantly to the outbreak of war in 1914'. Explain and comment on this statement.

8 Discuss the view that the Versailles Settlement was an unsatisfactory compromise between the demand for revenge and the hope of reconciliation.

9 By what means and at what cost did Lenin maintain the Bolshevik regime between 1918 and 1924?

10 Account for the relative lack of open opposition to the Third Reich within Germany before and during the Second World War.

11 Did Mussolini lose popular support from the moment that he tied Italy to the Third Reich?

12 'To keep the Russians out, the Americans in and the Germans down' – explain this summary of the purposes of NATO.

MOCK EXAM SUGGESTED ANSWER PLANS

1 Refer to advice on answering document questions in the introductory section (pages 10–11). Note the weighting of marks. Question (a) tests simple understanding of Document C. (Remember to read through the extracts very carefully.) (b) is a straightforward test of knowledge. (c) involves you in comparative evaluation. (d) is the most testing: you should note the variety of reasons for the failure of 1848 in Italy and then list the explanations offered in the extracts. A good answer could comment further on the discrepancy, which involves you in understanding the circumstances, origins and purposes of the source material.

2) It is important for you to do full justice to both the 'praiseworthy intentions' and the results of the Congress System. The Treaties of Paris and the Vienna Congress deliberations should be explained with emphasis on the treatment of France and the decision embodied in the Quadruple Alliance to pursue Congress diplomacy in the settlement or prevention of international disputes.

Emphasise that the desire for peace and the reconstruction of a European balance of power were inextricably bound up with the safeguarding of Europe against revolution. You should not neglect the second part of the question. Indicate a clear and detailed understanding of the congresses after 1815, Aix-La-Chapelle, Troppau, Laibach and Verona. Also show an awareness of the underlying conflict of ambitions between the major powers. The Congress System was not genuinely supranational. Avoid contenting yourself on this point with simply a comment on the rift between Great Britain and the Holy Alliance.

3   You may be tempted to treat this simply as an invitation to say why the revolutions in the Habsburg Empire failed. A good, or even adequate, answer should also explain the early triumphs of the revolutionaries, their significance and impact, not forgetting the wider context of revolutionary upheaval across Europe. It is important to give specific examples to indicate a grasp of the complexity of the relations between the nationalist groupings. Points for emphasis in evaluating their failure should include the uncoordinated (and sometimes contradictory) nature of the revolts, the tenacious loyalty of the military commanders such as Windischgrätz and their troops and the divisions among the revolutionaries, e.g. in Vienna. The Russian intervention must be mentioned. Do not overlook events in Italy, for instance the defeat of the Piedmontese at Custozza.

4   Do not simply accept that the causes were insignificant, or give short measure on this part of the question. An answer which concentrates only on consequences would be very unbalanced. The immediate causes, from the Holy Places dispute onwards, may appear trifling and suggest an 'unnecessary war', but you should remember the long-term issue (which was not finally or conclusively resolved by the Treaty of Paris of 1856). The fear of Russian expansion, Austrian, British and French apprehensions and aspirations should be dealt with. Analysis of the consequences should include both the immediate effects and, crucially, the impact on international relations, e.g. the diplomatic isolation of Austria (allowing unification of Germany and Italy), France's temporary role as the arbiter of European diplomacy and the domestic impact, particularly in Russia. You might also comment on the impact of the war on public opinion, particularly in Britain.

5   Be clear about the Napoleonic legend. 'Des Idées Napoleoniennes' was written by Louis Napoleon in 1839 in London. It was part of his effort to interest France in Bonapartist politics, while at the same time establishing his credentials as the leading heir to the Napoleonic legacy. He argued among other things that though Napoleon I had temporarily been forced to employ authoritarian methods, his role was fundamentally democratic and laid the foundations for a system of political liberty. Louis Napoleon claimed that his uncle's intentions had been obstructed by British hostilities. Britain had failed to understand the Emperor's wish for a federated and peaceful Europe. Louis Napoleon aimed at a national reconciliation transcending Left and Right in France under the Bonapartist idea. Examine his foreign policy in the light of this alleged mission, which also had a domestic political purpose.

6   The temptation for a candidate here, which should strenuously be resisted, is to reel off Alexander II's reforms, from the Emancipation of the Serfs onwards, with a general comment that they were only a partly successful effort. You should take a broader look at his reign, including the question of the nationalities in Russia, foreign policy (particularly the Eastern Crisis of 1875–80) and the development of opposition groups within Russia. You should not hesitate, also, to consider his 'achievements' from the perspective of what happened after his death in 1881.

7   Questions on the origins of/responsibility for the First World War are usually attempted by large numbers of candidates and often, as with Alexander II's reign, with prepared answers in which candidates signally fail to use the

broad range of information about the origins of the war and its background to relevant effect. The question does *not* read 'Allocate responsibility for the First World War', but calls on you to look specifically at Austrian policies between 1908 and 1914 and how these sparked off the conflict. So your focus here should be on the problems of the Habsburg Empire – the threat of Balkan nationalism and the perception that the South Slav question compelled Vienna to take a firm line against Serbia. Make sure that you register the significance of the Bosnian Crisis of 1908 (remember that Austria-Hungary had already been occupying Bosnia-Herzegovina for thirty years). So while you should not omit reference to the wider context, particularly German intentions and the Russian role, the central evaluation must be of the policies of the Dual Monarchy. German commitment to the Habsburg Empire allowed the latter to attempt an aggressive resolution of her Balkan difficulties. Comment particularly on the disagreements in Vienna policy-making circles and the general clumsiness of Austro-Hungarian policy.

8   Do not content yourself here with reiterating the key clauses of the Versailles Treaty and commenting on whether they were fair or not. Analyse the conflicting approaches of the US, British, French and Italian delegations over, for instance, the Rhineland, Poland, the Adriatic area and reparations. Explain, for instance, French fears and the British desire for German economic revival. Comment on the spectre in the background of events in Russia. Your analysis should carry you on after 1919 to consider, for example, the Ruhr invasion of 1923 and the Locarno Pact of 1925. A good answer will reveal the underlying conflict of objectives among the victorious powers and in particular the legacy of sharp rivalry between Britain and France.

9   Lenin's first action as Head of State was to oppose the broadening of the regime's powerbase through the inclusion of non-Bolshevik Socialists in his government. Gradually, the newspapers of the other Socialist parties were suppressed and their leaders were either forced into emigration or imprisoned. The long-awaited Constituent Assembly met in January 1918, only to be disbanded on Lenin's orders when it challenged the Party's right to govern.

   This authoritarian mould was also applied in external affairs, to the new Communist International as well as to the CPSU itself. Lenin insisted that foreign Communist parties joining the Comintern had to accept his 'Twenty-One Conditions', accepting the Bolshevik way as the only true path to revolution. The last serious challenge to Lenin within the Party came from those who wanted to refuse the terms of the Treaty of Brest-Litovsk. He showed mounting intolerance with intra-Party groups such as the workers' opposition. In 1919 he instituted a five-man politburo and in 1921 instituted expulsion from the Party for factionalism. He also, ominously for the future, approved greater powers being given to the General-Secretary, Stalin (something he subsequently regretted in his *Testament*). Lenin's earlier utopian dreams of worker control of industry and peasant control of land soon gave way to the police-state centralism of War Communism and the forced requisitioning of grain. Your answer should give a full appraisal not just of the immediate cost of these policies, but also their longer-term legacy in Stalinism.

10 You should not take this simply as an opportunity to explain the reasons for Hitler's popularity within Germany, in part the result of his initially successful foreign policy. You should explain how he suppressed potential opposition to himself and the Nazi Party. Stress the role of the state security services, the power of propaganda and control of the media. Illustrate your answer in a way which shows that you understand chronologically the developing hold of the Nazis over the German people. The words 'relative lack of open opposition' should lead you to point out that there was a range of opposition

within Germany. This was not just to be seen in the attempts on Hitler's life but also, for instance, in Cardinal-Archbishop von Galen's open denunciation of Nazism as inconsistent with Christianity; or the 'White Rose', the student protest in Munich. The vengence wreaked by Hitler on Stauffenberg and his co-conspirators in 1944 can be cited as evidence why there was really so little open opposition. One might further add that the Declaration of Unconditional Surrender by the Allies in 1943 helped to discourage open opposition within Germany.

11 Explain and assess the reasons for Mussolini's domestic political popularity briefly before dealing with the Second World War. Do you consider that his foreign policy was mainly an echo of Hitler's foreign policy and inherently fraught with danger for Italy? Show clear awareness of Italy's campaigns during the war. Because you may be better briefed on Mussolini and fascism pre-1939, you may be tempted to dwell overlong on his earlier popularity. Comment fully on the inglorious Italian engagements in the Balkans and North Africa and the need for German reserves, which greatly damaged Mussolini's reputation. Together with failure subsequently to prevent Allied invasion of Sicily and the peninsula, Italy's economic capacity for major war was exposed as very inadequate. Explain how disillusionment grew apace during the war, finally leading to the Duce's fall. You must, then, centrally evaluate the impact of the Rome-Berlin Axis on the fate of Italian Fascism and its leader.

12 It is important here to give each of the cited purposes due emphasis. The first two are likely to be more obvious than the third. But a considerable amount can be said about the postwar wish to 'contain' an economically revived Germany, and then a rearmed Western Germany within NATO. See, for instance, long and acrimonious debate over the European Defence Community (EDC) between 1950 and 1954. Remember that when NATO came into existence the Soviet Union had not yet exploded her first atom bomb. The problem was the superiority in numbers of the conventional Eastern Bloc forces. Emphasise the British pressure on Washington for a long-term US commitment to Western Europe. A good answer to this question requires you to say something, too, about the continuing purpose of NATO after 1955 and the Warsaw Pact.

INDEX